Creating Futures

Scenario Planning
as a Strategic Management Tool

First published 2006

Printed in France

Michel Godet

Creating Futures
Scenario Planning
as a Strategic Management Tool

ISBN 2-7178-5244-1

MICHEL GODET

Creating Futures

Scenario Planning as a Strategic Management Tool

Preface by Joseph F. COATES

Translated by Adam Gerber and Kathryn Radford

Second Edition

ECONOMICA

London • Paris • Genève

ACKNOWLEDGEMENTS

This is the second edition of Creating Futures and most of the content has been updated; particularly chapters one, two, and three. Chapter 3, *Clichés and AntiClichés About the Future*, is completely new. The first edition's success can certainly be attributed to the thousands of visitors to the Lipsor web site (http://www.lipsor.fr/) who have downloaded the toolbox for futures studies, which is available free of charge since 2005. None of this would have been possible without the generous support of the Entrepreneurs of the Future Circle, which now comprises more than 40 organisations.

This book was translated with assistance from the French Ministry of Foreign Affairs, specifically the Scientific and Technical Cooperation Department, in order to help the French school of *la prospective* become better known in the English-speaking world. The translation/adaptation of my work [1] for the first edition owes much to the literary talent of Kathryn Radford (lecturer, Université de Montréal and McGill University), who gladly attended corporate workshops in Paris to see our futures-thinking techniques in practice. My friend and close associate Adam Gerber (American futurist and researcher at Lipsor) has contributed enormously to this volume by translating and adapting much of the new content. Lastly, I am both grateful and honoured to have one of the greatest American futurists, Joseph F. Coates, write the preface to *Creating Futures*.

---

1. French handbook Manuel de prospective stratégique, Dunod, 1997, 2001, 2004.

Entrepreneurs of the Future Circle

Established in late 2003 and now comprising some 40 partners, the Entrepreneurs of the Future Circle contributes to the academic discipline of *la prospective* (futures studies) while advancing the prestige of the French school of *la prospective* throughout the world.

Thanks to the Entrepreneurs of the Future Circle, futurists from around the world now have access to these sophisticated software tools available in three languages; French, English and Spanish. In addition to the software, you will also find several important reference and out-of-print documents related to futures studies at our site, http://www.3ie.org/lipsor/.

These software programs and documents may be downloaded free-of-charge from the Lipsor website: http://www.3ie.org/lipsor/

Although futures studies is an intellectual "indiscipline", there is a need for rigorous methods to orient action towards a desired future. The toolbox of futures studies allow the user apply rigour to the foresight process by posing important questions, reducing incoherencies and creating a common language.

Six Tools and Software to Assist at Various Stages of the Foresight Process

Strategic prospective **workshops:** ask the right questions and chose the appropriate method.

Micmac: identify the key variables for structural analysis.

Mactor: analyse the strategies of various actors.

Morphol: sweep the field of possibilities with morphological analysis.

Smic Prob-Expert: reduce uncertainty with the aid of expert interviews.

Multipol: evaluate and chose the strategic options.

CONTENTS

PREFACE

A second edition is always a cause for celebration. For the publisher, it confirms his hope that the product he sponsored would continue to be successful economically. For the author, the implications are even more delicious. His message has been understood, studied, and used. One could rarely ask for more from a professional thinker and a proponent of better ways to think. To me the most striking mark of success is that the software indispensable to the tools and techniques which Godet describes, explains, and advocates has been downloaded from the Internet over 7000 times, at no cost. While a number of futures works in the English speaking world are accompanied by software packages in the form of CDs, the Godet approach – make it free with the help of the *Entrepreneurs of the Future Circle* – is far more socially valuable.

The second advantage I see in this new edition is pulling some of the good ideas out of chapter three to integrate into other chapters, and then creating an entirely new chapter three. He hunts down a particularly subversive form of thinking, or more properly, failure to think, in the form of six clusters of cliches. Other minor changes throughout sharpen, clarify, or expand on details.

If clarity is a virtue, Michel Godet is a saint. Two features of Professor Godet's career show through clearly in his new tour de force. First, as a university professor, he admires and practices clarity, consistency, and intellectual integrity. As a consultant practitioner – one of the most eminent in France – he brings to his treatment of scenario planning as a strategic management tool, a degree of practicality and flexibility which is admirable. His attitude and precepts if adopted would greatly benefit all of those who could be successful in the use of scenarios as a planning tool and in strategic management.

The Anglophones have too long dominated the world of forecasting and its applications to planning. Godet has been a primary actor in turning that tide and bringing the French experience of *Strategic Prospective* to an Anglophone audience with great force. As one might expect, there are cultural differences, but little that is fundamentally different when one looks past the differences in nomenclature and the difference in relative emphasis. His now widely available software packages should help in drawing Anglophone and Francophone closer together.

On the other hand, Godet makes a central point that what must be emphasized throughout formal planning is rigor and rationality. He notes that "The situation appears all the worse given the sad state of affairs in the United States where rational or formalistic techniques have been passed over for essentially intuitive approaches". There is no doubt that he has hit a resonant, if perharps a low base, chord there. There is far too much attitude, judgment, expert and lay sentiment entering into futures studies in general in the anglophone world, especially the US and UK. Reflecting that situation is the underuse of formal techniques and quantification.

Godet highlights the fact that by being less rational or what I prefer to think of as less systematic, the vocabulary becomes garbled, the terms confused, and the processes muddy. Godet's approach and prescriptions would carry us a great way toward rationalizing and clarifying our approaches to the future. Being rational and rigorous does not so much imply greater time and cost, but a fuller commitment to complete a examination of assumptions and possibilities.

His concentration on scenario based planning will satisfy many executives craving for clearer insights into the future and a more solidly based spectrum of alternative outcomes in terms of the choices that they must make. As a book and to some extent as a textbook, this work is beautifully organized. It begins with a smooth easy review of general factors and concerns. It moves into a crescendo of detail and ends with three outstanding chapters of case material. The cases are in enough procedural and substantive detail to convince the reader, at least this reader, that the processes Godet lays out and the technique that he describes will work in industry, aluminum and electric utilities, the military, the private sector, insurance companies, and in regional planning. His most extensive example is BASF facing agrofood and environmental challenges.

His approach is easy to take because of the grace, style, wit and humor with which he presents his model. After his easy beginning he moves on to key concepts in looking to the future, including a general look at "la prospective". He then moves into an expanded popular topic - why experts so often get it wrong. He next wages war on clichés, to emphasize how paralytic they can be in organizational thinking. With that clearing of the stage, he moves on to how to be rigorous in scenario planning, defining specific conditions, and the tools that are essential to ensuring rigor. This core of his approach is two chapters, followed by the case material. Readers enjoy, learn and profit from Godet's work, now available in three languages – French, English, and Spanish.

Joseph F. COATES
Joseph Coates, Consulting Futurist, Inc.
Washington, D.C.

HOW TO THINK ABOUT THE FUTURE NOW

Action is meaningless without a goal. Only an approach like scenario building can point the way to action while giving it both meaning and direction. Similarly, scenario building cannot readily be dissociated from strategy, hence the term "strategic scenario building" or "strategic scenario planning".

However, the complexity of strategic problems, as well as the need to resolve them collectively, means we require methods that are as rigorous and participatory as possible. Applying these criteria guarantees the most effective methods to identifying problems and finding acceptable corresponding solutions. At the same time, we must keep in mind the limits imposed by formalization and remember that people are guided by intuition and passion as well as rationality and logic. Our mental models are inventions of the mind and represent a world unwilling to be straitjacketed by equations.

As a result, we are resolved to use all the powers of reason while remaining aware of both their inherent limits and virtues. We should remember that intuition and reason are not opposite, but rather complementary faculties.

Back to the Future

We remember Gaston Berger's aphorism: *"looking at the future disturbs it"*. Perhaps, but if so, then imagining it together is already living the present differently and giving more meaning to action.

Let us start with the term *la prospective* [1]. Futures studies, or foresight as *la prospective* is usually translated, involves anticipation (pre- or pro-activity) to clarify present actions in light of possible and desirable futures. Preparing for foreseeable changes does not prevent one from provoking desired changes. *La prospective,* according to Gaston Berger, requires "seeing far, wide and deep; thinking about humankind and taking risks". Since the 1970s, we have lobbied within *Futuribles Association (http://www.futuribles.fr/)* to add three characteristics often neglected by our forerunners:
1) See differently
2) See collectively
3) Use methods as rigorous and participatory as possible to reduce the unavoidable biases in a group.

---

1. The term la prospective is usually translated into English as foresight or futures studies. This ancient concept quoted in the Middle Ages by French poet, François Villon, was revived by the philosopher Gaston Berger in 1957.

Planning, "la Prospective" and Strategy: What is the Difference?

The three concepts of *la prospective*, [1] strategy and planning are intimately linked in practice; as a result, *strategic planning*, *strategic management* and *the strategic prospective approach* will be mentioned throughout this book. Each of these approaches refers to a set of definitions, problems, and methods whose specificity is weak, given the vague terminology.

With all the buzzwords and false synonyms, some readers may wonder how we can make sense of anything related to the future. Some might ask if these approaches are not all quite similar. After all, do we not already have a series of practical methods that are actually more useful insofar as their limits are known? The answer is a resounding "yes". A toolbox for futures studies and strategic analysis does exist. Informed managers would do well to acquire this toolbox whose benefits include; creating a common language, effectively harnessing the power of collective thought, and reducing the inevitable biases among participants. To achieve all this, however, we must return to the fundamental concepts of *la prospective* and its history.

In order to be fruitful, the marriage between scenario building and strategy must be a part of daily life. It must be appropriated by all the actors involved, from the top of the hierarchy to the bottom. (Note that here the word *actor* is used as it is in management theory.) Although the union between scenario building and strategy may have been inevitable, it has certainly not cleared up any confusion in genres and concepts. Deep down, however, the ideas are much closer than is generally admitted. In fact the definition of planning put forward by Ackoff (1970), "to conceive a desired future as well as the practical means of achieving it" does not differ much from the one we suggest for strategic scenario building in which the dream infuses reality, where desire is the productive force of the future and where anticipation sheds light on the preactive and the proactive.

Managerial fads may come and go but they always have one common denominator – people need to be motivated through new challenges. Of course, the process of getting people involved is considered the goal to be reached no matter what the outcome. In this way, strategic analysis can generate a synthesis of collective commitment, contrary to the ideas expressed by Henry Mintzberg (1994). Indeed, the

---

1. With respect to terms, *la prospective* in French covers the concepts of *preactivity* and *proactivity*, as seen in Igor Ansoff's writings. The concept of *foresight*, another suggested translation, only partially renders the meaning of *la prospective* since in usage *foresight* is generally applied to technology with the inherent idea of a collective process surrounding anticipation (preactivity) of technological change, but the idea of proactivity is missing.

real difficulty lies not in making the right choices but in making sure that all the participants ask themselves the right questions. Remember the adage: A problem well stated (and shared by those concerned) is already half solved. This is exactly what Michel Crozier meant when he said, "The problem is the problem."

In the practice of foresight, one ought to avoid managerial fads and focus on sound strategic methods. For example, the classical analysis using threats and opportunities shows that we cannot limit our analysis to the current competitive environment in the name of short-term profits, as the early writings of Michael Porter might lead us to believe. The fact that many uncertainties hang in the balance within the general context, especially over the long-term, underscores the need for broad scenario building to clarify strategic options and to ensure continued organizational growth.

In the past, the European management market was flooded by tools and approaches designed abroad, mainly in Japan and the United States. Examples abound, but the most outstanding was the Strategic Business Unit (SBU) approach. Indeed many American firms actually became victims of the SBU approach. Yet in the end, the relative or even absolute decline of entire sectors of American industry, in comparison with Japan and Europe during the 1960s and again in the 1980s, made any debate over the superiority of the classic American approach moot. As Marc Giget (1998) put it: "The revival [of the American Economy] in the 90s was generated from analyses labeled *Made in America* which was inspired directly by foreign models." Hence managers rediscovered the virtues of positioning themselves against the best (benchmarking), the value of a complete rehaul of processes and structures (re-engineering), as well as the importance of lean organizations (downsizing) and lastly, the power of innovation (core competencies). Therein lies the difference between winning and losing companies, as Hamel and Prahalad point out: "We had to conclude that some management teams were simply more foresightful than others. Some were capable of imagining products, services and entire industries that did not yet exist and then giving them birth. These managers seemed to spend less time worrying about how to position the firm in existing competitive space and more time creating fundamentally new competitive space. Other companies, the laggards were more interested in protecting the past than in creating the future." [1]

Let us reconsider some of the terms employed above. Strategy uses foresight and innovation while *la prospective* uses preactivity and proactivity. Nevertheless, we are essentially talking about the exact same thing. Given this similarity, the term *strategic prospective* has been circulating since the late 1980's, especially in France. Better late than never.

---

1. Hamel G, C.K. Prahalad. *Competing for the Future*. Boston: Harvard Business School Press, 1994, Preface xvii.

We wonder if a strategist is capable of operating in a way different from that which was described by Gaston Berger "seeing far, wide, and deep, while taking risks and thinking about the human factor" (See Gaston Berger (1964).) We append to the above statement; "thinking unconventionally and collectively". To paraphrase Gaston Berger once more, "looking at the future disturbs not only the future but also the present". Again, we add a conclusion to his remark: "but anticipation encourages action". By now we are convinced that scenario building is often strategic if not through its outcome at least through its intentions. Similarly, strategy calls upon *la prospective* to clarify choices made with the future in mind.

The Use and Abuse of the Term *Strategy*

The so-called "rise and fall of strategic planning" has not exhausted people's interest in the subject. (This may be a relief for an author like Henry Mintzberg (1979).) Strategic planning will always be of interest to managers because of the independent nature of each of its components. "An organization can plan (take the future into consideration) without actually committing to planning (a formal procedure) even if it does draw up some plans (explicit intentions)." In reality, the issue is not really planning but rather the manner in which planning is carried out. The graft of strategic planning only takes root if it is integrated into the corporate culture and identity. To use another metaphor, the wheels of development depend not only on logic, but also on human emotion and behavior. Hence the idea of strategic management, which is almost a tautology according to Boyer and Equilbey's definition of management (1990): "the art of management is to make the organization serve strategy." Yet management in itself does not constitute a strategy. Strategy shapes management but also presupposes objectives and related tactics (contingent decisionmaking). One wonders how serious authors reject these distinctions. It is high time that these concepts be clarified so that the same word does not have different meanings and that different things are not named the same.

For traditional authors, such as Lucien Poirier (1987) and Igor Ansoff (1965) the notion of strategy refers to a firm's actions upon its environment and reflection on that action. Without hesitating, Lucien Poirier used the term *stratégie prospective* which we have called *Strategic Prospective* or strategic scenario building. Obviously, the two notions are distinct but often associated. However some authors, including Fabrice Roubelat (1996), maintain that *la prospective* has two sides to it. Roubelat bases his comments on Jacques Lesourne (1989) to conclude that "A strategic decision is either one that creates an irreversible situation for the entire organization or one that anticipates an environmental change apt to provoke such an irreversible situation." In other words, according to Lesourne, "A strategic decision would likely be a decision that forces the organization to ponder its very existence, independence, mission, and main field of activity." In short, this decision exists for a specific company and according to this definition, general forecasting sessions would not have any strategic value for the actor/company involved.

The main advantage of these definitions is that they avoid using the word *strategic* to qualify or inflate everything that merely seems important.

Of course prudence and common sense enter into the equation; consequently, our efforts are not limited to asking about risks of breakdowns or breakthroughs and strategy is not reduced only to decisions of an irreversible nature for the company. It is true that the borders are fuzzy here and impossible to redraw completely. The same may be said for decisions, for as Jacques Lesourne once put it: "major decisions are rarely made, they become increasingly improbable as the small decisions accumulate".

For any organization, *la prospective* is not philanthropy but rather reflection with a view to clarifying action, especially action of a strategic nature.

The Five Basic Questions Leading to Action

Like fraternal twins, *prospective* and strategy remain distinct entities and it is necessary to distinguish between:
   1) the anticipation phase, in other words, the study of possible and desirable changes, and
   2) the preparation phase: in other words, the working out and assessing of possible strategic choices so as to be prepared for expected changes (pre-activity) and provoke desirable changes (pro-activity).

The dichotomy between exploring and preparing a course of action implies the following five questions: (Q1), what could happen? (scenario building) (Q2), what can I do? (strategic options) (Q3), what will I do? (strategic decisions) (Q4), how will I do it? (actions and operational plans) and an essential prerequisite question (Q0), who am I? All too often ignored, the last question is the starting point of Marc Giget's strategic procedure (1998). However this preliminary identification also echoes Socrates' famous admonition, "Know thyself."

Only the *la prospective* approach with the preactive and proactive attitudes focuses on the question (Q1) "what could happen?" It becomes strategic when an organization asks itself (Q2) "what can we do?" Once these two questions have been answered, the strategy goes from (Q2) "what can we do?" to two further queries: (Q3) "what are we going to do?" and (Q4) "how will we do it?" The overlap between the scenario phase of *la prospective* and strategy is very clearly illustrated above. There are of course futures studies that contain no clear strategic component whatsoever, as well as strategic analyses of firms or sectors whose interest in the future is embryonic or even nonexistent. For the sake of clarity, the expression *strategic prospective* will therefore be reserved for futures studies having strategic ambitions and endpoints for those participating.

Five Attitudes towards the Future

Anticipation is imperative in the contemporary business climate due to the following two factors.

1) Social, economic and technological change is accelerating, hence the need for a long-term vision. Gaston Berger, the spiritual father of the French futures school, expressed this situation best when he said: "The faster the car, the stronger the headlights need to be."

2) The factors of inertia inherent to various structures and behaviors oblige us to sow now if we want to reap a future harvest later. As my grandfather used to say: "The longer a tree takes to grow, the earlier you have to plant it."

Lack of foresight in the past has led to the present situation in which yesterday's apparently irrelevant questions become today's urgent matters that require immediate attention, thereby drawing resources away from more important problems like long-term development. Although reactivity is not desirable in the short-term as an end in itself, the ageless advice of Seneca rings true here: "Not a fair wind blows for him who knows not where he goes."

Anticipation enlightens action and lends it meaning as well as direction. If there is no direction for the future, the present is empty of meaning. Similarly, a dream is not the opposite of reality but rather the incubator of it. All projects must be driven by desire.

In this sense, people can choose from among five basic attitudes:

1) the passive ostrich, who accepts change;

2) the reactive firefighter, who waits for the alarm to put out fires;

3) the preactive insurer, who prepares for foreseeable changes because an ounce of prevention is worth a pound of cure;

4) the proactive conspirator, who acts to provoke desirable change;

5) the anticipactive actor who savvily combines all of the above but adopts an anticipactive attitude; in other words, a blend of the reactive, preactive and proactive attitudes.

Another analogy is the college football try-out. A passive recruit will soon be back on the bench; whereas, a reactive player will chase madly after the ball and rarely get hold of it. A preactive player will try to anticipate the right moves but often defensively and incorrectly. Remember the old saying: A strong offense is the best defense. The team's star has to outplay the opponent's tactics and not be fooled by players who are running interference; i.e., those who follow conventional thinking. Leading and scoring require offense. When you play proactively, the other team plays reactively.

Decisionmakers would do well to emulate the fifth attitude, which blends the star player's ambition with caution and urgency. Try this decisionmaking exercise. From now on, when you prepare an action plan, create a table with three columns: one for reactivity, one for pre-activity and one for pro-activity. None of the three should be too empty or too full. Of course, in periods of crisis, reactivity will prevail while in periods of growth, changes must be anticipated and induced, particularly through innovation.

A Riddle: What is the *raison d'être* of the present and creative force of the future?

The world may well be changing but the direction of that change is not certain. Shifts and transfers trigger social, economic, and technological uncertainty that people and corporations have to integrate into their strategies for the future.

Futures-thinking exercises, *la prospective*, or strategic scenario building do not claim to eliminate uncertainty with predictions; instead they seek to reduce uncertainty as much as possible and to enable people to make decisions in view of desired futures. *La prospective* is above all a state of mind (imagination and anticipation) that leads to behavior (hope and will).

The attitude described above is an expression of free will and a rejection of determinism (Hugues de Jouvenel) and chance (Pierre Massé). Desire ilicits a goal, which in turn summons the will to achieve that goal.

By considering desire as a productive force for the future, we rehabilitate the concept of subjective utopia, thus reuniting imagination and scientific logic. Like many terms, utopian is too often used as synonymous with impossible. Etymologically *ou-topos*, coming from Greek, means a non-place; i.e., a place that does not exist. However, this does not exclude an eventual future existence. Utopia, as a virtual object of desire, is the source from which action takes its meaning and direction. We are thus able to understand why the structure of social relationships crumbles as soon as the level of social restrictions overwhelm personal liberties (desire). In other words, the philosophical goal of any futures-thinking exercise is to erase the line between reality and possibility.

Once again we are confronted by the dichotomy between dream and reality when discussing the present *vis-à-vis* the future, and once again we turn to Gaston Berger's wisdom: "The future is the *raison d'être* of the present."

All this talk about the future, however, does not negate the past. We need to make the link between the past, the present and the future. Regrets are simply lost opportunities in the past. Hindsight is always 20/20, nevertheless, when seen from the past, we can conider our current regrets as lost future opportunities, which might have been realized, if only we had acted differently. The image of an old couple comes to mind. "They do not want to relive their past love but to live their love now as they did before, when they had such a vast future ahead of them and which is now behind them. What they have lost and what they regret is not really the past but rather the future they no longer have before them." (Nicolas Grimaldi, 1971)

Generally what we suffer in the future is the result of past actions. Similarly, what we desire in the future is the justification for our present actions. In other words, it is not only the past that explains the future, but also the image of the future which leaves an imprint on the present. For example, one individual's consumption at any given moment does not depend only on his/her previous earnings or savings, but also on anticipated income, e.g. credit. This is precisely what Milton Friedman expressed in his permanent income theory. Decidedly, we have to look to the future to shed light on the present.

Ten Key Ideas

Practitioners of *strategic prospective* (futurists) do not claim to have predictive powers, and anyone who claims to have predictive powers is not a futurist. The future is open and remains to be created. Furthermore, the future is plural, undetermined and open to a wide variety of possibilities. Whatever happens tomorrow depends less on prevailing trends, and more on individual and collective decisions taken in the face of these trends. If the future is indeed the fruit of human desire, then the following eight key ideas should be kept in mind at all times.

The World Changes but the Problems Remain the Same

Why? The problems stay the same because they are linked to human nature. The basic motivators, e.g. wealth, power, love and hate, function today just as well as they did in antiquity. Politicians know the number of traitors has not diminished since Judas' time. The only difference is that a traitor's life expectancy has increased!

We have to study and know human nature to understand what is happening around us. We need to revisit the past to shed light upon the future while keeping in mind the message of Visconti's movie, *The Leopard*, "everything must change so that everything may start over!"

In fact every time we find a problem that we encountered some five, ten, even fifteen years before, whether it be a concrete situation, such as selecting an airport site or a social issue like unemployment, the idea of change as renewal comes to mind.

As did the year 1000, the year 2000 generated an excess of end-of-the-world predictions. However, now that Y2K is yesterday's news, perhaps we ought to stop trying to frighten or impress others with statements like, "two-thirds of tomorrow's products do not yet exist" or "the skills of tomorrow are unknown today!" In many respects, tomorrow's world will resemble that of today's. Children will go to schools where there are blackboards and chalk, even though their schoolbags will contain powerful portable computers.

Every generation has the impression that it is living in an era of unprecedented change and transition. Nothing could be more normal. The current era is exceptional to each of us because it is the only one we will know; hence, we tend to overestimate the speed and importance of changes, especially in terms of new technology.

Overestimating Technological Change

That which is technologically possible is not necessarily economically profitable or socially desirable. Let us take the example of telecommuting or the home office. It is improbable that telecommuting will develop to the point that it eclipses most office jobs. Many factors are inimical to this maximalist hypothesis. First of all, the current layout of suburban houses does not make them suitable for full working days on a regular basis. Second, work also means socializing and fulfilling a need to communicate with others. Human interaction is a social need that appears increasingly difficult to satisfy.

Interconnectedness and shared goals provide direction. People need to feel that they belong. Contemporary despair often stems from solitude and the problem is particularly acute among the unemployed who are excluded from the social network that a job offers. Obviously the information highway is a deadend solution in this regard. Treating solitude and satisfying the need for human contact will likely continue to be a fast growing market niche.

Internet: A Computerized Dumpster

In the practice of foresight, the tempation to overestimate technlogical change should be avoided. We concede that e-mail does represent a giant leap forward in communication, however, like our colleague Bruno Lussato, we tend to regard the Internet as a computerized garbage bin. Following the garbage analogy; indeed, there is anything and everything in a garbage bin, maybe even hidden treasure. However, that does not provide sufficient reason to spend one's time rummaging through the trash. There are skoupedologists trained to do just this type of sociological research.

Yes, we all need a garbage pail of some kind, but many people boast of devoting hours daily to communicating with the rest of the world on the Internet while they are incapable of exchanging a few words with their nextdoor neighbour. How can we consider this stampede to surf the Internet as anything other than a sign of the times; i.e., feelings of tremendous solitude and the need for human contact? The main advantage of cybercafés is that they provide those who long to communicate with a place where they can talk amongst themselves and not only with a screen. Of course some people achieve the same effect by taking their dog out for a walk. In fact, the statistics speak volumes because the number of households in France with a pet is equal to that with an Internet connection. Surfing the Internet does not replace the need for affection symbolized by the eight million dogs and eight million cats dwelling in France.

Technology is the Pandora's box of modern society in that information technology enables people to communicate with the entire world, and yet deprives them of human contact. Some people pay psychoanalysts a fortune just to have someone to listen to them. In terms of human contact, telecommuting does not really spell progress; hence, it will remain marginal.

Tomorrow's population will not work any less than today's. Tomorrow's workers will also try to find in their office job the kind of social ties and opportunities for mutual recognition that are needed for life to have some purpose. People do not want the life of solitude enjoyed by the cyberhermit. Obviously, the world changes, but over time people's behavioural patterns remain – often sadly – the same. People are people and we are all subject to emotions of fight, flight, pain and pleasure. When placed in similar situations, regardless of period or culture, we react in remarkably similar ways.

Let us not forget the human factor and that people are always at the core of any difference or change. There is no need to find a scapegoat in globalization or technology just to shirk our responsibilities. For many companies, regions or individuals experiencing difficulties, their troubles stem from internal insufficiencies and not some external force. The keys of success and causes of failure are initially internal.

The future of an individual or an organization depends largely on its internal strengths and weaknesses. We recognize the wisdom of the ancient Greeks, namely Socrates, who counseled: "Know thyself (we stress the second part; thyself first)". As we will see, this advice leads us to several key questions.

Deep down we know that there is no technological or economic solution to problems of a spiritual nature. Trying to apply technological or economic solutions to problems of an ideological or spiritual nature is like giving candy to a child seeking affection. The major issues for the future are linked to social fractures and the spiritual void which is the result of a society obsessed with material gain.

Yet people have selective short-term memory and fail to recognize the long-term and what it can teach us. The well-known expression states that history may not be repeated, nevertheless human behavior certainly is! Over the centuries, people have adopted and kept eerily similar behavioral patterns that led them to similar situations in which they behaved in almost the same ways. Their behaviour is thus predictable and the past thus provides us with insightful lessons for the future. Economic examples come to mind, such as cyclical scarcity and abundance in the food supply related to speculation on prices or long periods of inflation followed by deflation and lastly, the worrisome coincidences between the demographic transition and economic decline.

Economic structures and patterns are always characterized by heavy inertia, which should not be underestimated in terms of its potential to thwart change. Unfortunately in futures studies we tend to consider that which could change by forgetting to systematically list all that which most likely will remain unchanged, especially if nothing is done. Some inertial forces actually act like a brake on adaptation and development and they then become rigid if change – whether desirable or undesirable – has not been prepared far enough in advance. However, other inertial forces play a healthy role and, as any driver knows, the brake complements the accelerator.

From Key Actors to Bifurcations

The future should not be envisaged as a single, protracted line extending from the past. The future is plural and undetermined. This plurality and the degrees of freedom in human action essentially form a tangent.

The present is all the richer since the future remains open to a vast array of possible futures in which the desirable may dominate. In the words of Gaston Berger (1967), "old age is simply the shrinking of the field of possibilities". Phrased differently, whatever is no longer possible in the future is the fruit of our past actions; whereas, that which remains possible depends upon our present actions.

The broader the array of possible futures is, the greater the number of futures and the greater the uncertainty. Each possible future, or *futurible*, [1] is more or less probable but only certain ones are desirable to each actor. The actors' initiatives may be partially antagonistic and therefore, the future outcome may be considered as the result of the balance of power amongst those actors. Of course the balance of power is not static and the actors' strategies serve to orient probable results toward desirable results. In sum, creating futures depends not only upon chance and necessity but also upon human will.

The so-called real world is much too complex for us to hope to generate a logarithm of any hidden determinism it may hold. Even if we

---

1. Neologism based on the words *futur* and *possible*, created by Bertrand de Jouvenel.

could calculate such a formula, the uncertainty that is inherent in any measure, especially if social, would leave us with a range of possible futures at least in our minds. Yet since determinism is undeterminable, we have to go along *as if* no bets had been placed, and *as if* the revolution of will could singlehandedly dethrone the tyranny of chance and necessity.

During the seventies, Ilya Prigogine and Isabelle Stengers (1987) based their work on theories and experiments in thermodynamics and physical chemistry to advance their own notions of *order by fluctuation* and *fertile chaos* (Prigogine, 1990). They demonstrated that when far from the initial conditions of equilibrium, bifurcations appear which lead to other states of equilibrium. Near these critical points weak fluctuations, either internal or external to the system, may prove decisive in moving towards one or another branch of evolution. When transposed to social systems, these weak fluctuations may be chance upsets or individual actions. At these critical points, the fluctuations become dangerous whereas elsewhere they would have remained insignificant.

How can we recognize bifurcations? "What events and which innovations will be inconsequential and which ones are liable to affect the world order, determine an irreversible evolutionary choice? What are the zones of selection and the zones of stability?" (Prigogine, 1990) The same questions arise regularly in any futures-thinking exercise.

If we think about it, identifying the range of possible futures with scenarios is also recognizing the diagram of bifurcations. And if so, then the parameters of those bifurcations are also the key variables used in the analysis stage of futures-thinking.

Over the past few years, theories have converged towards a self-organizing concept that enables one to adapt them to whatever is "new" and to the creation of anything new. Everything happens as if the traditional arrow of time were reversed so that what we do today may be explained not by conditioning but by the goal that we have set and are striving to reach (Jean-Pierre Dupuy, 1982). Once again, the future is the *raison d'être* of the present. Let us add that desire is the force generating the future and the driving/guiding principle of self-organization.

Nevertheless, futures thinking is far from neutral. It depends on subjective choices related to how problems are approached, which hypotheses are tested, and what goals are pursued. In fact, starting a futures-thinking exercise and listing scenarios as part of actors' strategies is rather like a poker bid. Here we put our finger squarely on the ideological role that scenario building may play and on the danger of manipulation inherent in the process.

Political parties play with the future like Pavlov's bell that can be rung to mobilize or demobilize the masses. One example is to get people to accept the problems of the day more readily as a future project.

Obviously a leader can hardly tell the nation to tighten its belt so that tomorrow will be even worse! If we take it to extremes, there is the theme of the sacrificed generations. In this case the ideological spin is incredible and political groups speak of the future as if speaking about the future made it true. (Yves Barel, 1971). The danger of manipulation will be lessened once futures-thinking exercises or strategic scenario building are accessible to everyone; i.e., all those concerned may take part, not only executives and political leaders.

The image of the future that we create for ourselves is invaluable and must be analyzed since questioning actors on their representations of the future reveals a great deal about their strategic behavior. Moreover, even if this vision of the future seems wrong to us, we still need to take it into account.

At this point, many will want to justify the usefulness and credibility of futures techniques or methodology. Let us employ the analogy of a gambler at the casino. The uncertainty of the future prompts him to place bets and, like a good gambler, a good strategic futurist/expert wins more often than he loses.

Simple Tools for Complex Problems

Are only complex tools capable of measuring our complex reality? No. Modern history's great minds traditionally found relatively simple laws to explain the universe. Examples abound in the principles of thermodynamics or the theory of relativity. As the French mathematical economist and Nobel prize-winner Maurice Allais (1989) put it: "A theory in which neither the hypotheses nor the consequences may be squared with reality is of no scientific interest." Allais adds that a perfect model is impossible and that only approximative models of reality are possible. He points out that "of two models, the best will always be the one in which a given approximation will represent the data gathered through observation in the simplest manner." That should reassure readers who think all this is Greek to them and it should also shake up all those who confuse the term "complex" with "complicated" and hence simple with simplistic! The real challenge lies in convincing those who are used to making things complicated. It is always easier to complicate matters than it is to simplify them.

Here is one more definition: a system is not reality but rather a means to observe reality. Systems analysis is nothing more than a way of thinking observed as a way of thinking. It is also an act of epistemological faith since it supposes that the observer is capable of self-observation and observation simultaneously. In this sense a complex way of thinking, a complex vision of reality, does require a complex tool. Consequently we suggest confronting complexity with the simplest tools possible because a tool is there to reduce rather than increase complexity. We also suggest:

– testing complex tools on simple problems to be able to measure the added value of the complex tool versus the simple tool;

– approaching complex problems with simple tools in order to ensure that the complexity stems from the problem and not the tool.

It is worth repeating that an imperfect tool, be it an inaccuracy, a surplus or a lack of data, as well as the subjectivity of interpretations, is inevitable and encourages the use of varied, complementary approaches. Wherever possible, the sensitivity of the results generated by a model should be tested against the variation in input data and the use of another tool. Only solid, tested results should be considered credible.

If scenario building requires rigor to deal with complexity, it also requires tools that are simple enough to be appropriated. The following timeless recommendation rings true: "An operational imperfection is better than a non-existent perfection." In this respect, game theory has certainly advanced, at least theoretically, but it remains unapplied in corporations. On the other hand, the Mactor method (as seen in the case studies herein) used in analyzing actors' strategies may not be perfect but it is at least operational.

Ask the Right Questions and Quash Conventional Thinking

"The answer is yes, but what was the question?" Woody Allen

This famous line is all too often what happens when we forget to consider the validity of a question and rush like lemmings to find the illusory answers to false questions. Since there can be no right answer to a wrong question, how can we ensure that we are indeed asking the right questions?

Information is often stifled by conformism in the guise of consensus. As innocent as it might seem, consensus may incite individuals to opt for the dominant opinion and reject the minority view. In the end, any one individual who sees clearly will not likely be heard. Of course that does not mean that wild predictions should be given more credence, but rather that many conjectures and preconceived ideas should be considered with suspicion. Yes, there is always some discomfort in rousing people from years of intellectual habits; however, the scenario planner or futurist must act like the cheeky child who dares to say that the Emperor is naked and definitely not wearing new clothes!

In the past we have often been right in exposing conventional thinking. By deconstructing various problems, we've managed:

– to point out as early as 1978 that there would be a new oil crisis plus an energy surplus that would render nuclear energy less necessary; [1]

---

1. "Energy Horizon Keeps Receding?", *The Times*, 5 September 1978.

– dispute the thesis of the industrial decline of Europe in relation to the United States and Japan; [1]

– to cast doubt on the Japanese management "model of the week" fad; [2]

– to question the regularly evoked thesis of Germany's decline (at a time when Germany had become the world's leading exporter of manufactured goods); [3]

– to denounce the myth of technology as the way out of economic crises. [4]

Strategy is also affected by conformism and conventional thinking. How many investment and site selection choices have been justified with the mantra "the company needs economies of scale to compete internationally"? In reality, there are always smaller, more profitable companies even within the same sector. Why then does a company not opt to find ways to be more profitable without expanding? The correct question would be "how can we be more profitable at our current size?" The answer to this question may mean temporary lack of growth, like trees which are pruned only to grow back all the more beautifully. Profitability is really the best condition for healthy growth.

Despite a respectable track record in the futures field, we have few illusions about the impact of a statement or an article that goes against the grain of popular wisdom. However, we consider it almost a civic duty to say what others only think. Too many intellectuals keep quiet for the sake of their career, gobbing everything and prepared to sacrifice their own ideas for money, honor or reputation. Cowardice underlies the demure attitude of some, not to mention the "reasons of state", sometimes given as an explanation for remaining silent even about crimes.

Any good teacher knows that the best ideas or lessons are those that students find themselves. However, in the school of hard knocks, everyone knows that if the boss likes an idea and actually believes it came from him or her, then there is a much greater chance that it will be implemented. This is part of human nature. It is a fact of life that should be remembered whenever we have to convince anyone of anything.

---

1. "The USA: Recovery or Concealed Decline?", *Futures*, vol. 17, n° 3, 1985, pp. 196-201.

2. "Ten Unfashionable and Controversial Findings on Japan", *Futures*, vol. 19, n° 4, 1987, pp. 371-84.

3. "Germany: Paradoxical Power", *Futures*, vol. 12, n° 4, 1989, pp. 344-60.

4. "From the Technological Mirage to the Social Breakthrough", *Futures*, vol. 17, n° 3, 1986, pp. 369-75.

From Anticipation to Action through Appropriation

Vision may be a buzzword, but we insist on using it here, especially since breadth of vision is needed if anything is going to happen, first, on a small scale, and then within the larger scheme of things. Mobilizing intelligence is all the more efficient if it takes place within the framework of a specific project known to all. Internal motivation and external strategy are thus like two sides of the same sheet of paper. They are also two goals that can not be reached separately.

Intellectual and affective appropriation is a compulsory stage if anticipation is to crystallize into effective action. We turn to the ancient Greeks to conceptualize this idea, the Greek triangle illustrated below. "Logos" (thought, rationality, discourse), "Epithumia" (desire in all its noble and not so noble aspects), "Ergo" (action or realization). The marriage of passion and reason, of heart and mind, is the key to successful action and individual fulfillment (the body). Let us turn to the cover to see the same message in color: the blue of cold reason mixed with the yellow of warm feelings produces the green of brilliant action.

The Greek Triangle

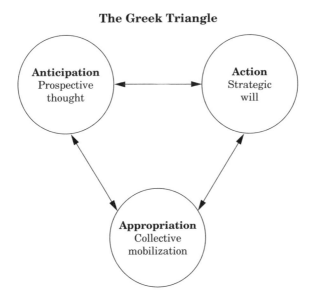

The Greek triangle can help us if we visualize the three points: Anticipation (blue); Action (green), Appropriation (yellow). The blue of anticipation turns to the green of action only with the yellow of appropriation introduced through the efforts of the actors involved. The triangle must be balanced to function properly. Appropriation means that all stakeholders are vested, not just the CEO and a few of his or her liutenants. Anticipation means relying upon on expert advice, and divorcing oneself temporarily from day-to-day problems.

The age-old dialectic between intuition and logic and the link between thought and action appears clearly here. Once it is time to act, it is too late to think. Moreover, when one thinks, one should take time and not be rushed by an emergency. Action is commanded by a reflex whereas reason is generally dominated by intuition. This impression fools us into thinking that the reflex to act happens without any prior meditation. William Blake (1790) put it nicely, "Without contraries there is no progression. Attraction and repulsion, reason and energy, love and hate, are necessary to human existence." In the end, there really is no opposition but rather complementarity between intuition and reason.

More Endogenous Projects and Fewer Scenarios

One aspect of foresight that must be mentioned here is the systematic use and abuse of scenarios. With respect to regions, rather than learning from the past and analyzing regions comparatively in order to shape development, many forget that foresight and scenario are not synonyms. Actually, scenarios hold little interest if not pertinent, coherent, and realistic for the region and its population. Here we remember one of our own rules: Ask the right questions. Granted, drafting desirable scenarios as a group may serve a therapeutic purpose; however, in this case the resulting scenarios are less important than the collective effort. Once a group has decided to consider the future together, it might as well ask the right question(s). Furthermore, the group might as well begin with those questions for which there is little consensus. Why? Tackling contentious issues tends to shake up the established order and break participants out of their usual patterns of thinking.

Furthermore, scenarios should not be confused with strategic options because participants in scenario building workshops are not necessarily those on the front lines. The anticipation phase should be collective and should involve the greatest number of people possible for this is participatory democracy at work. Indeed, this phase employs tools to organise and structure the collective thinking process on what is at stake in the future as well as the eventual evaluation of strategic options. On the other hand, for reasons of confidentiality or liability, the phase of strategic choices should involve a limited number of participants, e.g., the elected representatives only or a company's board of directors. This final phase requires less scientific methodology and decisions should be made after roundtable discussions and consensus gathering among the leading participants or those in charge. The tools employed here may be useful in choosing strategic options, but the emphasis remains on freedom of choice.

The use of scenarios becomes all the more an abuse of scenarios when the scripts deal with the future context of a region with the question (Q1) *What can happen?*: This natural query leads regions, like companies, to reinvent the wheel and world and in so doing people forget to ask the essential prerequisite question (Q0) *Who are we?* which implies identity, history, strengths and weaknesses. [1] Overall, we tend to forget what Socrates taught us: *Know thyself.* That essential prerequisite question underlies all else and necessitates a return to one's origins, roots or competencies, with the lessons of the regions' past failures or successes.

Future planning or scenario planning focuses on what can happen. In both regional and corporate applications, the essential prerequisite question suggesting self-knowledge, history, and desires for the future tends to be forgotten. Ironically, this question remains essential if we consider that the factors of development are endogenous and if we wish to focus on (Q1); i.e., reflect on contextual scenarios. This type of reflection does have its uses but it has it limits because the future is unpredictable and remains to be built or created. All regions will face the same restrictions and opportunities. The true difference between any two regions lies in the capacity of certain regions to accentuate their strengths and minimize their weaknesses. This implies self-reliance. Self-reliance is the singularly most effective behaviour and also the one within most regional actors' reach.

Diagnosis and a plan are not sufficient for a region or corporation to take action. *Why?* We return to (Q4), or *How?*, which must be answered through appropriation. Only through the correct use of participatory exercises and events upstream, to use a marketing term, can any foresight or strategic prospective endeavour actually function.

The development of any region stems from its own dynamic nature. Economic activity and employment are stimulated by the number of local initiatives plus the cross-fertilisation of those same initiatives. Globalisation, external constraints and technological change are therefore not really obstacles to be overcome but rather opportunities to be seized. In our experience, the process of participatory foresight using simple and appropriable methods has proved to be a powerful lever for promoting territorial development.

---

1. This five-step process rather than the usual three-step promoted by most authors of strategy stems from my collaboration with Hugues de Jouvenel and Jacques Lesourne in September 1997. When my first textbook on strategic foresight came out we realized that there was a (Q0) which we ourselves forgot at the first meeting. It just proves that no one is immune to blind spots, especially when directly involved in a project. Michel GODET (2001)

A Global Vision for 1001 Local Solutions

We end on a happy note. The future of our regions is open. Moreover, it depends less on trends or uncertainty about the future than on the ability of the actors to unite in collective efforts and build what we wishfully call "a society of projects".

Economic activity and employment are stimulated by the number of local initiatives plus the cross-fertilisation of those same initiatives. Globalisation, external constraints and technological change are therefore not really obstacles to be overcome but rather opportunities to be seized.

Areas open up to globalisation more successfully if they have deep roots, for this process heightens an area's need to affirm its distinct cultural and local identity. Globalisation and local cultures interact and mutually enrich one another. "Going global" does not mean losing but rather cultivating what makes an area different. In other words, it requires a global vision to find 1001 local solutions.

Local development is not made possible by infrastructure and even less so by subsidies, which at best can only support it. For example, Sainte Sigolène, in the Haute-Loire region, has become one of France's most important plastics centres despite its remote location and lack of a railway access. The key to local development lies really in individuals and organisations. Everything depends upon their ability to pool their energies towards a collective project rather than working against each other. An area achieves strength though unity not divisiveness, and as the American expression goes, "A house divided cannot stand." Society cannot be changed by decree; the doors of change swing open from the inside-out, as Jacques Chaize [1] has so aptly put it.

Herein lies an important message: instead of imposing top-down solutions that have little effect, policymakers should base their decision upon observations of what works in the field.

Participatory Foresight with Simple Tools

People need the future; in other words, they need hope. This collective need is best expressed if channelled through some form of method. Surprisingly, this corresponds to what psychiatrist Jean Sutter (1983) meant when he observed that people's principal and almost sole occupation was to live their future in advance. [2]

Let us give two quick reminders here: (1) action without a goal is meaningless and (2) foresight leads to action. In our experience, the complexity of the problems and the need to address them collectively

1. Chaize, J. (1992): La Porte du changement s'ouvre de l'intérieur, Calmann-Lévy.
2. Sutter, J. (1983): L'anticipation. PUF, Coll. "Psychiatrie ouverte"

call for methods that are as rigorous and participatory as possible to enable those involved to identify the appropriate problems and agree upon their solutions.

Although foresight requires a rigorous approach to address complex problems, the tools must also be simple enough to be easily used. Since the mid-1980s, the approach of Strategic Prospective Workshops has proven its effectiveness in meeting these criteria (appropriable, simple, and rigorous).

A Few Key Words

Prospective: Anticipate before acting. *La prospective*, an "intellectual non-discipline" (Pierre Massé) seeks to see "far, wide and deep" (Gaston Berger).

Prediction: Estimate of the future assigned a certain degree of confidence.

Projection: Extension or inflection into the future of past trends.

Scenario: coherent sets of hypotheses issuing from a given original situation to a future situation.

Five Basic Attitudes toward the Future

1) Passive   Ostrich accepting change as it comes
2) Reactive   Firefighter waiting for the alarm to ring
3) Preactive   Insurance agent preparing for foreseeable changes
               (An ounce of prevention is worth a pound of cure.)
4) Proactive   Conspirator (agent provocateur) who pushes for desirable changes
5) A combination of 2 to 4.

Planning

"Conceiving of a desired future as well as the real means required to achieve it." (R.L. Ackoff).

Strategy

Code of conduct for actors enabling them to reach their goals.

Tactics (plur.)

Ways and means of reaching goals within a strategy according to the circumstances.

Strategic Planning

Concept launched in the mid-60s, notably by Igor Ansoff, to refer to the fact that corporate planning should take turbulence in the company's environment (often called strategic environment) into account much more and adapt its goals accordingly.

Strategic Management

Concept launched in the mid-1960s by Igor Ansoff in order to emphasize the conditions that enable structures and organizations to adapt to an increasingly turbulent world.

Strategic Prospective

Concept from the 1990s, French School, in which *la prospective* is applied to strategic action and the corporate vision. In this way; *strategic prospective* acts as a management tool from anticipation to action through appropriation. This is also the case of technological *foresight* in terms of public acceptance of change and policymaking.

2

WHY DO THE EXPERTS GET IT WRONG?

The New Economy Was an Old Hat

American Growth Was Not New

What Have ICT's Really Done

Confusion Between the New Economy and New Technology

Every Generation Has Its own New Age

The Solow Paradox Is Still Timely

Growth Can Be Explained In Classical Terms and Remains Precarious

Long Cycles and the Temptation of Determinism

Fluctuations in Prices and Imaginary Cycles

Tales of Error

History is full of paradoxes regarding the future. For example, it was during the sixties when forecasting was easier and less necessary that futurology, futures studies, and *la prospective* were developed. In those days, econometric models driven by primitive computers could demonstrate, in practical terms, what people already knew: everything was more or less directly correlated to the national product, which was growing at 5% annually. Time was simply the best "explanatory" variable for what was considered a perpetual period of growth.

However since 1974 the future has stopped looking like the past. The horizon used in futures thinking; i.e., break points or discontinuities, had crept up on us. However no model based on data and relationships from the past could have foreseen these breaks or bifurcations because they were linked to the behavior of actors free to behave however they wished.

Although we might bruise a few egos in reviewing historical errors in forecasting, there are important lessons to be learned. In fact, it soon becomes obvious that errors in forecasting cause less damage than errors in analysis, diagnosis and prescription. The latter are created more by a lack of foresight and are thus worse than any false prediction. Canadian futurist Kimon Valaskakis uses a medical analogy to illustrate the potential for error in any futures exercise. The possibility of error lies at the following four points:

1) in diagnosing the disease;
2) in forecasting its development;
3) in prescribing the right drugs;
4) and lastly, in determining the correct dosage of those drugs.

The first error, a diagnostic error, is obviously the most serious, but numbers two through four are just as frequent. For most issues, for example, unemployment, the diagnosis was rendered public a long time ago, but the pill seems too bitter to swallow given the many socioeconomic taboos surrounding joblessness.

An effective futures-thinking exercise or forecast implies nonconformism, rigor, and consistency. Just trusting intuition, especially intuition unenlightened by logic, leads to desperate detours and even deadends. Remember that even while walking in the dark, we have to keep our eyes wide open and avoid preconceived ideas.

Whether errors in analysis come from models or not, they may be directly linked to experts whose erroneous viewpoints are spread on the simple basis of their reputation. The following historical example of conventional, conformist thinking and authority comes from Bernard Cazes (1986). In the fifteenth century, Christopher Columbus proposed his seafaring expedition to the King and Queen of Spain. The enterprise was carefully examined by an informal commission presided by the Hieronymite brother Hernando de Talavera, Queen Isabela's confessor.

Four years later, the commission rendered its opinion to the monarchs. To paraphrase Talavera, nothing could justify royal assent for such an enterprise based on weak logic and seemingly impossible to anyone with any knowledge whatsoever! The six arguments against Columbus' idea of a western passage to the Indies appear to follow a logical structure:

1) a journey to Asia would require three years;

2) the (Atlantic) ocean is infinite and perhaps unnavigable;

3) if Columbus were to reach the ends of the earth, he would not be able to return home;

4) there are no endpoints of land because most of the globe is covered with water and because Saint Augustine said so;

5) of five parts of the world, only three are inhabitable;

6) so many centuries after the Creation, it is unlikely that lands of any interest could have remained undiscovered.

Although the expert committee was wrong, Christopher Columbus was equally wrong. He remained convinced that between the end of the Orient and the end of the Occident there lay only one sea. As a result, he concluded that the Chinese coast was only five or six thousand kilometers from Europe. Columbus never did reach the Orient and discovered America without knowing it. He went to his grave claiming to have reached the Indies when he had only completed one-third of his journey. Furthermore, the Antilles did not look anything like what people knew of the Orient in those days.

Another historical example given by our colleague André Guillerme involves estimates of the Earth's age up to the eighteenth century and the catastrophic extrapolations that ensued.

Up to and including the year 1750, scientists estimated the Earth's age to be 5,200 years. In 1750, a Frenchman named Buffon calculated it to be one million years while his colleague, Cuvier, went as high as ten million. Nowadays, the Earth's age is considered to be approximately twenty billion years. Right up to the mid-eighteenth century, however, scientific calculations used five thousand years as a reference point for their extrapolations. On the basis of the observable erosion which had occurred over the past 5,000 years, they predicted that the mountains would disappear within the following two hundred years and that the planet would turn into swampland during the twentieth century. Similarly, given a "Little Ice Age" at the end of the eighteenth century, the same scientists thought that the Earth's temperature had settled at 1,000° in 3000 BC and consequently should reach 10° in 1880 and then 0° in the year 2000. Reports of academic societies also proved that the Champagne region of France was destined to become a desert based on the supposition that heavy deforestation would continue. No one anticipated the upcoming use of coal!

Well, that was then, some might say. Scientists of yesteryear did not have today's analytical tools. Granted, we are better equipped now, but often you would not know it from the results. Indeed, armies of economists focused their efforts on fuel and energy forecasting after the first oil shock. In hindsight, they were all wrong, dead wrong. Energy consumption in 1985 was actually half the amount regularly predicted in 1974.

That was then, but this is now. Can we say that current forecasts or predictions are any more reliable? The World Energy Conference (1993) forecast consumption rates of slightly more than 13 billion tonnes of oil equivalent (TOE).

Oil accounts for one quarter of that amount, in other words, only slightly more than what was predicted in 1985 for the year 2000. So far, the world demand has been systematically overestimated, especially for petroleum. Why? It seems that the slowdown in developed economies was never considered longlasting. In the future, of course, the opposite could arise if the probable upswing in several developing countries pans out. Remember that 1990 North American energy consumption of 8 TOE per capita was twice the Western European rate and five to six times that of developing countries.

Lastly, we know how a progressive increase in energy prices affects savings and increases the possibility of substitution. We can thus legitimately ask if the relative decrease in oil prices since the mid-eighties is not paving the way for new oil shocks that will be all the sharper because we have let down our guard.

Of course sometimes the experts get it wrong because they have biased information. However, often they simply attack false problems that mask the real issues. There are actually many possible causes of error. What follows is a summary and update of the classic list found in *From Anticipation to Action*, 1994.

Energy Forecasting Errors

Energy forecasting is notoriously fraught with error. The collective myopia conerning energy often leads to strategies which are based upon unsound evidence or a complete dismissal of potential energy ruptures. Moreover, the lessons from the past should have permitted us to avoid strategic errors and undesireable price shocks.

The First Oil Shock Should Have Been Expected

The first oil shock was a complete surprise, or rather, those who warned of such an event were completely ignored. With the benefit of hindsight, it seems obvious that the oil shock of 1974 resulted from the confluence of several trends which had been developing over the course of the 1960's (supressed oil prices, accelerating substitution of oil with coal, rising energy dependence among the Western countries vis-a-vis OPEC, etc.) and increasing political tensions between energy companies and OPEC countries. Furthermore, the geo-political shift of power which resulted from the formation of OPEC in 1960 should have captured our attention because it foreshadowed the upcoming energy crisis.

Errors Repeated

The oil shock of 1974 wasn't the first energy crisis that the Western world has known. In 1928, one could already envision the gasification of coal and the recovery of hydrocarbons from bituminous rock. The shortage that was apparent then, lead to an overabundance of energy due to the exploration and discovery of oil in the Middle-East in the years which followed the crisis. The original error in judgement was the result of a lack of imagination and a lack of reflection concerning the future. The ambitious energy programs in nuclear and coal, launched in France after the Suez crisis of 1956, had not yet even been concieved.

Forecasting Errors

Worldwide Energy Consumption

In 1974, the consumption of oil was 5.6 billion tonnes, and the expected consumption for 1985 was 11 billion.

In 1985, the consumption of oil was 7 billion tonnes, and the expect consumption for 2000 was 10 billion.

Thus, the forecasting error was an amazing 36% overestimation of worldwide oil consumption. If you consider the projections for just the industrialized countries, the gap between forecast and reality is even more pronounced. In 1974 the projection for the consumption of oil in indsutrialized countries was 6.5 billion tonnes, however the actual consumption of oil was only 3.5 billion tonnes – an overestimation of 45%.

Source: OECD

Beginning in 1975-1976, with declining oil prices in constant dollars, a number of experts believed that things were going to return normal – in other words, stable and relatively low oil prices. At the time, one barrel of oil cost 12 dollars, and the zietgiest seemed to be one of both complacency and denial. In the mid 70's I was working as a consultant and I went to great lengths to convince my clients that they ought to explore future scenarios in which oil prices might actually increase.

In fact, the recent oil-shock should have been anticipated as soon as the profit margins of oil-exporting countries began to dwindle in 1975 with the return of low oil prices. In 1977, sheik Yamani, Saudi oil minster declared, "It would be prudent to expect the price of oil per barrel to surpass 25 dollars by 1990." [1]

---

1. Le Monde, December 21, 1977

By 1979, the energy crisis had been taken seriously; perhaps even exagerated. A wave of panic washed over the Western world: There was going to be a worldwide oil shortage – and soon. Expensive prices at the pump were proof that the countdown had indeed started. In France, the response was to find alternative sources of energy. Nuclear energy seemed to provide the solution. At the time, nuclear seemed to be the only alternative which would outlast the impending oil crisis. According to accepted analyses, this approach was the only way to avoid disruptions in energy supplies which had the power to derail the French economy.

Errors in diagnosis lead to errors in prescription. The nuclear energy program in France had been grossly overdeveloped. We made the following observations as early as 1978:
 – cheap energy is scarce while expensive energy is abundant;
 – increasing oil prices, so long as they were gradual, were beneficial to an economy because they would lead to efficiencies, and encourage transition to oil alternatives;
 – there was a risk that the postwar boom, which had ushered in 30 years of unprecedented prosperity, was permanently over for structural economic reasons other than energy.

Given these conditions, an energy program devoted to 100% nuclear was a gamble that would only pay-off in the unlikely coincidence of an oil shortage and strong domestic demand for energy. Certainly, the development of nuclear energy was indispensible to France's overall energy strategy, but not at the envisioned scale. The economy never bounced back to pre-shock growth rates, the consumption of energy diminished, and oil remained abundant. The incertainties of economic recovery and the pattern of energy consumption required a far more flexible energy strategy.

That brings us to the current energy forecasts. The World Energy Council (2000) expected the consumption of total energy (in Tonnes of Oil Equivalent or TOE) for the year 2020 to be 13 billion TOE, of which a quarter would be oil. This amount is approximately the same for that which had been forecast for 2000 in the year 1985.

The scenarios for 2050 yield a range of consumption between 14 and 25 billion TOE. If there had been a systematic overestimation of worldwide energy demand for oil in the past, it's because the economic recessions over the last 30 years in developped countries were never expected to last. The per capita consumption of energy in North America is 8 TOE, 4 TOE in Western Europe and 1.3 TOE in developing countries like China and India. Given the sustained economic growth of the emerging Asian giants (China and India,) their relatively modest per capita energy consumption will not last, therefore there may now be a tendency to err on the side of underestimation with respect to future worldwide energy demand. Lastly, the supression of oil prices over the long-term usually leads to an abrupt upward correction attended by ruinous consequences for the economy. This is exactly what happened in 2005 after years of relatively cheap oil.

The Energy Horizon Keeps Receding

Given expected worldwide energy demand, the recourse to new sources seems enescapable, even if these new sources turn out to be less necessary than we had originally anticipated. At the current pace of production, the countdown to the end of the oil age has begun. The age of oil may last perhaps another 15 to 25 years. One era ends and another begins.

After having replaced coal in the 1960's, it was only a matter of time before oil would also meet its hour of decline. The spectre of an oil shortage and the lack of short-term profits in non-nuclear alternatives, lends credence to those who favor a return to a nuclear energy strategy in France.

Calling into question the pessimistic forecasts concerning hydrocarbon reserves serves the short-term interests of certain actors (energy companies, states, etc.) who wish to justify new research and investment in energies which would replace hydrocarbons. These same actors, attracted by cheap oil prices in the 1960's, had precipitated the transition from coal to oil. This was a strategic error. Notwithstanding the problems of polution, coal was a more sensible energy choice. At the time, coal was at least 5 to 6 times more abundant than oil, it could be extracted relatively inexpensively, and it was distributed more evenly across the planet's political geography.

The Effect of Suggestion

Forecasts do not exist in an vacuum, rather, they interact via feedback with the systems then intend to objectify. The result is often a boomerang. For example, announcing an impending shortage today is the best way to produce an abundance tomorrow.

The oil shock of 1974 wasn't the first energy crisis that the Western world has known. In 1928, one could already envision the gasification of coal and the recovery of hydrocarbons from butinimous rock. The shortage that was apparent then lead to an overabundance of energy due to the exploration and discovery of oil in the Middle-East in the years which followed the crisis. The original error in judgement was the result of a lack of imagination and a lack of reflection concerning the future. The ambitious energy programs in nuclear and coal, launched in France after the Suez crisis of 1956, had not even been concieved.

If we have learned one lesson from the history of energy it is that we mustn't assume that the future will be a linear extrapolation of present trends. *La prospective* should be concerned with rational analysis and the identification of those trends which have the potential to become future ruptures, even if that analysis calls into question accepted ideas like an inpending energy shortage. Numerous facts and signals cast serious doubt on the pessimism of most official energy forecasts. The era of cheap energy is most defintely over, however, expensive energy doesn't neccessarily mean rare energy, quite the contrary.

Source: Michel GODET, article which appeared in *Le Monde* and *The Times*.

The Four Main Causes of Error

Short-sightedness When Facing Change and Inertia

We have already mentioned two biases as sources of error: overestimating change and underestimating inertia. Overestimating change in 1965 led the Rand Corporation (Delphi [1] expert survey in hand,) to announce teaching machines and 100% accurate weather forecasts by the year 1975; automatic translation by 1979; and household robots for 1988. (For more information on these much awaited future technologies, see Bernard Cazes (1986)).

This excessive extrapolation of technological possibilities continues in the third millennium, as seen in the emphasis placed on distance education and telecommuting. Fortunately or unfortunately, many experts, managers and politicians forget that people crave social ties and that nothing replaces human contact. Think about how often you prefer to wait for the "real live" operator or a receptionist when you telephone a large business or organization.

Inversely, many technological changes considered inconceivable yesterday have become commonplace today. At the beginning of the twentieth century, American astronomer and mathematician, Simon Newcomb, thought that he had amply demonstrated the impossibility of ever seeing a device heavier than air fly. He considered the impossibility tantamount to a fact. (Denis de Rougemont, in Cazes (1986)).

One common denominator in technological change is uncertainty. Uncertainty prevails, and unexpected discoveries or innovations may arise, but we should never forget that what is technologically possible today will develop slowly because of inertia and socio-economic limits or restrictions. One example stands out: polymetallic nodules. Use of these nodules is technically possible but economically less profitable than existing mines, and, of course, there are considerable geopolitical issues. The life sciences and genetic engineering abound with examples of technically possible but socially or economically unacceptable changes.

Short-sightedness in the face of change leads to two types of symmetric errors: people either overestimate or underestimate the phenomenon. In our expericence, the former occurs more than the latter. Urbanization, as the agrarian world has transitioned to an industrial one in only a few generations, can teach us a lesson in underestimat-

---

1. "The Delphi method has traditionally been a technique aimed at building an agreement, or consensus about an opinion or view, without necessarily having people meet face to face, such as through surveys, questionnaires, emails etc. The Delphi method was developed at the Rand Corporation at the beginning of the cold war to forecast the impact of technology on warfare." http://en.wikipedia.org/wiki/Delphi_method

ing change. Again, the impact of television on families and villages has had a tremendous effect on structures and roles. Yet the family structures, e.g. authoritarian versus egalitarian, described by Emmanuel Todd (1983) seem to have existed for millennia. There are thus permanent features in life, despite the frequent appearance of structural changes.

Nevertheless, the prevailing *zeitgeist* of the twentieth century was that change had accelerated and that history constantly surprises us. One event that comes to mind is the fall of Communism in Eastern Europe (1989), crowned by the reunification of Germany in 1990. Only a few years, even months, beforehand, the domino collapse of several governments remained unthinkable. Yet the velvet revolution and equally surprising, although less smooth, revolts in surrounding countries rose from inertial forces like nationalism and cultural identity. These two forces had resisted decades of authoritarian efforts to stifle or eradicate them. Precisely because they were pent up, nationalism and cultural identity surged stronger than ever throughout Eastern Europe as if floodgates had been opened.

Of course an accurate appraisal of the forces of inertia and change depends on the horizon given in a study. It is important to distinguish among the short-, medium- and long-term, characterized by economic, trend-based, and structural variables respectively. In many fields, accelerated change shrinks the medium-term and brings the long-term closer. In other words, the horizon given in making many decisions may have changed. In some industrial sectors, like electronics, two to four years is already considered a long-term horizon whereas in aeronautics, inertia is such that ten to fifteen years must be used as a long-term horizon.

Prophecies and Political Lies

Almost any published report on any development or change in a given area of our lives will provoke reactions which, in turn, affect that development. This is the prophecy effect at work. Some are encouraging prophecies that help complete the effect of a phenomenon, e.g. inflation. In inflation the anticipation and announcement of an increase usually triggers a multiplier effect. Whereas others are dissuasive or discouraging prophecies which produce a reaction that counters or prevents a development from occuring. We often talk of self-fulfilling or self-destroying (also called self-destructive) prophecies.

Ironically, a good forecast is not one that comes true but rather one that leads to action. The prophecy effect is not always wrong and may even be sought after to correct a situation or reorient a development in a more desirable direction. Hence "foreseeing a catastrophe is conditional in that it requires one to foresee what would happen if we do nothing to prevent it." (Pierre Massé, Gaston Berger, 1967).

Catastrophic demographic projections given during the seventies provide an excellent example of a normative prophecy. If effective, the so-called prophetic information should lead to measures or behaviors that correct an undesirable development. However, in this instance, the prophecy went unfulfilled. African countries did little to control their spiraling birthrates; whereas European countries did nothing to stop the decline of an aging population.

In economics, as Keynes (1936) pointed out, a simple forecast change can through its effects provoke an oscillation similar in shape to a cyclical movement. As a result, the mere mention of a coffee shortage or the unavailability of a children's toy often paves the way for an abundance of the product a few months or years later. Agriculture and the raw materials sector are particularly susceptible to this effect since many investments, e.g. the futures market, depend on the time margin.

In political economy, the prophecy effect is much sought-after by leaders or politicians who play a permanent bluffer's game of poker. Political parties use the prophecy effect in a form of "lying by objective". Governments are better informed nowadays, according to Jean-François Revel (1988) in his book on lies and politics. As he describes it, the political lie has become a way to fool public opinion; whereas in the old days, the political lie was used to trick other governments.

Revel's blunt words should not discourage readers because we still have a role to play in creating futures. An anonymous political science professor once said that "one law deducted from the practice of pluralistic democracy is that a majority victory does not survive the application of its platform." The reason lies in the "broad margin separating an electoral platform from a governmental program. The platform expresses the desirable; the program, the possible." The supply is just meeting the demand. Who is to blame if – as Jean-François Revel (1988) put it – "The first force leading the world is the lie." ?

Self-Censorship and Insufficient Information

We all need to step back from the media floodlights and information overload in which secondary factors often take center stage. There is a real risk of "mind poisoning" from Garbage In, Garbage Out (GIGO). Not only is there useless, even deceptive information, there is also a lack of strategic information. This situation stems not so much from chance or progress as from countless petty struggles played out at the same time around the world. In fact, information should often be considered like a series of bids, as in poker, the game in which a bluff may well count for more than the truth.

Given this state of affairs, Revel (1988) asks a serious question: How can we explain the rarity of "accurate" information in the free world when those gathering information seem to care more about falsifying it and those receiving information seem to care more about avoiding it? He does offer an explanation of sorts: "regulating the circulation of information (in a positive sense) is the determining element of power and the need to believe is stronger than the need to know. There is an ill will which leads us to take precautions and hide the truth from ourselves so that we are surer of our resolve when we deny it in front of others. There is a refusal to admit a mistake, unless we can attribute it to one of our qualities. Lastly, we have the capacity to put in our mind these systematized explanations of what is real, in other words, ideologies, which are like machines capable of both sorting favorable facts that suit our convictions and of rejecting all others."

Relevant information on either the future or past is a rare commodity. Spreading and exchanging information are not neutral, gratuitous processes. "Informing the other person, giving him elements that he does not have, is disclosure or showing one's trump cards rather than bidding." (Michel Crozier, Ehrard Friedberg, 1977).

Decoding information or misinformation according to the power dynamics within a society or a company means cross-checking, reviewing sources and filtering the data on the basis of the actors who create and distribute it. Otherwise anything goes. Clichés, hollow promises and motherhood statements abound simply because they meet the expectations of the reader or listener, "rub the right way" or fit the zeitgeist.

Never neutral, information must always be checked against the source and the channel. What is hidden is often more important than what is shown. The media and the government dazzle us with statistics and official commentary to the point where we become blind. Any skeptic should look up the unemployment rates in the annals of the statistics department. They will find that unemployment is generally presented as a rate and a variation from one year to the next. Rarely, however, are any absolute values given so that the reader can calculate and compare one period to the next, one country to another. These figures do exist but happen to be less accessible and often are provided much later than the sacrosanct unemployment rate.

As a result, information or its omission often serves specific interests. Every reader really should ask two questions: what's to gain and who benefits here? Many desk drawers are lined with politically ill-timed studies. Many relevant reports are gutted or sanitized. Similarly, many realities remain unreported because no one dares to speak out. The most effective and powerful form of censure is the self-censure that researchers and managers adopt when they do not wish to displease their clients or superiors.

Faulty Interpretation

A prediction or forecast generally precedes from a single "reading" of a single situation or event when there are actually many possible interpretations. The resulting error in interpretation is a source of many forecasting disasters. As Bertrand de Jouvenel (1964) pointed out, "because Marx looked at history as a class struggle, the revolution of 1848 is in his eyes was just a parody of the first French Revolution (...) but others see in this revolution an awakening of the nationalities which would soon spread across Europe." In essence, there is no reality free of perception and the perception of facts depends on the theory used in reviewing them. Objective facts do not exist other than through our subjective perception. To paraphrase Oskar Morgenstern (1972): "Data do not become scientific information except through theory."

Errors in interpretation are more difficult to discern because a false theory can provide accurate predictions. Inversely, a valid theory may be proved much later or never. Einstein's theory of general relativity stands out as a brilliant example. An error in interpretation is acceptable in the sense that interpreting is like betting that one has accurately read a phenomenon and also that the reading will be verified. The wager is necessary here since there are no absolute truths and only relative ones. Any proposition is true, but so is its opposite. The most important thing is to retain a sense of proportion.

Misinformation – More and More!

Misinformation or disinformation, noted as a consequence of political lies and self-censure, makes us wonder about the media. Although not a systematic process, misinformation may be explained using the media's commercial goals, e.g. sales figures and audience ratings. One of France's finest journalists – one whose ethics remain impeccable – enlightened us in 1986 with the following statement: "The media are not there to inform but rather to make money on information." A sad commentary, indeed, but one that should not be ignored.

The sloppy reporting, sensationalism and self-promotion that run rampant in much of the media will never be headline news. Reporters may love to talk about themselves, as seen in hostage-taking episodes in Lebanon during the 1970s or the expulsion of certain journalists and confiscation of their cameras in various parts of FYROM (Fomer Yugoslav Republic Of Macedonia.) As in many other professions, there is a code of honor or even Omerta's law. Often journalists interview or quote their colleagues as part of the newscast. Some even go so far as to become both the source and the story! The viewer who surfs the channels during news time or during weekly digest shows finds panels of reporters chatting amongst themselves. The painfully obvious diagnosis is that style and packaging (the container) has taken the place of content, especially when there is no content! In other words, the quality of information plummets and the media end up talking more and more about themselves.

Add to the media malaise, some say sclerosis, the mania for public opinion polls and the result is a debate over empty phrases coming from surveys on anything and nothing. Examples abound: a survey on the need to hold a referendum; i.e., a survey on a survey! Soon the telephone will ring at suppertime and someone will ask whether you would like to know what you think about what you want. The illusion of direct or participatory democracy hides direct demagogy.

Would any medium ever mention a book about the media mess? Would the author take the risk of being blacklisted professionally? Brave without being stupid, we think that the profession is egotistical enough to want to taste some criticism of the content not just the container.

The Abuse of Power

The press is often called the fourth branch in a democracy, followed closely by the legislative, judiciary and executive branches. The label flatters members of the profession but the cliché reveals a danger in that only oppressive regimes claim to use the press as public opinion. The media's role is to serve as a spokesperson, a mirror of society, a relay between the people and their government. Given the journalist's professional duty to investigate, the media also serve to counterbalance the first three columns.

Politicians use the press for advertising while the press uses politicians to anchor its privileged status as spokesperson, or vehicle, in public opinion. The result: coverage of the political scene reaches the saturation point. What we usually see is staging or orchestrated events in which a few big wigs appear and make a sound bite which is then rehashed or interpreted by teams of reporters.

In the age of TV and computers, image counts more than sound. However, an image is only a partial, even a deformed, reflection of a whole. There are editors, mixers, graphic artists, and computer wizards involved, too. The reporter or anchor often passes off these clips as reality with no commentary. What is really eighty seconds of an interview is presented as a "special report" while someone who witnessed an accident gives a few impressions which become an "exclusive live-witness item". The less valuable the news content, the fancier the packaging with file footage or archive material to fill in the gaps.

Information as a Product

In television, the Nielsen or other audience rating systems and the competition among major networks dictate what we see. A network's results may be measured in market share which translates to advertising dollars. As a result, information is orchestrated to catch the public's attention. Hence information must surprise, shock, and then disappear but only to be renewed endlessly. Competition pushes the networks to reduce the "shelf life", or air life, of a news item and to promote scoops or flashes instead, even though these may not be reliable or complete. Rumor thus replaces information. Fortunately there are some watchdogs who dare to point out such examples as the false news story about babies in incubators at an Iraqi hospital during the Gulf War, to name but one.

Information once was called the "oil of the 1990s" because of its cost and value. Given budget restrictions, the news covers a few subjects briefly. Many newsrooms and reporters rely on the same raw data, dispatched over the wire, without taking the time to crosscheck or complete the information. Overall the reporter, news anchor and journalist see their profession reduced to delivering anemic information pumped up with superlatives like *historic, exclusive* and *just breaking.* As a result, the average citizen is made irresponsible and bloated on a diet of non-information.

Yet rigour in processing information is of vital importance if people are to make relevant judgments. Unfortunately, misinformation feeds upon itself and becomes a habit tolerated out of ignorance or apathy. The public starts to think "wrong" using seemingly correct logic. One word is used for another and through false synonymy *resistant* is substituted for rebel and Eastern Europe now has only reformers. Communists are labeled conservatives, socialists, even liberals.

Effective misinformation is all the more insidious because it alters judgment and blunts common sense. Meanwhile the media are decieving themselves and others through competition heightened by sensationalism. The dictatorship of novelty favors anecdotal events and stories to the detriment of important trends and actions that really do make history. Moreover, many of these events are told rather than captured live. Of course this does not mean that filming a disaster equates to explaining it. In the end, what good is a 20-second commentary given by a specialist questioned during a televised newscast? Based on our own experience, the audience remembers the face but not what was said or even the subject of the news clip. Even testimonials from eyewitnesses may be fraught with errors.

Credible but Unreliable Witnesses

Most facts rely on testimonials; unfortunately, accurate testimony is exceptional and jurists or criminologists know it. On this last point, Jean-Noël Kapferer (1987) concluded the following:

– "witnesses give false information with the same assurance as they give accurate information, and always in good faith;

– what we say we saw reflects stereotypes in our mind more than what we really saw;

– if several witnesses concur, it it not necessarily an indication that
their claims or declarations are true. It may mean that several people
share the same stereotypes and mental clichés and yet they perceived
the facts in an identical but erroneous manner."

How can we avoid analysis and forecasting errors with information
that is insufficient and incomplete? How can we escape misinformation
as clichés multiply and media sclerosis increases? For our part, the
answer is doubt, verifications, and taboo hunting. On the part of the
media, the answer is greater rigour and stricter ethics. Intellectuals
also have some responsibility for misinformation but they know when
to keep quiet especially when speaking out might harm their reputation or career which requires types of communication other than vul-
garization. Silence or pseudo-scientific jargon makes many academics
and intellectuals partners in the crime of misinformation. All too often
those in the know remain silent. Consequently there is very little official censorship because self-censorship operates so effectively.

In terms of growth, technology, competitiveness, employment and
training or in demographics and ecology, common sense and experience soon clash with what is "politically correct". Anyone speaking out
soon earns a reputation as an agent provocateur whereas it is reality
that is provocative! By speaking our mind, we have often been told
things like, "you're 100% right… but we can't say that! It would kill us
in the polls". It seems sense is revolutionary. Saying aloud what many
whisper deep down inside does not sit well in our conformist societies.
The futurist must not, however, remain silent since the torchbearer of
the future must point out the pitfalls so that we can avoid them.

What Makes a Good Expert?

Our answer is simple but does not make matters simpler or solve the
problem. Bright lights are often in the minority, an enlightened few.
We then have to ask which minority sees the most clearly.

In many fields, notably in technology, an expert's forecasting judgment is often the main information tool available. This characteristic
explains the success of methods like the Delphi (see Linstone, 1975)
which seeks the convergence of opinions through a consensus guided
gently – some might say manipulated – by the organizers. These methods are appropriate when decisions are pushed forward based on the
consensus reached; however, the same methods are often more misleading than helpful in forecasting or scenario building. Remember
opinions converging in a consensus do not necessarily mean and,
indeed, rarely imply statistical consistency. The fact that everyone
agrees on one opinion does not lend it any additional credibility.

There is often confusion on consensus and expert opinions. The
reader should consider the following analysis of experts' forecasts or
predictions from the first half of the twentieth century.

Evaluating the Experts

In Issue no.5 (Vol. 8, October 1976, p. 411-419) of "Futures", George Wise of the General Electric R&D Centre analyzed the accuracy of forecasts on technological progress and the effects of various American innovations from 1890 to 1940. The author based his study on a corpus of 1,556 forecasts related to the following:
– technological progress (confirmed or not) in 18 specific technological areas;
– social, economic or political impact expected from these changes.

From the bulk of Mr. Wise's study, we can draw five conclusions:
1) Authors of long-term predictions (10 yrs +) were wrong more often than they were right.
2) Experts view the situation slightly more accurately than do the non-experts.
3) Predictions by experts outside their own field are no less accurate than those from specialists in the field studied.
4) Forecasts related to a continued *status quo* in technology, at any particular time, are not more accurate than predictions on innovation.
5) Effects of technological progress are less foreseeable that the changes themselves.

It seems that the reliability of any expert reaches a point of diminishing returns. After that moment, specialists lose sight of the bigger picture or lack critical distance from their own previous opinions or recommendations; in other words, those which made their reputation.

In any field, it is easier to think like everyone else so as not to justify any divergent point of view. On the other hand, any divergent viewpoint does require justification. Here is a practical exercise: managers, consultants or leaders who state opinions should ask only those who think like they do for a justification and not ask those who doubt them. The results can be revrealing.

All in all, the isolated expert can really get it wrong, regardless of reputation. Statistically, it seems wiser to seek the services of a group of experts because we have often observed that the consensus of the group, or the average taken of the various individual views, will yield better results.

No Right Answers to Wrong Questions

No doctor can prescribe the right remedy based on a faulty diagnosis. Unfortunately managers, politicians and even experts run the risk of diagnosing a situation incorrectly when they follow popular or fashionable ideas.

Consultants and leaders have to go against the tide of popular wisdom and conventional thinking to see clearly and ask the right questions, even if it hurts. Yet the majority of experts are conformist and conservative. Sticking with the majority is a comfortable choice because that way the others can do all the explaining. Often the correct forecast; i.e., that is the one which sees the situation correctly, comes form a minority of imaginative, daring experts. Of course it may be difficult to recognize the "right" minority point of view among the others. For the futurist and scenario planner, the lesson remains simple: "If it is difficult, even risky, to defend a new idea among other possible ideas, fear not! Go ahead and challenge the dominant vision; test the rationale behind prevalent ideas."

The consultants, managers, in fact all participants in a futures-thinking exercise, must question what they may take for granted and the "wisdom of the day" that consensus rarely checks. French Nobel prize winner, Maurice Allais points out the tyranny of dominant ideas and adds that only through the constant questioning of the established truths and flourishing of new ideas flowing from creative intuition can science advance. Yet all real scientific progress clashes with the tyranny of preconceived ideas within the major institutions which uphold them. Allais (1989) points out that the more widespread the thinking, the more stubbornly rooted it seems to be in human psychology, and consequently, the more difficult it is for a new concept to be accepted, regardless of its potential.

Light throws shadows. We should add here especially spotlights. Logically then, if the media promote certain problems, they mask others or make them disappear.

Let us use the theory of statistical testing as an analogy. There are three possible risks of error. The risk of error lies in…

1) preparing for something which will not happen and giving empty answers to false problems. This risk frequently arises in environmental and agri-food issues;

2) not preparing for something that can happen and is anticipated: a real question thus remains unanswered;

3) not asking the right questions because they might disturb people or they are politically incorrect, e.g. the demographic and economic implosion of Western Europe.

For example, it has not been proven that global warming is the result of human activities. However, if the principle of precaution requires hard decisions made on the basis of soft information, these decisions should not be too hard and should not be based on information that is too soft. The principle of precaution, or precautionary principle, must not rein in innovation. The future must be kept open and experimenting should continue, even with genetically engineered products, also called genetically manipulated organisms (GM products or GMOs). The same principle should be applied to demographics and economic growth. Although not yet demonstrated, it would be better to consider a possible link between the two and begin researching the various causes and effects. Otherwise, young people in the West (especially Western Europe) will remain a minority, sacrificed on the altar of conventional thinking. The main risk threatening Western societies today has little to do with the environment but everything to do with the demographic and economic implosion related to the "baby bust or crash" which has followed the famous baby boom. On the Old Continent, nothing has been done to prevent this major risk. In terms of retirement programs, every possible solution has been studied, except a plan to rejuvenate populations through an increased birthrate and more immigration. Why? Both birthrates and immigration remain taboo issues in countries like France and Spain.

The first mental habit to cultivate is doubt. Doubt leads to questioning, investigating and confirming. Descartes, whose Cartesian spirit has fallen out of fashion these days, considered doubt his first premise. "[I] never accept anything as the truth unless I knew it obviously to be thus. In other words, I painstakingly avoid precipitation and prevention and do not understand anything more than that which, in my judgment, was so clearly and distinctly presented that to my mind that I had no opportunity to doubt it."

Three Mirages from the 1970s and 1980s

Not long ago, during the 1970s, energy was the cause of all human woes. Only yesterday, in the 1980s, technology was humanity's savior. As a result, in the 1990s training became a priority but it was renamed a "nonmaterial investment". Europe fell victim first to the technology mirage and then to the education mirage.

From Energy to High-Tech: One Mirage Replaces Another

In 1974 the economic crisis was explained primarily in terms of energy. To summarize: Transcend the constraints of limited fossil-fuel resources in order to recover and start strong economic growth. This rationale explains how the French nuclear energy program began.

With hindsight, it is worth observing that in both the North and South, the most economically dynamic countries e.g. Japan, Germany and South Korea, remained heavily dependent on others for energy. Countries with oil, e.g. Great Britain or OPEC members, stagnated industrially. Moreover, not one of the OPEC countries belongs to the group of newly industrialized countries, once popularly referred to as NICs. Everything happened as if the limitation were a stimulus and as if the oil money had led to a complaisant attitude. It is also worth noting that from 1974 to 1977, technology in general – excluding energy technology – was virutally a non-issue in the debate on how to get out of the economic crisis.

From 1978 onward, before the second oil shock, the technology mirage chased away the energy mirage. During this time, official reports resounded with the phrases like "new technological society".

The technology mirage justified an enormous waste of public funds. Note the past tense is used in this case, but the mirage persists. The main idea was not to be left behind during this third industrial revolution. This kind of thinking led to schools equipped with computers which soon became dated and unsalable thus contributing to the failure of the "computers for everyone" plan. After "computerizing the classroom", as this phase was called, long-distance teaching in which the computer replaced the chalkboard was discussed. Educational television was yet another idea, one that led to more channels and less quality on the air. It seems that the same inverse ratio of quantity and quality applies to technology.

On another front, did governments really have to dig into the public coffers to finance research on high resolution TV and cable television? Perhaps there are needs that are not real needs as well as basic needs that are not well served. What about the need for security, human contact, living space, and peace of mind? Whose needs are really being met in our society? The answer is not clear when we think of how the elderly are treated sometimes or how the countryside is ravaged.

Initially, major corporations also fell victim to the technology mirage. For example, in the early 1980s. Renault attributed its sagging productivity rate to technological causes. It soon became apparent, however, that with a comparable level of automation, Renault's performance remained half that of the Japanese carmakers. The difference lay not so much in technology but in individuals and organizations; i.e., the human factor.

The above observation shows just how relative the importance of technical, and financial solutions can be in the development strategies of a company. Any strategy based solely on modernizing technology appears more often that not to be a bottomless pit sucking money. More importantly, this type of strategy diverts management's attention from the real problems of competitiveness that are not only technological but also socio-organizational. The techno-trend can be traced throughout management literature starting around 1982. Before then, technology was scarcely ever mentioned, to the point that the term does not appear in the index of corporate strategy manuals. In the end, however, it is not the volume of material or immaterial investments that matters but rather their effectiveness.

The technology mirage continued, buoyed by a new mirage called training, rebaptized "human capital". However, a shiny new label does not change the contents of an old box. Training remains an expense which must be both suitable and effective. Many trainers should be trained or retrained themselves! And nothing can top collective self-training because only when you teach someone something do you really learn it yourself. The same movement can be traced in modern pedagogy.

The Computer versus the Chalkboard

Most major industrialized countries dived headfirst into beginner computer courses given at school during the 1980s. Each country wanted to "keep up with the Joneses" and the phenomenon spread quickly, especially in countries that produced hardware, like France and Great Britain. Modernizing education, adapting the school system to the new technical and economical context tempts commissioners and politicians to provide material solutions (more computer labs, more consoles and workstations) to problems that are of a nonmaterial kind.

Educators fear a generation of computer illiterate children, but the real risk lies in creating a generation of computer users who are simply illiterate. The computer remains a container that can process information. The wealth and value of that information comes from the computer user or programmer. The rationale in training children in computers at the end of the twentieth century resembles that of teaching pupils auto mechanics at the beginning of the century. As Bruno Lussato (1988, 1996) said "the issue of using the computer in the classroom is no more important than that of using chalk."

Yes, new information technology may facilitate the transmission and acquisition of basic knowledge. However, it seems increasingly obvious that the image on the screen does not enhance learning and that nothing can replace the direct human contact of traditional teaching practices.

In reality, new information technology should not revolutionize the education system any more than traditional media did. After all, the media have a different mission; i.e., sell information and attract an audience or a readership. Ironically television channels multiply like fruit flies, but no one has developed a successful educational channel, at least not in Europe. The stellar success of the Internet will do little to change this situation. Although access to data has become almost unlimited, it takes time and knowledge to sift through the information, just to separate the sheep from the goats. Think for a moment about how many people have an encyclopedia at home. And just because they have it, how many consult it regularly? The encyclopedia meets an infrequent need while many other needs must be met and all within the twenty-four hours available daily!

These new media may, nevertheless, prove useful in developing parallel training systems that would allow those who do not live within the geographical territory of a school board or those who do not want an imposed system to try their luck by paying for this additional service. The "new media" may inject a competitive spirit into a compartimentalized marketplace and, as a result, correct the serious regional disparities existing in education. Other outcomes might be a form of quality control (upstream) through centralized production and efficiency (downstream) in lower dropout rates or higher graduation rates.

Yet the original question of how to integrate new information technologies into the educational system has become secondary to one of the new stakes; i.e., the development of parallel educational systems organized by local groups, companies or associations, thus introducing new forms of competition on an educational market heretofore protected by distance or limited access.

The Diploma Disease

The true story (Michel Godet, sworn witness) began just as a fairy tale should. One fine day in the early 80s, a top French civil servant was touring Honda's auto plants in Japan. He found out that 90% of the Japanese auto assembly line workers had attended school up to the age of 18. He heard the words "final year" and understood high school diploma. Remember that all of this conversation was held in broken English by a Frenchman and a Japanese executive. The civil servant returned to France to tell his minister that obviously the Japanese were outperforming the French in the automobile sector because they have high school graduates on the lines whereas France has illiterate manual labourers. And thus the slogan "80% of a generation with a high school diploma" resounded throughout France.

Alas like Cinderella's pumpkin, it soon came out that everyone goes to school in Japan until the age of 18, but no one is failed so that "face" and the social cohesion of groups are maintained. The real selection process begins after what could be called the last year of American high school. Fierce competition begins then as difficult entrance exams for admission to the major universities must be taken. Training for these entrance exams starts with evening and summer courses at a very early age. Those working on the assembly lines are those who could not get into university.

However the real question that French civil servant should have asked is: How do our German neighbors build Mercedes with Turkish guestworkers? The answer lies in training, not in geography or schooling. When the major French industries closed their training facilities, they gave themselves an additional handicap vis-à-vis their Bavarian competitors, who benefit from a system in which state and industry share responsibility for training.

As the new millennium began, France already had almost 75% of one generation at the high-school graduation level. Perhaps the next Education Ministry objective should be that 80% of the next generation of those high school graduates know the three Rs! Irony aside, the stakes are high here. What France needed to do was follow the German example and develop training and apprenticeship programs, not a general education imparted by teachers who have little life experience other than teaching. According to the OECD, France has 8 million illiterates; i.e., people unable to read and understand an administrative document. (Of course many administrative forms mystify scholars with post-graduate degrees!) Nevertheless, it is continuing education or training that should be promoted as the true source of social and economic renewal because reinforcing basic education only accentuates the initial social inequalities.

Strangely enough, the education mirage has not completely replaced the technology mirage. Instead one feeds the other. The rationale is that the children must be prepared for the third industrial revolution. Nonsense! Tomorrow's jobs will require a high level of professionalism not more skills. What does "professional" mean? Essentially it means liking what you do and wanting to do it well. In other words, the opposite of the uninterested, bitter graduates that the diploma disease generates.

Confusion over words and meaning in training creates the illusion that knowledge equals skill and that skill is equivalent to experience. Why then do companies not recruit executives over the age of fifty or simply adjust retirement programs accordingly?

The paper chase in general education is all the more difficult to justify given that tomorrow's jobs are not only in new or high technology as many people believe. Technological change in industry and service translates to an increased need of high-level specialists but the number required is limited. There will be more positions filled by less skilled workers who will monitor machines and provide services; in other words, the tertiary sector. There will be a tremendous need for secretaries, healthcare workers, sorters, wrappers or packers, waiters and waitresses. In these jobs "book learning", as sanctioned by a diploma, will not be as important as cooperative behaviour, attention to detail and creativity in applying various skills or techniques. Training in the workplace or in company training centers is the main vector leading to the professionalism needed for the "jobs of tomorrow" or even today! Hire to train rather than train to be hired should be the byword.

Made in Japan

Now here is a label that may be interpreted in many ways. Some fifteen years ago managers in Europe and North America were chanting the same mantra: imitate the Japanese management model to catch up with Japanese productivity rates. Ironically the French automaker, Renault, bought Nissan in the mid-nineties.

Of course while the fascination with Japan Inc. was at its peak, I made comments that clashed with the popular ideas of the day. Nevertheless, my analysis from the end of the 1980s stands today. [1]

Basically, any attempt to explain the fierce competitiveness of Japanese industry at that time must take into account the overwhelming desire to work in order to escape the scarcities that Japan knew in the 1950s. The country had no resources other than its people and their labour.

The Japanese concepts of productivity and quality had been imported from the USA during the 1950s. At that time, American productivity rates were the highest in the world. As the proverb says, no man is a prophet is his own country, so American management specialists like W.E. Deming and J.M. Juran, considered the fathers of quality, saw their ideas applied in Japan. (See Dimitri Weiss, 1988.) Initially Japanese companies created small groups mandated to improve processes and products to the latest productivity levels. The idea of total quality, which was originally the concept of quality all together as a collective goal or shared responsibility, made the concept of quality control redundant. American authors would use the word "excellence" later on. Quality became a resounding success in Japan for various reasons, including prevention. Remember that Japanese products were exported around the world with no need for an expensive after-sales service network.

Other cornerstones of the Japanese management system were put forth as reasons for success. First of all, lifetime or lifelong employment. This aspect of the Japanese corporate world only affected 20% of the salaried workers, but it does reveal the strong sense of almost feudal loyalty that Japanese employees had towards their employer.

Similarly, the individual is perceived as a member of a group or clan in Japan. Hence we find another pillar of the Japanese management system: consensus. Group or peer pressure explains the apparent social harmony that reigns in Japanese businesses. Japanese proverbs like "drive the nail that sticks out" may apply to consensus-building, too. Of course in the Japanese system, workers who got out-of-line would hear from both their superiors and their colleagues.

Who would not toe the line under these circumstances? Do like the others becomes the golden rule. In other words, the famous Japanese corporate consensus is a result of collective self-censorship more than any form of debate or negotiation. It is better to give up one's ideas rather than rock the boat. In any event, an individual Japanese worker could never live down the loss of face created by rebellion or dissension.

---

1. See "Ten Unfashionable and Controversial Findings on Japan" in Futures, August 1987.

Another Japanese cliché in manufacturing: longer working hours. Official statistics reveal theory more than the harsh reality, given that production restrictions and the strains of belonging to a group are such that many employees "spontaneously" stay late at night and come in on the weekends to reach the goals set by the company. Peer pressure is so strong that employees do like their colleagues and give up a large part of their leisure time.

Motivating and mobilizing human resources was also at the core of the Japanese management system. At Honda, for example, the employee who could come up with the most proposals on how to improve productivity received a handsome bonus. Despite all the clichés that readers may have heard, the Japanese miracle stems from basic production organization. The idea was to do well what had to be done through order, method and, of course, tremendous staff motivation. None of the above lay beyond the reach of any company of any nationality. In fact Japanese-owned and managed electronics plants in France's northern coastal region, Brittany, actually achieved better performance rates than their counterparts in Japan.

As in show-business, we have saved the best for last – a finale of sorts. One of the most famous Japan Inc. management anecdotes ruffled politicians' feathers and made headlines. Like an urban legend, it probably would have circulated via Internet had Japan not sunk into an economic crisis in the early 1990s.

The background almost surpasses the story itself. Everything started with a shocking remark attributed to the Japanese president Matsushita. It translated roughly to "We are going to win and the industrialized West will lose. You can not do much about it because you carry your defeat within you. Your organizations are Taylorian and what's worse your minds are too (...) we are post-Taylorian."

Quoted variously but broadly in the mid-eighties, Matsushita's remark worked like intellectual electroshock therapy. Suddenly the Japanese lead could be explained by a management model which one needed to understand in order to emulate. Yet we have known since 1987 that the famous quote is a historical half-truth. A French author, Henri Sérieyx, revealed the other half in the preface to Isabella Orgogozo's 1987 book and reconfirmed it in the 1989 publication entitled *Le zéro mépris* (a clever punning title like "Zero Intolerance").

The Japanese management system became a true fashion based on a false analysis. Rather like a rumor reflects one facette of reality or the old adage "where there's smoke there's fire". Moreover everyone knows that Japanese politeness resembles false modesty and may actually mask a certain arrogance. Given the Japanese reputation, Matsushita's remark was plausible. Imagine, a Japanese leader was finally telling us what he really thought! Of course this was not the case and the real story now begs to be told or retold.

Once upon a time, we were invited by the Management Centre of Europe (Paris, 1990) to speak before three hundred top managers from around the world. The panel included renowned experts like Henry Kissinger. Among the other speakers was R.T. Pascale, a Harvard professor and the premier specialist in Japanese management. Halfway through his presentation in English, he quoted Matsushita's famous remark. Astonished, even embarrassed, I wondered what to do as a colleague and conference participant. I opted to ask questions and check sources like a good reporter. In speaking with one of Professor Pascale's assistants and co-workers, it came out that he had only started using that quote two or three years prior. In fact, his last conversation with President Matsushita took place in 1982. Curious, even stubborn, I discretely buttonholed the professor himself. Slightly red-faced, to his credit, he said that he had read this ten-line quote one day in its English version. He added that when he met Matsushita in 1982, the elderly leader spoke scarcely audible English. The whole episode sounded like the children's game of broken telephone. Nevertheless Professor Pascale said that he believed what he understood that day from the Japanese president to correspond exactly to what he read later.

Somehow the quote, like a rumor, has already done its job and discrediting the statement means little now. Moreover, Sérieyx's book has not been translated into English and even the francophone professor had never heard of it.

The one redeeming feature of Matsushita's supposed prophecy is that it triggered a real revolution in Western corporate minds. Results included quality circles, corporate projects, and self-training, to name a few. Someday history will cover the Japan Inc. period and show the healthy albeit unexpected role that the Japanese model played in the West.

The New Economy Was an Old Hat

Renewed growth, lower unemployment rates, and no more crisis! Long wave economic growth; such was the hope given by the new economy at the end of the 90's.

This new economic picture, which evoked the optimistic postwar boom years, questions its own basic assumptions. For example, why did the experts not see this "new growth" coming? Was it really the result of "new technology"? Will the blue skies stay blue? Lastly, was this growth not at the mercy of an oil shock or an American stock market crash and did it remain precarious?

American Growth Was Not New

The forecasters talking about the new economy and long growth cycle are the same ones who neglected this perspective only three years prior when the Left returned to power in France. Few experts dared then to declare that we had seen the light at the end of the proverbial tunnel. Most recommended effort and sacrifice. (Further proof that the age-old notion of blood-letting to have evil or illness removed remains with us.) Yesterday's myopic view makes us suspicious of tomorrow seen through rose-coloured glasses. Converging analyses make no difference either. Together, forecasters generally will mistake the number of angels that can dance on the head of a pin and even the size of the pinhead.

Once again the economic movement was born in the United States in the mid-90s, when it looked like the revival begun in mid-1992 would last, given a favourable context of low inflation, low interest rates, record-breaking job creation figures and nearly negligible unemployment rates. By the summer of 2000, the USA had enjoyed nine years of uninterrupted growth. Although initially Europe lagged behind the United States because of restrictive European monetary policies in the early 1990s (high interest rates, cost of German reunification, budgetary policies for EU convergence), the Old Continent has also been experiencing growth for over seven years now.

We hastened to point out that this phenomenon of long prosperity was not as exceptional as some might maintain. Since 1960, the USA has gone through other long, even steadier growth periods. For example, there were nine years between 1961 and 1969; five years between 1975 and 1979; seven years between 1982 and 1989, although interrupted by much shorter recessionary phases (one or two years on average). The following chart provides a fine overview.

Characteristics of the Last American Cycles

Cycles	Number of Terms	GDP Growth in volume (%)
Q1 1961 - Q4 1969		
Expansion	36	4.7
Recession	4	–0.1
Q4 1970 - Q4 1973		
Expansion	10	4.8
Recession	7	–1.3
Q2 1975 - Q4 1979		
Expansion	20	4.2
Recession	2	–0.2

Characteristics of the Last American Cycles

Cycles	Number of Terms	GDP Growth in volume (%)
Q3 1980 - Q3 1981		
Expansion	4	2.4
Recession	4	−1.6
Q4 1982 - Q2 1990		
Expansion	31	4.1
Recession	3	−1.6
Q3 1991 - 2001		
Expansion	37	3.5
Average		
Expansion	23	4.0
Recession	4	−0.9
Q1 1961 - Q4 1969		
Expansion	36	4,7
Recession	4	−0,1

Source: le Point mensuel Aurel-Leven SA Washington Plaza. March 2000

What Have ICTs Really Done [1]?

There were new things in the American economy. The first thing is that, this time, inflation has been contained despite low unemployment. As a result, the Federal Reserve Board wisely opted to allow growth to continue while not raising interest rates. The healthy American economy has been masterminded by Alan Greenspan, head of the Federal Reserve Board from 1987 to 2006. This longevity is also due to continuity and consistency. The second new thing is that the growth appears less volatile, in other words, less vulnerable to impact on stock market activity. Yet we have to attribute the American economic phenomena to the efforts upheld by the various companies to keep production and distribution lean and mean, e.g. zero inventory. This rationalization would have been unfeasible without the levers of technology and new possibility of sending data in real time, at a derisory cost, to scattered networks linking manufacturers to consumers.

All of the above was remarkably well analyzed by Philippe Lemoine [2] and Michel Didier. [3] Indeed, for Lemoine, "the new economy is

---

1. ICT: Information and Communication Technology
2. Philippe Lemoine: "Qu'est -ce que la nouvelle économie?" La nouvelle économie et ses paradoxes Cahier Laser n° 3 juillet 2000.
3. Michel Didier Quelle croissance longue pour l'économie française? Revue de Rexecode n° 66 1er trimestre 2000 (ce N° est entièrement consacré à la nouvelle économie).

the computerized exchange as opposed to the old economy still dominated by the strategic model implied by the computerization of manufacturing and management." The old economy sought to increase productivity through downsizing, and social plans were a way to bolster stock market levels.

The old economy could also be characterized as one of "retained value" or "value retention" even within the computer industry in which Moore's famous law has been in effect since 1965, halving the cost of performance-equivalent products every 18 months. In other words, "the best gets cheaper... its the law of price inversion, the products are improved and increasingly cheaper." [1] It is also the inversion of value chains. The demand is increasingly affecting the supply. The client ends up offering the manufacturer an opportunity to "bid". This is a classical trend among mature markets. In order to keep the demand high, manufacturers must listen carefully to the customer. The new aspect introduced by computers ensures greater transparency in terms of the information available to consumers. Also isolated manufacturers can thus improve the relationship between their own supply and demand, two previously compartmentalized concepts. In short, they could encourage competition while also lowering prices.

The new economy is therefore a virtuous model of lower prices, innovation in the offer to meet ever more diversified needs, inventory reduction and greater rotation of inventory, increased hiring and services so as to fulfill the consumer's expectations. Philippe Lemoine, researcher and Vice-President of the Galeries Lafayette group, provided a surprising illustration of this model by comparing a French "hypermarket" (combined food and soft-goods store,) to Wall-Mart. Similar in format, Wall-Mart employs twice as many employees for the same annual revenues. How? Lemoine points out Wall-Mart's competitive edge lies in the rotation of circulating capital. Stock turns around 25 times a year in the USA versus 10 times a year in France. Another example that Lemoine gives is the merchandising of personal computers made to order and delivered within eight days. The company, Dell, invented a distribution model that really rotates stock. In fact, Dell never has more than five days worth of inventory on hand; in other words, one-tenth the amount of inventory held by its competitors!

We should add here that certain activities experience exponential growth through networking. It is an example of Metcalfe's law; i.e., the usefulness of a good or service simply increases by the number of users, as seen in the spread of the fax machine. Among the surprises of the new economy, Michel Didier points out that lower prices have fallen to the point of being free. It is true that information has a set investment cost and a very low, marginal operating cost. However, "economic theory teaches us that in a balanced market, the price of a

---

1. see Philippe Lemoine

good is equal to its marginal cost. If the marginal cost is zero, the price is set to drop right off the page. (...) In the case of the Internet, the explosion has been especially shaking given the network effect played out immediately and globally."

Confusion between New Economy and New Technology

Yet does all of this explain away the unbelievable twists and turns on the NASDAQ? Early in 2000, AOL.com and Time Warner shared a stock market capitalization seven times that of General Motors. Some companies, which may never be profitable, saw their value plummet as their losses were announced. If that is the new economy, then the old one will likely return with its reality principles.

Virtual exchanges may be much easier, but at one point or another, reality sets in and the product must be manufactured, delivered on time and with a profit. And let's face it, logistics and organization of the production line and distribution system are not new. Mastering information technology is not enough to excel in these two areas. The well-publicized bankruptcy of Boo.com is but the beginning of a long series of wake-up calls. It is interesting that the giants of mail-order sales in France (La Redoute, Les Trois Suisses) are hurrying to put their catalogues on-line. Of course, there is nothing really new in all this. People speculated on tulip bulbs in the 18th century, railroads in the 19th century and utility companies in the early 20th century.

It seems that the past is repeating itself. Although there may always be something new in the economy, ranging from production in real time, or supply-based demand, to lower inventory and prices, these concepts theoretically touch all sectors of the economy. It is therefore ridiculous to reduce the new economy to the sectors of information technology alone and exclude the others with the rather odd period condescending label of "old economy". One thing that characterizes the old economy is value retention, limited competition and passive consumers. Most of the productive sectors integrated new technology to improve performance and productivity a long time ago. We should remember that some pockets of activity, e.g. local telecommunications, are still part of the old economy given old-fashioned, protective regulations.

Every Generation Has Its Own New Age

We can perceive the New Age phenomenon accurately as the association of new technology and liberalization, say Bill Gates plus Margaret Thatcher. In other words, there may be many new things in the economy, but they refer primarily to the classical concepts of competition, pricing, and transparency of markets that are facilitated by ICTs. Of course that does not justify consulting runes or the latest New Age craze, talking about new growth or even less Kondratieff's cycles.

We smile when reminded that each generation, even our own, is tempted by the idea of a New Age. This was the case in the United States at the start of the 20th century. History records Roosevelt's New Deal in the 1930s [1], and more recently we have heard or read the New Management plus the New Society. Of course the expression New Age now generally refers to the movement begun in California in the early 1980s. This "Age" focuses on ways of living and thinking. France saw its own New Age, with new economists and new philosophers. Of course advertising uses and abuses the word "new" to the point where it appears on almost every label.

Nevertheless, our memories are short and it is tempting to refer to Kondratieff's long cycles with technology as the driving force behind growth; whereas a purely economic, monetary and, lastly, liberal explanation should be equally attractive, if not more so. Besides considering why Kondratieff always enchants newcomers and oldcomers alike, we should delve deeper into the current and future growth in the United States and Europe, on the role of the ICTs and on the risks of a recession caused by an oil shock or a crash.

The Solow Paradox Is Still Timely

The ICTs have played a determining role in competition, lowering prices and inventory, thus facilitating, as in liberalization, healthier growth that is less inflationary and less volatile. Yet we have to weigh the quantitative portion within the economy and in terms of growth itself. This type of measurement is only beginning to be used, but official statistics bureaus including the OECD and Insee give similar estimates. In the United States, new technology represents 2% of the capital stock* and 8% of the GDP with service sales. It also explains 15% of the growth, in other words, .6 of the growth of the past few years. In France, we have nearly 5% of GDP attributed to ICTs and that would explain 10% of the growth, or .3 of the annual GDP.

Yet the new economy experts would say that a driving force need not be enormous to fuel the economy and boost productivity. Is this the end of Salow's paradox? Already in 1987, the Nobel Prize-winner for economics pointed out that we can see computers everywhere except in productivity statistics. The MIT professor is regularly reminded of his words. He replied prudently "It may possibly be the end of the computer paradox, but I'm not sure." [2] It is true that the acceleration in

---

1. This period was very active and many "new" books were published: New Theology, New Nationalism de T. Roosevelt (1910), New Diplomacy de W. Wilson (1915), New Freedom, New Federalism, New Idealism, New Deal de F.D. Roosevelt (1932), New Republic, New Realism (1912), New Democracy (1912), New History (1912).

2. see interview in Le Monde de l'économie, 18 April 2000.

labour productivity in recent years is far from the figures seen in the 1950s when there was nary a computer in sight.

Yet deep down we know that current statistical tools are incapable of proving the possible link between technology and growth. The same incapacity does not, however, prevent anyone from proving the contrary. In other words, we can all cast doubt, give hope and even stir up controversy. In fact, this atmosphere helps perpetuate the Nikolai Kondratieff legend.

Growth Can Be Explained in Classical Terms and Remains Precarious

Our preferred hypothesis is the following: classical economic factors play a more important role than technology in the new growth. Heading the list, consumer confidence, which Alain Peyreffitte showed to be essential in development, followed by the reduction of budgetary deficits surplus in the USA during the Clinton administration, cheap money, investment in R&D (double in the USA versus the turnover since 1980), replacement or upgrading of technological equipment (double the spending in the USA compared to Europe), more efficient organization of companies, market liberalization and stimulation through competition, maintaining demand through a decline in prices and an increase in quality.

The above-listed factors of the new economic climate, were it to remain stable, could inspire hope for sustained growth for many years to come. Unfortunately, not all the pillars of the American economy are solid. The first crack appears in the incredible foreign trade deficit: $170 billion in 1998, $350 billion in 2000, and more than $600 billion in 2005. The USA enjoys an enviable privilege which allows them to finance deficits of such magnitude with their currency. Dollars lost in trade return in the form of capital investment.

American consumers use a "negative savings" technique which enables them to live beyond their means through the rest of the world's savings, notably Japan's. Average Americans will even borrow to play the stockmarket and possibly get rich, as the past few years have shown.

The high foreign debt that the United States contracted when the American dollar was strong can always be repaid using devalued dollars. Yet in the meantime, the greenback remains high and the low American inflation rates appear to be the result of imported deflation rather than the effect of new technology on the competition.

Thanks to the Euro, Europe did not experience the various upsets in national currencies. Traditionally these currency matters lead to stop-and-go policies staggered from country to country. As a result, the parts prevent the whole from functioning properly. Today, the Euro zone is operating in sync as a whole, especially since 91% of what is produced in

Europe is also consumed there. However, the value of the Euro has increased 25 percent with respect to the dollar. This valuation hurts the competitiveness of those European countries like France and Italy, who have not yet made the necessary structural reforms to their economy.

As a political and monetary entity facing the future, Europe is still too fragile to do anything but suffer the rollercoaster ride of the US dollar. In fact, unlike the USA, Europe is threatened by a foreseeable demographic implosion. Before dealing with the current clichés about the future, let us try to understand why Kondratieff's cycles come back into fashion regularly.

Long Cycles or the Temptation of Determinism

We have already mentioned that the hypothesis in which the new economy has been ushered in by new information technology remains unproven. Yet we recognize that the opposite is also not proven, given our apparent incapacity to measure the phenomena. Some analysts have dusted off Kondratieff's famous long cycles in which the market economy is punctuated every 50 years, according to the rhythm of innovation, e.g. the railroad between 1845 and 1870; electricity and the automobile between 1895 and 1914; oil and durable consumer goods between 1945 and 1973, and now, information technology and biotechnology.

The analysts have already divided into camps on the same battlefield. Neomarxists, always ready to spout something when inbred capitalist crises arise, alongside liberals of varying stripes who follow Schumpeter in his belief in creative destruction, and who claim technology, innovation and entrepreneurship play the determining role.

As a futurist, I consider the future to be the fruit of individual and collective will. I can not help but be skeptical about explanations of social change in which yesterday's religious determinism has given way to a form of technological determinism with scientific pretensions. The social sciences have little to do with the physical. Let's face it, people do not behave like electrons, their movements constrained by equations, and we should gladly remember that we have a certain freedom when facing the future. Quite some time ago, in conversation with Jacques Lesourne, we realized that if long cycles exist, they are socio-organizational rather than technological. Naturally that type of thinking does not make headlines.

Fluctuations in Prices and Imaginary Cycles

Yes, we admit that we have tried to back up our views within a context that is more ideological than purely logical. There are indeed many long fluctuations in prices and interest rates but they are not cyclical. A better term would be alternating. Moreover we know that they are not linked to industrialized capitalism because they can be traced from the end of the Middle Ages. Already in the 1940s, analysts concluded that the long waves identified by Kondratieff stemmed essentially from statistical techniques and time series that are considered far too limited. The dating of most turning points was arbitrary.

In fact it is currently impossible to choose between rival interpretations, except ideologically, because the empirical basis, (when it even exists) remains quite weak. (…) The core of the theory and debate revolve around the issue of prices and this aspect is always sidestepped through the use of particularly sophisticated statistical methods used to process time series that do not allow one to decide conclusively. Also the results have not always been irrefutable in confirming the reality of long cycles.

It would thus seem that Kondratieff's long cycles are imaginary. Accordingly Paul Samuelson ranks them with sci-fi. Wassily Léontief, on the other hand, excludes the idea of periodicity over long periods in which the structure of the economy undergoes radical transformations. We refer to these Nobel laureates because it is unlikely that they are merely making conversation.

The recurring theme of long cycles stems from our incapacity to explain crises. If there is a Kondratieff cycle, it is a movement of long duration affecting the prices of raw materials; in other words, what used to be the only known factor. Nevertheless, the era of the gold standard has faded in memory, and the prices of manufactured goods are determined by other factors. During the past century, there have indeed been many long phases of nominal decreases and increases of prices. However not since 1945, after which the increase has been constant at one or two digits. Wassily Léontief is certainly correct in speaking of radical changes. It is no longer the gold price cycle that punctuates the long fluctuations but rather the raw material price cycles and, in the first instance, energy prices, which can affect economic trends.

The new growth could not be perpetuated globally without generating new oil shocks which would bring into question the whole premise [1]. There is no real danger, but the situation is simply the consequence of two events: growth fueled by cheap energy and the termination of energy substitution programs in the US. It is well known that energy is wasted more in the USA than elsewhere and that statistically, American consumption per capita is exactly twice the European figure. In the end, the United States will be in trouble here in the long-term due to their increasing dependency and high level of energy consumption per capita.

The spectre of information technology and its unmet promises are not the only clichés which have currency these days. The critical mass

---

1. see Andrew Oswald "fuelling false hope" Finantial Times September 10th 1999.

of enterprise is yet another myth we ought to dispel. It is an oft-ignored fact that the smallest businesses in any given sector are also the best performing. In the last few years, the critical mass myth has found renewed justification in globalization and the mega-mergers of large multinational corporations. These events give one the false impression that there is a battle of titans taking place on a global scale, yet now that some of these giants with feet of clay have collapsed, it is useful to recall that in reality, more than one out of two, perhaps even two out of three, mergers fail. This is essentially due to the incompatibility of formerly separate and distinct corporate cultures. Indeed, only about one out of ten mergers creates value for the acquiring firm.

Regional foresight, or alternatively urban and regional planning, has also fallen victim to the myth of critical mass. The politics of development tend to favour urban areas at the expense of rural ones, presumably in order to agglomerate jobs and services. Of course, one doesn't know whether the agglomeration is the cause or consequence of these policies. In any case, the facts belie the cliché. Certain rural areas, like Choletais Vendéen, have succeeded in assuring their own economic success by coordinating the activities of several constituent towns. Rather than migrating to big cities, the youth of Choletais Vendéen tend to stay, because there are jobs and activities in Choletais Vendéen. Furthermore, the rate of new business creation per habitant is among the highest in France.

Meanwhile, American growth has settled at 3.6%, on average, over the past few years while European growth remains far behind at 2.2%. How can we explain this difference, if we put aside the already doubtful technology argument? The answer lies in the question, yet the question would not even be asked if we noticed that growth in per capita GDP is the same on both sides of the Atlantic. In blunt terms, the number of heads increases on one side and stagnates on the other! The demographic implosion in the Old World can not provide a greater contrast to the dynamic American population which is expected to grow by 50 million between now and the year 2025.

3

CLICHÉS AND ANTI-CLICHÉS ABOUT THE FUTURE

The Link between Economic Growth and Demographic Dyanmics

Refusal to See the Link between Economic Growth and Demographics

The Turning Point of October 29, 2004: the European Youth Pact

The March 2005 Good News: Europe Confronts the Demographic Challenge

High and Low Demographic Pressures

France as a Driving Force in European Demographics

The Multiplier Effects of Demographics

The Family, a Public Affair

Development Factors Are Endogenous

Age and experience have taught me one thing: Even if everything has already been said, not everyone has said it, nor furthermore understood it. Therefore, a simple realization is often a personal epiphany. After 30 years of foresight and futures thinking, I've let my curiosity run free attempting to anwer the questions often posed to me. My work consists of assembling a puzzle, whose pieces may be understood separately but are rarely assembled to reveal the meaning of the whole. My speciality then, is to reveal the pattern in the tapestry, along with the knots that we often refuse to see. Obviously no longer a pure economist, I wonder whether I have become more of a historian or even a sociologist without actually realizing it – at least if one believes the journalists who often introduce me as such. Personally, I find work resembling more and more that of a demographer.

A futurist's work entails seeing the whole in the parts; hence my ongoing desire for exploration and discovery. Thirty years of feeding a curious mind has led me down various paths ranging from energy, international trade, technological change, corporate competitiveness, training, employment, food safety, agriculture, local development, job creation, management, and the environment. Three decades of an independent spirit have also led to diagnoses that often contradicted popular opinion. Nevertheless, I consider the process of challenging preconceived ideas a form of intellectual hygiene that is always salutary. At the risk of being accused an *agent provocateur* or having my ideas and images turned into caricatures, I have often taken unpopular positions. Yet, I find the political gridlock and myopic policies which seem to dominate European politics far more provocative. Having visited various regions, near and far, including Africa, California, Japan, Latin America, South East Asia, and the Middle East, I am struck by just how little culture I possess. Culture, a fragile construction, constantly evolving, is transmitted through discoveries constantly restarted. Fortunately on my travels, I found something natural and familiar, like the thread Ariadne left in the labyrinth. My thread can be expressed in one sentence: *Developmental factors are endogenous – the source of both success and failure is almost always found within.*

The above statement may appear simplistic, but this thread can cut like a razor. The greatest favour that we can do for regions, corporations or individuals experiencing economic problems is to refuse them a hand-out. What they need is a sense of responsibility for their own future combined with a feeling of being accompanied along the way. Technology is an important component, but it is not essential to competitiveness. The myth of the *new economy*, promoted at the end of the 1990s was as erroneous as the Japanese management fad was in the late 1980s. The real key to development is entrepreneurship. Entrepreneurs, who are often the formerly unemployed, are the magicians of growth. Entrepreneurs stand out because of their personal dedication to their project, their vision, and their ability to lead. Many soccer fans will remember that as soon as the French team returned after losing in Seoul, the coach was quickly and rightly replaced. The same brutal law applies to companies in trouble – government subsidies and bail-outs only prolong the agony caused most often by the ineffectiveness of incompetent executives. In terms of spurring economy activity and employment, public funds would be better spent on healthy companies to encourage their further development. In other words, give financial assistance to companies who are *not* requesting it. This seems counterintuitive, but it is the most effective policy.

Truth is Stranger than Fiction

Ariadne's thread led me on far-flung missions that were both enlightening but also disappointing. I realised that I could not do much for places like Zambeze, whereas in France, I discovered lively regions, rich in terms of their culture and solidarity. It became clear to me that culture and tradition are roots that allow local development to fit into globalization and take part rather than be taken. Certain European regions, such as the Italian industrial districts, Brittany, Alsace and the Rhone-Alps provide proof.

Truth is indeed stranger than fiction. Most of our dreams and projects have already been realised by others. The good news is that by emulating those who have succeeded, we can save time and energy. The bad news is that there are places where there are simply not enough people or capital to sustain anyone's dream. The French region of Correze is one such place. With its green solitude, neglected cemeteries, and lack of railway access, Correze, belongs to a neglected strip of territory that the French government calls "the empty diagonal". In fact, half of France falls into this category of region, which is deserted but not a desert environmentally. The only thing missing in these regions is people. There is nobody to dream or to start a project. The cradle has given way to the coffin in these regions as most adolescents have long since migrated to big cities. There was no reason to hang around these regions and unlike salmon, no one returns to spawn.

If human energy and initiative are the sources of economic development, declining population should be our principal concern. Italy, for example, could lose one-third of its population by 2050. France has a healthier demographic balance sheet than its neighbours, but we must remember that France's principal market may crumble because over 90% of what it produces is consumed in Europe.

Rediscovering Family and Children

At this point in history when the socialization of old age has increased, perhaps we ought to stop considering the family as a private affair. Dependent young people merit the kind of collective guardianship that seniors receive in the form of pensions. Furthermore, those bringing children into the world are contributing to our collective social welfare and should be encouraged financially. If we view demography historically, we see how families with children have become the missing link in today's society. Demographic data on the family relevant to economics are rare, scattered and incomplete. In fact, I spent one year writing a book about the topic (2002 for *Le Choc de 2006*) and in 2005 I wrote a report entitled *The Family, A Public Matter*, (*La famille, une affaire publique*) mandated by the French Prime Minister through an economic council (CAE).

As a category in official documents, the family is often an aggregation with very little substantial data. Yet statistics do exist and by cross-referencing data one can fill in the blanks. The main message: Stable family and affective structures are important for success at school, personal development and productive social integration.

Parents have costs to bear, rules to respect and obligations to fulfil. Why then is there no legal code with penalties for infractions the way there is for driving an automobile? If education and a stable family situation are so important to early development, then why are educational standards so sorely neglected, and furthermore, why should we continue to tolerate deadbeat, absent, or tyrannical parents? Although society may be imperilled by such neglect, we have a duty to reform the system through public education, prevention and intervention. All the research confirms that social victims and those excluded from the economy through academic failure suffer from family problems. Victims often include those children raised in mono-parental or broken families. Couples separating should know that children do not change parents the way one trades-in an old car for a new model. There is no such thing yet as prosthetic maternity or paternity; however, there is an affective amputation. The psychological trauma, violence, or simply the loss of a childhood, never fully heal and predispose the survivors to various forms of illness, failure and exclusion. Prison statistics reveal the link between social and familial fractures. Among detainees, the percentage coming from broken homes amounts to double of that in the general population. I am not suggesting a certificate to be earned through parenting classes, but we must seriously look at the paradox of a society that imposes a myriad of codes and regulations only to preach indifference in home and school matters. Many schools already offer sex education courses; perhaps some parental training should be developed as well.

Indifference about the crisis of family in contemporary society tends to exacerbate the situation. After all, is it not contradictory to be **against** economic *laissez-faire* yet **for** family *laissez-faire*? In both instances, individual freedom can not be exercised without a framework of rules established in the common interest. The anti-globalization activists really should question family responsibility when considering inequalities. Economic differences are actually reinforced by social inequalities. In fact, by not intervening preventively, society finds itself unprepared for the rise in violence and thus reacts repressively. Society is also always granting more funds to prisons, security, social assistance, urbanization and even education. Yet these policies are often misguided because the problems are not simply material in nature. A family environment in which parents pay attention to raising children and encourage their development is a decisive comparative advantage in a child's personal, and ultimately professional life. On the other hand, absent or tyrannical parents pile a heavy load on their children in the form of psychological baggage that some victims find difficult to shed.

Unhappy families make for dangerous cities, but a carrot-and-stick penal system provides little remedy for such affective problems. Sometimes a disaffected youth simply needs the patience of a family member willing to listen. If such a person is absent, then society must find a surrogate. The judicial system has unfortunately played a participatory role in social disintegration. For example, by systematically granting custody to the mother, judges facilitate the rise of distant, even absent, fathers. Judges, like the media, are currently rediscovering the structural importance of a stable family, and some judges are requiring the whole family to take an active role in juvenile rehabilitation. The family of two parents remains the majority in France, where seven out of ten adults live as a couple. Eight out of ten of those couples are married and nine out of ten have been married only once. At the end of the day, three-quarters of all people under the age of 18 live with a mother and father together in the same household. As usual, however, we end up talking about the exception rather than the rule.

Happy families are an important component to a more virtuous society, however they are not enough. There are issues of living conditions, sustainable development, and lastly the search for some meaning to life because an accumulation of wealth cannot compensate for the loneliness that attends contemporary existence that is often bereft of meaningful social interaction. These areas must be considered collectively with new, commonly shared, more legitimate answers as part of better public governance; in other words, a real participatory democracy.

At their zenith, ancient Greece and Rome imposed not only powers, but also duties and obligations upon the richest and most powerful members of society. Paul Veyne lists the virtues of classical society; notably, private liberties in favour of the public. In other words, as Laurent Gille

(2002) revealed in his wonderful thesis, modern societies have forgotten that the accumulation of goods is not enough to lend some meaning to life. People also need to forge ties around a common project.

Obviously, the current aimlessness cannot continue for long. What we need to do is address the real issues about the future while ignoring the clichés. Examples: *no*, globalization is not to blame; *yes*, the French "exception" is exorbitantly expensive; *no*, technology is not the essential element; and *yes*, we have created illusions about productivity and tomorrow's jobs. What we really need to do is rediscover the human factor. Without people, there is no sustainable development and, after the demographic landmark of 2006 (the start of baby-boomer retirement), everything is going to change.

Growth, demographics, the status of the family and regional development are interrelated. In the following chapter, it will become clear what companies and regions can do to develop their own initiatives given the changing situation. As usual, foresight means always being a bit like the look-out or scout atop the nest of the Titanic. Even the best scout does not want to see the ship hit an iceberg and later say "I told you so!". Good foresight should lead to preventative action.

Globalization Is Not to Blame

Globalization: Good news or bad? Posed regularly in the media, this question seems new; however, globalization is actually a rather old issue, well known to historians, at least since the time of Fernand Braudel. In fact, Jacques Marseille reminds us that "In 1910, France exported 18% of its GDP and did not return to that level until the 1970s. Thirty-three million people left Europe for South America and the United States. Already back then multinationals existed like Michelin, Bayer, Kodak..." As a specialist of the so-called *belle époque*, Michel Winock smiles whenever asked about globalization as something new. Yet the answer to the question asked above is always ambiguous. Globalization is not ideal as it remains governed by balances of power that tend to be national hence blind to general and international interests. Development conditions are uneven, but some countries, even without natural resources, fare well while others with abundant natural resources simply fail to thrive. Examples of countries who have succeeded include; South Korea, Thailand, Taiwan, Singapore and of course, Japan. Those countries with abundant natural resources who have failed to thrive include; Algeria, Argentina, Russia, and most of the OPEC countries. If globalization were such an omnipotent force, then how can we account for vast economic differences – for example unemployment rates that vary from single to triple digits – which may be found among developed countries sharing a comparable degree of international openness and natural resources. In short, globalization is not to blame.

We should be suspicious of globalization activists who accuse the United States of using globalization as a vehicle to advance American hegemony – there is no conspiracy to globalization. If such critics make a legitimate case for an imbalance of power with respect to international relations, we should not then assume that such injustices extend to internal politics. Certainly, the process of globalization is not always fair. Nevertheless, accusing globalization leads nowhere because states, along with their political and social partners, are ultimately responsible for the proper management of their internal affairs. This is especially so in the case of developed democracies. The political elites are aware of the crisis in public management, (Faroux, Spitz, 2002) however, they are not brave enough to carry out needed reforms, (Bébéar, 2002) as this would mean abolishing their own privileges. Nevertheless, little will change so long as we continue appointing top civil servants according to allegiance rather than merit. The globalization debate very quickly sheds light on what we usually keep in the dark – our own responsibility and our own wastefulness. It is up to us to create social relations that are less affected by current balances of international power.

Interdependence and Balance of Power

Increasing interdependency does arise from globalizing economies and from the worldwide impact of problems involving health, security, natural resources and the environment. It becomes painfully visible when we see the lack of so-called "international regulation", a notion that has been overtaken by the concept of governance, evoked more and more in international affairs.

As the sociologist Daniel Bell highlighted some thirty years ago: States have grown too small for the big problems and too big for the small problems. The principle of subsidiarity, as in the directive to treat locally all problems that may be treated locally, and treat internationally those problems which can only be resolved in that way, seems to be the best approach. The worldwide economy is rather like a rudderless ship, propelled only by balances of power and unable to overcome some of its most vexing problems – for example, rising economic inequality. There is no world government, and thus even less world governance; i.e., there are no effective democratic rules for governing national governments. However, without such governance, there can be no effective governance of world affairs.

We are still in the early stages of building a system of international governance. As Michel Camdessus, the former head of the International Monetary Fund, said rather bitterly, "I was under the illusion that I could be an architect whereas I was only a firefighter. [...] The world does not really know how to reform without a crisis and when there is a crisis, the reform is too little." Wondering if anyone is in charge, Camdessus concludes that "the IMF plays a role without true democratic legitimacy and with a group of nations that agree on very few things." The new "World Economy", as Fernand Braudel called it, will take over from the *Pax Americana* some time soon. The Pax Americana continues to dominate the world without governing it by default, as there are no other regulatory means. The absolute value of power does not prevent the relative decline of the Pax Americana. The United States now represents 30% of the worldwide aggregated GDP versus 40% in 1955. The Americans are no longer powerful enough to insist on a regulatory role but they are sufficiently powerful to play a disruptive one. Although a minority blocker within the world system, the United States can still prevent any other regulator from taking its place.

Who has not been tempted to rally behind the hypothesis promoted by some economists concerning the unsettling volatility of currency exchange rates, e.g., an American dollar worth somewhere between 0.7 and 1.4 Euros? As compared to Europe, the United States claimed economic growth with far greater job creation – one-half the EU unemployment rate and a GDP per capita approximately 30% higher than the EU, expressed in terms of purchasing power parity (PPP). Nevertheless, the United States economy continues to operate with huge trade deficits and its legislators' inability to impose new taxes, including those on gasoline, which is still comparatively inexpensive there, is worrisome. Despite these apparent problems, the greenback is still relatively stable and remains the currency of choice for central banks of developing countries, who have long since given up gold for dollars. This situation hardly encourages efforts to correct imbalances of international power. The United States finances much of its foreign trade deficit through the rest of the world's savings; and therefore, unlike other developed countries, the United States has few external constraints that would otherwise prevent it from living beyond its means. As a result, despite a revival in its power, twenty-first century America may end up like Great Britain at the end of the twentieth century – a decadent power.

The above thesis is one often shared by Japanese experts, yet Tokyo's vocation is not to become the centre of a new "world economy". Japan's vision of reigning within the Pacific zone and leaving the old Atlantic world (Europe included) on the sidelines turned out to be a myth popularized in the 1980s. Japan actually represents 15% of the world's GDP; i.e., one half of that which the EU or USA represent. It is true that, despite hurdles, growth among newly industrialized countries in South-East Asia looks spectacular, however, this growth merely corresponds to a delay in development. GDP per capita in terms of purchasing power parity in South Korea is about half that of Japan but three times stronger than that of Indonesia or China. Moreover, the Pax *Nipponica* will not take over from the Pax *Americana* because the Japanese have neither the military power nor the demographic vitality of the United States. A Japanese-American co-management of the world system did seem to be the most realistic hypothesis at one time; however, the Japanese never believed in it. They are still dubious of American leadership and remain harshly critical of a country that they consider to be living beyond its means with a negative savings rate and an abysmal foreign trade deficit. Perhaps someday Japan will rediscover Europe as a more responsible partner. In the meantime, however, Japan has not found the road to growth, even during the few boom years of the new economy. The reason undoubtedly is the aging Japanese population whose share of the population is greater than that of other developed countries.

The great wild card is China. China's impressive economic development over the last two decades, averaging 9.5%, corresponds to a tremendous lag in development. The country's structural weaknesses are significant and its challenges are enormous. China must stabilize the macro-economic environment, reform its banking and financial systems, reduce sectorial imbalances, and lessen the risk of disruptions in its supply of energy and raw materials. This must all be done while avoiding social fractures in a country already marked by gross social and regional inequities.

At the same time, the economic weight of China combined with its role in international trade reveals this giant's growing integration in the world economy. Since China's great leap forward in the 1990s, the data have been turned upside down. In 2004, China had 7% of the world's exports; in other words, double the 1999 figure. The country ranked third after Germany (10%) and the USA and far ahead of Japan and France (still fifth with 5% of the total). Shifts in the GDP per capita expressed in terms of purchasing power parity are equally startling. The standard of living has doubled since 1995. Of course, the Chinese standard of living remains one quarter that of the Korean, one-fifth of the Japanese and French, and one-seventh of the American. Yet, given its demographic mass, China weighs-in heavily in terms of value-added at four times the French rate and twice the Japanese rate and two-thirds of the American.

However, we should not forget the lessons of history. Over the long run, China has regularly opened up then brutally closed in on itself once more. The reason for these cycles remains the same: there is a significant development differential between the maritime and interior provinces. This disparity threatens the very cohesion of the "middle kingdom", that restores its unity by turning in on itself. In the surrounding region, China's partners know the pattern well. They tread carefully when dealing with their giant neighbour. The Japanese have been especially reticent, given the contentious relationship that they have historically had with China. The Japanese sacking of Nanking in the mid-1930s remains part of the Chinese collective memory. History also teaches us that relations between the colonized and former colonies are never simple, especially when the economic hierarchy of the zone is the inverse of the cultural hierarchy.

No country, nor intergovernmental or international agency appears capable of taking up the baton of *Pax Americana*. Given the situation, building a politically strong Europe appears delicate and all the more difficult due to continued enlargement of membership. Nonetheless, a strong Europe is needed more than ever if we are to hear a voice other than that of the United States.

Globalization: The Frame and the Big Picture

Rather than focus on the gilded frame, we should consider the big picture which reflects our responsibilities. Developmental factors for regions are endogenous and depend on the economic dynamics of the assets which they possess. The more numerous and entrepreneurial the assets, the healthier the region tends to be. In short, problems are first and foremost internal; hence the overestimation of globalization and its affect on local and national economies should be seriously reconsidered.

This conviction is based on two important observations. First, all European countries are subject to the same external constraints, yet the unemployment rates range from single- to double-digit, e.g., between Spain and Portugal, or between Holland and Great Britain. The same discrepancy may occur within the same country. In France, for example, the Vitre region unemployment rate is approximately one-third that of the Valence region. Second, globalization occurs initially among countries that share proximity and form regional trading blocs. So, for example, French firms export 25% of their production while the remaining 75% is consumed domestically. However, 70% of French exports are sent to Western European countries where the social conditions are more or less comparable.

Everyone benefits from the internationalization of trade, and even if jobs are lost in some sectors, there is a net gain in wealth. Moreover, accusing the newly industrialized countries (NICs) of devaluing labour is no longer appropriate. In fact, Claude Vimont (1997) has shown that overall, foreign trade represents a positive net balance of jobs. There is also the ethical issue: How can we ask weak countries to accept the laws of competition when those laws are favourable to us and reject the same laws when they are problematic, either here or over there? We cannot refuse to import products manufactured by countries with relatively inexpensive labour because that is often the principal advantage such a country can claim. *Comparative advantage* is not a euphemism used by greedy capitalists in developed countries to justify the exploitation of labour in developing ones, as some globalization activists would suggest, with one important exception – child labour. Allowing these nations to open up to increased trade still constitutes the best means of improving their social condition.

Liberalization in international trade has encouraged unprecedented world growth. Ever since the GATT began in 1947, the average tariff has diminished by approximately 90% among industrialized countries. Trade has expanded twentyfold and world production, ten-fold. Attacking non-tariff barriers and the protectionist practices of certain countries, e.g., the United States, will be the next step before the next round of trade negotiations.

Certain countries like the United States still intend to decide whether governmental assistance should continue in sectors where they already lead, e.g., agriculture, services, and entertainment. The Americans do not hesitate in protecting themselves through unilateral anti-dumping measures, e.g., European steel, or through pressure that encourages self-imposed limits on exports.

An open Europe does not mean a discounted Europe. The Old Continent must use all its influence at the World Trade Organization (WTO) to organize free trade and oppose the application of the "law of the strongest". Europe should start lobbying to ensure that its partners accept the reciprocity principle. However, all this must be done without falling into the temptation of protectionism.

It is true that competition among low-wage countries has provided plenty of fodder for the press. Overall, the EU enjoys a balanced foreign trade with the rest of the globe. Trade represents approximately 25% of EU production. Furthermore, 70% of European trade is intra-European. Using unemployment rates to regulate trade and production is thus dangerous because the European nations have a common advantage in trade, even though this advantage is not shared equally among EU countries. In fact, trade has enriched some EU countries, while lack of trade has impoverished others. Such were the cases of Germany and Hodja's Albania respectively. In the end, over-protection of industry does not promote development. Like sport, competition requires you to train. For example, if you play tennis with better players, your game improves.

The real stakes, however, lie elsewhere. It turns out that developed countries can profit by focusing on industries with greater specialization and added-value while importing vast amounts of goods of little added-value or those goods requiring a large input of unskilled labour. The Germans certainly got this equation right and maintained a trade surplus before Reunification. In fact, despite a quick adjustment due to Reunification, they were able to restore this favourable trade surplus once their economic situation stabilized. Despite rising unemployment, the Germans enjoy two advantages rarely seen together: high incomes and plenty of leisure time.

Globalization will not induce a world-wide suppression of living standards. It is true, however, that the less-developed countries (LDCs) will have to catch up in terms of economic and social adjustments which will likely be more painful if not anticipated.

With respect to tariffs, subsidies and trade, there are a limited number of industries that should remain off the bargaining table and should be partially spared the brutality of the free market. These strategic industries include; defence, security, culture, environment and, of course, agriculture. Highly advanced countries like Japan, Switzerland, Austria and Norway continue to protect their own farmers through subsidies of 80% and more, while continuing to find their niche internationally.

Governance and Its Overly Soft Interpretations

The Commission in Brussels prepared a White Paper listing the principles of good governance applicable at all levels of government:
 – openness and transparency of institutions;
 – broader participation by citizens at all levels of political decision-making;
 – greater responsibility on the part of institutions and member states, efficiency in policies set out by clear objectives, consistency, and greater understanding of policies.

However, all these characteristics of good governance should not erase the definition of governance already adopted by international agencies like the IMF, OECD and UN, where the idea of checks and balances and the rule of law are central; otherwise we run the risk of diluting the definition of governance. Governance should be a participatory process that, according to François Ascher (1995,) "Articulates and associates political institutions, social actors and private organizations in processes which formulate and implement collective choices capable of generating active participation by citizens." The concept of corporate governance, with its strong oversight and vested shareholders, may also provide some inspiration (Cannac, Godet, 2001).

According to the late Peter Drucker's definition (1957; 1973), "Corporate governance consists of creating and respecting rules that guide and limit the conduct of those acting on behalf of the corporation." In other words, good governance is a set of mechanisms designed to ensure that the action of the administrators conforms to the will of the shareholders and their interests. Governance is not synonymous with management. Management designates the relationship between managers and their subordinates, whereas governance functions like a "government for the governors". Paraphrasing the definition given already by Alexander King in a 1991 report delivered to the Club of Rome, James N. Roseneau (1997) spoke of governance for all players who employ the command mechanisms to express demand, set objectives, distribute orders and follow up on policies.

Transposed to democratic politics, governance is often incorrectly understood as agency – the ability of governments to shape socio-economic systems as desired. Governance is not "the art of governing", either, as described by Kimon Valaskakis (1998), nor even the "art of steering the process of government action". Here are some simple definitions: **governance** is a relationship of power; **government** is the operational exercise of that power; and **governability** is the measure of that power on the systems involved.

A system poorly monitored is not very efficient. That is why a free press is an indispensible component to any functioning democracy. The Foresight section of the Economic and Social Council (CESR) of the Ile de France region claimed in a report from the year 2000 (Guieyesse) that indecision among those in charge [...] insufficient communication and transparency lead to distrust among citizens in terms of their political and administrative institutions. To paraphrase the same report: the quality of governance, that is the rules and procedures enabling one to "govern the government better", is actually an essential element to resolve the crisis of governability.

At the level of the state, the poor quality of monitory relations, which exists in principle between parliament and government, may be the main cause of inefficiency and the excessive cost of action in public administration. Good governance should therefore reinforce the evaluation of public policies through independent agencies.

More and more the concept of governance is raised in international bodies precisely where what used to be called international regulation is lacking. Furthermore, the lack of such regulation is substantial given the greater interdependence created by the globalization of local economies and the very planetary nature of problems like environmental disasters, natural resources management, health and security issues. There is no world government, so the term "world governance" is really a misnomer.

Deindustrialization: Where is the Problem?

Our fears certainly enjoy longevity. Relocating facilities abroad actually represents under 5% of French foreign investment. The remaining percentage bears eloquent witness to the healthy state of French companies which head out to conquer new markets, primarily in Europe, which is the principal market of French industry. The French, after the Chinese, rank second in the world when in comes to direct foreign investment; however, this good news simply does not make headlines like deindustrialization or relocation abroad. Official reports from the French government continue to reach the same conclusion: France remains a top-tier industrial power and there is less deindustrialization than there is industrial transformation and internationalization of activity. Future challenges lie in innovation and the ability of actors and regions to organize themselves as centres of competitiveness.

These reassuring, constructive messages fail to chase away fear; instead, other reports appear which conclude with the necessity of relaunching an industrial policy through large European projects. When a corporation is struggling, the reason is almost always a failure in management. It is often both useless and expensive to help a company without changing its management. Conclusion: We should help corporations that are successful so that they develop further and revive intiatives perhaps ready but filed away. At the same time, we should not be seduced by the promise of emerging technologies or fall into the trap of mature sectors in decline. What matters is keeping competitive activities going, regardless of sector. For example, France remains one of the world leaders in wheelbarrow manufacture with Haemmerlin, a company located in Saverne, which still manufactures 100% in France. Fortunately the French economy utilizes hundreds of thousands of little wheelbarrows rolling and refilling. Beyond the folksy image, 96% of the 2.5 million companies with less than 20 people on the payroll represent 40% of commercial employment. We have to keep them healthy so that they can thrive in France, Europe and elsewhere in the world. That is the true challenge for public authorities in search of some kind of industrial policy.

On this topic, Alain Fribourg, head of the firm Dirigeants & Investisseurs, which specializes in turning troubled companies around, wrote recently that "we intervene in most areas of economic activity and in industrial, commercial and service corporations. In our experience, when a company is in trouble, rarely is it the result of external causes. Management is the cause, most often. [...] In passing, there is much to be said about relocation abroad that has been badly handled because the company laboured under the illusion that it would save in manpower costs in terms of the service provided to a specific client. In turning companies around, we have repatriated certain factories that had unwisely been relocated abroad. It is, however, normal that French companies set up industrial sites near their foreign markets."

All in all, we talk far too much about deindustrialization in France. Yes, industrial employment figures are shrinking but our balance of payments in manufactured goods has not dropped dramatically. The trade deficit with China (7 billion Euros in 2003) remains lower than our deficit with Germany and comparable to our surplus with the United Kingdom and Spain. If we define French deindustrialization as the decrease in industrial employment within the overall employment rate, then it should be considered the sign of advanced development or tertiarization (greater tertiary/service sector activity). This is the post-industrial society familiar from the 1960s and perceived as good news in those days. It should grow because we are producing fewer and fewer products that require intensive labour and material inputs. Instead, we are producing increasingly sophisticated products. This is the case for all developed countries. The share of industrial employment for France did fall by 9 points over the past 25 years, but much of this drop may be accounted for by positive gains in productivity and the outsourcing of certain functions. At the same time, employment in business services increased by 7 points to represent 14% of the total employment figure in 2003. In the end, what matters for a company is maximizing its value added by mastering design, marking, product distribution and after-market services. The secret is producing for less that which sells (quality plus service) rather than trying to sell (even at a loss) whatever we produce. Let us hope that locomotives sold in China are not half-paid for by French taxpayers, as was the case with certain cruise ships.

Despite Great Britain's deindustrialization, Eurostat reports that 25% of employment there may be categorized as industrial and equal to 20% of the British GDP. This corresponds to the French figure, but Britain has recorded greater per capita growth annually over the past two decades with a yearly average of one point greater than that of France. Moreover, the British unemployment rate is one-third the French. There is no miracle at work here; instead, British economic performance may be explained by structural reforms of the labour market and public spending plus an employment rate higher by 10 points. Activity itself generates wealth and employment. Rather than waving the spectre of deindustrialization and relocation in front of the public, our leaders would do well to speed up reform. They could start with the state. Public spending in France is 7 points above the EU average, which automatically handicaps our corporations with respect to international competition.

Let no one despair over French industry, though. In the future every commercial entity will need to be closer to the consumer, produce according to demand, with the least possible stock, ensure expediency, and traceability of supplies (accountability). Sustainable development and corporate efficiency may thus play a curative role in manufacturing in our own backyard, especially in terms of health, food and security. Sustainable development is an opportunity for European industry.

The CAP: Yes to an Open Europe; No to a Discounted Europe

The Common Agriculture Policy (CAP) has been a tremendous success in Europe but it must be seriously revised. One reason is the integration of new members in the East. Their entry into the European Union implies reconversion and modernization of a type of agriculture reminiscent of what France had in the 1950s. Help with products should now be assistance with quality, improving the products but also the producers and the process. Logical farming which pays close attention to traceability and respects the environment is one step towards sustainable agriculture. Yet subsidies granted in rich countries lead to artificial international prices that are disconnected from production costs and too low for the less developed countries to compete. Cotton, for example, in both the USA and EU where 70% of the overall production is located, enjoys a subsidy per kilo (1 kilo = 2.2 lbs) which has surpassed the selling price. In these conditions, African cotton, although more competitive, cannot be sold at its proper value. Consequently, its production and export have not been developed as they normally would. The same applies to sugar, grains and most other staples.

Given the sheer clout of the United States, the international price of agricultural products is often a "dumping" price which ensures the selling-off of American surpluses. If revising the CAP according to the concept of sustainable development becomes reality, this must be done without the pressure of the United States. Should we really throw markets open to the winds of "free competition" thus greatly reducing direct aid to production? No. Remember that the winds of the free market are artificial, too, in that they are often fanned by the United States, who protects national agriculture more than any other country does. In fact, agriculture has become more than an election issue – it now belongs to those select issues with geopolitical scope. All EU countries are not equally affected though. France, for example, represents 20% of the net value added to European agriculture. The other members follow: Italy (19%); Spain (18%); Germany (10%); Greece (7%); The United Kingdom (6.5%). However, Europe should not let down its guard. Subsidies or assistance packages remain slightly lower in volume in the United States but higher per farmer ($20,000 in America versus $14,000 in the EU). On the other hand, employment in the European agricultural sector is threefold the American rate (7 million versus 2 million). Given the stipulations of the Farm Bill, American assistance should increase by 70% over the next decade. In other words, now is not the time to casually dismantle in Europe what the Americans are reinforcing at home.

We should really be using agriculture in the plural as there are several types ranging from the corporate agribusiness to the gardener. We should also not forget that peasant farmers shaped our countryside, and, without them, France would be disfigured. After all, scenery, whether natural or artificial is the face of a country.

There are some 65,000 large farming concerns in France. Many economically viable farms are based on a versatile combination of activities and services. We have as an example the eco- or green farmer who is involved in socio-economic activities, education, leisure (tourism) and the environment. With 80 million tourists annually, France is the top international destination. Moreover, two out of three French citizens spend their vacation in the homeland, most often in the country, at friends' or with family. Eco-tourism already fulfils an essential function. Thanks to this new farmer, cultural sites and local roots may be maintained, green tourism will grow and educational activities will be created. Agriculture is not an insignificant industry in France. France exports 10 billion Euros of agricultural produce annually, which is two-thirds of the revenue generated by tourism, and par with the export revenue of France's auto manufacturers.

Economic performance, local initiative, citizen's responsibility, environmental responsibility, and prizes in agriculture. The former are all proof that France's "peasants" may remain innovative in their region, while being actors in local development. France's agricultural success is a result of its farmer's courage and will to succeed. In this way, France – a European green space – will be able to keep its agricultural and peasant roots alive. The strong human presence of the farmer who not only inhabits but shapes the landscape will remain part of French culture. However, the average citizen must help the producer and pay for the quality as well as some non-negotiable products or services which are nonetheless useful to the community as a whole.

The main message from the agricultural sector: Globalization has its limits. If we do not protect the sectors that constitute part of our national identity and corresponding patrimony, we run the risk of disrupting our society by disturbing how we live and relate to one another. This risk should concern all of us, but it threatens developing countries even more. Developing countries bear the hallmarks of acceleration in terms of rural exodus and shattered social structures. The result is the urban jungle, accompanied by misery and pollution. In other words, ticking time bombs that future generations will inherit.

What to do? One thing is to recognize that some sectors are naturally protected from international competition. These are essentially services provided nearby, or goods whose bulk prohibits long distance distribution. There are also a limited number of sectors that should be protected and regulated, such as architecture. Otherwise, every city will soon look as if it were poured into the same glass, concrete and steel mould of the Modern-International style. Lack of cultural diversity will stymie the urge to travel among tourists seeking exoticism.

"Open to the outside and thus the laws of the market, while organized from within to preserve national traditions which sustain basic relationships." In a nutshell, this is the prevalent model of social liberalism in certain North European countries. Their unwritten motto: As much market as possible and as much state as necessary to free up trade while ensuring solidarity and favourable arbitration in the long term. Clearly the idea is to be *for* more market and more competition wherever public monopolies are entrenched (not to say sclerotic) and to be *for* greater public intervention wherever the law of the marketplace is blind to collective interests.

Flexibility with a Human Face: The Need for State Responsibility

With respect to the labour market, flexibility ranges from the American, or wild type, in which everyone can work without any guarantee of living above the poverty line to the French, blindly rigid variety, in which everything is done to maintain the established order and the workers' rights while buying the silence of the unemployed. We really must find a middle road; in other words, flexibility with a human face. In the United States, the unemployment rate is less than half that of France's and the term long-term unemployment may be applied to 6% of all those unemployed whereas the figure is 35% in France. Man is not a product, but unfortunately the labour market does indeed operate like any other market. Rare is expensive; common is cheap or at best moderately priced. Naturally, a drop is prices increases demand. It is regrettable but true that for greater growth, job creation depends on overall labour costs. This does not mean simply wages and employer's costs (holiday pay, worker's compensation, taxes, deductions, etc.) but also the statutory restrictions related to labour law on recruitment and dismissal. The lower the overall cost of labour, the more people are hired. The higher the overall cost of labour, the more companies automate, outsource or relocate. In this respect the minimum wage with heavy additional expenses may actually be a barrier that prevents the least qualified workers from being hired. Of course, the least-qualified usually happens to be the largest sector of the active population.

However, corporations exist to create wealth, not jobs. Being competitive internationally means remunerating production factors at their international value. This statement has not gone unheeded by the French government. In fact, France has created a substantial number of public sector jobs, approx. 1.8 million between 1997 and 2001. In France and other countries, these figures may be explained by increased economic growth and development of lower-level jobs as a result of the decrease in employer costs per employee, payroll taxes or employment expenses, on low wages.

Will "flexibility with a human face" lead to the replacement of the minimum wage by the "minimum income for activity"? Corporations are not in charge of ensuring social redistribution. It is up to the political constituency to correct the distribution of wealth through negative and positive transfers which enable each citizen to earn a minimum income (with some conditions) that is at least equal to the current minimum wage. With the "bonus upon employment", France may have begun removing the taboo of a negative tax which is paid as a supplement to the salary from the corporation.

A job offer, however, is not equal to job creation. There must be a match between the employer and jobseeker willing to work at the advertised rate. Unfortunately the passive penalization of unemployment does not encourage people to work. Despite the *bonus upon employment* the gap between unemployment insurance and the revenue coming from a low wage is not encouraging. Solidarity should not destroy individual responsibility. There should be neither revenue nor penalty without some form of activity or insertion provided in return. This is a matter of dignity for the unemployed and a question of efficiency for society as a whole. We must stop helping passively and start encouraging directly.

Technology Is Not Essential

Whatever our uncertainty, companies of the future will face similar trends, breakdowns and breakthroughs. As always, structures, behaviours and the very quality of the people involved will make the difference between the winners and the losers. In fact, this explains profitable companies in so-called declining sectors as well as dogs in so-called rising sectors. In fact, this explains why it is useless to bail-out a corporation the minute it starts struggling with excuses of technological change or unfair competition. More often than not, the problem is a management deficit, a lack of foresight, or the inability to innovate or motivate people. The same may be said of regional problems.

Technology, albeit important, will never be the essential factor. We need to stop considering R&D spending as the principal positive indicator for future development. Being effective in saving money is what counts in R&D budgets. International statistics prove that the most effective organizations in any sector are those with average R&D spending – they are effective with what little money they spend. The same observation may be made about states. Small countries may have lower R&D efforts than the big countries, but they have higher GDP growth.

The Magicians of Growth

Henry Ford is quoted as once saying: "Take everything away from me, but leave me the men and I will start it all over again." Competitive growth over the long term depends on innovation and risk-taking. Entrepreneurs are magicians in this aspect. Unfortunately there are too few entrepreneurs, which is a fundamental characteristic of the "French exception". The elites, often veteran public administrators, act as managers of what already exists. Management should not be confused with strategy; the former minimizes risk while the latter optimizes it.

Rather than launch defensives on existing markets, entrepreneurs ride out to conquer the future. They do not limit themselves to reacting; instead, they deliberately take offensive action inspired by *preactivity* (preparing for expected change) and *proactivity* (provoking desired change), thanks to anticipation and innovation. An innovative entrepreneur changes rules rather than submits to them. We already know activity is what creates employment. The entrepreneurial spirit should be encouraged even within existing firms (*intra*preneurship) or firms created with a view to new developments. However, we must keep in mind that innovation and technology are not synonymous. Innovation, literally the introduction of something new, is not limited to technological aspects of process or products. Innovation may also be commercial, financial, social or organizational.

Unemployment, the Researcher and the Entrepreneur

Government researcher and entrepreneur are no more synonymous than innovation and technology. Actually, top honours in entrepreneurship go to the formerly unemployed who create their own enterprise and represent almost one-third of those starting a new company. Only 30% of new entrepreneurs have more than a high school diploma, and at most 5% have a graduate degree. As for researcher-entrepreneurs, one needs a microscope to find this statistically insignificant species. Annually only a few dozen of the 30,000 researchers in the public sector launch a business. The skill set is just not the same for research and business; hence, we need to link creative researchers to managers so that they can turn patents or licences into profitable innovations.

The premature death of new businesses is not fatal. An average of one out of two new companies disappears after three years. If an entrepreneur approaches his or her project with diligence and has an experienced team of advisors, the survival rate reaches 80%. Unfortunately good advice is tough to find. Only 55% of business projects do a financial study and only 33% do a market study (Rieg, 2003).

In the middle of the year 2000, corporations associated with information technology represented fewer than 3% of all companies and only 5% of all newly created companies. Without any crystal ball we can see that the magicians of growth are not produced by new technology. Entrepreneurs use the latest technology as a tool, among others, to ensure progress and innovation in a field in which there is latent demand. This observation, well known in business circles, doe not prevent top managers from falling victim to "technological determinism", which replaced old-time religious fanaticism in modern societies and generated an avatar called the "new economy". The "new economy" fell out of vogue only to be replaced by the knowledge or knowledge-based economy, another avatar for the same technological phantom.

Knowledge-Based Society and Innovation: Beware of Technological Mirages

After the "information society" of the 1980s, and the "new economy" of the 1990s, those still mesmerized by the mirage of technology launched a new concept: the knowledge-based society. Europe became fascinated by the concept of the knowledge-based economy at the Lisbon Summit in 2000. In fact the fifteen members of the European Union set themselves the objective of international leadership in this new knowledge society. In other words, an aging Old World reassured itself that the future would be populated by grey-haired sages with youthful spirits who were champions of innovation. Some might consider the knowledge-based society just another catchy label for what amounts to more or less the same thing. Knowledge society, knowledge-based economy, Knowledge Management (KM)... all these concepts remain fashionable in business and in the corresponding departments of academia (Pesqueux, Durance, 2004). Yes, the ability of corporations to "learn" has become a key factor in competitiveness. Nevertheless, most of the organizational learning is a form of adaptation, rather than proactive preparation.

More information does not readily translate to more knowledge. Furthermore, one must learn to separate the wheat from the chaff. The downsizing or laying-off of workers over age 55, workers with the greatest human capital, provide ample proof of what is really happening today. Knowledge Management requires managing the knowledge of people which implies respecting rather than rejecting people.

Knowledge does drive innovation, but that is no reason to pursue the mirage of technology and high-priced R&D. Moreover, innovation is not only technological but also commercial, financial and organizational. Although important, technology cannot constitute the essence of innovation. We must stop considering R&D expenses as the main hopeful indicator for the future.

Productivity, an Indicator of Exclusion

The French cock crows about productivity which, after the most reliable calculations, stand at 8% higher than that of the American and 16% higher than that of the EU average. Yet the same sources report that the GDP per capita in France is barely higher than the European average and 30% lower than the American. What can it mean?

One idea comes to mind right away: The French perform "better" than the Americans on average, but the employment rate in the USA is ten points higher than that in France. The French figure is based on 100 people of working age in the 15 to 64 age bracket of whom only 62% have a job versus 72% of their American counterparts and 66% of their EU cohorts. In sum, we are so good that we can work less (those famous 35 hours) while producing as much as the others. Well, if we rolled up our shirtsleeves and used our brains, we could become the world champions. To increase per capita GDP in France, more French people need to work, and they need to work longer hours. If the GDP is 30% higher in the United States, the reason is their employment rate is higher and they work approximately 30 days more than the French and ten days more than the European average.

It is time to press our luck and once again go against the grain of popular opinion, even those illusions about productivity held dear by some of the most reputable economists. They all refer to productivity, previously known as the "apparent" productivity of labour, which has lost the adjective and concept of *apparent* which formerly served to remind us that productivity is measured very roughly by dividing the GDP per number of employed active workers. Without the word *apparent*, productivity appears less tentative, but appearances may be deceiving. Imagine schoolchildren running a 100-meter race. If the entire class participates, their average speed will be lower than it would be if the fastest half of the class ran.

The paradox of France's high *apparent* productivity disappears once we consider that France only employs the most productive members of society. The less fortunate are replaced through outsourcing or automation. Perhaps the time has come to stop glorifying our apparent productivity rate which is actually a statistical consequence of the high cost of labour and ultimately a waste of productive means. If we wish to increase the employment figures, we need to accept a temporary decrease in the average productivity rate. Insertion on the job market is a form of training which acts as a lever to develop skills in individuals and, in the end, improve their productivity. This is the way in which a society increases its wealth while reducing exclusion or marginalization. In the productivity race, as in any sport, the coach does not want to select the champs simply in order to eliminate those who don't meet Olympic standards. On the contrary, each one must enter the race and progress according to his (or her) own level. From this perspective, we need first to insert rather than assist, avoid distributing funds without some form of activity in return and, overall, revive part-time work, which has decreased in France and remains two points below the EU average.

Technology and Solitude

Humans are social animals and we require social interaction. Without such interaction life becomes meaningless. Young farmers in France express it eloquently: "We don't need hectares as much as we need neighbours." The number of households comprised of only one person rose from 4.8 to 7.1 million in France between the two censuses (1982; 1999). Even if retirement is comfortable, the loneliness of old age is not. According to the INSEE, three-quarters of those aged 60 or more say that they have no social activity (club, association); while two-thirds never spend holidays with family or friends. Lastly, fifty percent of those over age 60 described themselves as isolated or very isolated.

The situation is exacerbated by poor urban planning which is often dictated by the demands of automobile infrastructure, usually at the expense of social interaction. In France, and particularly in Paris, we are fortunate to have a highly accessible public transportation network. However, in cities such as those in the western United States, with indomitable sprawl and few transportation alternatives to the car, the lack of "social capital" as Harvard sociologist Robert Putnam (2001) describes it, is desperate. Martin Pawley (1977) said this about the automobile: "Western society is on the brink of collapse not into crime, violence, madness or redeeming revolution, as many would believe, but into withdrawal – withdrawal from the whole system of values and obligations that has historically been the basis of public, community and family life. Western societies are collapsing not from an assault on their most cherished values, but from a voluntary, almost enthusiastic abandonment of them by people who are learning to live private lives of an unprecedented completeness with the aid of the momentum of a technology which is evolving more and more into a pattern of socially atomizing appliances."

The great paradox of modern society is a lack of communication despite ubiquitous information technology. Everyone should feel more openly connected to everyone else, linked to the entire world, but there is no one nearby for a chat. Watch people at a lecture or seminar. At the break, many slip out to talk on their cell phone or check their email. They talk with people who are absent and ignore those who are present. There are others who pay a fortune to have psychoanalysts listen to them and still more who boast of spending hours on-line, communicating to the world when they cannot even recognize their neighbours.

All that is technologically possible is not necessarily economically profitable. The Concorde airplane as an example of such technology. Technology is merely a means to an end, where the ends may be considered human values. There is no technological fix to problems related to social dysfunction and the spiritual void can only be filled by human interaction.

The Shortage of Professionals and the Need for Selective Immigration

The race for diplomas is not justifiable in that the jobs of tomorrow will not be where we think. For years now the alarm bell has been ringing about the risk of too many graduates and not enough trained professionals. In France, we now lack enough gardeners, chefs, butchers, nurses, hospitality industry employees, unskilled workers, and taxi-drivers. In landscaping alone the need is so great that one in two job offers goes unfilled.

What we need to do is align corporations' overall need for skills with the corresponding offer in the active population. We can thus smooth out tensions in the labour market and structural insufficiencies in some of the disappearing trades which have lost their appeal because of a poor image, e.g., manual labour, health services.

Given today's context in which fewer generations are entering the labour market (decrease of approximately 20% in the number of births since 1975), we might think that normally educated young people seeking work would have their pick of jobs. They should be encouraged to study for less time and enter the active population earlier. The new trend is already visible since the unemployment rate among high school drop-outs (age 16) has dropped lower than that of high school graduates (age 18). Competition to recruit young people should highlight the shortages in the least valued and most restricting professions which also require the least qualifications. These are the sectors where the need for renewal will be substantial. Think of the 300,000 qualified construction workers and the 600,000 aides to mothers and the elderly. We will have to find them by 2010 to meet new needs and make up for those leaving.

These jobs in the tertiary sector with a high degree of conviviality require not so much a diploma but a high level of willingness and professionalism. Competence is the fruit of passion, or less poetically, *you have to like your work to do it well*. Those with university degrees will have to forget their frustration and bitterness in order to rediscover the pleasure of working, which alone leads to competence. We need to adjust the offer to the demand by revalorizing working conditions and salaries. That means an increase in prices for services provided by the trades that have been abandoned over time. Turning to immigration will be necessary if we are to satisfy the need for personal services, maintenance and similar non-tangibles. This immigration must follow labour market and regional needs. It is worth noting that, on average, North America and Great Britain attract immigrants who are twice as qualified as those who enter France.

Sustainable Development, With or Without Mankind?

An aging Old World mulls over the obvious: Material wealth does not prevent affective and spiritual poverty. We have always know deep down that Gross Domestic Product is not Great Domestic Bliss. In many areas, accumulation in terms of quantity has led to lower quality. Human relations are a case in point for we see that more means of communication has not prevented solitude from spreading more than ever. Growth that is richer in quality could also mean greater overall "wellness". Whoever said that consuming more material goods meant being happier? Growth is a little like having a drink. Rather than always having the same old table wine, progress means consuming the same amount, even less, of a fine wine.

Sustainable development is a fashionable topic. Its origins are both ecological and Anglo-American. The concept includes two often antagonistic forces: sustainability with respect to the physical environment and social acceptability. Two versions of sustainable development face off regularly: the *Romantic primitivists*, who think growth is bad as soon as it depletes existing resources stocks and *pragmatic greens*, who know that creation cannot happen without some form of destruction. The first group is poised to impose a green dictatorship on us in the name of protecting nature and would prefer to return to Eden or some idealized past that never existed in the first place. In the year 1000, the planet was actually warmer than it is today. Greenland was exactly what its name suggests, hence without ice, which may explain why the Vikings colonized it. The world is much colder today, and global warming as a phenomenon became perceptible only in the mid-twentieth century. Nonetheless, this may be only a minor fluctuation within centenary cycles that have witnessed several sweeping movements over the millennia. As the world changes, plates shift, with climatic and volcanic shocks that originate in nature's, rather than man's activity. Nature's barbarity does not, however, allow humans to become like the sorcerer's apprentice. We subscribe to the pragmatic vision of sustainable development but add a human and social dimension as well.

Development of megalopolises will no longer be sustainable if the rising stress levels, social tensions and various other imbalances continue unabated. In densely populated urban areas, the first species threatened with extinction is Man, and thus human dignity, independence, social cohesion and ultimately meaning to life.

What we must condemn here are short-term profitability practices that lead businesses to depreciate future values (positive and negative) and to undervalue the present. This is the process of inflating growth (fluxes) to the detriment of assets (inventory). It may be normal to consider the current value of a far-off advantage as negligible, regardless of the magnitude, but should we treat major risks in the same manner with the pretext that they too are far-off?

These practices pass along a negative heritage to future generations in the form of urban blight, disfigured scenery, polluted water tables, extinct species, hazardous waste, etc. Our children shall shoulder a heavy burden as they correct the errors of their parents, who have behaved as if there were no tomorrow. Lester Brown's famous comment about the Earth not being the heritage of our ancestors but a loan from our descendents resonates more than ever. How then should we exercise our responsibility, given that the wild cards in environmental issues make us doubt the statements as well as the suggested solutions?

Wild Cards in Environmental Issues

However the media and public authorities have exaggerated the threats posed by the apparent hole in the ozone layer, the greenhouse effect and catastrophes like Seveso, Three Mile Island and Chernobyl, the degree of environmental degradation and its affects remain contentious issues. We have to remember that at the beginning of the 1980s, most environmental problems were considered solvable. However, that calm reassurance no longer seems to be true. Many major environmental problems have become permanent front-page news, such as the hole in the ozone layer. Haroun Tazieff has since said that the famous hole, well known to be growing, would continue as it always had; in other words, randomly, according to volcanic rhythms.

Who wins with doubt? Researchers certainly do. They see more credits and funding increases. Governments also win because they appear to be reacting in a responsible manner. Of course, they are unable to solve national problems and prevent more public anger. Yet what we do not know about the environment far outweighs that which we do know. For example, the regular increase in CO_2 in the atmosphere (over 10% in the past 25 years) should theoretically generate atmospheric warming (greenhouse effect) of more than 2 degrees Celsius on average annually until approximately 2150. In reality, some experts disagree with the recent warming trend but remain divided as to the timeline of this phenomenon, its true causes and the magnitude of future consequences. In principle, the polar ice cap should not melt, but the amount of rain in zones like the Mediterranean may increase and could actually reduce certain deserts. Could it be that what worried us yesterday might be hope for tomorrow?

Once again, the long term in foresight, or futurology, must be considered as part of the long term of history. Unfortunately, human beings have a short memory, and historians dwell upon the past without questioning the present. Emmanuel Le Roy Ladurie (1993) in his book *Histoire du climat* wondered "if the small shifts of glaciers, recently noted here and there, constituted merely a passing blip, or were they the starting point of a new fluctuation, positive and the inverse of the regression of the previous century?". Ladurie immediately brushes the question aside by giving his non-answer: "The historian, unconcerned by futures studies has no vocation to decide in this issue."

At the end of the 1970s and in the early 1980s, the dominant theory was that deforestation in Europe and North America was caused by factory emissions of sulphuric dioxide. Dozens of measures implemented at the international level were supposed to limit the damage caused by pollution. Five years later, the theory had been changed. Then the guilty party was no longer acid rain but rather the deadly effects of ozone depletion. The sun and automobiles were to blame. As a result, the European Union decided to impose catalytic converters on vehicles within its member-states. No sooner was the ink dry on the law than experts had to admit the unthinkable: the forests were suddenly on the mend, in even much better condition than in previous decades. Of course, by that time, two collective errors had been made and two important industrial policies had been implemented. The winners in both cases were the laboratories specialized in measuring the atmosphere and forests. This was only the beginning of the sweeping tide of scientific ecology.

Among the unknowns, or wild cards, declining biological diversity stands out. Interest in diversity stems from the rising rate of extinction among animal and vegetable species. The attitude in developing countries towards diversity should not be one of complacency. In fact, given the unknowns in environmental issues, we should all cultivate doubt as well as prevention in order to instil the long term in our collective thinking. Nevertheless, doubt must not paralyse action.

It is important to avoid both the scientific and the green dictatorships. We should keep in mind the Heidelberg Appeal from the Rio conference in 1992. Launched by an international group of hundreds of scientists, the Appeal says "... we want to make our full contribution to the preservation of our common heritage, the Earth. We are however worried, at the dawn of the twenty-first century, at the emergence of an irrational ideology which is opposed to scientific and industrial progress and impedes economic and social development. We contend that a *natural state*, sometimes idealized by movements with a tendency to look toward the past, does not exist, and has probably never existed since man's first appearance in the biosphere, insofar as humanity has always progressed by harnessing Nature to its needs and not the reverse."

While the Heidelberg Appeal rightly identifies the irrational misanthropy of radical ecology, it neglects to place man squarely in the centre of the new agenda. Therefore, we need to include the human factor and put mankind to work for both humanity and the future.

The Price of Abundance

The evolution of the consumption of energy depends first of all on the pace of economic growth. Given this reliable correlation, one can expect that oil demand will increase in China and India. Will the thirst for energy among developping countries exhaust the resource? It is generally admitted that the planet will not be able to sustain a worldwide level of consumption (waste) equivalent to that of the Americans. Less than half of the raw energy consumed in the United States is effectively used – the rest is wasted. The Americans claim that their way way of life is non-negotiable, nevertheless, it would be best that the Americans, and all inhabitants of developped countries, rethink their growth in a more sustainable way.

The nominal price of oil is not the real price. In fact, in real 1973 dollars, the price of oil is cheaper today than it was in 1980. Prices which change slowly and progressively pose little threat to an economy, whereas abrupt changes can wreak havoc. Progressively increasing oil prices, up to $100 per barrel or more, would bode well for sustainable development, elicit further energy exploration (and therefore increase known reserves,) encourage the development of renewable energies and discourage waste. All of these conditions would likely cast the famous peak-oil (the moment where the production of oil crests and then declines due to exhaustion) to a more distant horizon.

Year	Nominal price	Real price (1973 dollars)
1973	4	4
1974	12	8
1980	36	18
1988	14	5
1990	20	6
2000	27	7
2003	34	8
2005	70	16

The sharp increase in the price of oil since 2003 will certainly be followed (just as it did in the years between 1974 and 1979) by a decrease in the demand and a considerable realocation of financial resources to exploration and recovery. On the consumption side, the possibilities and incentives for energy efficiency are directly proportional to the amount and cost of the waste.

Hydrocarbons (oil, gas and coal) represent 90% of worldwide energy consumption and oil alone is represents 40% of worldwide energy consumption. We ought to welcome higher oil prices, past and present. The little shock of 2003 which pushed oil prices from $25 to $35 had, in one fell swoop, increased proven reserves by 18% by making the recovery of Canadian oil from bituminous rock profitable.

The time horizon to oil depletion tends to fade as we approach it. The explanation for this economic phenomenon has less to do with new discoveries, and more to do with the subtle distinction between proven reserves and resources. Proven reserves are those which are immediately recoverable from existing wells given contemporary economic conditions and technologies. Given this distinction, we can make the following observations, all of which support the thesis of energy abundance.

1) Proven reserves, which is to say those which we are certain to recover, are systematically underestimated insofar as analysts often dismiss reserves which we are only *likely* to recover. On average, wells yield almost twice the oil and gas originally expected.

2) Given contemporary technology, an average of only 25-30% of the oil in any given well is recovered. Secondary and tertiary recovery techniques, which are currently under development, could increase the recovery rate to 50%, perhaps even 60%, according to certain experts. Doubling the recovery rate, of course, doubles the proven reserves.

3) Around 50% of the sedimentary basins are located under the ocean floor at depths of more than 200 meters. This untapped potential is often not counted among reserves.

4) Economic conditions are most likely to change. At $50-$60 nominal dollars per barrel, the price of oil is still pretty cheap. Oil prices will naturally rise as they align with more expensive substitutes. Therefore, according to certain estimations, we can expect a doubling in the price of energy.

With respect to energy strategy, it is more important to consider these potentially new hydrocarbon resources than it is to consider nuclear – long considered to be the natural replacement for oil. The goal of any sustainable energy strategy is transition to renewable resources. Abundant alternative hydrocarbons and more oil exploration/recovery could spare and augment our oil reserves respectively, thus obviating the need for intermediate technologies like nuclear.

Nevertheless, the hypothesis of abundant hydrocarbons is not in itself enough to exclude the possibility of a serious energy crisis resulting from political ruptures like oil embargoes. Given the considerable delay between price signal, mobilisation of capital, exploration, recovery, processing and distribution, indecision today could lead to another crisis of capacity some 5 to 10 years in the future.

Abundance or shortage? The question remains unanswered. Nevertheless, it's best to prepare for the worst, rather than count on the best. Therefore, lets develop a diversified energy strategy, cultivate precaution, adopt a flexible aproach and stop mortgaging our future by gambling on one particular technology.

Food Safety, GMOs and the Principle of Precaution

In the past and with the help of the CAP, farmers knew how to mobilize in order to win the battles of productivity and modernization. However, increasing the number of acres and bushels per acre or hectare means that, in the past 30 years, the same farmers have lost half of their neighbours. They have often forgotten the old ways, too. Some resources, for example soil, water, and scenery, cannot be treated indefinitely as renewable while the supply continues to be degraded in terms of both quantity and quality.

The intensification and artificial manipulation of agricultural practices came to light in the 1990s through the media reports on the Mad Cow crisis, bovine growth hormone, genetically modified organisms, and various other health crisis such as avian flu. These events forced food security into the spotlight.

The pressure to be productive has indeed led to many unreasonable agricultural practices, like the intensive use of growth hormones, unnatural combinations and illegally produced food. Raising chickens in under five weeks when nature requires five months really has to be considered excessive. On that note, the average cow would not have gone mad if left out in the pasture.

We have opened Pandora's box and now we have to deal with the consequences. Otherwise, with each new scandal revealed by the media, mistrust among the public regarding food will grow. The tainted blood scandal created a precedent that incites officials to act fast. After the dioxin-infected chickens, we may start to see sick salmon, which makes sense insofar as whatever animals are forbidden to consume is often redirected to aquacultural consumption. Another example of the domino effect in nature is the use of herbicides like atrazine, now forbidden in Europe. Atrazine was previously used in massive quantities along the French railroads and highways as if no one had ever thought of its impact on water supplies through runoff. There is also plenty of land that must be obliterated from the map because it is contaminated by household waste containing heavy metals.

This does not mean necessarily rejecting technological progress and preaching a return to "all-natural" products. If our life expectancy has increased, the reason is healthier, more balanced nutrition. Remember that the 100% natural state is not without its dangers. In the past, people died from ingesting grain parasites like the ergot. Without pesticides, people would not be able to eat as much as their appetite dictated. The consumption of "bio" products also presents risks. For example, the very symbol of healthy eating, the apple, must be treated to prevent diseases otherwise this common fruit develops dangerous toxins.

The intensive use of fertilizers and pesticides does have its limits. We need to protect the water table and optimize the use of entrants with integrated farming. Technology provides an array of new answers with genetically engineered or manipulated organisms (GMOs), which do indeed modify plants genetically to avoid the use of pesticides. Those answers are not completely free of risk or anxiety either. There are many more questions than answers. Manipulating nature elicits gothic images of Frankenstein, as seen in the now widespread English expression *Frankenfood.*

Society's attitude toward risk is often paradoxical. GMOs scare many people, and those who reject them according to the precautionary principle are correct. Why take a risk if there are no tangible advantages in the balance? Although GMOs have not yet killed anyone, they certainly generate opposition. Viagra, on the other hand, is socially acceptable despite recorded deaths because it has a genuine usefulness for those who take it. In order for GMOs to be accepted, we will have to wait for *pharmafoods,* or products developed using genetic modifications that enhance human health. An oft-cited medical example that no one criticizes is Limagrain which uses genetically modified tobacco to produce an artificial human blood coagulant similar to natural hemoglobin.

In any event, we can leave the choice to the consumer by developing non-GMO market niches. Of course that means accepting the inherent cost increases. The precautionary principle, or erring on the side of caution, must also keep the future open. In this sense, we should pursue experimental GMO production if only to keep the technological race running. Actually no one can seriously claim to outlaw GMO corn or wheat in France while still massively importing American soya which has been genetically modified for animal feed. After all, if the danger is real, then logically the entire agricultural chain must be protected.

The European Union's Agenda 2000 changed the landscape, literally. Not only were assistance programs to be reduced, but also funding was to be more closely linked to limits and objectives in agri-environmental orders. Contracts for regions and integrated farming were drawn up in this spirit, too, so that the potential for future development would be preserved. In other words, set the course for sustainable development in agriculture.

However, logical farming, or integrated farming, is an obligation in terms of method only; it does not guarantee results. Quality and security have been developed in agriculture. As successfully applied in industry, quality assurance and certification systems have been put in place on the basis that there is full traceablity for all products, from stable to table. Transparency and consistency across the agribusiness sector will enable farmers to regain the public's trust and esteem, as well as a sense of confidence in the future.

The wild cards in environmental issues should make us cultivate doubt and a preventative attitude so that we keep long-term not just short-term concerns in the forefront of the popular opinion. Yet prevention of risk must not lead to strong measures based on weak information. Risk prevention must prioritize concerns and keep people and the future as its focus. In the end, development will not really be sustainable if there are no people around to maintain diversity and variety in languages and cultures.

No Sustainable Development without Children

What would the ecologists say if the fertility rate of whales had shrunk over the past twenty years to less than half the level of renewal? As good environmentalists, they would appeal to public opinion in resolving this planetary ecological disaster. Yet this is exactly what is happening in Northern Italy and Catalonia, where the fertility rate has been falling for the past twenty years to arrive at fewer than one child per woman. Obviously this species is far from going extinct, but cultural variety is being threatened. Ironically it was in the name of variety that ecologists did oppose plans to put a highway through the Bercée forest in France. Part of their logic was to save a species of plume-eating beetles. Sustainable development keeps the future alive for generations to come, yet we seem to focus on bugs and whales while forgetting people.

The precautionary principle should be applied to economics as well as society, especially when we consider the troubling correlation between the lack of economic growth (recession) and the demographic transition (regression). The causal relationship has not been proven, but when in doubt, as in ecology, we should encourage research. In the meantime, we should operate as if demographic vitality were the first condition required in sustainable development.

As of 1987, the Brundtland Report defined *sustainable development* as that which meets the needs of the present without compromising the ability of future generations to meet their needs (Brundtland, 1987). Of course without those future generations, sustainable development becomes a moot point. The risk of a demographic implosion in Europe should be ecologists' first concern. Some "green fundamentalists" may consider the extinction of the White Westerner (*read* polluter and waster) is good news for nature. Again, humans as a species are not threatened, but Europe's cultural variety is. This cultural variety which constitutes Europe's identity deserves to be preserved in its historical biotope. It seems paradoxical to promote the conservation of plant or animal species yet forget mankind in the struggle for an open, culturally varied future. One day the "politically correct movement" will realize that we need to protect not only whales but also people.

The Link between Economic Growth and Demographics

A taboo topic that evokes past dictatorships in countries like Spain, Italy and Germany, family policymaking remains tainted with a conservative, rightwing image even in France. Oddly enough, those who initially promoted family policies just after the Liberation, Alfred Sauvy, among others, tended to be socialists. At this point in history, let us hope that the call for a *European Youth Pact* from four leaders located in Paris, Berlin, Madrid and Stockholm will rouse the entire Old Continent. In general, if the population is aging from the top down, the good news is that we are living longer; however, if the population is aging from the bottom up, we do not have enough people to replace the existing generation. The latter statistic is not fatal but certainly will impact our future, which already appears compromised and imbalanced simply because the next generation will be insufficient in number.

Despite relatively good demographics in comparison with its neighbours, France also has a dwindling youth base. A glance at the numbers available proves that in 1999, there were 2.5 million youths (ages 0-18) fewer than in 1975; in other words, 12.8 million versus 15.3 million! With a fertility rate hovering around 1.4, the Europe of tomorrow will have one-third fewer youths than the Europe of today. There is simply no guarantee that the next generation will be there to pick up the baton.

At the European Council in Lisbon in 1990, Europe adopted an ambitious program to take the lead in the new knowledge society. Fine, but what if there are no more young people to take up the torch, to carry on working? The projections for 2050 are dramatic. Italy for example, will lose one-third of its population. Wealth may indeed require educated citizens, but when there are not enough people, there is no wealth or future.

Europe should open its borders to immigrants in a more selective way, similar to the American system, and use more positive public and family policies to ensure integration in the host society. Successful integration comes through the national school system where native-born children and newcomers mix; hence the need for more children, a higher birthrate in Europe. The Eurobarometre (a statistics service) has shown that one out of every two women would like another child, but juggling work and family life make it too difficult. (European Commission, 2002, 2004) Aging from the top down is great news for those Europeans living longer and in good health. It becomes a problem when there is no next generation, no one to take up the torch. It is aging from the bottom up of the age pyramid that we must avoid. Again, what good is saving the whales if there are no children to see them or to use the latest supercomputers?

Refusal to See the Link between Economic Growth and Demographics

Alfred Sauvy (1980) decried people's "refusal to see" the reality of not renewing the generations and economic development that ignored future generations; in other words, that which is contrary to the very definition of sustainable development. Intergenerational solidarity does not mean making the young pay systematically for their elders' poor management and lack of foresight. If seniors have retirement problems, one reason is that they had fewer children. This follows the Sauvy "theorem": "Today's children determine tomorrow's retirement." In fact, the increase in dependency rates which threatens our retirement programs may stem from an increase in the numerator (a higher number of retired people) as well as from the denominator (number of taxpayers, for example, for demographic reasons, but also a result of Malthusian choices regarding seniors working, women working, etc.). It should not be up to future generations to pay off the public debt accumulated by their forefathers. Gerard Calot (2002) in his intellectual testament reminds us all that "a drop in the birth rate for a country is equalivant to less investment for a company. For a certain period of time there is a benefit: a more comfortable financial situation. This comes, however, at the expense of serious problems later on. Family policymaking is a long-term investment. [...] A low fertility rate is met more favourably by all the actors in a society, fewer educational expenses, fewer interruptions in women's careers, more money available in each household."

Contemporary political leaders know that a dwindling youth base in the population is a serious matter but they prefer to avoid the topic in the short-term as bad news because their efforts will not win them any votes. Occasionally they do say out loud what they are really thinking. This was the case of François Mitterrand who wrote of "a France poor in children in an even poorer Europe". In 1994, Jacques Chirac commented that the drop in the birth rate is the virus that will attack our competitiveness. Alain Juppé (2000) did use the expression "demographic suicide" but never mentioned it again. In general, everything goes on as if we want to avoid admitting consciously or unconsciously the confession of something better left unsaid.

Europe's leaders are, however, well aware of the phenomenon of aging from the top down. They know that our health and retirement systems must undergo painful reforms. The state must ensure funding will be available for those over 80, a segment of the population that will double in France by the year 2035 to surpass 6 million people. People often object by saying that old age has been redefined since 1680 when Pierre de Richelet stated in his dictionary that "A man is called old from age 40 to age 70." Perhaps we can live "young", healthy and independent up to age 80. Unfortunately beyond 85, most people are no longer independent. We might be able to extend the deadlines, but the younger citizens still active in the workforce will be fewer and paying more to maintain their elders.

The Turning Point of October 29, 2004: the European Youth Pact

For thirty years the topic of youth never appeared on the agenda of European summits of heads of states. The same silence was deafening at the Parliament in Strasbourg. Only when Sweden took over the EU presidency in 2001 was the taboo issue addressed clearly. To paraphrase the Swedes, the low European birthrate has negative effects on economic growth and, therefore, prosperity. The state must intervene so that people may manage their professional and personal lives better. Germany, a country with more coffins than cradles right now, recently had an interesting cover on the popular *Der Spiegel* magazine. The image was one of a couple with two children and a third child outlined only. Obviously the demographic issue is part of the *zeitgeist* there. Chancellor Gerhard Schröder has just launched an ambitious program promising parents greater daycare options by the year 2010 (CNAF, 2004). In 2001, he even had a long article in *Le Monde* describing the family as essential to the future (Schröder, 2001).

The negative economic situation familiar to EU countries since 2002 has not made broadcasting the demographic message any easier. The transition to the Euro and the enlargement of the EU to 25 countries took the spotlight. Once the referendum on the European constitution is over, we hope that the main issue in Europe will not be the so-called technology gap with the USA but the demographic gap. The shift in focus is not that great as the USA remains the country of reference. If demographics do top the agenda, the joint letter of October 29, 2004, signed by President Chirac, then Chancellor Schröder, President Zapatero and Prime Minister Göran Persson, will mark the end of the *Omerta* on population growth that has reigned in Europe up to now. This letter went unnoticed in France and was pointed out by a *Time Magazine* reader (Graff, 2004).

The March 2005 Good News: Europe Confronts the Demographic Challenge

The European Union has decided to confront the challenge highlighted by the Wim Kok report (2004). In its March 2005 Green Book, the Commission urgently insists that the Lisbon Strategy be put into effect (European Commission, 2005). The emphasis should be on the following:

1) Policies that target greater participation in the job market for young people, women and seniors, innovation and greater productivity;

2) Innovative measures to support a higher birthrate and controlled use of immigration to create new investment opportunities, increase consumption and the creation of wealth;

3) Reinforcement of solidarity between generations through the distribution of the fruits of growth, through some balance in the care of the very elderly, through the distribution of financing needs related to the social security and retirement programs;

4) Promotion of a new organization of work, and the definition of life-long training policies.

The European Union intends to develop a broad-based approach to the active lifecycle thus facilitating new transitions between age brackets over time. The issues brought together in the Green Book will be discussed at a conference in July 2005. They will certainly have an impact on the European Youth Pact. The Commission has put children and families at the very heart of measures taken to find ways to growth. In the end, we must ask two simple questions: *"What value do we attach to children? Do we want to give families, whatever their structure, their due place in European society?"*

High and Low Demographic Pressures

Developed countries possess over two-thirds of the world's wealth whereas they account for less than one-fifth of the world's population. In 2025 their share in the world's wealth will have decreased slightly for a population reduced by 16% of the total (Population Reference Bureau, 2004). If we consider certain hot spots in the Middle East, we see that Israel will increase its population from 6 to 9 million by then, followed closely by the Palestinian territories which will have doubled from 3 to 6 million. At the same time, Iraq will balloon from 25 to 45 million; Syria, from 17 to 28 million. Obviously today's hot spots or potential conflict zones are not being depopulated.

Among developed countries, the United States provides the exception to the rule and continues to expand. The American population has increased by 80% since 1950 and will grow by approximately 40% by 2050. In that year it will surpass the Europe of Fifteen by 20%, despite the fact that in 1950 the American population was less than half the European (United Nations, 2004).

Still, among developed nations such as Russia, the Eastern European countries and Japan will experience a demographic situation even more devastating than that of the European Union. For the period 2000 to 2025, the American demographic trend (increase of 66 million) will be superior in absolute value to that of Brazil (increase of 54 million) or the Indonesia's (increase of 55 million) and opposite to the Japanese (decrease of 2 million) and the Russian (decrease of 17 million).

The Japanese population will fall from 127 to 125 million in 2025 and then to 112 million in 2050. The active population will decrease by 2 million between the years 2000 and 2005. This decrease will continue by 12 million more between 2005 and 2025. During the same period the number of citizens over age 65 will explode, thus marking an increase from 25 million to 36 million. What kind of economic crisis will hit this country as it risks losing around 15% of its population by 2050? Japan entered an economic crisis as the 1990s began, yet no one has connected this to accelerated aging. The recent upswing in the Japanese economy is basically explained by an incredible leap in the Chinese demand.

Western Europe has at least caught a glimpse of its future. In 2025, the "Fifteen" will have almost the same number of inhabitants as in 2000 (378 million).

France as a Driving Force in European Demographics

With a fertility rate hovering around 1.9, France should be proud to come second to Ireland, the EU fertility champion in 2002 (Sardon, 2004). Without the French natural "surplus" of 210,000 people, the figure of the European Union (with 15 members) might be 73% less.

France boasts of its growing population and, indeed, will see an increase of 4 million by 2025. In fact, France is rightfully proud to have had more births than the reunited Germany since the year 2000, especially as Germany had double the French rate in 1939. Germany will lose one million citizens over the next 25 years and currently has a deficit of 120,000 births compared to the number of deaths in its population (Sardon, 2004).

Yet France should also be concerned, even alarmed, by its main neighbours who are also its principal clients. *Through immigration and the amnesty offered illegal migrants over the past few years, Spain will see its population rise by 4 million rather than drop by 3 million. Similarly, Italy's population will decrease by only 1 million rather than the 3 million projected in 2004, and overall, the perspective for Great Britain resembles that of France.*

In this context, the positive migratory balance of over one million people is what boosted the Europe of Fifteen's population statistics. Indeed annual net flows exceeded 200,000 for Germany, Spain and Italy, 150,000 for Great Britain (Sardon, 2004).

**Graph 1: The Demographic Implosion of the Europe of Fifteen
(1960-2050, in millions)**

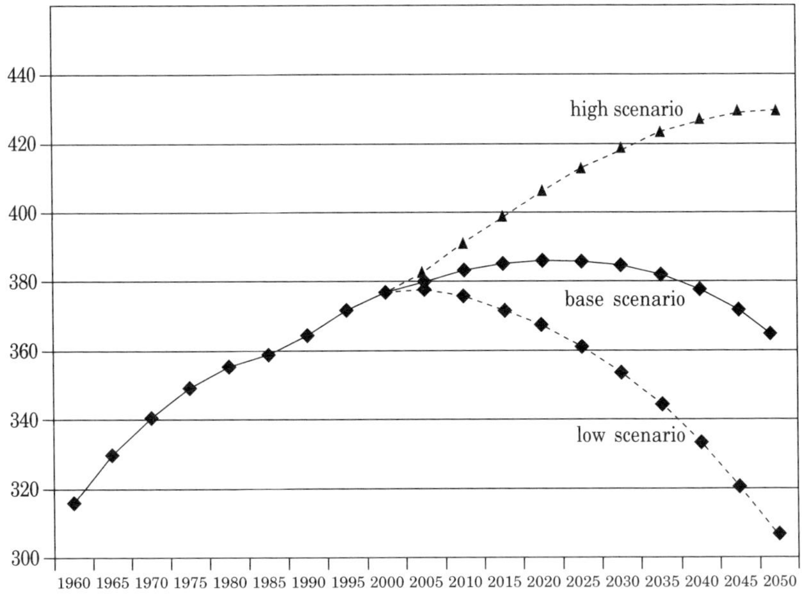

Source: Eurostat, 2005 for retrospective data, 1995 revision, 1999 for the projections.

Note: the three scenarios arise from the difference in the estimate for the fertility, lifespan and immigration rates for the Europe of Fifteen.

The demographic decline in Europe has long been expected. In fact, the UN even published a provocative report in 2000 which announced a decrease of 40 million inhabitants by the year 2050. The same report underscored the necessity of bringing several hundred million immigrants to counteract the effects of an aging population. Naturally such simple mathematics cannot predict the demographic outcome. Nonetheless, without immigration, there will be fewer active citizens available to ensure the production of wealth. When OECD experts considered the impact of an aging population on economic growth, they calculated that as of 2010, the average income per inhabitant would rise less than half as fast as it did on average in the past.

The EU should not count on Eastern Europe either. Its population will shrink like that of Japan. Russian will drop from 147 million to 129; the Ukraine will fall from 49 to 37 million and even the very Catholic Poland will decrease by 1,6 million inhabitants between 2000 and 2025. Beyond figures in absolute values, we can see that it is aging from the top down (more old people) and aging from the bottom up (fewer youths) that will affect productivity, entrepreneurial and competitively. Our Old World will really deserve its clichéd name soon! In this context, immigration appears necessary, but problems arise when the newcomers are concentrated in a few megacities where tension and urban apartheid become entrenched. We know that the integration of Islamic populations is not as easy as that of migrants from elsewhere in Europe. The East, which is draining out, is not a reservoir. Perhaps we should consider the potential of Latin America, where the population will rise by some 140 million by 2025.

In the meantime, the proximity of high- and low-pressure zones translates to migratory flows. Europe receives a growing number or new immigrants annually. In 2002, 1.3 million came: some 350,000 for Italy, 230,000 for Spain and 220,000 for Germany, and the United Kingdom follows with 150,000 while Portugal takes in 70,000 (Sardon, 2004). *Some 50,000 additional foreigners were arriving in France – officially – every year. That figure has now been doubled to 100,000, but given illegal immigration and occasional amnesties, the number is likely closer to 150,000 or 200,000, as seen in the nearest neighbouring nations.*

These flows should increase tremendously, given the lack of labour available in the rich yet aging North and the plentiful, young yet unemployed population in the poor South. There are already more youths under age 20 in Algeria than in France (15 million) and this is twice the Egyptian figure! The 8.5 million Spaniards under age 20 contrast sharply with their 14 million counterparts in Morocco. Who would not be tempted by the El Dorado of a job in the North, where there are not enough hands and heads?

As a solution, immigration raises several questions rarely asked because they are simply too delicate politically. The first question involves selective immigration. This implies quotas according to origin and profession. North America, Great Britain and certain Nordic countries use this system. Others, like France, take in those who reach the national territory. As a result, two-thirds of the immigrants who get to France have no more than high school or "lyceum" level whereas these categories are only 30% and 22%, for Great Britain and the USA respectively (OECD, 2001). The second question involves the reception and integration of foreigners. The *laissez-faire* in this area leads to new situations, including a Europe of urban apartheid and ghettoization where the living conditions degenerate and the original inhabitants leave (Maurin, 2004). The third question raises the issue of developmental ethics. In other words, do we have the right to loot the human capital of poor countries by attracting their best and brightest to our shores? Asking the last question in this way leads us to a negative realization: those countries will not develop with this approach.

The aging active population will have an especially noticeable impact on the European Union during the period from 2005 to 2050. In fact, between 2010 and 2030, the number of workers aged 25 to 54 could drop by 25 million, and even 45 million between now and 2050. There will not be enough young replacements in the labour force between the ages of 15 and 24 either because their numbers will fall by approximately 7 million between 2010 and 2030. The number of older active workers (55 to 64) will have to rise; however, they will not be enough to make up for previous population deficits as their numbers will increase by fewer than 9 million over the same period. This perspective of a dwindling active population in Europe heralds shortages in manpower in the least popular trades and reinforces the need for selective immigration.

Graph 2: Population Changes by Age Bracket in the Europe of 25 (variation 2005-2050, in millions)

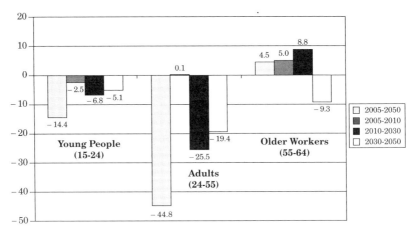

Source: Eurostat, 2005

**Graph 3: The Aging of the Population by Age Bracket
in the Europe of 25 (variation 2005-2050, in millions)**

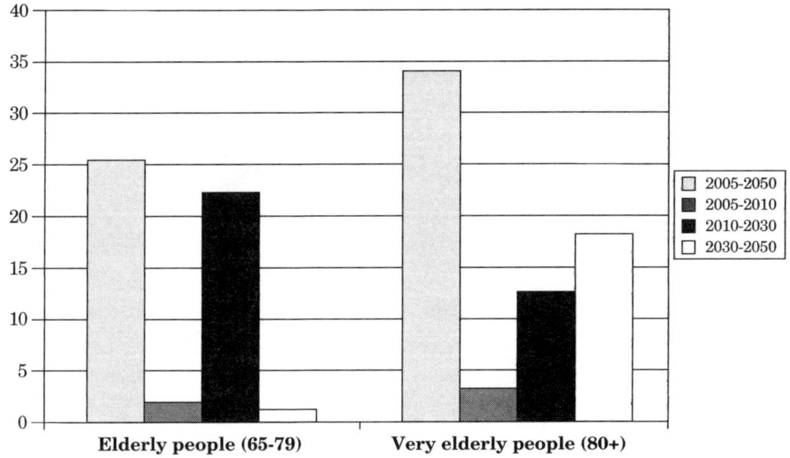

Source: Eurostat, 2005

Meanwhile, the ranks of young retirees, or seniors as Eurostat calls them, will swell by more than 20 million. Elderly people, that are those over age 80, will rise in number by an additional 30 million. The issue of independence and guardianship, as well as intergenerational solidarity, will certainly come to the forefront given that these generations are more numerous yet had fewer children than did their parents.

The Multiplier Effects of Demographics

At the Commission in Brussels and most other international and national bodies, the link between growth and demographics is rarely ever discussed. Reports on technology, innovation, and competitiveness abound; however, Man is considered little more than human capital to be trained. People are viewed as an investment or a long-term growth factor. Demography is treated only as aging from the top down with the subsequent problems created by retirement pension plans, health spending, and dependency on the state, but almost never in terms of the consequences of aging from the bottom up, in other words, the effects on growth and the position of Europe on the world stage. Even the ambitious Lisbon strategy for growth and employment relies essentially on information technology and a growth economy to ensure Europe's future and power on the international scene with a horizon line of 2010. Yet at the halfway point, the recent report by Wim Kok focuses on a knowledge-based society and sustainable development for an enlarged Europe. There is one new element: one page devoted to the aging of Europe. This greying Europe could decrease the EU's potential growth by one point (1% rather than 2%) from now to the year 2040; however no mention whatsoever is made of European demographic developments in contrast with American trends (see chart 1). This omission is all the more glaring as such comparisons are systematic in terms of research efforts, innovation and productivity figures.

**Chart 1: Comparative Demographic Developments
of Triadic regions (1950- 2050, in millions)**

	1950	2000	2050
United States	158	284	395
European Union (15)	295	378	335
Japan	84	127	112

Source: United Nations, 2004, Population Division of the Department of Economic and Social Affairs of the United Nations Secretariat, World Population Prospects: The 2004 Revision

As Alfred Sauvy used to say, economists refuse to see the link between demographics and economic growth so they fail to test it. Yet post-war prosperity and the baby-boom that went hand in hand with the American economic miracle likely stemmed from strong demographics. For some twenty years, the American fertility rate has been 2.1 children per woman versus 1.5 in the Europe of Fifteen. The American population also experienced major migratory influxes which continue. Comparing the European and American rates requires a technique that explains long-term differences. We have to wonder if a "demographic multiplier" effect is not involved. This hypothesis could not be developed fully within the framework of this paper, but some research tends to highlight this relationship (Doliger, 2003). If tested, we could understand why growth and especially gains in productivity from the 1950s and 1960s were on average double that of the 1980s and 1990s even though these last two decades saw more technological advances which theoretically yield gains in output.

This last point is not ignored by economists, who always refer to the famous Solow Paradox about seeing computers everywhere, except in productivity statistics! With the new economy, the question seemed answered: the USA underwent a period of strong economic growth with (apparent) productivity gains far above Europe's. Obvious proof of Europe's technological lagging? We may wonder about this explanation now that past statistics are validated and well-known. For example, in the 1980s, GDP growth per active worker was comparable in both zones at approximately 1.7%, with a slight European advantage. However, the initial results for the period from 2000 to 2004 reveal a clear-cut difference between the USA whose apparent productivity seems to rise at over 2% annually and the Europe of Fifteen whose rate is under 1%. The question begs to be asked: Is this difference due to the technology gap or the demographic gap? We put forth the demographic hypothesis. The demographic factor now plays a determining role as the gap is widening more than ever.

The entire population is not active, but the number of hours worked basically explains away the difference in productivity levels. Americans work 46% more than the French on an annual basis. Yet if they are working, then there must be a real demand to be met. Indeed, perhaps the demand is greater there because of demographic expansion.

If we reject the hypothesis of independence between the two variables (GDP *per capita* and Demographic Growth), then we can suggest a new hypothesis, that of a demographic multiplier which might be at the root of the major gains in productivity made in the US and not in Europe.

Economists usually explain growth with three factors and reference to the famous Cobb-Douglas production function. The factors are capital, work and technological progress. We know that productivity is the remainder of additional growth which cannot be explained by the increase in production factors (capital and labour). For lack of anything better, we attribute this increase in growth in the GDP per active worker to progress in information technology. In sum, it is a positive way of naming an unexplained remainder.

GDP growth depends upon two factors: GDP per active worker and the number of active workers. The increase in the ratio GDP per active worker is more significant in the USA than in Europe since the mid-90s. Yet how can we explain the productivity and economic growth of the 1960s – approximately double that of the 90s on both sides of the Atlantic – when there were no computers?

It turns out that the variation in the GDP per active worker is more important since the number of active workers and the number of job openings increase in a growing population. Technological progress, training and economies of scale combine to lower unit costs and improve quality; in other words, the added value is greater, or the GDP per active worker. The multiplier effect in demographics still plays a role in the United States, albeit a lesser one than in the 1960s, but not in a greying Europe. As mentioned, most economists fail to see the demographic multiplier because they simply do not look for it. Yet this hypothesis has revealed more on the gap between a rising GDP per capita in the US and Europe in the 1990s than did the so-called lag in communication and information technology. Long-term growth in developed countries is regulated by demography. The real issue for companies is market openings. Europe buys 91% of what France produces. Consider, however, the fact that the European population will stagnate by 2050. Furthermore, eastern European countries will see a decrease of over 20 million, while the American population will continue growing to add some 65 million more people. If we continue moving east, we can explain Japan's economic downturn in the 1990s by referring to a population aging more quickly.

According to the demographic multiplier hypothesis, demographic differences may explain the spread between developed countries in terms of job creation over the past 25 years. The fact that qualitatively young people learn new technologies easily certainly adds to the multiplier effect. In a comparative study based on an endogenous growth model, Baudry and Green (2000) showed how countries with solid demographic growth had a more rapid spread of modern technology and created more jobs. A test carried out on 18 OECD countries highlights a positive, significant correlation between demographic growth and employment from 1975 to 1999, the same period when new information technologies were spreading.

Anyone clinging to the single-variable method and refusing to see the link between economic growth and demographic dynamics should consider the following question: how can you reconcile the high and rising productivity of the USA, which is attributed to computer and information technology, and the abysmal drop in their foreign trade deficit (500 million dollars in 2004)? Remember that this all occurred with a weak American dollar! Obviously the time has come to reconsider the concept of productivity and to destroy the myth which leads us to forget the essential – without human capital any growth is limited for lack of new blood.

Chart 2: Evolution of Population and Employment between 1975 and 2000

	Evolution of population (in million)	Change in %	Evolution of employment (in million)	Change in %
United States	60	28	49	57
Japan	15	13	12	23
Main european countries *	20	7	12	11

Source: Eurostat
* France, Germany, Italy, Spain and United Kingdom

With the current fertility rate hovering at 1.5, tomorrow's Europe will have generations of young workers which are one-third smaller than today's. Plummeting birthrates in a country resemble decreased investments in a corporation. For a while, the company benefits financially only to pay the price later and the consequences may be costly. Government policymaking on family issues is really a long-term investment.

European countries are like orchards full of trees. After a fruitful life of 40 years, the grove matured without anyone having planted new seeds. If we are to invest and consume, we need to have faith in the future and should prepare ourselves. Unfortunately, these are characteristics that tend to be lost with age.

What underlies the dynamics of economics and demographics may be considered the same: a zest for life that is expressed in an economic initiative and the rearing of children. The corporate spirit is closely related to the family spirit! You can understand the impact of aging on corporations in France if you remember that in 2002, 40% of all entrepreneurs were 25 to 34 years old and two-thirds were under 44. Those over 55 represented only 8% of entrepreneurs. Between 2000 and 2025, those under age 30 will continue to decrease in number but it is the group at the peak of its productive life (age 30-49) that will plummet by 1.6 million. This fact is all the more shocking when you realize that the same group had grown by 4.5 million during the previous 25-year period.

An aging Europe and a demographic implosion in certain large countries paint a picture of grey hair and soft growth. There will be serious tension regarding the labour market and retirement. This will intensify given our collective illusions about the jobs of the future. We should brace ourselves for a shortage of young professionals in manual labour and the service sector. There will also be new territorial divides accentuated by population movements and unequal development of infrastructure. The knowledge society is all well and good as long as it does not break the backs of workers over 55 who are the carriers of that human capital.

Another thing would be to ensure that children finishing primary school can read, write and count properly.

Demographic dynamics impact the economy but also reinforce regional divides, all the greater when a society had ghettos by social class and a real urban apartheid in which troubled or broken families live in a certain neighbourhood. Under these conditions, the family can no longer be considered a private matter. It becomes a public matter.

The Family, A Public Affair

If there exists one single area in which immediate action is required, it is family policymaking. The clock is ticking and the hands cannot be turned back. Policy in this area affects demographics thus economics. As mentioned above, there can be no sustainable development without children. Also important is the social cohesion factor. Society already bears the heavy cost of broken families with pathetic results. If we let current fertility rates continue, if we let families neither blend nor mend but simply wear out, the social cost will skyrocket. However, any discussion on family policymaking requires frank talk about reality.

In a Europe facing dramatic demographic aging, France can still hold her head high. The French birthrate remains relatively good thanks to family policy passed unanimously after the Liberation. Although a bit dog-eared, this legislation now serves as a model in Europe. Its universal character has protected the French, through family allowances, a supplement that reduced the difference between households with children and those without and a primary school system which is unique because it is not only free but also excellent and accessible.

The universality of the French policy is a precious asset. If we dilute it to convert it into a means of reducing the inequality of household incomes, we lose on two playing fields, the demographic and democratic. The policy of fighting poverty must be added here but not as a substitute, especially as targeting the poor ends up having negative effects.

We can avoid confusing family policy and social policy by keeping in mind three aspects: vertical, horizontal, and universal. The vertical nature of family policy seeks to correct social inequality among families; the horizontal, however, tries to reduce the relative pauperization of families with children within each social category; the third is the universal nature mentioned above.

Yet the standard of living among families decreases with the number of children, at an average rate of 10% for the first child and again 10% for the second, then 5 to 10% for the third and so on. Perhaps this would explain the constant drop in the number of large families. Yet such families are necessary simply as a replacement for the previous generation given that 10% of all women of child-bearing age do not have a child and 20% have only one.

Families with children should receive assistance because they do save the collectivity a substantial amount. One child placed in a foster family or in a public institution costs the community six to ten times more respectively than the surplus income of 2,400 Euros per child received on average, per family

A decreased standard of living is not the only variable to consider when explaining the difference between wanting a child and statistics. Throughout Europe, one out of two women would like another child but has given up the idea because she cannot balance work and family life.

The number of women working in France is another precious advantage that must continue to be encouraged. Women in the workforce will not prevent children from being born if we prioritize all the measures which enable couples to balance their work and home lives. Men and corporations must understand this. Sharing responsibilities at home has become part of the conditions affecting women who want to have children.

Women have control over their fertility and seek some balance between their reproductive and professional activities. They should have working and living conditions which enable them to have a child without sacrificing opportunities. Nonetheless, women continue to delay motherhood. This situation is still reversible if we provide young mothers specific rights to training, housing and employment.

The family is a public matter in the sense that children are involved. Yet sex and affection remain a private affair. The state should not reward financially unions or their dissolution. Yet the state is doing precisely that by granting tax benefits to those who are married and to those without children.

It is true that more and more couples are breaking up. Currently over 40% of married couples end up divorcing. A full 65% of those couples have children. Separations among those living together (common law) come even earlier and more frequently. The most upsetting issue is the number of children subjected to the separation of their parents. In fact, soon one out of three children by age 16 will have lived through his/her parents' separation. Relations with the father, in 40% of the cases, are dangerously weak or completely non-existent. Studies show that children suffer from their parents' not getting along. The ensuing conflicts and separations affect their physical and mental health as well as their studies and socialization (at-risk behaviour, violence). Judges regularly see in their courtrooms delinquents without a father or without a father present in the home.

In sum, families with children still make up the majority at 54% in the French population while representing the minority at only one-third of households and electors. A strong political will is needed to defend the interests of a generation not yet born. Without that will, we seriously wonder about the future of our development and ongoing intergenerational solidarity.

4

How to be rigorous with scenario planning

Five Conditions and the Tools to Ensure Rigor

More and more scenario planning functions as a collective thinking exercise or the mobilization of many minds when the winds of change blow through a company's strategic environment. It is also being successfully applied to regional organizations and local groups. The popularity, appropriation and increased use of scenario building means that specialists no longer monopolize the techniques. Sadly, however, there has been a decrease in methodological know-how and rigor.

The situation appears all the worse given the sad state of affairs in the United States where rational or formalistic techniques have been passed over for essentially intuitive approaches. Although commercially successful, these fuzzy approaches do not justify the meandering and detours involved. In this sense, if there is indeed a rationale to the procedure adopted by a group (Simon, 1982), a futures-thinking exercise must remain heuristic as opposed to either an algorithmic or a guesstimate approach. Of course that does not preclude the use of rigorous techniques when appropriate. This is the perspective of scenario building as "the art of the long view" to borrow Peter Schwartz' title (1991).

Despite the fine quality of Schwartz' book, not very many people have a mind as brilliant as his or the ability to execute this fine art without any method or technique. The philosophy and steps presented in his approach come close to ours but his lack of technique makes "the art of the long view", difficult to appropriate or reproduce.

This general loss of rationality coincides with a loss of memory to the point where words and names are forgotten. Too many would-be futurists and budding consultants dive headfirst into scenario planning with no background knowledge. Little wonder they look surprised, even bewildered, when someone mentions morphological analysis or probabilization.

At the end of the 1980s, French economist Jacques Lesourne, (then at the EDF, France's national power utility) sent out an important message. He called for more research in the field of scenario planning. Then, just as now, people tended to confuse simple and simplistic tools. The times have not changed. Nevertheless the scenario method, as designed twenty years ago, remains useful because it imposes a minimum of intellectual rigor through the qualitative and quantitative analysis of prevailing trends and actors' strategies. Moreover it highlights seeds of change, conflict and tension, and allows for the construction of complete, coherent scenarios.

Scenarios: Use and Abuse

If you had a penny for each time you used the word scenario, you could still get rich soon since the word remains fashionable. Unfortunately its scientific nuance in futures-thinking exercises has been diluted.

Given the context, two questions must be asked:

1) Does simply baptizing as *scenario* any combination of hypotheses make an analysis, even the most convincing analysis, credible in terms of managerial science?

2) Is it absolutely necessary to draft full, detailed scenarios in the planning process?

The answer is *no!* "No!" on both counts because scenarios and planning are not synonymous. A scenario is not a future reality but a way of foreseeing the future, thus throwing light on the present in terms of all possible and desirable futures. Reality as the litmus test, combined with some concern for efficiency, should be used to guide futures thinking in order to gain a better mastery of history.

In other words, we have to ask the right questions and form real hypotheses that are key to the future in order to gauge the consistency and feasibility of the possible combinations. Otherwise there is the risk of leaving 80% of the probable futures unexplored. With the methods used in calculating probability, e.g. the Smic-Prob Expert, we can evaluate the probabilities in an exercise that takes little time for a working committee.

Ironically, the true value of a tool can often be seen when it almost went unused. This was our experience of the iron-steel industry in the early 80s. The probable scenarios remained unexplored because of conventional wisdom or clichés which blur the vision of futures-thinking groups or scenario-builders. In fact without probability testing, managers and consultants alike can pen nice tales more suited to Hollywood than to any particular commercial enterprise. In Brussels, administrative capital of the European Union, the Forward Studies Unit's report called *Europe 2010, Five Possible Futures for Europe,* appears to have fallen into this trap. [1]

It seems obvious, but a scenario is not a future reality. A scenario is simply a means to represent a future reality in order to shed light on current action in view of possible and desirable futures. The test that only reality provides combined with concern for efficiency guides futures thinking so that scenarios are only credible and useful if they meet the following five conditions that we believe instill rigor: relevance, coherence, plausibility, importance and transparency.

The last condition, transparency, is vital to appropriation. Without dwelling on transparency, which unfortunately became a buzzword in the 1990s, we point out the contradiction of consultants who do not submit their rationale to any system or tool that could detect errors or inconsistencies. This is not to say that probabilization of scenarios solves all problems. It is important to consider the much less probable scenarios which may be important in terms of breaks or bifurcations

---

1. Godet, Michel. Foresight. vol. 2, n° 1, Feb. 2000.

and the major impacts implied. Actually, transparency is vital to the credibility and utility of the scenarios produced. Transparency reminds us of old-fashioned teachers who preached that clear writing was clear thinking. Another traditional schoolroom lesson: A question well asked is half answered. This last chestnut certainly applies to scenarios.

Yet all too often reading scenarios becomes a chore as the busy reader must make an effort to tease out the relevance and consistency of the scenario. The frequently low literary level of the scenarios does not help matters. Usually the reader skims through the scenarios without looking for the contradictions and since a few scenarios already seem relatively credible, he/she stops there.

Without the fifth condition, transparency, there can be no appropriation by the actors, players, or even the public, the very people who we often want to be sensitized through the scenarios. Of course transparency and attractive scenarios do not guarantee quality. There is also the risk of what is known as scenario entertainment, rather like "infotainment". Catchy titles, emotional terms and high anxiety do sell, as in Alvin Toffler's *Future Shock*; however, the genre remains fiction similar to Orwell's *Nineteen-Eighty-Four* and does not help a company or region in creating futures.

Let us go back to our second question: Is it absolutely necessary to draft full, detailed scenarios? We answered with a resounding *no* before. Why? Once again we underscore the difference between scenario planning and scenarios in general. Many futures-thinking exercises get bogged down when a working committee decides to dabble in the scenario method. People lose their focus and forget that a scenario is not an end in itself. A scenario only acquires meaning or direction in the form of results and consequences, in other words, action.

The scenario method implies a long timeframe that may extend to 12 even 18 months. Of course that estimate does not take into account the time needed to strike a committee, build a team and make it operational. Even participants in the Organization for Economic Cooperation and Development's three-year program, Interfuturs (1976-79), regretted having too little time to get to the end of the various scenarios. (For details on this program, see Lesourne, Malkin, 1979.) Of course in an ideal world, we would add a year to follow up the collective process by distributing and evaluating the results.

As a rule, working committees, groups or teams must produce a final report after one year of meeting. The other extreme may also happen and as a result, executives start a futures or scenario planning process that lasts only a few weeks. Although rarely ideal, any opportunity to reflect as a group allows participants to shed at least some light on their decisions for as the proverb goes, "It is better to light one candle than curse the darkness." In the end, common sense dictates the following pre-questions:
– what can we do in the time allotted and with the means available?

– how can we ensure that the results are credible and useful for the participants or report recipients?

The French Iron and Steel Industry

An Example of Scenario Building to Reduce Collective Biaises
Between 1990 and 1991, several months of participation in a futures-thinking exercise on the iron and steel industry in France (horizon 2005), enabled participants to identify six relevant and consistent scenarios constructed around three general hypotheses: H1 (low GDP growth, below 1.8%); H2 (severe constraints on the environment); H3 (strong competition from other materials).

Black (S 1)	poor growth in GDP and strong competition from materials
Morose (S 2)	poor growth in GDP with no strong competition from others materials.
Trend-based (S 3)	continuation of the current situation.
Ecological (S 4)	strong constraints from the environment.
Pink Steel (S 5)	strong growth of GDP and competition favorable to steel.
Pink Plastic (S 6)	strong growth of GDP and competition favorable to other materials.

Use of the Prob-Expert software enabled participants to pick out just six scenarios which covered only 40% of the field of probables:

S5 Pink steel and S4 Ecology	$(010) = 0.147$
S1 Black	$(101) = 0.108$
S6 Pink plastic	$(001) = 0.071$
S3 Trend-based	$(000) = 0.056$
S2 Morose	$(100) = 0.016$

Three new, far more probable scenarios thus appeared which the experts had not even selected, let alone identified, because these scenarios went against implicit or shared conventional thinking. This type of consensus, all the stronger since it remained unstated, is the source of major collective biases. Of the three remaining hypothesis configurations (60% of overall probability), each has an implementation probability superior to the most probable of the scenarios previously retained.

S7 Ecological black	$(111) = 0.237$
S8 Steel green	$(110) = 0.200$
S9 Plastic green	$(011) = 0.164$

The pair (11) in the two scenarios (S7 and S8) had been eliminated because, in a context of low growth, serious constraints from the environment seemed to be an improbable luxury. The pair (11) had also been eliminated because serious constraints from the environment (H2) seemed somewhat favourable for steel. But why did no one imagine plastics that could be bio-degradable with greater efficiency as suggested by scenario (11)?

From this point of view, it would be preferable to limit the number of scenarios to a few key hypotheses, perhaps four to six. Beyond six (and sometimes even beforehand) the combinations become mindbog-gling and participants give up. On the other hand, reducing the num-ber of scenarios to four by combining two hypotheses (a technique sug-gested by some) oversimplifies matters. Scenario building on the basis of five or six fundamental hypotheses will provide the group with a backdrop for strategic thinking, and questions like what to do if *x*? or what to do so that *xyz* happens? This shortcut does, nevertheless, require some reflection ahead of time, especially consideration of the key variables, trends and actors' strategies.

As mentioned, one inevitable logistical problem in scenario building and method choice is time. Worse, if there is a change of team and cap-tain, the project suffers. In fact, few futures studies or scenario planning efforts survive the departure of the leader or originator of the project. In major corporations, where mobility has become part of working life, a one-year limit or scheduled intermediary results make a lot of sense.

Confusion of Scenarios and Strategies

Pure synonymy is rare in any field hence the confusion in manage-ment over terms like *scenario* and *strategy*. One point to remember is that scenarios depend on the type of vision adopted, e.g. exploratory, normative and plausible. Whereas strategies depend on attitudes toward possible futures.

It seems that the normative concept creates the most confusion. As a result, we prefer to speak of *anticipatory* scenarios. In the case of sce-narios, normative is taken in the sense of retroprojective, or working back from the future. Expressed bluntly, there is no "goal scenario"; there are only strategies. The following chart illustrates how attitudes affect scenarios.

Attitudes towards the future	Corresponding scenarios	Corresponding strategies
Passive	None	Go with the flow
Reactive	None	Adaptive
Preactive	Trend-based	Preventive
Proactive	Desirable alternatives	Innovative

It is always tempting to take our desires for reality. However just because certain views of the future or scenarios appear desirable, we do not have to draft the strategic plan of an organization according to this proactive vision alone. We need to be preactive too, in order to pre-pare for expected changes in the future corporate environment.

Remember that all possible scenarios are not equally probable or desirable. In fact uncertainty may be gauged in the various scenarios which can then be plotted on the field of probable scenarios. Essentially the higher the number of scenarios is, the greater the uncertainty. However this ratio stands only in principle since the content of the various scenarios may be very different. The most probable scenarios may be either very similar or very different to one another.

Experience shows that in general one-third of all the possible scenarios cover 80% of the field of probable futures. This translates to ten scenarios out of 32 possible scenarios for five basic hypotheses. If uncertainty is low; i.e., there is a limited number of scenarios that cluster on the graph, that concentration forms the main part of the field of probable futures. In this case, a risky strategy could be selected, rather like a gambler's bet, on one of the most probable scenarios. If uncertainty is high, over half the possible scenarios are needed to cover 80% of the field of probable futures and the most probable are highly differentiated. In this last case, a flexible strategy would be best. In other words, a flexible strategy that includes the maximum number of reversible choices. The risk here is to refuse to take a risk, to adopt a strategy that rejects risky but potentially quite profitable options and then turn inward sticking with choices that yield rewards as low as the risks involved.

Again, it seems that success may spoil the term scenario. More than a terminological nuance, there is a difference between scenarios applicable to the general environment of a corporation and actors' strategies. We cannot stress this distinction enough and we remind managers, executives and decisionmakers of all stripes to distinguish between phase one, exploring future stakes, and the normative phase two, defining possible or desirable strategic choices in order to face the future. The distinction between these two phases becomes all the more important because the choice of strategy depends on the level of uncertainty – high or low – weighing upon the scenarios and on the degree of contrast among the most likely scenarios.

We also warn against confusing scenarios, which basically project desires and anxiety onto the future, with strategic options, which imply ambition and reality in foreseeable developments within the corporate environment. Why this warning? Because the actors found on the front lines are simply not the same as those in the back office. The anticipatory phase which looks at change should be collective with the participation of as many of the players as possible. Hence the need for futures studies or scenario planning as tools that help organize and structure the collective process and eventually the evaluation of strategic options in a transparent, efficient manner.

Of course, given legal issues like confidentiality, the strategic choice phase relies upon a limited number of people, usually the company's officers or board of directors. This last phase does not really need any specific method. However decisions must be made after consultation and some consensus among the executives, according to the corporate or group culture and the personality of the management team. One last reminder, the tools are useful in preparing choices but should not become a straitjacket.

The Nail and the Hammer

Although our problems may appear unsurmountable, we are not stuck in the stone age without tools. We do not have to reinvent the wheel since yesterday's tools are still useful today as long as they fulfill the following five conditions that we have set:
- stimulate the imagination;
- reduce inconsistency;
- create a common language;
- structure the collective thinking process;
- enable appropriation.

Of course intellectual tools do not come with a manufacturer's guarantee! We must always remember their limitations and respect freedom of choice. The simple hammer and nail analogy sums up the situation. We either ignore the hammer when we have to drive a nail (the nail's dream) or we think that every problem resembles a nail and use only a hammer (the hammer's pitfall) while the nail happily stays put.

The key words here are appropriate use and appropriation. Paradoxically, as consultants, we spend half the time encouraging the use of strategic tools like scenario planning; the other half, discouraging beginners from misusing the same tools.

Of course we are not claiming that these tools equal the formulae used to calculate material resistance or magnetic fields in physics or biochemistry. Instead, the toolbox that we have humbly developed enables decisionmakers to consider realities full of unknowns as objectively as possible. Moreover, correct use of these tools is often hindered by the lack of time or money inherent to collective thinking exercises.

Why then do we insist on these tools at all? The answer in one word, rigour. Their principal common feature is that they inspire intellectual rigor which, in turn, encourages participants to ask the right questions and reduce inconsistencies using their own logic. In other words, they meet the five criteria which we feel inspire and guide people in their reaction to the future. Naturally there is also the talent of the planner or consultant who can add a dose of common sense. In fact using these tools makes sense only in group futures-thinking exercises where they structure thought and provide participants with a common idiom. The tools are not unlike a deck of cards used for a game of solitaire. Indeed, working in isolation, a futurist or a management consultant can really only count on his or her own intellectual rigor. Since collective exercises require rigour to deal with complexity, the tools should be simple enough to be appropriable by the group.

Tools to Reduce Inconsistencies and Collective Biases

Scenario building enables managers, decisionmakers or entrepreneurs to keep the mind active and the intellect sharp. Time-tested methods ensure the effectiveness of strategic planning. In fact the common heritage of strategic analysis and futures studies serves us best when we want to show how various approaches converge or complement one another and may be organized in one super toolbox, rather like an old-fashioned fishing tackle box. Once the problem has been recognized, this intellectual toolbox helps us organize our thoughts while remaining creative.

The toolbox was set up according to a problem-based system which enables users to start the futures-thinking process which may lead to scenario-building. The five types of tools enable users to ask the right questions and identify key variables, analyze actors' strategies, scan possible futures, reduce uncertainty, obtain a full diagnostic of the company in terms of its environment, identify and evaluate strategic choices and options. The following list of tools reveals how practical the toolbox can be. Naturally this list is not exhaustive and there are other equally effective tools. However, we decided to highlight the ones that we had developed and used successfully. In this way we can vouch for the increased rigour and greater communication that these tools generate when used with the right blend of caution, common sense and enthusiasm.

A Specific Toolbox for Futures Thinking

Initiating and stimulating the process
– strategic prospective workshops

Making a complete diagnosis of the firm in relation to its environment
– competence trees
– strategic analysis tools
– strategic diagnosis

Asking the right questions and identifying key variables
– structural analysis and the Micmac method

Analysing issues and actors' games
– the Mactor method

Scanning the field of possible futures and reducing uncertainties
– morphological analysis
– the Delphi method
– the Régnier Abacus
– the SMIC Prob-Expert method

Evaluating strategic choices and options
– relevance trees

Multipol and multicriteria analysis

Scenario Planning: An Integrated Approach

Given past and potential oil shocks, the eighties and nineties witnessed a boom in the use of scenarios for strategic planning at large corporations within the energy sector, e.g. Shell, Electricité de France and Elf.

The French School and la *Prospective*

The French school's approach, which relies on the analysis of trends and the risks of discontinuities (breakdowns or breakthroughs), shakes up the present and calls for strategic action. Strategy, or strategic analysis, covers possible choices and the risks of irreversibility in decisionmaking, and refers to scenarios. In fact, as Michael Porter's books show, scenarios have been a major reference point since the 1980s. We focused on developing the tremendous synergy between scenario building and strategic analysis in the early 1980s, starting with the combined use of competence trees, as developed by Marc Giget (1998), and the scenario method.

The integrated approach to scenario planning blends futures scenarios, competence trees and strategic analysis. This approach to scenario planning seeks to recenter the corporation in its environment while taking full account of its specific traits, especially its core competencies. The objective of this approach is to suggest strategic orientations and actions on the basis of a company's competencies according to scenarios applicable to both the company's general environment.

In order to compete for the future, as Hamel and Prahalad (1994) suggest, companies must rely on their core competences and mold them into key factors for commercial success in their field. It is not always enough to struggle for greater performance and increased market share. Through benchmarking, a corporation must also innovate, drawing again upon its core competencies to create new leadership activities. The modern strategic approach sounds like the ancient Greek motto, "know thyself". Simple as it may seem, corporations that do not know their own strengths or weaknesses can ill-prepare for future development. At the risk of sounding like a self-help book, the only way to know what you wish to become is to know what you are, where you have been and the history behind it all. The same applies to a corporation.

By combining these two diagnostic techniques, a company can start to position itself within its competitive environment. However we have to go beyond the simple analysis of the company's portfolio of strategic activities. Here the competence tree helps us picture the company in its entirety, with a growth dynamic in the form of environmental scenarios.

From Five Resources to the Competence Tree

The diagnosis of a company's resources and competencies must take place before anyone can consider its general and competitive environments. If we are to ask intelligent questions about changes within the strategic environment, we have to know the company's products, markets, techniques, staff and background, if only to home in on the environment under study.

Traditionally the internal diagnosis includes the financial, operational and functional components to which we add two more categories, technology and quality. These last two highlight the strengths and weaknesses of the five basic resources needed if a company is to succeed.

Five Basic Resources

An organization, be it a small firm or a major corporation, may be defined as a legal and economic production entity generating goods and services. As such, this entity comprises five basic resources which can be categorized as human, financial, technical, productive and commercial. They all play a role in the goals and limits of the entity. As an organization, this entity must simultaneously do the following:

– make the capital invested profitable while financing further or future development (idea of operationality and profitability);

– stimulate research to encourage innovation in processes and products that are likely to both meet market needs and guarantee lasting competitive advantages;

– turn basic products into finished or semi-finished products efficiently (idea of productivity and added value);

– sell as much as possible at a profit (idea of market share, sales figure and sales margin).

As a human collectivity, this commercial entity can create, adapt and grow but may also decline and die out. Strategic management of our hypothetical business must ensure a coordinated shift towards a desired future through its five resources. Objectives, strategic tools and tactics may be associated with each of the five resources. Nevertheless, these objectives (technological, economic and social) are contradictory. In this sense strategic management is an ongoing negotiation between divergent objectives within a more or less turbulent environment.

Of course given a particular financial structure and level of profitability, the value of a company as perceived by its owners or administrators depends on the perspectives within the areas in which the company is active and also on the trust that the administration has in its managers or executives who should be capable of providing some vision and of forging a coherent strategy.

Value Chain, SBA, Core Competence and Competence Tree

Any production (output), be it goods or services, requires an input that may be transformed, processed, or enhanced. This creates a functional chain that originates in R&D, snakes it way through design, production, distribution and ends in after-sales service.

This functional chain is normally associated with the "value-added chain", a concept revived by Michael Porter (1985). However the notion of added value/value added is in part an illusion given that until the product is sold, the company knows only the additional manufacturing costs related to the product. To paraphrase Michael Porter, "value is what customers are prepared to pay". Actually, it would be more accurate to speak of "added-cost chains" and then the division of added value (difference in value between the sales price and the added costs) throughout various functions of a company.

Core competences here refer to the technological, financial and administrative know-how that a company has. A function may be described as a relatively homogenous field of activity or competence. For example, the same department or professional function usually does not produce items with high and low unit-prices, with long as well as short shelf-life, both mass manufactured or handcrafted, for both a mass-market and industrial clientele.

The competence trees created by Marc Giget in 1983 seek to represent the company in its entirety without reducing it to its products and markets alone. In these trees, the roots, (generic skills or competencies and know-how) and the trunk (manufacturing capacity) are just as important as the branches (product-market lines). The representation of a company as a competence tree grew out of the strategic analysis of Japanese firms. It seems that implictly or explicity most organizational structures in Japan were presented in tree formation. For example, three concentric circles would symbolize research, production and merchandising. The result was a one-dimensional tree.

Illustrated is an economic view of the competence tree. Here we can see the difference between technological trees in which the trunk (manufacturing) does not exist. Also the branches appear to spring directly from the roots. As Marc Giget (1989) points out, these are two concepts with distinct aims. Technological trees were usually drawn up by the research or communications departments which appreciated the simple, positive form presenting a coherent, exhaustive image of the company's activities to the public.

The full competence tree requires considerable effort, especially an exhaustive listing of data on the corporation itself as well as its competitive environment. This comparative gathering stage is vital to the strategic diagnosis of the tree, e.g. the strengths and weaknesses of the roots, trunk and branches. The diagnosis must also be retrospective, in other words, it must look back before looking forward.

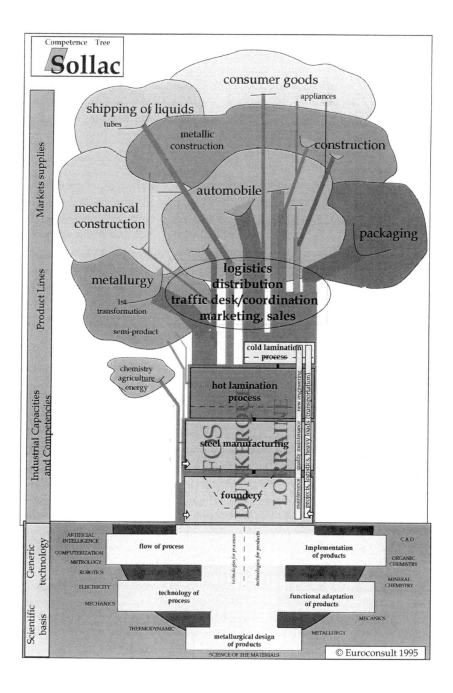

The tree image works well in that it shows how a company should not die with its product. Just because one branch is diseased, the forest ranger does not saw off the trunk. If a branch is sick, the sap of its competences should be redistributed to new branches, new activities that share its genetic code. There are some famous examples like the manufacturer of cigarette rolling papers who converted to special packaging or the slide rule distributor who switched to selling calculators.

However the tree image has its limits, too. The dynamics of a tree are not unidirectional from the roots to branches only. As in nature, the branches feed the roots through photosynthesis as well as humus, a mulch formed by dry dead leaves and soil. There are incredible biological combinations but there are also inescapable incompatibilities. If we stay with the tree analogy, a pine cannot become an oak and a cherrytree cannot grow pears.

Strategic planning and management, based on competence trees, required a competitive environment to complete the picture. The need to see the big picture hence the need for other tools reflects the strength of the French school *(la prospective)* which has been enriched by tailoring techniques (scenario method) to meet a real demand.

Origins and Definitions of the Scenario Method

As the title of this book indicates, there are many possible futures and no single path leading to one or the other. The description of a possible future or *futuribles* plus the path to that future make up a scenario.

The word scenario was introduced into futures studies and common management parlance by H. Kahn over a quarter of a century ago in his book *The Year 2000*. Given the literary genre, the term was associated with the imagination applied to either a rosy or apocalyptic prediction. Of course there was a rich futuristic or Science Fiction tradition already established, from Jules Verne *(The Time Machine)* and Anatole France *(Ile des pingouins)* to George Orwell *(Nineteen-Eighty-Four)*.

In France the scenario method was first applied by the DATAR, a governmental organization, during regional futures studies. Ever since then the method has been adapted to many sectors ranging from agriculture to industry and services, and also applied to various geographical or political levels, e.g. regions, states, countries, or even the entire world.

In the United States, researchers like Coates, Gordon, Helmer or Dalkey developed several rather formalistic methods for scenario building. Most were based on expert advice or opinion, e.g. the Delphi questionnaire and Cross-Impact Matrices. Naturally their findings were published regularly in *Futures* (UK) and *Technological Forecasting and Social Change* (USA).

The rigorous method of scenario building dominant in France uses tools developed primarily for systems analysis. Many of these tools were developed in the early 1970s at the Rand Corporation in the United States and later in France at the Sema, a private consulting group, as part of Futuribles International, at the French army's centre for futures and evaluation, and at the DATAR.

The approach that I have personally developed in various posts with various teams over the past three decades stands apart because of its use of mixed systems analysis tools and procedures. There are tools or methods like the Micmac which identifies key variables; the Mactor which analyses actors' strategies; morphological analysis which helps build scenarios and the Smic-Prob-Expert which helps determine how feasible scenarios are. Yet these very helpful methods – mathematics in general – remain underused.

One vital message that we spread in workshops and classrooms is the potential of these tools. As we pointed out earlier, they stimulate the imagination; reduce inconsistencies in thinking; create a common language; structure the collective thinking exercise and enable participants to appropriate the techniques. Of course tools should not serve as a substitute for reflection and should not restrict freedom of choice.

Strangely enough there is no single scenario method but rather a host of ways to create scenarios. Scenario-building techniques range from rather simplistic to more or less complex. There does appear to be consensus, however, on restricting the label "scenario method" to a process requiring a certain number of very specific steps. The usual steps are systems analysis, retrospective analysis, actors' strategies, and scenario drafting. They flow into one another logically as seen in the following figure.

Usefulness and limitations

Traditionally scenarios have been classified as possible, plausible and desirable. Their classification usually corresponds to their nature or probability as trend-based, reference, contrasted or anticipatory.

The trend-based scenario, probable or not, corresponds to an extrapolation of trends at all the points where a choice must be made.

Often the most probable scenario continues to be called trend-based even if it does not correspond to a pure and simple extrapolation. In the distant past, when the world changed at what seems a snails's pace now, the most probable scenario was in fact the continuation of trends. However, today when looking torward the future, the most probable scenario in many instances seems to correspond to deep breaks or even breakdowns in current trends.

Extrapolating from trends may lead to a much more contrasted situation with regard to the future. In this case the trend-based scenario is also an exptrapolation from trends and not the most probable scenario. No wonder words become confused in usage. To be more precise, we call the most probable scenario a *reference* scenario whether it is trend-based or not.

The Scenario Method

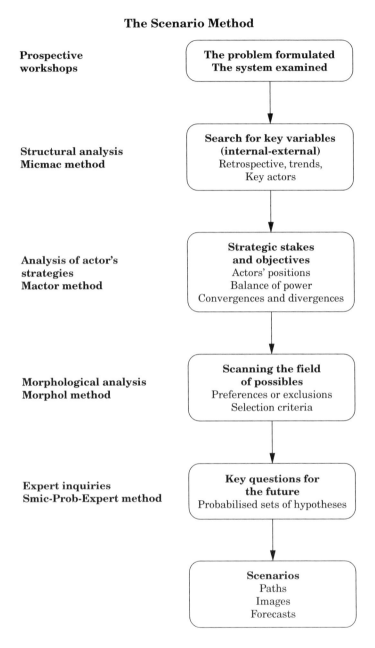

Prospective workshops — The problem formulated / The system examined

Structural analysis / Micmac method — Search for key variables (internal-external) / Retrospective, trends, Key actors

Analysis of actor's strategies / Mactor method — Strategic stakes and objectives / Actors' positions / Balance of power / Convergences and divergences

Morphological analysis / Morphol method — Scanning the field of possibles / Preferences or exclusions / Selection criteria

Expert inquiries / Smic-Prob-Expert method — Key questions for the future / Probabilised sets of hypotheses

Scenarios / Paths / Images / Forecasts

On the other hand, a *contrasted* scenario is the exploration of an intentionally extreme theme, in other words, a future situation determined ahead of time. A trend-based scenario corresponds to an exploratory operation probing development heading in a particular direction for a specific situation. Inversely, a historical, contrasted scenario corresponds to an anticipatory operation that is both normative and imaginative. In this case we usually set a future scenario that is highly

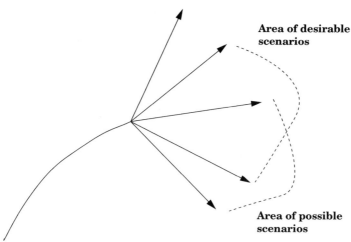

Area of Possible Scenarios

Area of desirable scenarios

Area of possible scenarios

contrasted in terms of the present and then we work backwards to reach that future. In doing so, we draft the developmental/evolutionary scenario which may lead to that future.

The desirable scenarios may be found somewhere in the possible cone but they are not all necessarily plausible and all the plausible scenarios are not necessaily desirable.

Our Rediscovery of Morphological Analysis

Just when everyone was ready to reinvent the wheel, morphological analysis resurfaced. During a futures-thinking exercise with the French military on future weaponry at the end of the 1980s, we rediscovered morphological analysis and it became the most used tool in that case.

Oddly enough, morphological analysis had long been used in technological forecasting but very little in economic or sectorial futures studies. As a tool, however, morphological analysis works well in scenario building and in generating strategic profiles. (See chapter 6, ICW case study.)

Since the early 1990s, morphological analysis has been used systematically in future studies on air transportation, computerization in Europe, development in the Catalan region of north-western Spain, and scenario planning at AXA Insurance. (Please see the full AXA case study in chapter 7.)

The usefulness of morphological analysis became all the more apparent when the French Corn Growers Association came to us in 1998. Their time was limited to four or five business days. Not the ideal timeframe, but it was feasible. We suggested using morphological analysis for the two classic stages: scenario building and strategic planning. The first analysis provided development scenarios related to what would be at stake in the future of corn growing, especially the technological, economic and regulatory environments of this particular sector. Each scenario asked corngrowers strategic questions which could have different possible answers. Once again morphological analysis enabled the participants to organize their thinking as a group on the most relevant and consistent strategic responses.

Relevance, Coherence and Plausibility of Scenario-Building through Morphological Analysis

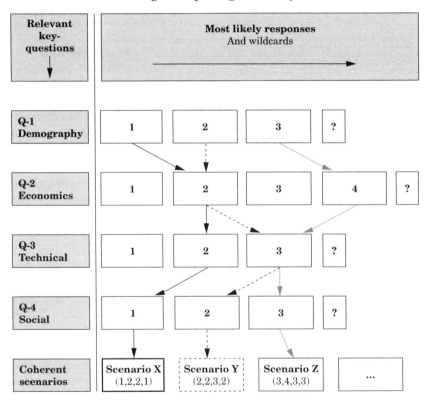

? stands for all other possibilities
At least 320 possible scenarios : 4 × 5 × 4 × 4

Relevance and Coherence of Strategies
through Morphological Analysis

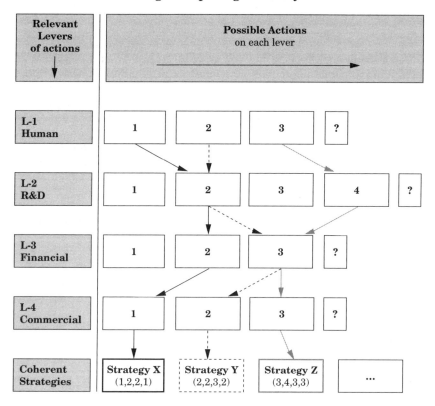

? stands for all other possibilities
At least 320 possible scenarios : 4 × 5 × 4 × 4

Morphological Analysis: Usefulness and Limitations

The areas of application of morphological analysis are many: exploratory scenario building, areas of innovation, and R&D.

Although the method has been used primarily in technological forecasting, it lends itself well to the construction of scenarios, in which the demographic, economic, technical and social dimensions, or components, can be characterized by a certain number of possible states, or hypotheses (configurations). A scenario thus becomes nothing more than a path, a combination bringing together a configuration for each component.

Morphological analysis stimulates the imagination and enables users to scan the field of possibilities systematically. There is just the very real risk of being swamped by the various combinations. It takes a bit of navigating to get through the morphological space using the selection criteria provided by the Morphol software.

The first limitation of morphological analysis stems from the choice of components. By leaving out one component or simply a configuration that is essential to the future, you run the risk of leaving out an entire facet of the range of possible futures. Note, however, this range is not restricted and evolves over time.

The second limitation, of course, stems from the sheer bulk of combinations which can rapidly submerge the user. One of the solutions is to introduce selection criteria, constraints such as exclusion or preference factors, and to exploit the useful morphological subspace.

Scenario Method and Strategic Planning

The integrated approach outlined here combines the scenario method and competence trees. The core scenario method appears in boxes 1,3,4, and 5 in the figure on page 82.

The first of the four steps seeks to analyze the problem put to us and to set the parameters of the system that we are studying. Here the scenario method or any futures-thinking exercise must be placed within the organizational context. Workshops generally serve to start up the process.

The second step is based on a full X-ray of the company, from its know-how to its product lines, illustrated by the competence trees.

The third step is to identify the key variables of the corporation and its environment using structural analysis.

The fourth step seeks to capture the dynamics of a company, a retrospective look at the company within its environment, its development, its strengths and weaknesses vis-à-vis the main actors in its strategic environment. By looking at the corporate battle field and the strategic stakes, we can ask key questions for the future.

Step five attempts to reduce the uncertainty weighing on key questions for the future. Various methods may be used at this point, for example, surveying experts for their opinions so that we can pinpoint the prevailing trends, faultlines or breaks and tease out the most probable environmental scenarios.

Step six highlights the coherent projects, in other words, the strategic options which are compatible both with the corporate identity and the most probable scenarios, given the corporate environment. Step six flows into step seven, which is the evaluation of strategic options. A rational approach to strategy should use a multicriteria method, but this is rarely the case. Step seven ends with reflection in anticipation of decisionmaking and finally action.

Step eight is crucial in that the participants move from thinking to deciding. The strategic choices and hierarchy of objectives come from the board of directors, executive committee or administrative equivalent.

Step nine is devoted to the action plan. This step involves drafting "goal" or "objective" contracts, setting up coordination and monitoring systems, and a strategic watch (*veille* in French, or vigil) that looks outside the company.

Steps eight and nine involve a smaller group within the company but they are important in that the decisions must be followed up with action. Although fewer people are involved in these steps, the information, decisions and objectives have been enriched through the consultation process. They crown the efforts of a group united in its efforts and motivated through a collective process designed to shed light on future action.

Note that the integrated approach is not entirely linear, and may offer opportunities for collaboration amongst phases. Sometimes implementing the action plan and the results of the strategic watch can lead participants to reconsider the dynamics of the company within its own environment.

The Advantages and Disadvantages of the Approach

The integrated approach can be a double-edged sword. It combines logically and sequentially most of the tools used in futures studies, scenario building and strategic analysis. Each of these tools works, but the logical order within the approach need not necessarily be followed. Similarly, the scenario method is rarely followed through from A to Z, usually because there is not enough time. Fortunately, as with any good toolbox, the tools may be used separately or in combination.

In any event, the choice of method is not dictated by the nature of the problems but the means (time and money) available.

As the previous figure shows, the integrated approach provides the rational skeleton but does not prevent the irrational circulation of ideas. Appropriation of the tools by the group paves the way to successful action without opposing the limits and confidentiality of strategic decisionmaking.

Scenario Planning Complete Process

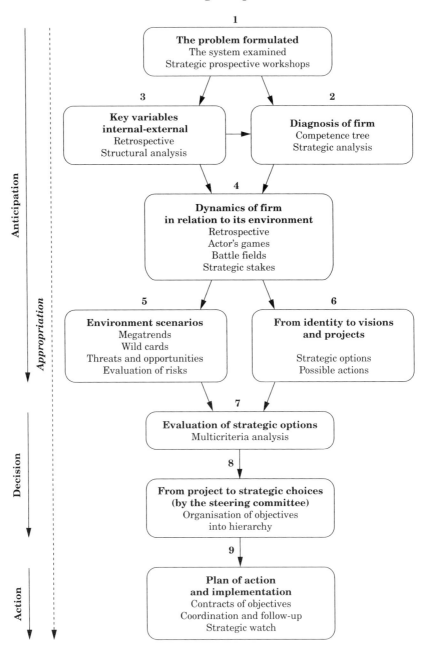

© Marc Giget (Euroconsult) Michel Godet (Cnam) 1990.

The integrated approach initially provided companies with a way of representing their structure as a competence tree. It has also been adopted by groups working on the future of territories or regions like Catalonia. There are, of course, many other general or sectorial issues for which the classic scenario method suffices.

The shift from futures-thinking to strategic action supposes appropriation by those involved. In other words, the personnel – not only the executives – should be as active as possible in the various steps of this process without altering the confidential nature of certain strategic choices. Success in moving from anticipation to action means moving through the three corners of the Greek triangle. (Please see chapter 1 and the front cover for color version.)

There really is no need to start all over again, as we already have tools that enable us to improve the pertinence, consistency, plausibility, importance and transparency when thinking about the complexity of our various futures.

Scenarios as Strategic Management Tools

There is a major distinction to be made between companies that carry out highly restricted futures studies for their executives' use in making strategic choices and companies that use scenarios as a collective tool – a way to mobilize people and intelligence because of turbulence or change. Major corporations like Lafarge, Péchiney, Mercedes and Nestlé belong in the first group; Renault or federal ministries, e.g. supplies and services, in the second.

The obvious difference lies in communication. In the first category, a group like Lafarge, provides an example of a traditional futures-thinking exercise which had an impact on strategy. Already by the mid-seventies, this group had foreseen a decline in the use of cement (– 1% annually by the year 2000). Lafarge decided to invest in an up-and-coming field, biotechnology, and bought the Coppee group, another capital-intensive business. This common financial feature was not enough to build a common future and Lafarge has since chosen to refocus on materials. Companies like Lafarge are always looking to the future and, indeed, Lafarge has already anticipated the consequences of European construction and a more open Eastern Europe.

For companies belonging to the second category mentioned above, a futures-thinking exercise serves as a means of mobilizing and managing people. In the examples mentioned, especially Renault, staff involvement allowed this corporation to face changes with greater awareness. It seems probable that restructuring at Renault in the 80s (one-third of the personnel downsized between 1985 and 1989) was facilitated by the awareness achieved through a program called MIDES (acronym for Industrial, Economic and Social Change). Thousands of executives and managers participated in this collective futures exercise. In this type of situation, transparency is mandatory. In fact Renault produced a workbook specific to the program. The workbook served as both a sounding board and a bullhorn for ideas generated by the futures studies group at Renault.

Between the two extremes lies one common point and several intermediate situations. The common point is the cyclical nature of futures studies, performed every four, five or seven years. The long-term backdrop must, however, be sturdy enough to last several years. If we adapt the traditional car analogy mentioned in the first chapter, an extra highbeam makes the road ahead easier to navigate.

The intermediate situation is that in which a company is using futures-thinking exercises to mobilize its managers or as a tool to determine strategy This was the case for Shell and Elf, two corporations that have been using scenarios for over twenty years and even consider this practice a key component of strategic management.

On a patriotic note, we have to mention that the scenario tradition at Shell was started by Pierre Wack, a Frenchman. Indeed, Wack (1985) drew upon concepts introduced by the founders of the French school (de Jouvenel, Berger, Lesourne). Their ideas were little known across the channel and unknown across the Atlantic. It is worth noting that Shell was the not the only one to anticipate major change in the oil sector. Another French pioneer, Jacques Lacoste at Electricité de France, the national power utility, presented a report entitled *An Abundance of Oil but for How Long?* to a futures group within the the the "General Commissarat of Planning", an organ of the French government.

Planning à la Shell

This timeline illustrates exactly how Shell shifted from highly quantified linear predictions to an acceptatnce of uncertainy and descriptions of possible futures based on analysis by scenario.

1945-1955	Physical planning
1955-1965	Planning by projects selectively
1965-1972	Unified Planning Machinery (UPM System)
1967	Start of the Shell study using 2000 as a horizonline
1969-1970	Exercise called "Horizon Year Planning" (15-year horizon)
1971	Scenario experiments at the London Head Office
1972-1973	Introduction of the scenario planning method
1975	Introduction of cyclical scenarios for the medium-term
1976-1977	Further exploration of societal analysis in planning
1978-1979	Further exploraton of geopolitical and political risk in planning
1979-1980	New approach to the long-term plus development of planning skills within the Shell Group.

The method Pierre Wack described now operates like a well-oiled machine. The planners at the Shell Group acquired excellent experience in analyzing crucial factors impacting their field of activity, identifying the relations between the various actors and describing the processes of change in the balance of power among these actors. All analyses were presented to decisionmakers within coherent plans for further consideration.

Scenarios were developed on an international level by one department at the Shell Group. This particular department operated like an observatory monitoring the environment around the globe. It also produced world scenarios for the development of the economic, energy, and other environments. In these scenarios various events or phenomena were analyzed, e.g. demograpahics, political shifts of power, trends in values and lifestyles, technological and economic changes, monetary issues, energy demand on the basis of the preceeding factors, energy supplies, the special position of petrol, possible developments in relations between oil-producing and oil-consuming nations, price structures for crude oil and hypotheses on how these prices might change.

Using the international environmental scenarios presented by the Group, Shell's subsidiaries would draw up their own scenarios that included specific national and local conditions that could affect their business activities.

Designed as tools to help people think strategically, national scenarios must not be too numerous but they must come from an in-depth, rigorous analysis, be usable, cover a full array of possibilities probable.

One of Pierre Wack's spiritual sons is Peter Schwartz who actually took over from Wack at Shell in 1984. Two years later Schwartz returned to the United States and set up the Global Business Network (GBN) a network of futures consultants and scenario planners who serve an international club of businesses. Peter Schwartz popularized scenarios in the English-speaking world and, somewhere in the eighties, even convinced his friend Michael Porter to integrate scenarios into his own methods.

Scenario Planning (adapted from Peter Schwartz, 1991)

1) Identify the focal issue, question or decision.
2) Pinpoint the key forces in the micro-environment.
3) Determine the driving forces (drivers) in the macro-environment.
4) Rank by order of importance and uncertainty.
5) Choose the "logics" or rationale behind the scenarios (axes).
6) Flesh out the scenarios.
7) Consider the implications of those scenarios.
8) Select the "signposts" or leading indicators.

In 1981, all oil companies stocked up reserves of crude oil in anticipation of the recently errupted conflict between Iraq and Iran.
Thanks to the method mentioned above, Shell managed to get rid of its
surplus before the market became saturated and the prices started to
plummet.

Correct Use of Scenarios: The Elf Example

Without wearing out the French flag, we have to describe the textbook
case of Elf, a large fuel company. Elf carried out three futures-thinking exercises over fifteen years; that is once every five or six years. In
1969, the first effort had a 1985 horizon; in 1978 the horizon was 1990
and the last meetings through 1985 to 1987 had a 1995 horizon. We
were fortunate to be involved in a new exercise begun in 1996 with a
horizon of 2010. At this point, professional ethics prevent us from
going beyond the methodology used at Elf. For more details, interested
readers may refer to François Didier's report on the Elf case, published in French by Paul Alba (1989). What follows is a brief outline of
the Elf experience.

In 1969, a small team of internal and external consultants was created. The team, led by research director Bernard Delapalme, produced
a report. Looking back now, we see that although the oil shocks had
not been foreseen, the vulnerability of Elf's position on Algerian oil
had been identified. Hence the team's recommendations to diversify
geographically, e.g. the North Sea, and horizontally, e.g., chemicals
and pharmaceuticals. These recommendations were followed with the
known outcomes. In terms of technology, however, the development of
combustible fuel batteries, e.g. electric cars, and artificial proteins
were vastly overestimated. In fact two or three years later, Elf interrupted its research in this field. Of course the rise of computers and
growing awareness of environmental issues had been foreseen and an
information and research centre was already in place. Overall, the
report card for this first exercise was good. The team recommended
doubling Elf's size in relation to its competition by 1985 and this goal
was reached. [1]

Second Exercise in 1978-1979 with a 1990 Horizon

Elf's strategy manager, François Didier, took over this futures study
and had eight people working fulltime over several months. The objective was to define strategies according to three identified global
growth scenarios (conveniently labelled as grey, rosy and black). As in
the previous exercise, changes in the energy sector went undetected.
Although the West was in the throes of an oil shock, the price per

---

1. In 1999 Elf was purchased by Total, a smaller, more profitable chal-
lenger.

barrel was dropping in constant dollars. However, this time caution was applied on the topic of technology. Nevertheless, the focus was placed on innovation, not only technological but also economic and organizational.

Also stressed was reorganization of chemical activities while developing the biotechnological axis with Sanofi, a pharmaceutical company. One recommendation in particular stands out from this study – from the GRETS (acronym for groups for reflection and study on strategic themes). Some such twenty groups did operate throughout the eighties.

The Third Exercise in 1985-1987: Elf with 1995 as a Horizon

Still under the direction of François Didier, the study lasted 18 months and involved several dozen people. It took place in two stages: exploratory, to build environmental scenarios; and normative, to define strategies given these scenarios.

Throughout the exploratory phase, a dozen teams per branch and by transversal theme (environment, research, geopolitics) were created. Throughout the normative phase, three typical strategies were studied: natural resources, commodities and "high tech-high growth".

Like the previous exercises, this one was carried out without any special methodology but with tremendous professionalism in terms of group animation and respect for deadlines. The collective effort was broadbased at key moments and included various meetings with the president, with division managers, and other levels or functions.

We were fortunate enough to follow the exercise as an invited consultant answering to the steering committee. The consultant as observer plays a thrilling yet sometimes challenging role. It involves listening without speaking for hours and then making a report, possibly critical, on what was said by the various participants, some high up on the corporate ladder.

In this case, two external consultants were used in another constructive way: they were offered – not imposed – as facilitators to teams in need of leadership. As P. Alba (1989) worded it in his conclusion on the Elf experience: "Once a company is very large, it cannot just hop up and down at will." Elf Aquitaine thus opted to base future development on its three industrial axes (oil, chemicals, health and hygiene products) and only those three axes. It is worth noting that this last exercise included a message written by the company president and distributed to all personnel on July 17, 1987.

Both Elf and Shell use scenarios regularly because of the high level of outside involvement they have developed. Errors in strategic diagnosis and forecasting have been made, though. And as any process may be improved, we think that these groups could benefit from using existing futures tools more often to enhance the pertinence, consistency and feasibility of their analyses. With regard to the issue of transparency in this case, not much more could be done to render the facts at Elf without betraying the confidential nature of that study.

Correct use of scenario building and strategy has been part of the corporate culture at the Parisian Transit Network Authority (RATP) since 1972 and Electricité de France (EDF) since 1985. We will see just how EDF used scenarios in chapter 6.

Examples of Specific Tool Combinations

In the late 1980s, the French military carried out a futures-thinking exercise on an individual weapon for infantry for the year 2010. As consultants to the General Direction of Armaments (DGA), we went back to square one in a structural analysis project that had been dragging on for three years. By creating a hierarchy of 57 variables with the Micmac method, we managed to narrow the list to 15 key variables. Upon reflection, we realized that nine of these key variables were features of the weapon itself, e.g. type of projectile, energy source, and range. Six of the variables were criteria to judge arms (cost, competitiveness, antipersonnel effectiveness). Morphological analysis of the nine components of this weapon, each component generating several configurations, led to 15,552 theoretically possible technological solutions. By using the Multipol method for multicriteria selection and the Morphol method to take into account the restrictions of exclusion and preferences, we were able to reduce the morphological space to fifty and then twenty solutions worth exploring futher in terms of both cost and technological know-how. Ten years later one of these solutions made headlines in France. It was the PAPOP or "polyarm-polyprojectile". This weapon enables a hidden foot soldier to fire on a stationary, moving or armored target with a specific projectile. (See chapter 6 for the full ICW 2010 case.)

Recommendations for the Future of Territories

We have had various opportunities to hone and test the tools mentioned thus far in several futures-thinking exercises on territories as diverse as the Basque region, Ile de la Réunion, France's Lorraine region, and the Ardennes, to name but a few. In this brief section, we show how lessons can be learned from both the successes and the failures.

The credibility, utility and quality of a territorial exercise require the strictest respect of various conditions. One condition that must be respected is the role of the outside consultant. Participants should never outsource the entire thinking process on a region's future.

In any study, regardless of its quality, the final report is far less important than the process leading up to it. Hence the need to use local expertise and take advantage of the exercise to create a desire for change, at least intellectually. In this situation the study is almost secondary to the participatory thinking process that it brings about. Actually, by encouraging this type of futures-thinking exercise at a local level, we do spark a desire to bring together ideas and find consensus around one or two projects designed for that territory.

Participatory Yet Confidential

Although some futures studies must remain confidential, especially analysis of actors' strategies, the overall process must be considered one of appropriation. Each participant is an actor and this applies throughout the company or territory. The process has to prepare people mentally for desirable change in the company's environment and culture.

This decentralization in the process implies a minimum of centralization around the company's strategic poles. There must be some consensus and usually the steering committee ensures that there is. Generally the steering committee reports to the board of directors or executive committee depending on the company's structure. The latter organizes and coordinates the technical teams or groups within the collective futures exercise and ensures that the various orientations are taken into account.

In principle, an anticipatory process may be open to all personnel. In fact, experience shows that success is greater when there is freedom of expression and individual motivation within the limits of the strategic objectives put forward by management. These objectives may be detailed in a "charter" unveiled at the launching of the futures exercise. This charter usually outlines the rules of the process. If the rules are posted from the start and respected throughout the process, participation will not usually interfer with the confidentiality involved in strategy and will perhaps even make a strategy more acceptable.

The following comments, collected after a strategy seminar held by a major corporation in the service sector, sum up the desired effect.

"Participants were not only consumers but also producers of thoughts on the future... working in small groups enabled participants to be actively involved and to generate an avalanche of ideas that were not only diverse but expressed freely. Over a hundred factors of change were identified."

The spokesperson went further to add that "the groups strove to distinguish two dimensions that are often confused: the importance of change and the mastery of change. We talk a lot about some changes but they are not important only because we 'know how'. Inversely there are important stakes we do not even talk about because they are taboo. The workshops showed that the company masters changes the best when they are technological. On the other hand, the company does not really master social or economic changes."

To this last point, we add that changes in mentality or behavior, in particular, management rules in the human resources department, are the keys to competiveness and flexibility.

Lastly, futures studies and scenario planning, whether for a company or a region, provide a unique opportunity for participants to get beyond short-term restrictions and contradictions in order to become aware of the need to modify habits and behaviors in anticipation of future change.

However if this collective process is to be successful, internal expertise must be tapped and the futures-thinking exercise should be used to crystalize the competences often scattered throughout an organization. After our workshops the problems are usually better formulated, thought out and understood. The exercise has hopefully been a group effort that involved not only those who will continue the work but also those who requested it in the first place!

Instead of rushing headlong into building general environmental and competitive scenarios, participants should remember Seneca's words, "know thyself". We humbly add "as completely as possible". In other words, a full diagnosis of the company in terms of its environment and the use of appropriate strategic analysis tools extend ancient philosophy to creating futures.

A Few Concepts

Megatrends
Movement affecting a phenomenon over a long period. Examples: urbanization, globalization.

Seed Events/Weak Signals
Factors of change which are now barely perceptible but will make up tomorrow's prevailing or megatrends. In fact a latent variable is what P. Massé called a "seed event, or a miniscule sign given current dimensions but immense in its virtual consequences".

Actors
Those who play an important role in the system through variables which characterize their projects and which they more or less control. Example: the consumer society, multinational companies, to name a few, are actors in the energy sector.

Event
Notion defined by E. Borel as "an abstract being whose sole characteristic is that it happens or does not happen." We can consider an event as a binary variable, one that can take only two values, usually 1, if the event takes place, 0, if the event does not occur. Such an event would be called an isolated event.

5

Initiating the Entire Process

The Strategic Prospective Workshop

Workshop Outlines
Anticipating Change and Inertia
Hunting Down Clichés
Negotiating between the Short- and Long-Term
Drawing Competence Trees

Illustration: Regulation of the Telecommunications Industry (Horizon 2010)
The Context of Futures Thinking
Major Changes and Clichés Detected during the Workshops
From Key Issues to Actors' Strategies
Leading to Four Initial Scenarios
A Few Lessons From the Basque Region 2010 Excercise

Practical Guide for Strategic Prospective
The Components and Functions of the Technical Group
Starting with Workshops
Practical Advice
Recommendations for Regional Foresight

The *Strategic Prospective* Workshop

How did the futures workshop develop? To answer that question, we think back to a period of several years when we trained forty-odd newly promoted executives at Renault. The seminar topic was "future watch" *(vigilance prospective)*, or a form of foresight similar to technological foresight. In 1985, we were asked to design a more participatory method so that the attendees would be more than consumers of foresight and actually become participants actively thinking about foreseeable change and the strategic consequences of such change. The following three types of workshop took shape:

1) Anticipating and mastering change;
2) Hunting down clichés (conventional thinking);
3) Negotiating the short- and long-term.

From 1989 to 1990, a fourth type came naturally from the concept of competence trees, e.g. the past, present and future of an organization or a territorial collectivity. In this sense what began as a training tool, the competence tree, became a full futures-thinking exercise for a group, be it a corporate department or regional council. Creating the tree enables members of the group to outline problems and priorities according to the stakes, identify possible strategic actions and, most of all, simulate the entire process; in other words, outline within a few hours what would later take place in detail over several months. That group, be it a working committee or an informal assembly, is thus better prepared to become aware of potential obstacles. The group can then lay out an efficient plan adapted to the specific nature of both the problems at hand and the approach adopted by the group.

Futures workshops, or futures-thinking exercises, are suitable for groups of ten to one-hundred people with a shared experience or interest. They must be people who want to think together about possible and desirable changes with a view to charting a common course and mastering those changes.

The ideal number for a group is thirty. The main group can always be broken down into sub-groups or cells of five to ten. These sub-groups can then participate in different workshops. The laws of group dynamics tend to support at least two sub-groups on anticipating change. This division allows the group leaders or facilitators to later reconvene the two groups as one and compare notes. A sub-group for the clichés or conventional thinking workshop is a must. This workshop usually provides participants with a chance to release tension and speak more openly than usual.

In an ideal world, there would be 30 workshop participants meeting over two days. Obviously thinking about the future requires some mental preparation, a bit of a warm-up and a break from routine thinking. Given the logistics, the actual workshops should start only in the afternoon of the first day to end in the evening of the second day. The morning of the first day should be an introduction with debate about futures thinking. This initiation includes analysis of the causes of forecasting errors, warnings about clichés and landmarks in planning, e.g. probable trends and major uncertainties. It also shows participants how behavior and structures must be adapted, even transformed, in times of change. This introductory lecture should be thought-provoking, not dry or academic. Ideally participants will want to roll up their shirtsleeves and get started.

Overall, this two-day seminar aims to present the most important, most easily appropriated concepts and tools to participants. Through immersion, the futures workshop seeks to harness the collective thought process and apply it to strategic action. The workshops themselves allow participants to identify and prioritize as a group the stakes that their company or region has in its future environment. Note that the environment may be general or competitive, local or international. After two days, participants are ready to define their priorities and goals, draw up schedules, list methods and organize the follow-up to the workshops.

We have presented these workshops a hundred times over the past fifteen years. Each time the process must be adapted to the context, but little else changes in terms of alternating the participants' passive consumption and active production. The two-day format is preferable for tapping into the group dynamics without overwhelming participants and losing their attention. One day is simply not enough to introduce, explore and apply the concepts and tools mentioned above. And the last thing we want to do is frustrate participants who have just discovered their role in creating futures.

Futures-thinking exercises can spark incredible interest and enthusiasm in participants, as best seen in the BASF example. (Please see the full case study in chapter 8). In short, BASF Agriculture in France met with its distributors over three to four years. The process began with an initial encounter in Venice in 1995.

The workshops serve initially as a launching pad for two processes: collective thinking and mastering change. In some instances, however, it seems that the workshops are actually useful sooner than expected. In the case of BASF, it seemed smart to translate future stakes (results from workshops in terms of related goals), the identification of sub-goals, courses of action, projects and studies contributing to these goals (determined with pertinence trees) and to align the potential reality with studies and projects already under way. As a result, we soon could pinpoint the projects or research missions already undertaken but with an unspecified aim and the main stakes that required new courses of action.

Workshop Outlines

One of the most valuable pre-seminar tools is a basic questionnaire asking participants to list:
- changes that they have confronted in the past;
- ways in which they reacted to change;
- changes that they expect in the future;
- ways in which they expect to react.

Usually anonymous, the input provides the facilitator or group leader with a crash course in the company's problems and history plus the position of each participant. A summary may be prepared and presented at a plenary session before the workshops begin.

What follows below are thumbnail sketches of the four workshops mentioned earlier.

Anticipating Change and Inertia

This workshop takes place in two phases, exploratory and normative. The first phase answers the question "what can happen?" while the second leads to the question "What can I do?".

Anticipating Change (Exploratory Phase)

List the technological, economic, social and organizational changes that each participant perceives or wants. Each participant then makes his/her own list (15-20 minutes). These ideas are collected and regrouped as each participant around the table is called upon to comment. The entire workshop should take one to two hours.

A simple point system enables everyone to see the five or ten main changes and future stakes among the fifty to seventy originally listed. Although simple, this system places the ideas in a matrix which could be called generically "Importance × Control". The selected changes are graphically displayed and the current level of mastery is evaluated, too. The axis (ordinates) gives the importance of the so-called critical changes while the abscissa (coordinates) gives the current mastery of those changes.

Mastering Change (Normative Phase)

- Identify strategic objectives in terms of stakes.
- Take actions and choose the means to reach objectives.
- Assess the strategic gap or, roughly, the difference between an objective and what will happen if you do not act.

During the normative phase, participants ask the following questions:

- Who are the other actors (players) implicated by these changes?
- What "levers", "drivers" or "brakes" are involved in the actions?

– How can we improve our control when dealing with important changes?

– How can we reduce the impact of changes that we do not control?

– In short, how can we reduce our weaknesses and maximize our strengths?

Position with regard to changes and inertias
Matrix: importance versus control

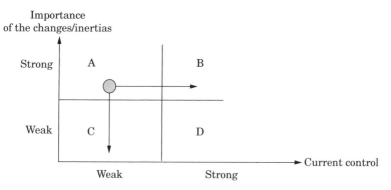

○ Critical changes & inertias
How to reduce their importance?
How to increase their control?

The four zones break down as follows:

Zone A: Critical changes affecting future stakes. Important changes that we have not yet mastered.

Zone B: Important changes already mastered.

Zone C: Unimportant changes that are not yet mastered. (Guiltless Weaknesses)

Zone D: Important changes that are mastered. We probably talk about them more because we master them. (Useless Strengths)

From critical changes to action

Critical Changes	Stakes for Company	Corporate Objectives Given These Stakes	Ideas to Apply
1: ...			
2: ...			
3: ...			

Hunting Down Clichés

A cliché, whether true or false, is generally accepted without questioning. As a result, you may have often heard remarks like...
- "Young people don't know as much as previous generations did";
- "Americans (Brits, Spaniards, etc) are not good at learning languages";
- "Consultants are expensive."

In this workshop, participants list individually and then collectively examples of conventional thinking that they hear in their field. Sometimes mentioning a few clichés breaks the ice. Participants soon catch on.

The Top Ten Preconcieved Ideas from Various Workshops

1. The customer knows best.
2. Might makes right.
3. Women take more time off work than men.
4. Consultants are expensive.
5. A good consultant seldom intervenes.
6. Medicine is a product like none other.
7. Bigger is better.
8. Change has to start at the top.
9. Decentralization makes more people responsible but also dilutes responsibility.
10. Insurance companies are a band of thieves.

The facilitator then asks the following questions:
- can some of these examples of conventional thinking be considered partially true, at least?

If so, why and which ones?
- how do you explain the popularity of these clichés, this type of thinking?
- what results do you see from this type of thinking?
- is there a lesson to be drawn from this analysis?
- what can be done to correct a cliché if it is negative and what can be done to utilize a cliché if it is positive?

Here is a personal favorite: "Consultants are expensive."

Does this idea have any foundation in fact? Why?

- Gray matter has no price tag.
- Service exceeds the billed time (e.g. proposal writing, research, analysis, reports).
- The cost-benefit ratio must always be considered.
- It is a net cost for the company.
- The consultant has a high level of expertise.

– The consultant is efficient and knows how to deal with the problem quickly.

Why does this idea prevail?

– Daily rate versus a salary.
– Recommendations seem obvious when *expost*.
– Weight of history.
– Misunderstood profession.
– Advice is not considered and investment.
– It is not easy to judge what the ROI (return on investment) will be.
– Some recommendations are not followed and thus become expensive!
– Quantity is favored, e.g. the thickness of the report not the quality.
– The consultant's look.
– Since it is expensive, cost is a good excuse for not using a consultant's services.

Consequences of the above

– Undervalued profession.
– Image problem.
– Potential for quick earnings attracts new consultants.
– Small-to-medium-size firms seldom use consultants.

Lessons to be learned...

– Clichés and conventional thinking are based on incomplete and biased information.
– Resistance to something new is strong partly because people have a system of references that they know and trust.
– Any excuse may be a good one to avoid asking difficult questions.

Negotiating between the Short- and Long-Term

Here we ask participants to draw upon their experience.
– What are the advantages and disadvantages of a course of action set out over the long-term, e.g. beyond one year?
– What are the advantages and disadvantages of a course of action set out over the short-term?
– What problems in choosing the short or long-term have you experienced in your field?

Although used less frequently than the others, this workshop suits audiences who admit that futures-thinking exercises hold little appeal for them. We have met negative reactions to futures-thinking among comptrollers as well as human resources directors. Yet no matter what their thoughts on the future may be, they have all faced choosing between the short and long-term in buying equipment, e.g. credit conditions, cost amortization, or in hiring people, e.g. which skills will we need in the future? This workshop provides decisionmaking criteria that enable participants to weigh the advantages between the short- and long-term.

Drawing Competence Trees (Past, Present and Future)

In the1980s, Marc Giget, head of Euroconsult, came up with the concept of a competence tree to assist managers in strategic thinking. Competence trees serve to analyze and evaluate the overall technological, industrial and commercial skills of a company. Properly used, this tool enables one to mobilize the key people involved at a corporation as well as quantify accurately and exhaustively that company's competences.

The purpose of the exercise within a workshop is not to come up with a detailed analysis and exact evaluation but rather to use the principle of the competence tree so that the participants or working committee develops a collective vision of reality for the company, city or region under study.

The workshop outline goes as follows:
1) Draw the past tree (20 years) and the present tree according to
– roots (vocation, competence, skills, know-how);
– trunk (implementation, organization);
– branches (product or service lines, markets).

2) Pinpoint the strengths and weaknesses on the tree according to the company's environment, the actors and implementation of strategies.

3) List major changes in the environment, e.g. technological breakthroughs, socio-economic shifts and political movements, that could affect the tree. Note whether these changes are desired, feared or perceived.

4) Match up the parts of the tree (roots, trunk, branches) that correspond to these changes and outline the advantages and limitations of other actors.

5) Build a competence tree for the future, e.g. which products or skills should be kept, discontinued or further developed.

The Competence Tree and Its Dynamic

Roots: know-how and skills
Trunk: organization of production
Branches: product-market lines

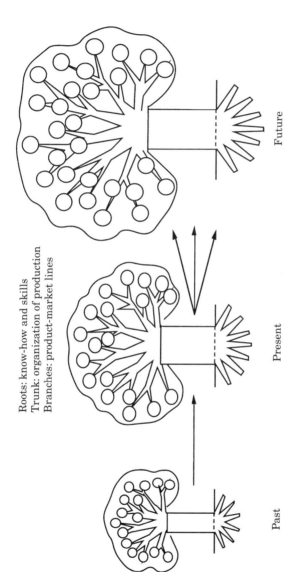

Past

Present

Future

The past is unique; analysing it allows us to understand the constants and continuity of the company's business, to improve our knowledge of the company project in its historical reality.

The future is uncertain; its analysis allows us to identify the threats and opportunities presented to the company, and to define the issues and challenges it faces, in order to determine its desired future and to incorporate this future into the company's strategy.

Giget, La conduite de la réflexion et de l'action stratégique dans l'entreprise (Euroconsult, 1988).

Illustration: Regulation of the Telecommunications Industry (Horizon 2010)

The results presented in this section come from a futures-thinking seminar called "Determining Factors in Regulating the Telecommunications Industry (Horizon 2010)". This event took place February 3-4 in 1999 at the French Secretary of State for Industry. The comments and opinions expressed in our report and this section present the different points of view of those in attendance. Nevertheless the opinions are those of the author and co-author, Stéphane Leroy-Therville, do not necessarily reflect those of the specific department or companies involved. Note the full report of this futures-thinking exercise was published in French in the LIPS working paper series, Cahier n° 12 "The Future of Regulation in Telecommunications".

The Context of Futures Thinking

The legislative document which establishes the French federal secretariat of industry, information technology and postal service gives the Sub-Directorate of Telecommunications Regulations responsibility for analysis of the future of those sectors falling under its mandate. Subdirectorate management took the initiative of launching a series of futures-thinking exercises on regulation of telecommunications companies for two reasons.

First of all, the Telecom Review, a revision of the European regulatory framework was starting that year, so France needed to define its position. What was needed was a snapshot of the current situation and an idea of how circumstances may develop along with possible orientations. At the national level, it soon became apparent that principles of economic doctrine were needed to take into account increasingly numerous technologies, converging networks and services, as well as the specific a nature of the local network, often called *the last mile*.

Another vital component in this process was sharing experiences and exploring ideas. This was achieved by bringing together representatives from all the various units of the system under study. In fact representatives from the telecommunications regulatory bodies and administrations from the French telecommunications regulatory body (ART), from the European Union, and also various users such as the French Telegraph and Telecommunications Union (AFUTT) took part. Consultants along with certain experts known in the field also participated. Operators, manufacturers, service providers and distributors were either consulted, later on, or brought on board later as participants in working groups.

During the seminar itself, two workshops (Anticipating and Mastering Change and Hunting Down Clichés) were held. The results from the workshops are presented here first, followed by overall comments or observations.

Major Changes and Clichés Detected during the Workshops

1) Converging services and infrastructures in telecommunications, computers and audiovisual equipment. The main feature that was immediately noted was the mobile versus traditional stationary distinction.

2) Regulatory model, in other words, the level and basis of regulation.

3) Balance between sectoral regulation and competition.

4) Development of e-business/e-commerce.

5) Globalization, in other words, the spread of networks and markets around the world.

6) Sectorial and trans-sectorial alliances among companies involved in the information society.

7) Technological developments (digitization, packet-switching, Internet protocol).

8) The local system and ungrouping, last mile, legal rights, etc.

9) Consideration of market demand and pressure.

10) Standardization, in terms of harmonization, be it *de facto* or already underway.

11) Importance of satellites, groups of satellites and geostationary satellites.

12) Development of added value from transmission to content.

13) Role of the State: Actor or Arbitrator?

All of the above appears in the following diagram.

Hunting Down Clichés about the Telecommunications Sector

This workshop follows the format of the so-called change workshop. The first step involves listing clichés or pearls of conventional thinking both individually and collectively. In this exercise, a cliché, or preconceived idea, is part of what we call conventional thinking. It is an idea that has been accepted by the participants or by the public without any debate or critical thinking.

Proving or Disproving Clichés

The process of confirming clichés and debating them proved very stimulating in this field. The following charts show how the process goes right to the core of each cliché.

Among the 17 main clichés, the first one was:

"Promoting universal Internet access is vital to France's competitiveness."

Statements that disprove...

This is only one dimension among many.
The economic rules affecting the Internet have not yet stabilized.
The Internet is not safe and does not make the public feel safe.

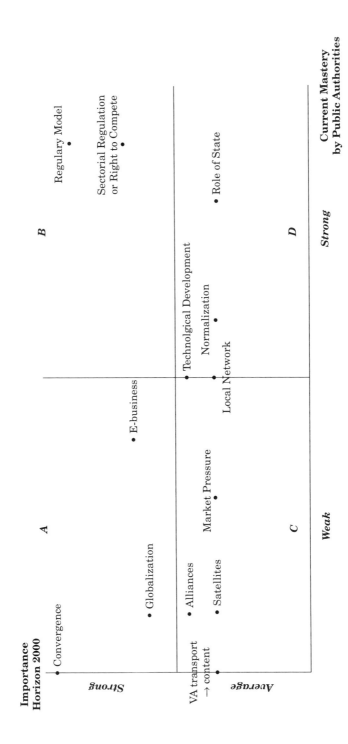

Zone A: Critical changes, future stakes. These are the major changes that are not mastered currently. One strategy here might be to increase mastery or reduce the importance of the stakes in this zone.

Zone B: Major changes well mastered.

Zone C: Unimportant changes, not well mastered (no serious consequences).

Zone D: Unimportant changes, well mastered (do not focus on this zone).

There is a danger of building a virtual society, at the expense of the real society.

The Internet is is just a fad.

France is not behind technologically.

The important thing is to master usage and not spread the tools.

Universal Internet access plus illiteracy?

Statements that prove...

There is an increase in business on the Internet (e-business or e-commerce).

There is a "club effect" at work among the actors, thus increasing new uses.

Telephone services, such as VoIP, are developing on the Internet.

Increased productivity is linked to the circulation of information.

This decreases the price of information.

It is a tool serving research and innovation.

It is a self-fulfilling prophecy.

This facilitates the economic reach of certain regions, thus breaking down enclaves.

The younger generation is interested (an age gap may form).

It is a competitive component in the telecommunications sector.

It is a weapon in the war against illiteracy.

The second cliché off the top of the list: "Telecoms, computer and multimedia firms will merge."

Statements that disprove...

Limits to wireless technology may slow down any attempts to merge.

Global regulation is required; an idea that does not please either the economic actors or the regulators.

Industrial logic is contradictory over the long-term, (questions of diversity and mass distribution).

In multimedia, mergers might slow down the penetration of certain markets.

Statements that prove...

Technology allows for it.

There is already a convergence in the technologies involved.

The actors' strategies are heading that way.

There is a will within the industry to provide a complete offer, all around the world.

The movement has already begun.

Distributors must maximize their channels; producers must show their programmes.

From Key Issues to Actor's Strategies

An initial analysis of the results from the three workshop groups reveals a high degree of similarity among participants' perspectives.

Key differences appear in the importance that they assigned to foreseen changes or to the corresponding clichés. In this sense, the changes cited the most often by the first two groups are convergence (networks, services, sectors), the regulatory model, problems at the local level and management of scarce resources. The main clichés or preconceived ideas elicit exactly the same topics. The telecom, cliché workshop is typical, yet especially enriching when we look back now.

At this stage; four issues appeared:

Issue 1
Converging services, networks and markets.
Issue 2
The Evolving Regulatory Model.
Issue 3
Problems in the "Last Mile" or Local Network.
Issue 4
Management of Rare Resources at the National; Regional or International Level.

On the basis of their analyses, the working groups decided that French public authorities had a rather mediocre mastery of these issues. Yet these are key stakes which need to be monitored closely.

Workshops provide an initial image of the system, but conclusions must be translated into action. Two strategy workshops follow the "changes" and "clichés" workshops so that participants can plot possible courses of action. Workshops and follow-up usually take a few meetings. In this case, two groups were formed. Half the participants worked on the analysis of actors' strategies; the other half worked on building scenarios through morphological analysis. Their results follow with comments.

By analyzing actors' strategies, confronting their agendas, and considering the balance of power, participants can see how strategic stakes are evolving. They can then ask key questions about the future. In this instance, the group used the Mactor method to consider issues and consequences of foreseeable conflicts. (For the Mactor method, see the BASF case study, chapter 8, or *From Anticipation to Action* published by Unesco, 1994.)

The main changes identified during the previous sessions of this workshop were translated as stakes for regulation. The participants then identfed the actors associated with each "battlefield". The group thus built a list of actors who play a leading or supporting role in the telecommunication sector or whose views could fall in the balance when making certain decisions. The group then constructed a matrix "Actors × Actors" which pinpoints the powers that each actor has over the others, analyzes the balance of power associated with the stakes set out initially and then lists, as follows, the information.

This group tackled the issues through seven stakes. The actors influencing each stake were then listed in the next column.

Stakes	Associated Actors
E1: Regulation Model	European Commission, government, ART, CSA, operators, media
E2: Anti-trust Legislation	European Union, government, WCC (Geneva), Justice Dept./Min.
E3: Convergence Voice-Data	Industrials, operators
E4: Mode of Access to Subscriber	Industrials, operators, ART, government,
E5: Interoperablility/compatibility	Industrials, operators, ETSI, public authority
E6: Frequency Management	Public authority, NGOs
E7: Market	Government, consumers, operators, media

A list of actors was then drawn up as follows:
A1: Europe (standards, justice dept. EU).
A2: Government.
A3: ART.
A4: CSA.
A5: Territorial groups.
A6: Investors.
A7: Historical operator.
A8: New operators.
A9: Equipment suppliers.
A10: Distributors.
A11: Corporate customers.
A12: Private customers.
A13: Media.

With a Few Improvements for Better Thinking

First of all, the list of actors seems too limited, especially in terms of legal power. Legislation could play a key role in competition over the next ten years. Think of the AT&T case which launched the telephone wars in the United States. The state's opinion on the various law suits brought to court by local collectivities also indicates the role that the legal system may have in the European telecom landscape to come. Yet, in general, the European justice system does not have the same checks and balances or self-regulating tradition as the American, and the telecommunications sector is currently regulated sectorally and controlled by public agencies.

Here the working group decided to water-down the national and European judicial power potential into the actors considered public authorities. Nevertheless, a more detailed analysis will surely rank the legal system as a full-fledged actor on its own.

Second, the list excludes international aspects and focuses on Europe. The external world is considered benevolent, at best, and non-existent, at worst. Yet, nowadays, most battlefields are chosen by the Americans who essentially oblige the Europeans to follow along. The decisions made in Asia, notably Japan, will also likely have an influence on several choices for the future. The list could be extended by taking international pressures into account.

Leading to Four Initial Scenarios

A path, in other words, a combination associating a configuration from each dimension is a scenario. Without considering the incompatibilities, the array of possible futures according to these dimensions and configurations generates $2 \times 3 \times 3 \times 3 = 54$ scenarios. By introducing limits like exclusion and preference, this "morphological space" may be reduced. Within the time allotted for this exercise, the group was able to tease out four paths without analyzing them.

The four paths or scenarios were given easy-to-understand and retain titles:
1) Much Ado about Nothing.
2) The Information Society.
3) Happy Few.
4) Major Trusts.

More and More Technology; Less and Less Security

This exercise helped participants map out the major forces in telecom scenarios developed by others over the previous few years. When aligned, the various scenarios reveal a few gaps. First, the technology dimension was highlighted whereas most experts agree that while technology will remain a basic tool in actors' strategies and their transactions, it is not shaping the market as much as before. Indeed from this point on, marketing and the service/product offer itself are dominating the system and from an increasingly short-term perspective. The reign of engineers has given way to that of merchants before what may be the advent of the consumer. Nevertheless, the inertia factors, considered very strong in the telecommunications sector, must be kept in mind at all times.

However, consumers are concerned about the security of their transactions as well as risks of violation of privacy. Security systems may well condition the development of new communication tools. Indeed, this dimension seems to have been glossed over in the scenarios presented.

Although catchy, the title given to the first scenario should not act as a smoke screen. Even if the effects of opening up this sector to competition did not have the impact expected; even if the national champions and local monopolies have held their ground, the telecommunications sector will never be able to go back to the situation at the beginning of the information age. The behaviour of both the actors and consumers has already been not only greatly but also permanently modified.

The weakness in the second scenario, "Information Society", lies in the plurality of the information society. There are many societies not one, if we take into account usage and possible changes in lifestyle as well as in products that are truly accepted. Of course, the impact of technology may be positive or negative, thus this scenario could easily be refined and subdivided.

A Few Lessons from the Basque Region 2010 Exercise

The territorial foresight exercises done for the Basque Region with a horizon of 2010 is exemplary in more ways than one. [1] Started in 1992 with the support of the regional French government agency, and with the participation of active territorial forces in workshops which brought over one-hundred people to St Palais (elected representatives, economic agents, academics) for two days. These endeavours led to the publication of entire pages in the regional newspapers and continued to do so for some two years. A structural analysis was carried out and scenarios were drafted. The group involvement process led to an outline of the development of the territory and serve as a reference to this very day.

We thus were able to test in the field during the Basque exercise the main idea expressed by Philippe Gabillet (1999) [2] throughout his work entitled "Savoir anticiper"; in other words, "the same tools, the same mental and intellectual processes enable a collectivity, a group, even an isolated individual to project itself/himself into the future". The charter of the Basque exercise was simply transposed from the one we had helped create for the Mides Operation at Renault in 1984. The same collective and participatory methods applied to the 1992 Basque country exercise and almost the same rules of the game as those used at Renault.

---

1. Although often quoted, few articles have been written on this topic notably because of the modesty of François Bourse, the main facilitator, who succeeded me in the follow-up to the initial launching seminar. The Basque exercise is nonetheless outlined in the group publication "Projectique" published by Economica in 1996, under the direction of Jean-Michel Larrasquet et al.
2. Philippe Gabillet, "Savoir Anticiper". ESF Editeurs, 1999.

Basque Region 2010

A Charter Designed to Put Futures Thinking into Action. (extracts)

A Need, A Will

In the face of an ever-changing world, what do we want for the Basque Region? That the territory changes with us, without us or against us? To liberate the Basque region from the tyranny of hazard and determinism and to restore the future as the fruit of will, some foresight was needed. Futures-thinking exercises are no longer the domain of only a handful of specialists or the fare of large corporations only. In the case of the Basque region, like other territories, does not want to only suffer its fate but rather to master it.

Foresight, be it for a city, region or any other unity, provides a unique opportunity to surpass the short-term constrictions and limitations and make all those involved aware of the need to change habits and behaviours in order to face change. To do that, we must rely on local expertise and use the exercise as a chance to crystallise skills that are often spread out in the region.

A State of Mind

The Basque Region 2010 exercise was also a state of mind, inspired by the following:

Opening and anticipation
– Understand better what is going on around us and know how to distinguish limits and opportunities so as to influence them or adapt to them in order to face them.

Pluralism and cooperation
– Recognize and accept our differences.
– Take into account contradictory opinions, e.g., knowing how to listen, one of the fundamentals of cooperation.
– Know how not to abandon one's options or responsibilities, this is the basis of relationships in the social world.

Method and imagination
– Set out the problem properly and seek to solve them.
– Promote participation from each individual present.
– Stimulate imagination and creativity.
– Highlight all the possible choices, their advantages and disadvantages.
– Associate all the actors involved at all levels of thinking and decision-making processes.
These are the principles that guarantee that a solution corresponds to both the problems and needs of those involved.

Autonomy and responsibility
– Take into greater account the aspirations of the people working or active in the organisation of everyday life.
– Base authority on the capacity to motivate men, to pool their skills together
– Define fully at every level of local life and in an organized manner, clear and measurable objectives.
These are the principles that guarantee each participant a zone of independence equal to the measure of the responsibilities that he/she is assigned.

Practical Guide for *Strategic Prospective*

First, one unofficial statistic: many futures-thinking exercises have motivated many people in a rich, collective process; whereas not too many have led to real, implemented action. Without harping, the voice of experience urges us to improve the functional side of creating futures with some practical advice.

The first condition (a *sine qua non!*) is to identify the source of the origin and the nature of the request for a futures-thinking exercise. In marketing terms, who is the client? If we continue the checklist, there are at least five key questions.

1) What position/power does the client hold within the corporate hierarchy?

2) What is the real problem or issue presented?

3) Who are the other actors involved?

4) How can they become involved in the process?

5) How does this exercise fit into the corporate culture of the client?

The most important yet often ignored condition is time. What is the timeframe or the final deadline? We have memories of major corporate clients (Renault, the Post Office, William Saurin, Péchiney) who had good intentions but was unable to embody those intentions due to a subsequent change of leadership. Many futures projects suddenly die when the pioneering executive who started the process leaves the company. Successors rarely continue projects started by their predecessors. It is important to have corporate executives personally committed to the project and active in the steering committee. It is also important that this committee have enough time for the collective thinking activities without dragging them on for too long.

The Components and Functions of the Technical group

The mandate and tasks of each group or committee must be made clear from the start. (A checklist including request source, problem, report recipients and deadline should be given.) Intermediary documents and the final report should be the responsibility of the technical group which reports regularly to the steering committee.

Each group should have some type of leader or representative chosen by the group once it has been formed. This leader will also act as facilitator and coordinate the various tasks performed by group members. This "pilot" must be prepared to follow the course previously elaborated and complete the mandate. In other words, the leader must set an example by monitoring activity, modifying tools but not goals, and, of course, meeting deadlines.

Launching Workshops to Initiate the Process

In our experience, a two-day, on-site seminar starts the futures process off right. Participants become group members initiated in the ways and means that may prove effective in the futures-thinking activities to follow. In this way, the group is not only consumer but also producer. The product remains the same: thought on the future. The group is ready to dive in when the workshops outlined earlier begin.

After the two days, the group is better prepared to determine the topic and define the work method jointly. The method is not fully validated until a later meeting by which time participants have had time to step back and look objectively at the process.

Organizing and Assigning Tasks

Our rule of thumb...
   – three or four meetings as the process is getting started;
   – at least three meetings annually when at "cruising speed";
   – then three to four meetings clustered near the conclusion. Again, experience shows that it is smart to set the dates of meetings and their objectives at least five to six sessions ahead of time.

Basic Housekeeping Tips

   – Always present an agenda and take the minutes at meetings.
   – During meetings every group member should give a progress report on his/her area.
   – At the end of each meeting, each participant's tasks and the agenda for the next meeting should be reviewed.

Over the course of the full futures-thinking exercise, specialists (internal or external) should be called in for advice on specific fields or applications. If possible, the expert could make a presentation, answer questions and a summary could be circulated almost immediately. If necessary, assistance or expertise may be subcontracted, e.g. in specific technical or sectoral issues.

Forming a team or working group is never easy. Group dynamics always require some effort. The hardest part is choosing an in-house leader or facilitator who can invest company and even personal time in the process. The facilitator prepares meetings, writes summaries, takes notes and encourages groups members' participation by delegating tasks. The group leader or facilitator must also foresee the various stages, problems and methods and schedule accordingly.

Here the outside consultant may prove very useful. An experienced expert not only enhances methodology but also reacts to the group's ideas, and stimulates debate. The outside expert is not needed at all meetings. The in-house facilitator should call upon a specialist or consultant only as needed.

Choosing the Right Method: Efficiency, Motivation and Communication

No single method is imposed, but choosing a method determines how efficient the meetings will be. In other words, without a method, there is no common language, no exchange, little consistency, and few structured ideas. Nevertheless, choosing a method is not the be all and end all. We do not want to become a prisoner to the results of one method. As mentioned before, a method is a tool, among several, that helps people think better, together, about the future.

A rigorous method is a necessary factor if the group is to stick together and stay motivated. Partial results contribute to this group dynamic and should be distributed. Lastly, the choice of method must correspond to the problem(s) presented in the initial seminar, the time-frame and the way in which the results will be presented. The tools chosen must be sufficiently simple as to allow the users to appropriate them.

In the end, advice, be it on using coloured pens or from contractual consultants, should be taken and taken and adapted to fit the organization's needs. The one definite obligation is preparation (agenda, objectives, method selection, proposals, etc.) Of course in the futures workshops, we use less systematic but nonetheless effective working methods e.g. imposed "time- out periods" of silence a rare feature in any group activity and a simple voting system.

A Process Rather than a Final Report

The credibility, utility and quality of a futures-thinking exercise depend on the participants' respecting certain conditions. A common breach is to subcontract thinking about the future to an outside firm or consultant. Far too many corporations and even regions have thought that hiring a well-known management consulting firm was the best idea. They missed the point. In any futures study, the final report counts for less than the process leading up to it. It is, therefore, more important to draw upon local or internal talent and use the futures-thinking exercise as a way to change the way people think and behave. The idea is to "think globally but act locally" so that participants can truly be part of the creative process in a company.

Before undertaking the more or less onerous exercise of forward-looking strategic analysis, it is advisable to take time to reflect on the nature of the problem posed and the approach to be used to find and implement solutions. This will make it possible to avoid wasting time on false problems and to frame the problem clearly, which is half the battle towards finding a solution. When beginning this process of reflection, which can often involve dozens of people for many months, it is also useful to plan that the overall procedure follow a timetable of intermediate objectives and deadlines and by choosing methods that are not only adapted to the nature of the problem identified, but also to the time and resource constraints of the futures-thinking group.

Whatever the procedure adopted, it is useful to begin this collective reflection process with a two-day seminar devoted to training participants in Strategic Prospective analysis. This seminar enables participants to discover and familiarise themselves with the main concepts and tools of collective Strategic Prospective analysis. The purpose of this seminar, in which several dozen persons may be involved, is the total immersion of participants in foresight thinking aimed at strategic action. Such workshops try to frame the problem clearly and dispel any prejudices and stereotypes that distort perception of the issues. They make it possible collectively to define and prioritise the future challenges facing the enterprise in its national and international environment. At the end of these two days, the participants are able to specify the priorities, objectives, timetable and method to be used to organise their Strategic Prospective reflection. [1]

Although there is no single, set method for this process, it is indispensable that a method be chosen for the meetings to be effective, for without a method, there can be no common language, exchange or consistent framework for ideas. However, the method is not an end in itself, and the results produced must not be followed slavishly, for it is only a tool to help ensure the relevance of the reflection process. A rigorous method is also an invaluable factor for promoting the cohesiveness and motivation of the group, as are the intermediary results, which should be disseminated.

Lastly, the method should be chosen in the light of the problems identified (see the initial seminar) and the time constraints, and with a concern for communicating the results. The tools should be sufficiently simple to be easily used by participants.

Recommendations for Regional Foresight

Since I have had the opportunity of becoming either familiar or directly involved with a number of forward-looking territorial exercises (Basque Country 2010, Reunion Island, Lorraine 2010, Ardennes, Ille-et-Vilaine, Pyrénées Atlantiques, Martinique, etc.), I would like to share some of the lessons learnt from their successes and failures.

First, certain conditions must be met to ensure the credibility, usefulness and quality of regional foresight. It is essential that the process of contemplating an area's future not be outsourced completely.

In any study, regardless of its quality, the final report is less important than the process leading up to it. In this respect, it is important to

---

1. A comprehensive description of forward-looking analysis workshops was published in the *Cahiers du Lips, No. 12, "L'avenir de la réglementation des télécommunications, Etats des lieux et ateliers de prospective"*, by Stéphane Leroy-Therville, March 2000.

rely on local expertise and to use the forward-looking exercise to trigger a process of change, at least in people's minds. The goal is not so much one of completing a forward-looking study than initiating a process of participatory reflection and discussion. Stimulating thinking on overall issues at the local level can make actors want to come together and agree to support one or more projects for an area.

The use of three colours for the three phases of regional foresight

– Using three colours (blue for "foresight", yellow for "ownership" and green for "action"), it is possible to organise regional foresight in three separate phases for which three types of documents can be produced:
– a blue book. The purpose of this document is to provide an overview of the past, present and future environment of the area. On the basis of summary key figures, it includes elements of a diagnosis; it identifies problem areas and indicates probable trends, major uncertainties and possible future crises. This document, which is intended as a monographic study, can largely be outsourced to an external consultant;
– yellow books in which each operational centre makes its proposals for local action to prepare for the overall changes foreseen in the blue book (pre-activity), but also to achieve the strategic objectives and local projects (pro-activity). These yellow books can be prepared by departments in enterprises or in local and regional authorities, and embody the collective ownership of the forward-looking regional foresight;
– a green book proposing an overall strategic plan for the area of the region and city, listing each objective and the corresponding action. It is a synthesis of the blue and yellow books. This green book is a strategic document that commits leaders and elected officials. It is therefore produced under their sole responsibility.

The tools of business foresight can be used just as effectively in territorial foresight since both methods aim at planning and organising a collective reflection process while they also facilitate communication and promote more creative and collective thinking.

However, regional foresight is more difficult than business foresight for the consultants involved. The origin and purposes of their mandate are rarely clear, the actors have many and often contradictory expectations and the financial resources are not always adequate for the objectives targeted. In short, the consultant is the perfect target when the inconsistencies become too great. The safest approach in terms of image – and the one that is simplest to communicate and easiest for consultants – is to settle for a traditional study report. Unfortunately, this solution has little operational value or lasting effect, for it ignores the fact that unless local actors appropriate the process, it will be impossible to bridge the gap between foresight and action.

6

CASE STUDIES IN INDUSTRY AND DEFENCE

The Aluminum Industry

Few cases of structural analysis applied to industrial problems are ever presented publicly. In general, such analyses can not be published because of the confidentiality risks implied. Moreover, by the time the publication embargo has been lifted, the material is usually outdated. Fortunately this is not the case for the Aluminum 2000 futures-thinking exercise, begun in 1985 on behalf of the Péchiney Group. In fact, the specialists rereading the report found that ten years later the analysis had stood the test of time and appeared almost "clairvoyant". [1]

Part of this case study was published in 1989 with Joseph Vialle, then in charge of planning at the Péchiney group. Sections of the aluminum case were presented to Petrobras executives during a conference in Brazil. The conference organizers were kind enough to grant us permission to reproduce the material here.

For Péchiney, structural analysis was only the first step. Scenario building followed from 1986-1987 as a tool to shed further light on participants' strategic choices. Structural analysis proved particularly rich in that it enabled participants to sketch scenarios for the international aluminum industry. As mentioned in the first chapter, a change in corporate leadership interrupted the process, so who knows what might have happened otherwise. Nevertheless, the intellectual investment of the executives who participated was well spent. It always pays to have executives sit down occasionally and reflect upon the long-term. Interestingly enough, the decisions made later, e.g. downstream integration, with the buy-out of American Can, reflected to some extent the conclusions drawn by the Aluminum 2000 group.

A Young Metal with an Uncertain Future

The study aimed at pinpointing the key determining factors in the world aluminum industry with 2000 as a horizon. Structural analysis was the tool of choice. The aluminum system could be characterized by 75 inter-related variables.

The process of teasing out variables and reviewing the mechanisms connecting them was enriched by a series of some twenty interviews, two-thirds of which were conducted with outside experts. After the interviews, a number of the points raised could be considered probable trends or major uncertainties for the future of the aluminum industry.

---

1. Note that many of these analyses were performed under G.Y. Kerven, then president of the aluminum branch.

The Consequences of Political Uncertainty and the International Economy

Uncertainty awaits on five fronts: geopolitical (mining countries), economic (growth rates in various zones), monetary exchange (currency fluctuations), socio-economic and regulatory. As a corollary, other probable trends put forth for the year 2000, back in 1985, included international monetary instability and fluctuating growth rates. In order to adapt and survive in the face of uncertainty and change, participants saw the need to increase their vigilance and flexibility as well as diversify risks and opportunities.

Technological Explosion in Materials: Threat or Opportunity?

The raw materials sector is experiencing tremendous technological expansion, whether in composites or more traditional materials, e.g. ferrous metals, glass and wood. Why should aluminum be any different? Mixed materials are not deadly competitors and may actually represent potential markets. Everything depends on the will and strategy of the manufacturers involved.

Enlarging the Competitive and Strategic Environment of Aluminum

Manufacturers can find giant competitors along this "multi-material axis", notably international petrochemical conglomerates. One glance at the earnings of these corporations confirms how important this new challenge is to the aluminum sector.

In the eyes of many experts, strengthening the role of the London Metal Exchange (LME) seems inevitable. Nevertheless, the aluminum manufacturers may still be able to guarantee their clients stable prices. In fact, even though the LME might be called upon to play a role in generating fluctuations over the short-term, this should have little impact on the long-term competitive pricing trend in aluminum.

Recycling is a potential advantage for pure materials like aluminum. Why? The separation of composites is difficult. Therefore, the collection and disposal of composite materials may hinder further development of these materials which are at the mercy of a regulatory framework that opposes what has been called "the composite trash civilization".

Choice of Materials by Function and Service

A rapid review of the main uses of aluminum indicates that there will necessarily be a decrease if the main manufacturers limit their role to that of supplier while customers increasingly seek service (a response to a function). Service will no longer be the domain of an isolated material, given the mixes and massive choice of materials available.

Aluminum manufacturers must focus their marketing efforts on supplying a "service package". Of course this focus would affect R&D, too. Packaging is a perfect example. Here innovative materials go hand-in-hand with tooling innovations and conservation methods, hence closer links to firms downstream.

Approach and Results

In this case, structural analysis was started in May 1985 and ended in October of the same year. Drawing up the list of variables took several collective thinking sessions and involved several Péchiney executives as well as other experts. These meetings were enriched through a series of twenty-odd interviews inside and outside the Péchiney Group. During the listing, variables were divided as internal and external. Internal variables referred to the international aluminum system; external variables, to the geopolitical, social, and economic environments plus technology. By synthesizing ideas, participants succeeded in drawing up a final list of 75 variables.

The structural analysis matrix was filled in by a working committee or group created specifically for the task. Included were Messrs Bercovici, Fevre, Thomas, Vialle (Péchiney) and Messrs Barré, Chapuy and Godet as consultants. They were joined by two materials experts, Mr. Chalmin and Mr. Giraud. The group met over three days during which group members systematically asked about all the eventual interaction between variables. This group asked over 5,000 questions on the direct relationships between the variables and their intensity. The following intensities were established: strong (3), average (2), weak (1) and potential (P). Note that structural analysis also takes into account potential relations although they are practically nonexistent today. The idea is that these relationships may become probable or at least possible in the relatively near future.

Among the variables which seem to have the most influence on the aluminum industry in the world (still horizon 2000), the following eight stand out no matter which classification method is applied. Their determining role appears firmly established.

The most influential variables are as follows:
– competitiveness of materials: this variable is fairly dependent and the most influential across the board. In other words, the future of aluminum depends on a variable with a very uncertain development/evolution;
– financial situation of the aluminum companies: this variable appears second when ranked according to influence. Perhaps surprising, this result indicates that the future of aluminum is shaped by the financial capacity of the firms to implement their strategy and resist the ups and downs of demand and price;

– strategy of the leading clients: The position of this variable, both very influential and quite dependent, confirms the determining yet unstable nature of the main aluminum clients. Yet their choices and behavior will increasingly influence the strategy of major manufacturers;

– price stability: Here the key role of this variable can be confirmed. Its highly influential yet not very dependent nature seems to indicate that manufacturers may suffer price fluctuations;

– Alcoa, Péchiney, Alcan strategies: These three variables are the most unstable within the system. In other words, they are the most influential and the most dependent. The upshot is that the strategies of the main manufacturers are interdependent. It is worth noting that the variable "competition/cooperation among manufacturers" is ranked third in terms of potential influence whereas it ranks 41st in direct classification;

– transformers' strategies: This variable plays a vital role in the aluminum system. It is comparable to the variable "leading client strategies".

If we examine the more or less dependent nature of the variables in the aluminum system, we see that the most dependent variables are often the most influential. In fact, of the nine most dependent variables, six belong to the ten most influential. These are the actors' strategies variables already mentioned.

It is not at all surprising that strategic-technological foresight which depends on actors' strategies is also highly dependent. Among the dependent variables, we also found corporate research policy, innovation in aluminum products, recycling, competitiveness, and political corporate image. These are all closely linked.

Priority Variables Classified as Direct, Indirect or Potential

The Most Influential Variables (to be mastered)	Competitiveness of Materials Financial Situation among Aluminum Companies Leading Client Strategies Price Stability Alcoa, Péchiney, Alcan Strategies Transformer/Processor Strategies Price of Non-standard Products Management Criteria (quality, productivity, profitability
The Most Dependent Variables (to be monitored)	Strategic and Technological Foresight (*veille* in French) Corporate Research Policy Recycling Relative Competitiveness of the Companies Political Image of the Companies Strategies of the Second-Rung Companies

Some results raise more questions than answers. It actually seems that the relative competitivity of the companies involved is far more influential and less dependent in terms of indirect and potential effects than in terms of direct effects. Should we conclude then that in the future the competitive gap between the various companies will become more determinant and less "variable"?

In any event, the results concerning the demand variables are remarkable. The direct classification introduces a dichotomy between the rather dependent variables, e.g. consumption markets (packaging, construction) and demand variables that are almost independent of the system considered part of the professional markets (aeronautics, energy). In other words, part of the demand for aluminum is independent.

What surprises us should not confuse us, though. Instead some of these realizations urge us to think in a more in-depth and imaginative manner. In general, most of the results from the structural analysis confirm an initial intuition. Yet we remain on guard against the temptation of concluding that this type of analysis is unnecessary. In fact, it is always easier *ex post* to say that something was obvious than it is to reject *a priori* certain pieces of "evidence" rather than others.

Overall, what surprised us was the fact that the demand variables are not very dependent. This is intriguing in that they normally should have appeared as result variables. Moreover, the variables characteristic of professional markets and mass consumption have increasingly more influence when we integrate the indirect and potential effects. This result could mean that manufacturers have less mastery of the marketplace than expected. If demand from leading clients drove the market, then the competitiveness of the materials would tip the balance.

Another interesting result drawn from structural analysis: the relatively influential character of the macroeconomic variables (monetary fluctuations, industrial production) and social variables (lifestyle and consumer habits). Most of these variables lose their relative influence on the system when the indirect and potential effects are taken into consideration.

Emerging Variables Ranked Indirect and/or Potential

Emerging Variables (Influence)	Demand Variables New Markets for Aluminum Innovation in Product and Market New Competitors in End Markets Strategy of Manufacturing States Competition-Cooperation among Manufacturers Rate of Use of Capacities (electrolysis, semi-products)
Emerging Variables (Dependence)	Free Market for Standard Products Dowstream Integration for Industrial Clients Upstream Integration for Mass Market Linkage, Networks, Partnerships

Should we conclude that the future of the international aluminum industry depends less on political, economic and social uncertainty than the strategies of the main actors within the industry and their capacity to innovate both technologically and commercially? We lean towards that general view.

Elements for Building Scenarios

Positioning variables along the influence/dependence axes and monitoring their development provides vital information that guides our thinking to possible scenarios for the future of the aluminum industry for the year 2000. (Note that although this horizon has now been reached, the material presented herein has not been changed and reveals the pertinence of the exercise.)

The structural analysis with a horizon of 2000 provided the raw data needed to analyze how the industry would develop and to highlight the relationships between groups of variables.

Yesterday, an Ideal?

The past situation is described in the following diagram which picks up the part of variable positions on the direct axis. This is an "ideal" (perhaps yesterday?) or a stable situation in which demand is dominated by the strategy of the large companies and the production context (variables 23 to 29).

The Past Situation in the Industry

PC: Production Context: Exit and entry barriers, Manufacturing flexibility, Innovation in processing, Rate of use of capacities, Recycling.

S: Strategies: Leaders' Strategies, Transformers' Strategies.

D: Demand: Professional Markets, Greater Public Markets.

Today's Ambiguous Situation

Demand is becoming independent in terms of the leaders' strategies. These strategies are less dependent on the production context than on the influence of the control variables.

The Current Situation in the Industry

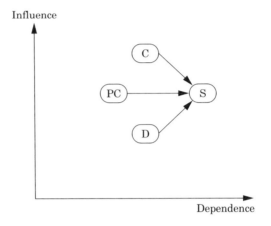

C: Control Variables: Competitiveness among Materials, Financial Situation of the Companies, Price Stability, Leading Clients' Strategies

Tomorrow's Industry: The Risk of a Separation between Manufacturing and the Market(s)?

The aluminum system is evolving in such a way that the potential indirect relations lead to the risk of a split of manufacturing and markets.

The fact that the demand is becoming independent points toward a potentially difficult situation in which the control and demand variables are influential on the strategies, thus playing more on themselves than on the production context.

Two Contrasted Strategies

The "split up" scenario envisions the manufacturers' strategy as one under the influence of both demand for the product and the control variables. The production context is no longer the determining one. In fact it has shifted into one of dependence on the system.

Strategy 1: Aluminum in either a defensive or an introverted position

Given the inertia in the aluminum industry, manufacturers adopt a stance somewhere between defensive and introverted or inward-looking. The nuance depends on whether or not they react to the influence

of the old control variables (C) and the new control variables (NC). Two new actors in particular might acquire a pivotal position and encourage this type of development, namely:
– new competitors on the end market;
– producer/source states.

Faced with this enlarged strategic environment, major aluminum manufacturers appear weak and threatened as they are divided by the strategies or actions of their traditional competition. Is this divide and conquer?

The results of strategic analysis in terms of indirect and potential relationships reveal that the system under study would tend to develop towards this strategy; i.e., between defense and introversion. Why? The demand is losing in terms of dependence and gaining in terms of influence. Domination by manufacturers thus becomes only a vague memory. Moreover, the strong increase in indirect and potential influence of new control variables confirms the above. In this strategy, manufacturers managed to cooperate and make objective alliances, a common front of sorts to face the threat of new competitors and competitive materials.

Strategy 1: Aluminum: From Defensive to Introverted Position

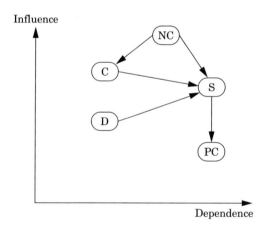

NC: New Control Variables:
– New Competitors on the end markets
– Role of manufacturer/source states
– Competition-cooperation among manufacturers

Strategy 2: Aluminum, from Innovation to Offensive

A second strategy foresees aluminum manufacturers moving into an offensive mode through product innovation. Manufacturers thus open up new markets and take control of a portion of the demand (D2). In fact, they readily adapt the production context to the development of another part of the demand (D1). The success of this market segmentation strategy depends on a fairly substantial mastery of the control variables (C + NC).

This strategy is far from being excluded by the structural analysis since the "innovation" and "cooperation among manufacturers" variables are potentially highly influential on the overall aluminum system.

In conclusion, the great disparities in material use from one country to the next can not be explained by the intrinsic performance of the materials but rather by the strategy and behaviour of the main actors operating in a particular country. As a result, the aluminum industry's future depends on the manufacturers' capacity to be:

– flexible, even when facing political, economic and financial uncertainty on an international level;

– innovative, both technologically and commercially, in order to offer a broader range of mixed materials, which include aluminum, and thus meet the needs of functions and systems. Increasingly, the client will demand that the supplier be a multi-material provider. Obviously marketing will play a pivotal role in this area.

In sum, structural analysis enabled the participants to create a hierarchy of key variables for the future of the aluminum industry by weighting the role of certain economic and financial restrictions which, after all, are the same for the competition. The ability to innovate, meet the needs of the market and create other needs will enable one aluminum manufacturer to succeed rather than another. The conflictual or cooperative nature of the actors' strategies and behavior will also play a determining role.

Strategy 2: Aluminium: From Innovation to Offensive

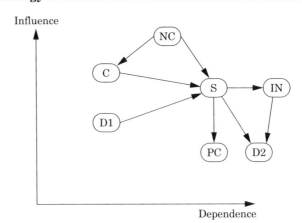

IN: Innovation:
– Production innovation
– Commercial innovation

EDF: The Utility of Futures-Thinking

This chapter section was prepared by Assaad-Émile Saab, in charge of the "Mission Prospective" at Electricité de France, in order to provide a brief history of how futures-studies exercises and strategic scenario building have evolved in a major European corporation. Rarely do we have the opportunity to reflect on how a corporation or an institution thinks about the future. The EDF case reveals just how far we have come in terms of tools, concepts and breadth of thought.

A Forecasting and Planning Tradition

Although named differently at different times, *la prospective,* foresight, or a futures-thinking process has existed at Électricité de France (EDF) since the utility's inception. This process has always been considered an integral part of forecasting and planning. Naturally accurate forecasts of future demand were essential to a company mandated to ensure the production, delivery and distribution of electricity. Beyond these basic functions, there was the need to set rates that were both fair and economically feasible. Interestingly enough, this type of forecasting at EDF also led to the development of exemplary econometric tools. Of course, in the past, the production of electricity was tremendously important for a country rebuilding and then experiencing rapid development. In fact, the magnitude of the investments required made electricity part of the national plan.

Always necessary, always present at EDF, futures-thinking has nevertheless gone through several stages.

During the 1950s and 60s, growth in electricity production remained fairly regular at 7% to 8% annually. In terms of consumption, figures doubled in one decade – a famous statistic. In those days, futures-thinking exercises were not called such and relied essentially on extrapolation. The general idea was to outline demand for electricity over the long-term, e.g. 10 to 20 years. The institutional environment was considered stable and only the economic parameters of growth were needed to generate a forecast.

Suddenly the 1970s and the oil shock hit. Futures studies or any future-thinking endeavor needed to integrate discontinuities or breaks in economic growth and consequently became more exploratory. After this watershed event, it became necessary to develop different scenarios using various hypotheses on how energy prices would develop while taking into account the growing number of uncertainties.

During the 1980s, EDF was obliged to ask new questions. At this point, after the previous decades in which scenarios were based on either energy or economics, EDF had to consider the institutional and political context in which it would continue developing. Changes in this context, or environment, stemmed from the new Europe and the decentralization of the French state. Simultaneously, technology was developing at a supersonic pace while competition among different forms of energy (electricity, gas, fossil fuels) grew fiercer.

Lastly, in the 1990s, new themes became obvious priorities:
– first, the development of the institutional framework within a new European context;
– second, adoption of a European Community directive within the national electricity market;
– third, the "green wave" with sustainable development included as not only an economic but also as a social stake in terms of intranational solidarity and social justice;
– fourth, new borders of national and international development considered as specific opportunities to draw upon the competitiveness and productivity made possible through growth in multiservices and international business.

The Necessity of Futures Thinking

An exploratory procedure applied to just one company's future appears inadequate, given the need to reflect broadly on the corporate environment and to question the uncertainty affecting the institutional, economic and technological dimensions. In short, EDF needed to define its stakes in the institutional, economic and technological fields. The question was how to do it. Management wondered if the traditional forecasting and planning approach would be adequate. Jean Bergougnoux, manager of the economic research department, sought the help of Jacques Lesourne in laying down the groundwork of a futures-thinking approach. A team within the economic research department was created to work with Lesourne and to assess the results of futures-thinking exercises.

The first step involved identifying through a systemic and structural analysis the important parameters, major trends and the actors within EDF's internal and external environments. This step enables management or other participants to determine EDF's means and its margin of maneuver. The scenarios envisioned were not to focus solely on energy and economics anymore. Instead they would include social, political, technological and institutional aspects. EDF could no longer simply cross a few hypotheses and actors' strategies to define the most probable scenario. Contrasted scenarios had to be multiplied in order to see a multiple and uncertain future, as well as estimate the company's capacity to develop and adapt to that future. In response to EDF's needs, the following scenario-planning method was developed from 1986 to 1987.

A New Organization: Prospective and Strategy

In 1988, the chief executive officer of EDF introduced a strategic directive in which futures thinking required a strategic aim and did not need to shed light on possible futures. This strategic management process followed four stages:

1) exploration of both environment and future;
2) definition of strategic axes;
3) decisionmaking in accordance with strategic orientations;
4) evaluation of the results and appropriateness of the implementation of these orientations and strategies given the initial objectives.

At this point in EDF's history, futures studies, scenario planning, or *la prospective* had to be clearly linked to strategy, hence the new term prospective stratégique or strategic futures thinking. Given the need to introduce change into the company itself, a "strategic economic futures research" section (DEPS in EDF's corporate organizational chart) was created. In tandem, a futures committee headed by Christian Stoffaës was set up. The "futures mission" within the DEPS was mandated to ensure that the studies produced by the various working groups would be implemented and monitored.

An Effective Program

Several studies were carried out simultaneously every year, so that some forty reports were finalized from 1988 to 1998. At the outset, Jacques Lesourne had suggested as an objective that at least half the studies started by the committee and monitored by the mission should be delivered to the strategic management committee; in other words, with the executive organ that meets with the president and CEO as well as the key managers or officers at EDF. Within the first three years, 80% of the studies were indeed sent to this decisionmaking level. This percentage serves as an indicator of the quality of these studies and the activity of the project leaders.

The futures approach also serves to initiate a collective thinking process within the various units and departments themselves during the preparation of strategic plans. Already in 1989, futures-thinking committees were struck in operations departments in order to shed more light on the decisions for which they were responsible. As a pedagogical exercise, futures thinking was thus extended to an increasingly broader circle. Futures-thinking seminars were initiated at departments in EDF-GDF (Gaz de France) for managers. In fact these seminars became part of the training program for new unit managers.

A Joint Futures-Thinking Exercise

By 1990, other French firms were expressing interest in EDF's methods. The CEO decided to launch a club called Prospective et Entreprises (Futures and Firms) whose members still include large public corporations like Gaz de France, France Télécom, the French railroad (SNCF), the French Post Office, and ELF (now privatized), but also other members, like L'Oréal, the Ministry of Defense and more recently, the Parisian Public Transit System (RATP).

The purpose of the club was to provide a forum where people could meet, share experiences, debate issues, and possibly undertake joint studies on the major stakes and developments affecting the member-corporations within their respective environments.

The club has carried out several timely studies over the past few years. In fact the studies have often foreseen topics of national interest. From the top of the list:

- future of contracts between the state and public corporations;
- French public corporations and EU law;
- future of public utilities in Europe;
- future of social relations within statutory companies in Europe;
- future of retirement plans in France and Europe;
- future of intermediary agencies;
- future of capitalism in France.

The Futures-Thinking Philosophy at EDF

Anticipate in order to Decide

Traditional forecasting and planning methods suited an economic context of regular growth within a stable institutional framework. However, over the past three decades, companies and organizations have recognized the limits of such methods in the form of demand, global competition, industrial restructuring, geopolitical and institutional changes. In today's world, extrapolating from the past to forecast the future is no longer enough.

On the other hand, strategic decisionmaking does not only consider investment choices, the traditional domain of planning and economics. All the major choices involving the future are strategic, e.g. relationships with major partners, alliances, organizational management, investment in human resources.

In the face of uncertainty, the futures-thinking method serves to imagine hypotheses clustered around scenarios, to suggest reactions or strategic options, and to evaluate the alternatives; i.e., compare possible choices.

The First Link in the Managerial Chain

Futures-thinking activities are the first stage of integrated strategic management, as Jean Bergougnoux defined it in 1988. One should ensure that the future has been thoroughly explored before making any decisions. In this respect, a futures-thinking exercise is not a purely intellectual exercise of gathering data, and providing academic conjectures or drafting forecasts. The purpose of the futures-thinking enterprise is to provide those in charge and those making decisions with what they need to know in order to make sound decisions.

The Principles of Corporate Strategic Prospective

The systematic monitoring of developments includes detecting trends and important signals through what is traditionally called scanning in English (veille in French) and observation of the environment. Equally important are a follow-up of strategy and the actions of the company's major institutional, technological, and commercial partners.

The use of experts in future studies enables researchers or managers to base their work on specific analyses carried out by specialized professionals handpicked from either inside or outside the company. Besides expertise, imagination must be mobilized to shake off traditional ways of thinking and to get off the beaten track.

Reactivity and flexibility in terms of adaptation are needed because no single strategic option may be considered valid in as much as the circumstances have not changed. In other words, managers, executives, experts, and all other participants must think and reconsider the situation. Given potential threats and opportunities, futures thinking and scenario building help to imagine the possibilities and propose alarm systems.

The connection between futures thinking and strategy must be respected. They actually form a duo that is complementary yet contrary. Thinking about the future is a functional activity; in other words, an advising activity designed for decisionmakers. It must be clearly distinguished from strategic decisionmaking and its implementation, which depends upon the corporate hierarchy. Futures-thinking activities suggest open action, with a freewheeling, imaginative yet analytical spirit. Once the line between futures thinking and strategy has been drawn; however, strategy must be stable and shared by all in order to be implemented effectively.

Organizing Futures Thinking

Organizational Principles and Structures:

Between 1988 and 1998, futures-thinking activities enjoyed a more structured framework than in the past, and dovetailed with EDF's three-level decisionmaking system, as follows:

1) The futures-thinking committee is responsible for leading and coordinating studies. It comprises the six main mangers or officers of the company (HR, economics, futures thinking and strategy, finance, legal, research, development, marketing) as well as experts from the central administration, and the individuals responsible for futures thinking within the operational departments. The futures-thinking

committee sought not to do everything alone but rather to assist EDF's experts and decisionmakers in their reflection by asking questions and providing techniques or analytical tools.

2) The strategic management committee (CGS), presided by the CEO, brings together members of the administration and the officers. As the main entity mandated to define EDF's strategic orientations, this committee receives various studies from the futures- thinking committee, as well as reports from different committees within the administration. It occasionally receives studies from the operational departments themselves.

3) The economics and futures-thinking department (DEPS) unites the departments in charge of investment planning and rates, among other functions.

This organizational structure ensures the link between futures thinking and strategy by distinguishing the role of experts from that of operational decisionmakers and that of other instances within the company. It also differentiates between the futures-thinking activities of general management and that of the separate operational units.

Managers for production and transportation, for EDF-GDF services, and for equipment are called upon to develop futures studies in their own area. In general, each operational unit in the company is asked to develop its own futures-thinking and strategic methods as they relate to a decisionmaking area considered its own within the preparation of its strategic plan.

Recent restructuring at EDF will probably lead to a revised version of the existing structure but will not likely challenge the overall spirit.

Some Methodological Tools

Most of the tools available ranging from the Delphi to the Mactor method were applied at EDF. Mentioned below are structural analysis, actor analysis, scenario building, and multicriteria analysis.

Structural analysis enables managers or any other participants to draft relevant questions as it provides a systematic panorama of the interactions and mutual dependencies of the parameters that influence the future of a company. This type of analysis also helps identify key variables according to their role as a driver or lever and their impact on the company.

Analysis of actors' strategies, that is the choice of coalitions and their contents, constitute the basic elements of strategic options. In fact, the developments are largely a function of the strategies and movements of major corporate partners.

The combination of multiple hypotheses that can be formulated for the future soon becomes a quagmire. By building coherent scenarios, as well as paths that link these scenarios, we can make contrasted futures understandable and then judge the probability of these scenarios occurring.

Strategic options constitute the choices available to a company in decisionmaking. The consequences of these alternative strategic options are assessed in light of a specific scenario being carried out. Multicriteria analysis evaluates the consequences according to the grid of objectives set by the company including the corporate mission and the company's basic interests.

Open evaluation is an essential rule in this process. A futures-thinking exercise sets its own ethics, primarily to never conclude in a definitive manner. A futures study should simply provide decision-makers with a grid for evaluation purposes plus the instruments needed to make informed strategic decisions.

Permanent Foresight at a Strategic Company

A strategic company must constantly pay attention to what is going on both inside and outside its walls. The futures-thinking committee is responsible for:

– distributing studies which may be made available to the public at large;

– holding training seminars as well as lectures/debates suitable for all those responsible for futures endeavors;

– analyzing and evaluating the current observational and monitoring structures (or creating them) in the departments within all those areas affected by corporate strategy (be it institutional, industrial, technological, commercial or social).

The above structures primarily observe the environment of the company, detect any indicators of change, alert decisionmakers to sensitive changes, and encourage strategic reactivity at the top administrative level.

A Group Learning Experience

Futures thinking at EDF was also designed as a collective pedagogical process that would prepare people to face greater uncertainty and accept the major changes ahead. For when there is a shared future vision, strategic choices virtually impose themselves.

EDF did not opt for a specialized, centralized department but rather a structure that relies upon work carried out by several multidisciplinary teams, dialogue among various managers or directors and the breaking down of traditional barriers. The overarching goal is a permanent exchange of information and ideas as well as the creation of new ways of thinking about the future.

At EDF, studies on the future have always relied on internal expertise first. Outside opinions from universities or consulting firms are nevertheless systematically encouraged through a budget provided to project leaders.

Major Topics

Before the futures thinking committee was created, EDF had undertaken two major futures studies, "EDF and the Future" and "The Future of the Electronuclear Industry". The procedures and methods used therein contributed to the strategic themes and orientations of the initial studies carried out by the futures-thinking committee.

Since 1988, numerous subjects have been explored, thus providing background material for fifty-odd studies under the auspices of the futures-studies committee. As a result, dozens of experts and various departments within EDF worked together. These studies generated a flood of environmental scenarios, some of which did not take into account neighboring notions expressed, albeit in different terms, in other research papers. This multitude, although creative, lead to a certain opaqueness which was lifted only by ensuring that the procedures were set out and linked better. This is the price to be paid in the decentralized exploration of a multiple or pluralistic future. By summarizing the various efforts, a document called "Environmental Scenarios" was produced. It suggested five possible scenarios for the institutional development of EDF. This document provided a base for the studies that the new futures-thinking groups would produce. On the basis of that document, we could outline the following five centers of interest and five transversal themes:

Centers of Interest

The centers or poles of interest create clusters of different studies around a few major interests.

– International pole: brings together the studies related to the future in the EU electricity sector, ranging from the British to the East-European and including internationalization of electricity, the EDF's potential role as a European actor in North Africa (the Maghreb).

– The technological/economic pole directly related to electricity: includes studies on thermal decentralized production, on the partnership between EDF and basic industries, on fuel price developments, means of production, nuclear energy (irradiated fuel, technological foresight in the electronuclear sector, possible nuclear surprises). The study on global warming is also closely linked to technology, whether it focuses on the role of CO_2 or reflects upon how to avoid CO_2 emissions by using electricity produced from nuclear power plants. Lastly the effects of technology on distribution have been explored in future studies on EDF's clientele and client-computer-EDF interfaces. This is the case of the so-called "smart meters".

– The general technological pole affects EDF's situation as an actor in telecommunications or the role of EDF with regard to computerization. It also includes the future of the nuclear industry.

– The institutional pole structures EDF relationships with its various partners, e.g. public authorities, local groups, rural spaces, water legislation, and management of hydraulic resources, industries involved in changing electrical equipment and, in a slightly different register, the situation of EDF as a commercial actor and the future of the EDF-GDF mix. This pole also accounts for corporate research studies on ideological developments and changes related to electricity.

– The internal managerial and social pole covers the social future and role of managerial control as well as the future of human resources with 2010 as a horizon.

Major Transversal Themes

Five major themes stand out in almost all the futures studies:
– the powers of local groups;
– the relationships between the state and company;
– the nature and degree of European integration;
– the deregulation of the electrical system (which enters into the more general deregulation framework);
– the technological changes in electricity production and distribution.
Other key themes:
– the environment, given that EDF strategies must take into account the public's awareness and demands concerning ecology, especially water management;
– the future of irradiated fuels;
– electrical networks;
– industrial safety;
– climatic changes.

Challenges for the Years 2010-2025

EDF in the World to Come

At the dawn of the new millennium, changes appear to be occurring faster than ever before. Fifty years after its inception, EDF is now crossing the threshold into a new world in which international development, management methods, the European electricity market, restructuring of electro-technological and nuclear industries inform the corporate environment. Even if historical movements are progressive, historians like to use dates and events as hooks. After the "after-directive" context (company directive delivered June 20, 1996), the future ceased to be written in the singular. Instead scenarios became plural; the strategic options, very open.

At this point, the president of the EDF requested a futures studies along the lines of "what could EDF look like like in 2010 or 2025?"; "what are the stakes (medium-term 2010) and (long-term 2025)"; "what is involved in terms of preparing EDF and the next decisions to be made?"

Three major themes stand out as priorities in the medium-term: development of the institutional framework in terms of European Union dynamics; renovation of the social; and new frontiers in development. The technological theme should be envisaged as long-term, given the uncertainties surrounding the horizon of technological ruptures (breakdowns or breakthroughs) and the relative weight of the demand for energy and the environmental pressure on technology. The future of the nuclear energy industry is a special case to be considered when reflecting on the future of technology. The absence of CO_2 emissions tips the scales in favor of nuclear energy or balances out the implied waste disposal problem.

Institutional Framework and the European Union

The European community directive on electricity has already changed certain aspects of the EDF's institutional structure, legally established in 1946. Yet still other changes may be expected, especially at the executive level and in the roles played by the respective regulatory agencies at the local, national and European levels.

It will also be necessary to work on the notion of "industrial and financial group" since the EDF group's development should be considered in terms of "maintaining the status of an EPIC" (Public Company of an Industrial and Commercial Nature). Also at stake here is the principle of specialization which becomes an issue of limiting our sphere of activities to our core competencies and developing some room to maneuver with Europe.

Equally important in terms of the institutional framework will be:
– monitoring the process of restructuring in the electricity industry in Europe and the world;
– keeping a clear vision of the legal and economic stakes for the EDF group at a national and European level;
– promoting active strategies that mobilize staff and encourage initiative in terms of dealing with current or potential competitors.

Social Renewal

Beyond problems in changing working relationships, the fundamental question is: What should be done now to keep the social component integrated in EDF's desirable futures? EDF feels that it has time but not much and should act soon!

Without further delay, EDF must outline its paradigm for the company's development in order to guide the various actors involved.

Otherwise, there is a real yet underestimated risk that changes and decisions will be postponed and the potential or opportunities afforded by changes in EDF's environment will be jeopardized.

In order to flesh out the key long-term questions on national and international development, the following elements of a long-term policy should be considered:

– the international sector offers tremendous opportunities. EDF should seize well targeted opportunities in order to benefit from its sources both in terms of the competitivity and productivity inherent in international growth;

– downstream development is not an end in itself but rather a means of reinforcing EDF's positions and of preparing for the competition's attack;

– EDF's durability lies in lasting alliances with local groups. This solid foundation should be consolidated and supported in both qualitative and quantitative terms.

Technological Challenges and Sustainable Development

Visibility right up to the horizon 2025 remains high. Although during this period the world demand for energy should double, the primary source of energy and the conversion methods are ostensibly the same. The foundation of electricity production will remain fossil fuels, existing nuclear energy, increased hydroelectric equipment, and the development of renewable energy, where possible. The main uncertainties will come from environmentalist pressures. Here the overarching question is whether sustainable development is possible in both the developed and developing worlds.

Will we see harmonious use of the earth's resources in the upcoming thirty years? Will regional imbalances grow? Will we rise to the challenge of paying the ecological price of growth?

Strategy and Futures

Perhaps more than in other large companies, EDF's futures-thinking and scenario-building procedures are organically and institutionally tied to strategic decisionmaking. It is not enough to supply decisionmakers with a backdrop for global scenarios or to draw their attention to one particular eventuality. The idea is to define, evaluate and provide probability rates for a limited number of strategic options. From this perspective, penetration of the futures-thinking process throughout the organization is essential even beyond the pedagogical goal of making people aware of the future. Assessing a posteriori the results of futures- thinking studies when confronted with both reality and the strategic options that those studies inspired thus becomes extremely important.

Futures thinking, strategy and operational decisionmaking must interact while remaining distinct. In this way, the strategic company can succeed in acting not only on the current "front" but also on uncertain futures which yield both threats and opportunities.

ICW 2010: Looking for a New Individual Combat Weapon

This case study, part of a project code-named ICW 2010, includes information from research carried out on behalf of the French Ministry of Defense, Armed Forces (DGA), in 1989. In fact, we thank Mr. Michel de Lagarde of the DGA for his kind permission to publish this remarkable example.

The ICW 2010 exercise was supported methodologically by Michel Godet, who was assisted by Pierre Chapuy and Isabelle Menant of the Groupe d'Etudes Ressources Prospective Aménagement (Gerpa). With the help of complementary studies, the ICW exercise led to the design of a prototype "multi-arm-multi-projectile" weapon, abbreviated as PAPOP in French. It is an individual combat weapon (ICW) with indirect aiming that enables an infantry soldier to fire upon stationary, armored or moving targets with specific projectiles.

The ICW 2010 remains remarkable as one of the rare published cases in which a futures-thinking exercise led to concrete action. What makes this case all the more fascinating in terms of futures-thinking endeavors is the rediscovery of morphological analysis. Somehow morphological analysis had been ignored since the late 1970s. Since then, however, scenario building "by method" has become almost systematic, be it for partial or full scenarios. Perhaps the inventor of morphological analysis, Fritz Zwicky, did indeed succeed in making invention a routine!

Actually this case also reminds us why morphological analysis was forgotten. The method quickly leads to a morphological space rich in scenarios and technologically possible solutions. So the quandary becomes choosing only a handful. The famous, out-of-print book by Eric Jantsch (1967) on the topic developed the selection process at length; however, microcomputing, notably the Morphol software package, has helped in navigating through morphological spaces. In this instance, computers also enabled us to develop Multipol, a simple and appropriable multicriteria selection method for uncertain futures.

How to Define a New ICW?

The mandate from Armed Forces Headquarters was for a "brain trust", or expert panel, including representatives from the Infantry Center for Tactical Studies and Experimentation, the army's technology department and the DGA. The objective was to carry out a study that would define and design a future weapon system for infantry. Participants included Lt. Col. Fluhr, Lt. Col. Navec, ICETA (chief engineer) Durand, Messrs Dupuy, de Lagarde, Rouger, and Senior Medical Officer Gorzerino.

The initial idea was a study on what this weapon could be in terms of tactical use of the infantry, the potential of various types of technology, as well as the ICW's technological and industrial limitations (horizon 2010). The objective was to highlight the most promising techniques and technologies which could then be acquired or developed to meet the specifications determined for this new weapon.

This pre-feasibility study was designed to define a weapon corresponding to NATO's specifications for an individual combat weapon (ICW). These included the following:
– incapacitation of targets that are heavily protected and invisible behind a mask or in a shelter;
– increase in the area of engagement and efficiency of the grenadier-infantry soldier;
– incapacitate moving targets from a specific distance.

If the last two can be achieved by improving classic weapons firing small caliber ammunition with kinetic energy, the first specification would impose a radically new design.

Approach Adopted

With a view to organizing their reflection, participants (the brain trust) decided to use structural analysis to highlight key variables likely to affect this future weapon. Why structural analysis? The simple answer is that the method was very frequently used at that time and was found in the first chapters of my book.

Yet three years down the road, the group had not reached any satisfactory conclusions. Some of the difficulties encountered stemmed from the French army's rotation system at headquarters. For example, the futures-thinking group included officers from across the country, named to posts in different places and at different times. Over three years, the constant turnover had affected the quality of the exercise. Another problem was the seemingly innocent shortcut that the participants discovered. They used to fill out the structural analysis matrix individually rather than collectively in a workshop. At the risk of being redundant, we emphasize here that this type of activity must be a structured group effort.

As a result of the problems outlined above, the DGA contacted us to help pick up the pace. We can not really say whether or not the tool already chosen was the most appropriate; however, it was most important for the group's self-confidence and faith in futures-thinking tools to demonstrate how to carry out a successful structural analysis.

We advised the group to employ the following futures tools:
– strategic futures workshops, anticipate missions, capacities and equipment with a horizon 2010;

– structural analysis and Micmac to pinpoint key variables in the strategic environment, ICW military effects, limitations and specifications;
– morphological analysis to scan the field of possibilities and find practical solutions in order to profile the ICW;
– Multipol method for multicriteria analysis in an uncertain future to select the most interesting solutions.

The work really consisted in drawing up a list based partially on workshop results. This voluntarily limited list would, nevertheless, represent the system variables for the future ICW and enable us to construct a structural analysis matrix. Filling out and processing this matrix allowed participants to position these variables on planes, along axes, according to their influence and relative dependence. Analysis of the variables led to a graph and the selection of key variables used in the study of four technical components and six essential selection criteria. On the basis of these elements, the futures-thinking group carried out a morphological analysis. Using the Multipol method, participants could trace the most compelling configurations of the ICW in terms of strategy, technology and economics with the horizon 2010.

Structural Analysis and Key Variables

The futures-thinking circle was reinvigorated through workshops and opened slightly to include new participants. Members of the working committee led a collective session on the following:
– the future environment, in order to identify the stakes and threats. Each group member was asked as an individual (silently) and then collectively to list strategic, technological, economic, and socio-organizational changes, as well as determine desirable, feared, and anticipated consequences. They also were asked to identify the actors involved and the stakes;
– the armed forces' missions, capabilities and equipment adapted to this environment. This dimension would allow participants to see which capacities needed to be adapted. Again individual and collective reflection focused on the characteristics required according to capability and equipment.

Also on the agenda, a hunt for clichés, organized by the armed forces, again with a 2010 horizon. Here each participant was asked to list individually then collectively the clichés or conventional wisdom "out there" on the army, its missions, capabilities, equipment, and relations with NATO partners, in 1989 and from then to 2010. Lastly, the group proved or disproved each of the main clichés presented.

The List of 57 Variables

The structural analysis method seeks to highlight key variables, hidden or not, in order to ask the right questions and encourage participants to think about counter-intuitive aspects or behavior within the system. In this instance, structural analysis was enriched by the use of the Micmac approach. (Note: Micmac is the French acronym for Matrix of Crossed Impact Multiplications Applied to a Classification.)

What is surprising does not have to be confusing but should elicit serious thinking and trigger extra imagination. For example, structural analysis aims to assist futures-thinking groups, but it does not replace them. The method does not detail systemic operations but rather highlights the main characteristics of the system's organization.

This particular structural analysis ran for three months. The working group drew up a list of variables following the workshops. These 57 varieties were then classified in different groups: environmental variables (Friend/Enemy, Combat, Technico-political); effect variables (Negative for Enemy (ENI) and positive for Friend); restriction and quality variables (ICW use).

Using variable "index cards", each variable on the list was defined completely by the members of the working group, and then validated collectively. Participants took an initial census, per variable studied, of the relations of influence and dependence with the other elements on the list and then ferreted out the technological elements, with possible configurations, as seen below.

Structural Analysis and Key Variables

The direct influence of each variable on the set of other variables are illustrated in matrix form. Each element of the matrix represents an influence (0 = no direct relationship of influence on the two variables considered; 1 = a direct relationship of influence). We also took into account the level of influence between two variables. The following convention was used: 1 = low relationship; 2 = average; 3 = strong; P = potential relationship. Note that P may indicate what is now a nonexistent or almost nonexistent relationship, but the system may make it probable or at least possible in a relatively distant future. P levels were also given 0-3 ratings.

The working group filled in the matrix during a three-day meeting. Participants systematically considered all the eventual relations between variables.

Some 3,249 relationships; i.e., 57×57, were considered direct influence given priority status. For example, direct influence i on j or direct influence j on i, by excluding the indirect influences, those which pass by an intermediary variable. Obviously it is important to distinguish the direct influence relationships from those that are not! In our experience, a good matrix rating would reveal 15% to 25% direct influences, according to the dimensions of the matrix. The rate reached here (23%) thus seems correct.

List of Variables (A): Environment

Variable Category	N°	Variables Retained
Friend	1	Characteristics inherent to soldier bearing ICW
	2	State of soldier bearing ICW in combat
	3	Individual equipment of basic unit
	4	Group equipment of basic unit (Friend)
	5	Organic arms of basic unit (Friend)
	6	Firing support possessed by basic unit (Friend)
	7	Basic unit's actions (Friend)
	8	Operational capability of the basic unit (Friend)
Enemy	9	Characteristics inherent to eneny soldier
	10	State of enemy soldier in combat
	11	Individual weapons and equipment of enemy soldier
	12	Group equipment of the basic unit (Enemy)
	13	Organic arms of the basic unit (Enemy)
	14	Firing support that the basic unit possesses (Enemy)
	15	Concept of enemy force use (Enemy unit action)
	16	Characteristics of enemy's modes of action in combat
	17	Operational capability of the basic unit (Enemy)
Combat	18	Priority enemy targets for the ICW (Enemy soldier on foot)
	19	Secondary enemy targets for the ICW
	20	Numeric balance of power
	21	Theater of war
	22	Conditions of operations
Technical-Economic Aspects	23	Technical changes affecting the IWC 2010
	24	Interoperability/Functionality of ICW
	25	Political image of a French ICW
	26	Army's budgetary limits
	27	French industrial policy
	28	Industrial policies of Frace's partners

List of Variables (B): Effects to Be Produced

Variable Category	N°	Variables Retained
Negative Effects on Enemy	29	Pinpoint antipersonnel effect sought
	30	Area antipersonnel effect sought
	31	Antivehicle and anti-light-armored vehicle effet
	32	Antitank effect sought (degradation, firing function, mobility function
	33	Antihelicopter effect sought (dissusion)
	34	Antimine effect sought (detection, forward release)
	35	Degradation of the enemy's means of firing assistance
Positive Effects on Friend	36	Detection acquisition and localization of enemy
	37	Continuous all-weather combat
	38	Symbolic nature of ICW

List of Variables (C): Restrictions & Qualities

Variable Category	N°	Variables Retained
Concept	39	Concept of dependability of the arms system
	40	Functional organization of the arms system
	41	Power source
	42	Mass of arms system with initial issue
Technical	43	Nature of projectile
	44	Aiming
	45	External ballistics
	46	Terminal ballistics
	47	Fire power
Use	48	Ease of use in peace time
	49	Ease of use of ICW in approach-march combat situation
	50	Minimal amount of prepartion time to fire ICW
	51	Ease of use of ICW in firing
	52	Discretion and invulnerability of ICW
	53	Overall tactical efficiency of antipersonnel (Friend)
	54	Appropriateness of ICW to threat
$	55	Cost of ICW possession over 25 years
	56	Competitiveness
	57	Distribution of ICW

ICW Variable Card n° 29

VARIABLE CATEGORY	:	Type B Negative effects to be produced on ENI (Enemy).
TITLE	:	Effect sought: timely anti-personnel at a set distance (imperative).
DEFINITION	:	✓ Incapacitate an enemy solider, in the open at a set distance. ✓ Once hit, the enemy soldier must not be able to return fire and must be incapacitated for at least 7 days. ✓ Being incapacitated means: – definitive destruction (death); – long-term suppression (7 days). Lethality must be preferred over suppression.
KEY POINTS	:	✓ Incapacitate an enemy solider at specific distance? ✓ Immediate or temporary incapacitation? ✓ Immediate of temporary suppression?
INFLUENTIAL VARIABLES	:	18, 30 à 36, 54, 55.
INFLUENCED VARIABLES	:	2, 5, 7, 10, 11, 23, 30 à 33, 35, 38 à 40, 42 à 47, 53 à 56.

Participants should always keep in mind the limits of structural analysis. The first limit stems from the subjective nature of the list of variables. Caution has, of course, been exercised in that information has been gathered and condensed in the "variable cards". Moreover, given the logistics involved, the number of variables can not exceed a few dozen. An arbitrary regrouping of the subvariables is the next necessary step. This is both the advantage and disadvantage of the method.

The second limitation stems from the subjective nature of filling in a matrix. A matrix is never reality. It is a means of looking at reality, like a snapshot. To use the photograph analogy, structural analysis reveals things that translate part of reality, as well as the talent of the photographer and quality of the photographic equipment. In fact, examples from a French governmental commission (Commission Boissonnat) on labor have shown that structural analysis may actually reveal group subjectivity, lead participants to hold their reactions in check to encourage consistency in the group or challenge certain clichés.

With the limits of structural analysis in mind, we can review the results obtained and their essential contribution. The method serves to structure ideas around a problem systematically. The obligation to ask thousands of questions prompts participants to discover relationships that would never have been considered otherwise. Overall, the structural analysis matrix serves as a probe and provides the futures group with a shared language.

The more a variable has an effect on other variables, the more influential it is. The same applies if that variable is influenced by others more than it depends on them. In the end, each variable is matched with an influence indicator (within one basis point of the total influences normed for the system) and a direct dependence indicator for the entire system.

By reading the matrix, we can classify the variables by their
– level of direct influence: importance of influence of a variable on the whole system, obtained through the total of links created per line;
– level of direct dependence: degree of dependence of a variable, obtained by the total of links created per column.

Plan Influence/dependence

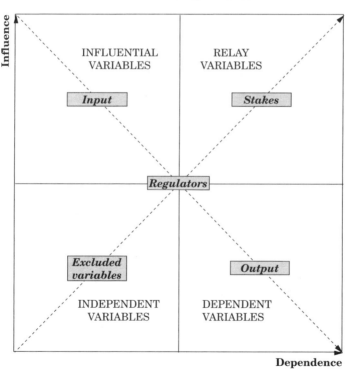

The full set of variables may thus be positioned one basis point within the plane of influence (ordinate) and the plane of dependence (coordinate) since the values of influence and dependence are normed.

Secondly, if we take into account the feedback effect in which each variable is involved, we can hierarchize the variables according to

ICW 20100 Structural Analysis Matrix

	N°	Variables Retained	1	2	3	4	5	6	7	8	9	10	11	12	13	14	15	16	17
VARIABLES A		**ENVIRONMENT**																	
FRIEND	1	Characteristics inherent to soldier bearing ICW	0	3															
	2	State of soldier bearing ICW in combat	0						2	2									
	3	Individual equipment of basic unit(Friend)	2	0															
	4	Group equipment of basic unit	2	1	0					2									
	5	Organic arms of basic unit (Friend)	1			1	0		2	2									
	6	Firing support possessed by basic unit (Friend)	1					0	2			1							1
	7	Basic unit's actions (Friend)	1	1			1	0				1							
	8	Operational capability of the basic unit (Friend)	2					3	0										
ENEMY	9	Characteristics inherent to enemy soldier									0	3							
	10	State of enemy soldier in combat									0								3
	11	Individual weapons and equipmentof enemy soldier	1	2							2	0							1
	12	Group equipement of basic unit (Enemy)									2	1	0						2
	13	Organic arms of basic unit (Friend)		1							1		1	0		2			2
	14	Firing support that the basic unit possesses (Enemy)	2								1				0				
	15	Concept of enemy force use (Enemy unit action)	2	1	1	1	1	3	1		1	3	3	3	3	0	2	2	
	16	Characteristics of enemy's mode of action in combat	3					1								1	0		
	17	Operational capability of the basic unit (Enemy)									2						3	0	
COMBAT	18	Priority enemy targets for the ICW (Enemy soldier on foot)			2	1	3	1	2										
	19	Secondary enemy targets for the ICW			1	2	2	P	1										
	20	Numeric balance of power	3				3	3	3		2								
	21	Theater of war	2	3	3	2	2	3	2		2	2	2	3	2	2		3	
	22	Conditions of operations	3	2	2			3	3	1	3	1	2			3	3	2	1
TECHNICAL-	23	Technical changes affecting the ICW 2010			2	2	2	1				2	2	2	1				
ECONOMIC	24	Interoperability/Functionality of ICW																	
ASPECTS	25	Political image of a French ICW	1																
	26	Army's budgetary limits			1	1	1												
	27	French industrial policy																	
	28	Industrial policies of France's partners																	
VARIABLES B		**EFFECTS EXPECTED**																	
NEGATIVE	29	Pinpoint antipersonnel effect sought	1				1		1			3	P						
EFFECTS	30	Area antipersonnel effect sought	1				2		1			3	P						
ON ENEMY	31	Antivehicle and anti-light-armored vehicle effect	1				1					1							
	32	Antitank effect sought (degradation, firing function, mobility funtion)	1				1					1							
	33	Antihelicopter effect sought (dissuasion)	1				1					1							
	34	Antimine effect sought (detection, forward release)	1							1									
	35	Degradation of the enemy's means of firing assistance	1				1		1			1							
POSITIVE	36	Detection acquisition and localization of enemy	1			1	1			1									
EFFECTS	37	Continuous all-weather combat	1					2	2			1							
ON FRIEND	38	Symbolic nature of IWC	3							1									
VARIABLES C		**RESTRICTIONS & QUALITIES**																	
CONCEPT	39	Concept of dependability of the arms system	1																
	40	Functional organization of the arms system																	
	41	Power source																	
	42	Mass of arms system with initial issue	2	1															
TECHNICAL	43	Nature of projectile		2								1	2						
	44	Aiming	1																
	45	External ballistics																	
	46	Terminal ballistics		P								2	2						
	47	Fire power	2				1		1										
USE	48	Ease of use in peace time	1							1									
	49	Ease of use of ICW in approach-march combat situation	1							1									
	50	Minimal amount of prepartion time to fire ICW																	
	51	Ease of use of ICW in firing	1																
	52	Discretion and invulnerability of ICW			P														
	53	Overall tactical efficiency of antipersonnel (Friend)					1		1										
	54	Appropriateness of ICW to threat	1				1		1										
ECONOMIC	55	Cost of ICW possession over 25 years																	
	56	Competitiveness																	
	57	Distribution of ICW	1									P							

18 19 20 21 22	23 24 25 26 27 28	29 30 31 32 33 34 35	36 37 38	39 40 41 42	43 44 45 46 47	48 49 50 51 52 53 54	55 56 57

Plan Influence × Dependence : Micmac

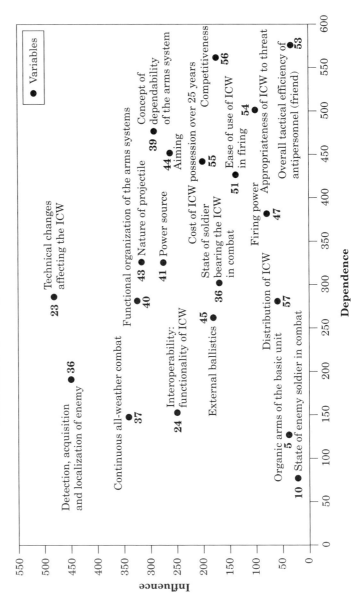

influence and dependence. In effect, the Micmac method does allow participants to see the influence that one variable exercises on another through a third, a fourth, even a fifth. The direct and indirect influences of the variable represent the system the most realistically. Highlighted are the determining factors (main determinants) of the situation under investigation. The input variables and result or output variables help participants understand the organization and structuring of the system under the microscope.

The Micmac grid or plane follows in a simplified form; i.e., it does not retain the ICW external variables, which are essentially input variables, and the excluded variables. According to the working committee, the so-called key variables which have an above-average influence are also essentially relay variables. The variables with above-average dependence are output variables

What to Do with the Key Variables?

True confessions from an expert consulting team: after structural analysis, we felt a bit sheepish. How could we use these results to look for new technological solutions for the ICW? This question seemed unanswerable, an intellectual roadblock of sorts, until the umpteenth rereading of the variables reminded us of morphological analysis, as invented by Fritz Zwicky in the 1940s for American military applications.

In concrete terms, we simply needed to recognize that nine of the key variables were technological components of the ICW and that six were evaluation criteria, e.g. continuous all-weather combat, pinpoint antipersonnel effects, side effects, possession costs, competitiveness, ease of use in peace time. The last criteria were put aside initially.

These nine technological components of the ICW (functional organization of the weapon and projectile, energy sources, type of projectile, aiming, materials, etc.) may lead to several configurations, possible technical answers, which may have already been at least partially listed through the "variable cards". Although the numbers may still boggle some, the next steps are simpler, so to speak. There were thousands of possible technological solutions so that the question was where to start and how to decide on a limited number of new solutions that meet the objectives set out.

The ICW's Morphological Space or 1001 Solutions

The ICW was considered a nine-component system in which each component can take a specific number of configurations. In the example given here, the source of energy may take the following configurations: solid, liquid, gaseous or electric. Here are a few other configurations as defined during this exercise:

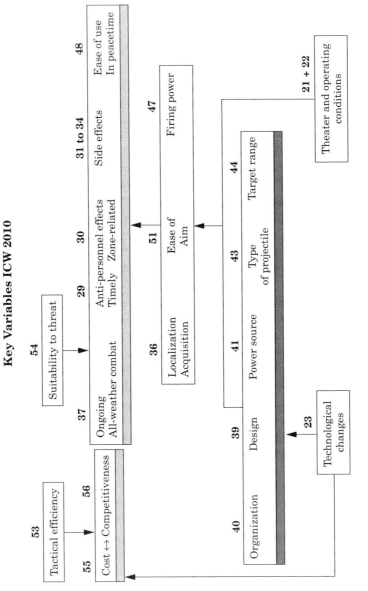

Key Variables ICW 2010

– Monoarm, or one type of launcher (e.g. FAMAS);

– Polyarm, or several type of launchers (e.g. M16);

– Single (mono) projectile, or the firing of one projectile of one type only, at a time;

– Polyprojectile, or the simultaneous firing of several projectiles identical (or not) or the successive firing of different types of projectiles.

The array of technological solutions identified through this decomposition is called "morphological space". Each solution corresponds to a path in the morphological space. This path links the configurations of each component at a rate of one configuration per component. The ICW morphological space represents 15,552 combinations, or nine components with respectively 2,3,6,3,6,3,2,2, and 2 configurations.

Using this method raises several issues related to the limits and the illusion of massive mathematics. First, the selection of components is delicate and requires serious, in-depth thinking like that also carried out in this study using structural analysis. Actually the number of components and configurations multiplies quickly so that the system soon becomes unwieldy. On the other hand, an overly limited number of components would impoverish the system, so there is a need to find a compromise like the one adopted in the AIF case. The compromise always implies retaining those components which are the most determinant. It is important to pay attention to the independence of the components, also called dimensions, and not confuse them with configurations, also called hypotheses.

This scan of possible solutions within today's imagined field may appear exhaustive because of the exponential mathematics. Yet the field has not been definitively surveyed because it evolves over time. By omitting one component or simply one configuration essential to the future, we run the risk of ignoring a facet of the field of possible futures.

To prove our point, let us switch to a hypothetical past case, if this method had been applied to the function "knowing what time it is" in the early 1950s or 1960s participants would have imagined everything except the quartz watch!

Lastly, the user or participant can end up drowning in numbers. The very stating of solutions becomes difficult once up in the hundreds. For a system with four components and four configurations, we start with 256 possible combinations already. How can we outline the useful morphological subspace, or subset of useful solutions, under these conditions?

A Vast Morphological Space: Fifty Solutions Selected

Reducing the morphological space is not only desirable but also necessary because the human brain can not explore one by one the possible paths generated and it is futile to identify combinations which will be

ICW Morphological Space

Compnent		N°	Configurations					
Functions	ARM	40	mono-arm 1	poly-arm 2				
Organization	PROJECTILE		none 1	monoprojectile 2	polyprojectile 3			
Type of projectile		43	kinetic 1	explosive 2	incendiary 3	chemical 4 biological	rays 5	multiple-effects 6
Aiming		44	direct visual 1 (market, optical, line of fire no target device)	indirect visual 2 (sreeen)	non-visual 3 (radar IR, laser)			
Power source		41	solid 1	liquid 2	gas 3	electricity 4	nuclear 5	mechanical 6
WEAPON DESIGN								
Maintenance			modular 1	non-modular 2	consumable 3			
Functions		39	functional chain 1	fonctional bloc 2				
Internal kinetic of ICW			moving parts 1	non-moving parts 2				
Materials			classic materials 1	non-classic materials 2				

rejected once the selection criteria (technical, economic, etc.) are taken into account. Some choices have to be made in order to identify the fundamental components with regard to the criteria. In the case of ICW, we opted to follow a four-part procedure.

Selection Criteria and Policies

Here participants had to identify the economic, technological and tactical selection criteria that would enable them to evaluate and pick out the best paths (technological solutions) from the array of possible paths (morphological space) prior to morphological analysis. The following criteria were retained from the structural analysis: continuous all-weather combat, pinpoint antipersonnel effects, side effects, possession costs, competitiveness, ease of use in peace time.

Different weighting systems for the criteria defined the various policies. In this respect, two policies were defined: economic and military in accordance with the principle that participants had to retain solutions corresponding to all the military objectives and economic restrictions. The economic policy successfully integrates the cost of owning the weapon over a 25-year period and competitivity but also covers the continuous combat or side effects; whereas the military policy favors something suitable to the threat, e.g. continuous combat, antipersonnel effects and side effects, but also considers competitiveness.

Weighting Criteria for Each Policy

Criteria	Policies	
	"Economic"	"Military"
❶ Cost	6	1
❷ Competitiveness	4	3
❸ Continuous, all-weather combat	3	5
❹ Anti-personnel effects	1	5
❺ Side effects	2	3
❻ Ease of use in peace time	2	1

Pinpointing the Main Components and Technological Incompatibilities

Prior to assessing the solutions, we believed some pruning was needed. It was decided that an initial reduction of the morphological space would mean keeping only those components, among the nine key variables identified, which seemed to be the most determinant given the criteria already mentioned and the policies defined using these criteria. For this to work, the components were classified according to the criteria. To determine the main components, each one was graded on a scale of 0 to 5 in terms of impact on the criteria, e.g., none, very weak, average, strong, very strong.

After working individually, group members reached a strong consensus that enabled them to retain the following four components:
 – organization of the weapon;
 – organization of the projectile;
 – nature of the projectile;
 – aiming.

The result applied to both policies considered, the economic and military, after a weighting of the coefficients per policy.

This procedure enabled us to examine, as a priority, four main components out of the nine initially considered. The original morphological space of 15,552 possibilities was thus reduced to a useful subspace of some one-hundred solutions. In other words, the group was able to reduce the space by a factor of 150.

A review of technical incompatibilities then enabled participants to eliminate a healthy 50% of the solutions.

From Evaluating Solutions to Choosing the PAPOP

We then evaluated the various remaining solutions according to each economic and military policy; in other words, for each weighting of the criteria. Our assessment enabled us to set up a classification of these fifty-odd solutions. (The Multipol software classifies this type of data quickly.) To do so, we graded each solution according to the six criteria retained. By applying the corresponding weight to each policy, we got two grades for each solution. Two classification systems were thus created, as the following diagram shows. When compared, we could discern the hard core 22 solutions which included:
 – best solutions for the overall set of criteria and the policies (in top ten classification);
 – average ranking solutions or those with one grade in one classification system and rising in the other classification system (from tenth to twentieth position);
 – excellent solutions in terms of certain criteria only and maintained by a particular member of the working committee.

According to the chart, the combination 2363 is classified first, according to military policy and fifteenth according to economic policy.

The twenty-two solutions were found in the deep core of the useful morphological space and then regrouped by family. In other words, they appeared according to their similarity or identical solutions to one of two configurations.

Each of these families and the twenty-two solutions was analyzed and evaluated in detail with special attention paid to the configurations linked to the five secondary components.

ICW Morphological Space with Four Key Components

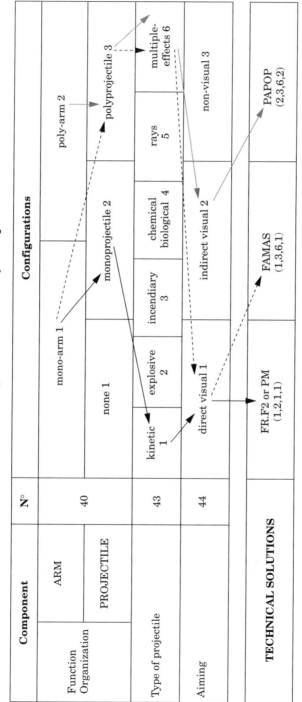

Wrap-up and Comparison of Economic and Military Rankings (Extracts)

Solutions				Military Policy Ranking	Economic Policy Ranking
OA	OP	P	V		
2	3	6	3	1	15
1	3	6	3	2	4
2	3	6	2	3	9
2	1	5	3	4	18
1	2	6	3	5	5
1	3	2	3	6	13
1	2	2	3	7	8
2	3	2	3	8	35
2	3	6	1	9	13
1	3	6	2	10	6
1	3	6	1	11	1
2	3	1	3	11	34
1	2	6	2	13	3
1	3	1	3	14	22
2	1	5	2	15	20
1	1	5	3	16	23
2	3	2	2	17	33
1	2	6	1	18	2
1	3	2	2	19	20
1	2	1	3	20	12
2	3	2	1	21	27

Abbreviations: OA: Organization Arm; OP: Organization Projectile; P: Profile of projectile; V: Aiming.

This last phase enabled the group to advance the following conclusions:

– analysis and reflection on the different components of the arms system, so that the nature of the projectile plays a determining role in defining the ICW;

– given the horizon, use of a radioactive arms system was excluded for considerations related essentially to the battlefield environment. (Note that the concept of a biochemical warfare system was also excluded);

– the four remaining concepts could be classified in two categories: innovative concepts with multi-effect, explosive or incendiary projectiles, a classic concept using kinetic projectiles which would be an improvement on existing systems.

The study also revealed a certain number of conclusions considered transversal:
- interest in a single-arm weapon for mass use;
- ease of use and cost;
- key role of fire-control in continuous all-weather combat;
- advantage of a single projectile weapon being multi-effect and the innovation of a "polyarm multiprojectile" weapon of less complexity yet high performance overall in terms of the evaluation criteria.

After these additional studies, the PAPOP was designed. The "infantryman's weapon for the 21st century", it is original as a multi-arm-multiprojectile weapon that uses an explosive ammunition launcher and a kinetic ammunition launcher. The PAPOP met the needs expressed in terms of the following essential criteria:
- explosive ammunitions set-off by a triggering device programmed to follow a path to achieve a high probability of hitting camouflaged targets;
- high caliber, which, combined with strong initial strength, leads to a strong, specific impulsion. The idea being to obtain a high probability that the target will be incapacitated with its NATO protection;
- effective fire-control, assistance in programming for the soldier firing and indirect aiming will allow the soldier to fire from a sheltered spot.

At this juncture, two lessons in morphological analysis should be reviewed. First, morphological analysis imposes a structured form of thinking about the components and configurations to be considered and allows for a systematic scanning of the field of possible futures. Although perhaps initially overwhelming, the mathematical formulae must not paralyze the thinking process in some form of "analsis paralysis". The useful morphological subspace can be reduced to one- tenth or one one-hundredth of its original size. To do so, selection criteria are introduced. For example, the multicriteria method Multipol, plus the restrictions of exclusion or preference. The Smic-Prob-Expert method allows for the probabilization of the combinations of configurations.

Lastly, after this exercise, the group declared that the use of the various methods had been a productive "detour" in structuring and organizing its thoughts, especially on the definition of ICW key variables using structural analysis to unearth the technological components and selection criteria as well as to analyze and evaluate the concepts of weapons systems using morphological analysis and multicriteria evaluation. The participants also emphasized how much more useful these methods were when the user remains aware of the inherent limits and respects certain conditions for their application.

7

CASE STUDIES IN THE SERVICE SECTOR

IT5: Global Scenarios

In May 1992, the ECRC (European Computer-Industry Research Center) embarked on a futures or foresight study of the European IT industry with the year 2000 as a horizon. Entitled "Information Technology in the year Two Thousand Think Tank" the code name soon became IT5 for obvious reasons. Michel Godet and Pierre Chapuy helped the IT5 group of economists and researchers from Bull, ICL, Siemens and the ECRC pool examine the impact of new technology, regulation, and globalization. Structural and morphological analysis, cross impact analysis plus global scenario building were the key tools used by the group. In fact this case study develops the scenarios drafted by the IT5 group for the international environment. With hindsight, we can appreciate the group's perspicacity and effective use of futures tools.

Only four possible scenarios were selected out of the dozen suggested. Note that the content of the other subsystems has been kept confidential due to its strategic nature. Part of this case was published in an article co-authored with Gérard Comyn, Managing Director (ECRC) in *Futures,* April 1994.

The group started its activities with a structural analysis where the interrelationships between some 60 key variables of the system were studied. These key variables were grouped into five subsystems:

1) international (geopolitical and economic) context of the 1990s;
2) autonomous technological determining factors;
3) infrastructures of the IT and communication systems;
4) strategies and actors' games;
5) market trends.

Each of these subsystems led to a morphological analysis seeking to identify the various possible states or configurations for each variable or component of each subsystem. The possible scenarios correspond to combinations of possible states. This case study presents the scenarios built by the IT5 group for the international context (first subsystem) only.

Scanning Global Scenarios

It is important not to confuse the dimensions or key components of the scenarios (demographic, technological, economic political, social...) with the configurations that each of these components can present. This is where morphological analysis works wonders.

There is only one initial hurdle: A system made up of four components, each having four configurations, will in principle have 256 ($4 \times 4 \times 4 \times 4$) possible states. How can we steer through this morphological space without being swamped by the sheer number of possible combinations? One answer is provided by the combined utilization of morphological analysis and probabilization of combinations of configurations (interplay of hypotheses) through the Smic-Prob-Expert method.

The originator of the morphological method, F. Zwicky, envisaged a method that would turn invention into a routine, commonplace procedure. Morphological analysis often proves useful in stimulating the imagination, helping to identify hitherto unknown products or processes, and scanning the field of possible futures scenarios. The principle underlying the method is extremely straightforward. The system or function under study is broken down into sub-systems or components. These components must be as independent as possible and yet listed as exhaustively as possible to represent the totality of the system. This field of possible combinations is called the "morphological space". (See case studies in chapters six and seven for examples.) Naturally there are constraints, e.g. technical incompatibility, which make several families of solutions unworkable, thus reducing the morphological space. It is also possible to give preference to those combinations of configurations which appear more propitious than others, in terms of such criteria as development costs, safety factors, feasibility, etc.

The Geopolitical Context of the 1990s

IT5 participants stated the obvious: the world is changing. The geopolitical, monetary, energy, technological, economic and social environment around us, will undergo profound upheaval in the next ten to fifteen years. By definition, futures-thinking activities with a time horizon of 2000 are easier to run than up to the year 2010. In particular, the horizon 2000 enables us to disregard the consequences of the main change to occur in the coming decades, a major demographic change.

The Seven Components from A to G

We try to identify these earth-shaking changes through various components:

A.	Demography and its imbalances
B, C.	Geopolitical context and the role of the Eastern countries
D.	European uncertainty
E, F.	Conditions of globalization and trade
G.	Perspective of growth.

A. Demographic Imbalances and the South-North and East-West Migratory Flows

The demographic explosion of the poorest countries and demographic decline of the richest countries is a prevailing trend which, if sustained for two or three decades, will modify the situation worldwide and disrupt our societies. For instance, the population of Europe in 2020 will be comparable to that of Nigeria or Brazil. In 1990, the population of the southern shore of the Mediterranean exceeded the population of the northern shore. If the current trend were to continue, by 2030 the southern shore would be twice as populous as the northern shore.

The apparent demographic stagnation in developed countries stems from their slowing birth rate, a trend which started in the mid-1960s in both Western and Eastern industrial countries. The United States, Japan and Europe are no longer able to ensure the replacement of current generations. Moreover, in terms of age, third world countries have increasingly larger and younger populations. The perspective of migratory flows from eastern countries will certainly raise pressure to introduce controls and limit the immigration flows, which will inevitably engender new problems in East-West relationships.

Of course these projections are not forecasts and will probably not correspond to the future reality, especially given migratory pressures. By the year 2030 some of today's minorities could represent 20% of the total population in countries like Germany, France or England.

Three configurations are taken into account for the demographic trends in the Western countries:

A1. Aging of the population, immigration control, ethnic conflicts.

A2. Migratory flows from the eastern and southern countries to the West, with the corresponding integration problems.

A3. New babyboom in the West and acceptable migratory flows.

B, C. Uncertainties due to the Lack of a Regulator

The absolute value of a power does not prevent its relative decline. The United States currently represents only 22% of the world's aggregated GDP, as compared to 40% in 1955. The USA may no longer be powerful enough to impose itself as regulator (as in a bipolar world), but it is still powerful enough to play a disruptive role, since it retains a minority freeze on the world system and is thus capable of preventing any other regulator from taking its place in a multipolar world.

In other words, fluctuations in American economic policy could themselves raise inflation rates around the globe. In the meantime, we share the hypothesis presented by certain economists about the uncertainty over exchange rates, with the dollar between 0.8 € and 1.2 €. Although the scale of this uncertainty may be hard to accept, it would be irresponsible not to take it into account.

On the other hand, Japan, which may have approximately 10% of the worldwide GNP, has no vocation for becoming the center of a new "Economic World". Japan is politically isolated in its zone, but has always been turned to the West, be it nineteenth-century Europe or contemporary America. The popular myth of Japan as the hub of a pacific zone, which would relegate the old "Atlantic World" to its periphery and, as a result Europe, remains a myth.

The absence of a regulating force is all the more critical, since in the heart of third world countries internal social explosions are to be expected as well as a multiplication of regional and local conflicts. The seed of tomorrow's social explosions lies in today's trends: Galloping demographic rates, flagrant inequality (i.e. luxury rubbing elbows with extreme poverty), massive urbanization in gigantic megacities that resemble shanty-towns more than cities.

Beyond the multiple uncertainties of the international imbalanced and turbulent environment, two permanent factors may be stressed:

– international monetary instability (the monetary system is a reflection of the geopolitical system) and, in particular, the persistence of heavy fluctuations of the dollar in comparison with other currencies;

– "self-centered" development of developed countries on their own, e.g., for most of the products and services, four-fifths of the solvent markets will remain in the USA-Europe-Japan triad.

Relatively speaking, certain strategic and military giants are economic dwarfs (Russia) whereas economic giants (Japan, Germany) are military dwarfs. This lack of balance is a source of tension. Obviously the bipolar "Cold War" world no longer exists, but can the multipolar world succeed without major upheavals?

Indeed, demographic and political shocks, irregular development, reinforced nationalism plus the absence of a regulator could combine to generate conflict and breed a climate of international insecurity. Unfortunately, in these conditions, management of an increasingly interdependent world has little chance of working by means of dialogue, foresight and concerted policy.

Defence issues are central. Will the East and West ally their forces to become the police of the United Nations? Will Europe remain "Atlantic" (NATO) with regard to defense, yet part of the European Community with regard to economy? The Eastern countries shift to a free market economy will not work right in the beginning. A possible failure of internal reforms in Russia and the new republics in the East could represent a threat to Europe. History tells us that an external war frequently played the role of an outlet to internal contradictions of countries; the Russian military potential remains colossal and Europe must not decrease its defence.

Let us make an intermediate conjecture: Instead of accepting ever increasing help from the West, Russia could refocus on the internal problems of its split empire and leave to the United States and its allies the task of defusing the time bombs which are bound to explode in third world countries.

Three configurations were taken into account with regard to the geopolitical context:

B1. Tensions and conflicts, without regulation of interdependence.

B2. Limited conflicts in the countries of the South and the East, uncertainties in the West.

B3. New international order and emergence of an interdependent, multipolar world.

Finally, the role of Eastern Europe seems very uncertain. Three configurations will be taken into account:

C1. Splitting, regional wars and a significant flow of refugees.

C2. Unequal development, social and regional tensions.

C3. Economic convergence and integration of the East and the West.

D. Europe's Uncertain Future: Division or Integration

Europe, the greatest solvent market in the world, constituted the new commercial El dorado of the 1990s. Europessimism, which prevailed up until the mid-1980s, fell out of fashion. The effect of the announcement of the great domestic market and the perspective of monetary integration played a positive and stimulating role and acted as an effective mobilizer. In short, the Old World has gained confidence in itself.

The history of European integration and union, its successes and crises, has been marked by the permanent confrontation of the community's desire for economic and political integration and the states' preoccupation with safeguarding their national sovereignty.

The overall impression is that the road to a united Europe is narrower than ever. The easiest part has been accomplished, but to go further, the states will have to strip off layers of national sovereignty at the monetary, fiscal and social level. Many states are simply not prepared to do so. In addition, the enlargement of Europe with new countries remains a risk that renders the laudable objectives of coherence and political cohesion among member countries even more difficult.

The expansion of economies to a world scale will entail new restructuring and painful delocalization on the social level; in other words, lost jobs. The risks of fragmentation in Europe, such as divergence in the capacity to adapt to economic globalization, are considerable as well as the risks of reinforced regional protectionism.

Three configurations will be taken into account for the level of European integration:

D1. Failure of the Europe of Twelve and a return to the national scale.

D2. Europe of Twelve, stable but only by economic integration.

D3. Political integration of Europe of Twelve and enlargement to include new members;

E, F. Conditions of Competitiveness, Exchange and Globalization

Technological, industrial, and relentless commercial competition between companies for market share in what has become a global marketplace will persist. Transnational space remains the arena of this competition among the large multinationals which have a tendency to create worldwide oligopolies with large sectors of activity. This competition is heightened by cooperation and strategic alliances, notably in the technological field, which tends to further reinforce the entry barriers for firms which are not co-opted in the oligopoly.

New production and organization techniques bring hope (increased productivity, new products and services) but also threats (jobs, liberties). Everything will depend on the political and social choices made in connection with the new technologies and the rate of their diffusion. Note this issue reappears in a more developed form later on as it constitutes a major uncertainty.

The differentials of competitiveness among companies will increasingly be based on the quality of the organization and mastery of information systems surrounding the new technologies. After hardware and software, the so-called "orgware" (tools which facilitate collaboration) will be a determining factor in productivity within competitive situations.

Five major trends are at work for the years to come:
– mass production of variety by small scale production systems;
– comparative advantage of low salaries, less relevant than automation processes and the development of communications;
– flexibility of the production machinery, which is indispensable for adapting to fluctuations characterizing the markets in renewal;
– need for alliance and cooperation with other companies at the level of precompetitive research, or development and industrialization due to the globalization of markets which alone will enable expenditure on technology to be profitable;
– reinforced coupling of scientific research and marketing within an effective strategy for the administration of the technological resources of companies.

At the European level, the regulation and introduction of norms will be a factor that reduces uncertainties with regard to the rules of the game. However, this factor will also generate new areas of competition, hence turbulence. International competition experienced mainly by the manufacturing industry, until now, will spread to activities which thus far have usually been "protected", e.g. banking and insurance.

Lastly, the very conditions for the establishment of these new regulations are evolving: more and more frequently, the CEC and international organisms such as the WTO or even the American Congress will become strategic sites for decisions.

Between transnational and regional, the national range provides comparative advantages which are frequently extremely diversified through three distinct mechanisms. In the first place, public policies of states with regard to matters of education, norms and public markets will define the technical environment of companies. In the second place, social and national dynamics will determine collective attitudes with regard to the division of added-value, the rules of the game between social groups and the relationship of individuals to their work and to the company.

All these trends are heading toward an extension of free trade and Europe's opening up to international competition. Nevertheless, the question of massive delocalization looms in the industrial sector, and now also in the service sector. These areas require information processing with repercussions on employment, especially in Europe, which is less protected than its partners. Overall delocalization will make protectionist maneuvers most probable by one country or by groups of countries.

Three configurations may be considered in terms of the conditions of exchange and competition:

E1. National protectionism (end of GATT).

E2. Regional protectionism (regional barriers and free exchange between regional blocs).

E3. Extension of GATT and free trade, fierce competition between enterprises.

The following configurations will also be taken into account for the globalization of economies:

F1. Reduced.

F2. Variable, according to regions and sectors of activity.

F3. Intensive.

A Key Question: Will the New Technologies Spread as Fast as Planned?

Overall, progress will probably remain slow due to the power of inertia, an inherent force in productive and social systems. Indeed, numerous points of resistance to the effective introduction of the new technologies can be observed.

Resistance is, without doubt, stronger in the tertiary sector in that this sector has temporarily been subjected less to the pressure of international competition. At the end of the 1970s, it was understood that within only a few years, office automation would invade a full range of services, especially banks and insurance companies. Yet if we look around today, office automation did not eliminate many administrative jobs. Numerous factors concur to explain this slower-than-expected penetration. In the first place, we have to deal with managing the time made available by the latest technology; i.e., production management. What would be the purpose of investing to obtain greater productivity, if it could not be converted into expanded production or into decreased manpower? Think of the situation of saturated markets or weak growth or idle personnel. A reduction of working hours can only be progressive if it remains distributed fairly among the sectors.

Moreover, the generalization of office automation brings relative transparency to the working world, something that flies in the face of established hierarchies. Consider for a moment that computer technologies are not neutral towards power structures. We really should not be surprised then that certain actors (frequently executives) deep in the heart of a corporation, feel jeopardized, and resist innovation.

Also, we have to remember that what is technologically feasible is neither necessarily economically profitable nor socially desirable. One concrete example is telecommuting or working from a home office. It is very unlikely that work at home will develop to such an extent that a large percentage of office jobs will disappear. Several factors work against this maximal hypothesis. First, the current conditions of urban living: close quarters, an ill-suited apartment environment render a full working day unpleasant. Second, people are people, and work represents a socialization process corresponding to needs less and less satisfied otherwise.

G. Slow, Irregular, Unequal and Interdependent Growth

Interdependence is more than a trend or fiction; it is a measurable reality. Indeed it may be quantified through multiple indicators, as the share of ever increasing national productions dedicated to export. This greater opening up to the outside world means that no nation can claim to control its proper growth alone. If we return to the traditional car analogy: the accelerator is international, only the brakes are national.

It is now impossible to introduce structures and rules for the international and national game which has been adapted to the new context of interdependence and technical and economic changes. A general and concerted economic revival hardly seems possible. In passing, it should be noted that growth will not be stimulated by aging populations, either.

Irregularity more than sluggishness will seriously impact investment decisions and entail forecasting errors and sudden sways in attitude, swinging from optimism to pessimism. Periods of recession will be followed by periods of recovery, as if compensatory forces were at work to keep growth at a weak average of 2%. Historically, if we take levels of development into account, the result is surprising at four to five times more in absolute value than an average year drawn from the nineteenth century.

However, GDP is not the only indicator that should be taken into account. One must not confuse the rhythm of growth (a flux) with the level of development (a stock). GNP is a flux which renews itself each year. Also, the quality content of this growth flux is far more important than its actual annual increase. Our aging populations will definitely be more vulnerable than ever before to such aspects as quality of environment and living conditions.

The majority of experts have made conjectures for the upcoming years which would have seemed improbable only a few years ago, e.g. a rate of inflation below 5%, positive, realistic interest rates, plus a very weak and irregular growth.

Yet their hypotheses are not solid. It is to be expected that there will be new oil shocks from now on up to 2005, which would destroy growth, assuming it should start off again in a strong and lasting manner. However, this perspective of new oil shocks fades farther away, the farther growth is out of sight. In fact, as in 1988-1990, sustained growth for two to three years could occur by means of the compensatory force of the recession of the preceding years. Basically, conditions for the return to strong and durable growth still need to be met. In an increasingly interdependent world, the absence of an international regulatory force is cruelly felt. If there is no alternative by the year 2000, eighty percent of the world's demand will still be addressed to the developed countries of the triad. In other words, world's demand will not increase on account of the population's aging and it runs the risk of fluctuating more and more in accordance with the rhythm of optimistic or pessimistic cycles of anticipation.

The gap between North and South, East and West will continue widening. This lopsided development would become an additional source of tension among neighbors who are developing fast and are moderately populated versus those subjected to the struggle of underdevelopment and overpopulation. Consider the example of Haiti and the Dominican Republic, two very different countries on the same island.

At this point, four configurations were taken into account for GDP, the average growth rate of the 90s:

G1. The recession (less than 0.5% of growth).
G2. A weak and fluctuating GDP (1.5% on average).
G3. An average growth (2.5%).
G4. Strong growth (over 3%).

The combinatory analysis resulting from the high number of components and configurations seems inevitable. Initially there were a considerable number of possible scenarios, 2,916, or the product of $3 \times 3 \times 3 \times 3 \times 3 \times 4$, the number of configurations. This number, however, may be reduced through morphological analysis. Here, the most a priori relevant and coherent ways have been retained by the group which extracted four of them, each of them being represented by a color: black, gray, blue and pink.

A1 B1 C1 D1 E1 F1 G1: Black scenario

A2 B1 C1 D2 E2 F2 G2: Gray scenario

A3 B2 C2 D3 E2 F2 G3: Blue scenario

A3 B3 C3 D3 E3 F3 G4: Pink scenario

IT5, International Context Morphological Analysis

Demographic Trends in Western Countries	A1 Aging of populations Migrants control ethnic conflicts	A2 Migrant flows from east and south to western countries Integration problems	A3 New baby-boom in Western countries and acceptable migration flows
Geographical and Geopolitical Context	B1 Tensions and conflicts No regulator of interdependence	B2 Limited conflicts in the south and eastern countries Uncertainties in western countries	B3 New international order of a multipolar, interdependent world
Role of Eastern Europe	C1 Disintegration regional wars refugees	C2 Unequal development Social ad regional tensions	C3 Economic convergence and integration of the countries (east and west)
European Integration	D1 Failure of the Europe of 12 Come back of smaller Europe	D2 Stable Europe of 12. Integration of markets only	D3 Political integration of Europe of 12 Extension to new members
Conditions of Trade and Competition	E1 National protectionism (end of GATT)	E2 Regional protectionism (regional barriers and free trade within the block)	E3 GATT extension free trade Strong competition between firms
Globalisation of Economy	F1 Reduced	F2 Variable according to the regions and sectors	F3 Intensive

Annual rate of growth of the GNP	G1 Recession Less than 0.5%	G2 Low with fluctuations 1.5%	G3 Medium trend based 2.5%	G4 Strong More than 3%

However, relevance and coherence do not necessarily mean likelihood.

Likelihood of the Global Scenarios

The diversity of scenarios (black, gray, blue and pink) does not prejudice their individual and overall likelihood. In other words, do these scenarios include the majority of the most probable ones? To answer this question, the SMIC method and the Prob-Expert software were used. In effect this method actually assigns probabilities to the scenarios; i.e., combinations of realized or unrealized hypotheses, from information on individual probabilities of these hypotheses and conditional probabilities. Nevertheless, the transition from morphological analysis to cross-impact requires further explanation.

In order to find the most probable scenarios, the IT5 experts met in London on May 7, 1993. This was an opportunity for them to give their opinions on the proposed configurations and the probability of their occurrence. For instance, the configurations of the component European integration; i.e., D1 = failure, D2 = stability, D3 = integration, were estimated on average with the following probabilities: $P(D1) = 0.4$; $P(D2) = 0.4$; $P(D3) = 0.2$

As the configurations are assumed to be exhaustive and exclusive, the total probability is one. This assumption of exhaustiveness is often questionable. Hence we recommend adding a new configuration per component. This new configuration was simply called "Others". In this sense, we have exhaustiveness by definition.

In this case study, the group of experts considered the probabilities of "other configurations" as negligible and did not add any new configurations to the following five subsystems:

1) international (geopolitical and economic) context of the 1990s;
2) autonomous technological determining factors;
3) infrastructures of the IT and communications systems;
4) strategies and actors games;
5) market trends.

Moreover, for several reasons, the use of the SMIC-Prob-Expert software is restricted to six fundamental hypotheses. Therefore, it is not possible to consider all the components and combinations. We can only rely on some of them.

Six hypotheses which characterize the various subsystems were considered:

H1: Political integration of Europe (D3).
H2: Extension of free trade (E3).
H3: Low and irregular growth (G1 or G2, i.e. less than 1.5%).
These first three belong to the international context.

H4: Integration with telecoms (this hypothesis comes from the subsystem called "Information and communication infrastructures" which envisages situations like access from home to optical fiber facilities).

H5: Active support to R&D (This hypothesis comes from the subsystem "strategy and actors game").

H6: Slowing down of the IT market increase: This hypothesis of an average increase of less than 8% in turnover comes from the subsystem "market trends".

The efficient use of this method requires that the number of hypotheses and consequently the number of variables which describe the scenarios be limited to five or six. The experts cannot assign a probability to the full set of thinkable scenarios (which means 64 scenarios for 6 hypotheses). Of course the total of the probablility of these 64 possible scenarios is equal to one as these scenarios (combinations of hypotheses) are exclusive and as it is sure that one of them will occur.

The Smic provides a direct response to this problem. In fact, with this method it is only necessary to know:

– the simple probability of the realization of a hypothesis within a given period of time; take $P(i)$ as the probability for the hypothesis i to be realized;

– conditional probabilities of realization of pairs of hypotheses; take $P(i/j)$ as the probability of the hypothesis i occurring, knowing that the hypothesis j occurs and $P(i/not\ j)$ is the probability of i occurring, knowing that the hypothesis j has not occurred.

The Smic method corrects the raw probabilities given by the experts to obtain coherent results, i.e. results which satisfy the classical equations of conditional probabilities. In any case the experts cannot give coherent answers, i.e. answers which verify the classical rules of probabilities:

$$P(i) = P(i/j)P(j) + P(i/not\ j)\ (1 - P(j))$$
$$P(ij) = P(i/j)P(j) = P(j/i)P(i).$$

At the same time, the Prob-Expert software calculates the probabilities of the scenarios. As the system cannot be fully determined – there are more unknown variables than independent equations – there is an infinity of vector solutions for the scenarios. Using the SIMPLEX method allows the extreme solutions for each scenario to be selected. Usually the "Max of Max" solution is preferred; i.e., the solution which gives the highest value to the most probable scenario.

The experts' skepticism regarding European unification appears immediately. Hypothesis H2 gets a probability of only 0.2 for the advancement of political integration. That corresponds to the D3 configuration in the morphological analysis. The same experts have then assigned a 0.5 probability to the D2 configuration (stability of Europe limited to market integration) and 0.3 to the configuration D1; i.e., the break-up of Europe and the return to national states.

Another indicator of the coherence of the experts' answers is the quadratic remainder resulting from the optimization done by the Prob-Expert software. As for linear regression, it is best to minimize the difference between the initial information and the data which verify the probabilities axioms. The lack of coherence in the data would be shown by a remainder greater than 0.2; whereas in the current study its value is only 0.102, which proves the data's coherence.

The scenarios generated by the 6 hypotheses (H1 to H6) are classified by decreasing order of probability. The cumulated probability of the 64 possible scenarios is equal to 1 (by definition, as an exhaustive set of exclusive situations). The equiprobability is around 1.5% (1/64).

Usually the probability of the most probable scenario is about 15% and one third of the set of scenarios covers 80% of the total of the probable scenarios. In this case the result is exceptional as the solution which maximizes the most probable scenario assigns the value 0.40 to the so called S28 scenario (001001), which means more than four chances out of ten. This corresponds to the unfavorable situation which extends the current situation with:

not H1: The political integration of Europe is not realized.

not H2: The expansion of free trade does not work.

H3: Slow and irregular growth (less than 1.5%).

not H4: The integration with telecoms does not work.

not H5: R&D is not actively supported.

H6: The development of the IT market is slowing down.

The other scenarios are much less probable. In fact, the following four scenarios teased out of the group are five to six times less probable but maintain a certain likelihood.

Group 1: Recessive set back; almost 6 chances out of 10. This group corresponds to the gray and black scenarios previously envisaged.

The overall probability of this group is 57%. The group is characterized by 001... as answers to H1, H2 and H3, which means a context with the withdrawal of the aging Europe turning in on itself, or even the breaking up of the European Community with likely limitations to free trade, all these events leading to low or very low growth. This recessive setback is not favorable to the IT markets, since integration with the telecoms could not be achieved, maybe due to the resulting lack of support in R&D.

Group 2: Recession and incomplete opening up (less than 1 chance in 10).

This group of two scenarios has less than one chance in ten to succeed. The weak growth or even recession is very likely due to an incomplete opening up; i.e., only from the economic point of view within one particular scenario which outlines a Europe broken up by free trade and the recession; or only from the political point of view with S43: Europe as a political fortress without a firm free trade agreement, or even with a breaking up of GATT (now WTO).

In a recessionary context Europe's opening outward cannot be complete and it becomes impossible to achieve the political integration of Europe simultaneously with the extension of free trade. The support of R&D does not help avoid a slowdown in the IT markets, especially since the integration of IT with the telecoms has not been achieved (idea of "not H4").

Group 3: Growth by the opening up of Europe
(less than two chances in ten)

This group of seven is characterized by sustained economic growth and it is the most heterogeneous. If the opening up is incomplete (four scenarios) the IT markets can remain dynamic assuming successful integration with the telecoms. If the opening up is complete (political integration of Europe with extension of free trade) as in the three scenarios, the evolution of the IT markets is uncertain and does not depend on either R&D support or on the integration with telecoms but seems to be dependent on the political and economic success of Europe. This complete openness corresponds to the pink scenario from the morphological analysis and has fewer than seven chances in a hundred to succeed.

Group 4: Self-centered development
(more than 15 chances in 100)

This group is characterized by regained growth (idea of "not H3"), the non-extension of GATT or even a decline in free trade and by a freezing or even an explosion of European unification. The development of the IT markets is rather favourable except in the case of one scenario only where the conjunction of R&D support and integration with telecoms cannot prevent the IT markets from decline possibly due to the regionalization of trade.

This group of four scenarios is close to the blue scenario which is characterized by average growth, by a maintained "economic Europe" but without extension of free trade. The likelihood of this blue scenario is then about 10%.

In sum, the black and gray scenarios (recessive setback) are unfortunately the most probable, with more than 60 chances in a hundred. The blue scenario (self-centered development) has only 15 chances in 100 to succeed. The pink scenario (growth by opening up) is far less likely to happen (7 chances in 100). It is as likely as S42, or the scenario in which Europe exploded by free trade and the recession and twice as likely as S43 in which Europe is a political fortress with an exploding GATT due to the recession).

It should be noted that the following hypotheses; political expansion and economic closure of Europe, increased economic openness raising the possibility of a setback in European construction, had been rejected a priori as they did not appear in any of the initial scenarios (black, gray, pink or blue) selected in the initial table of the morphological analysis.

Scenario S37 (110110) is in principle the most desirable (a triumphant Europe from both the political and economic points of view, in an expanding economy, with integration achieved with the telecoms, sustained support of R&D and recovery of the IT markets). It is assigned a null probability. The same situation applies in most of the international context scenarios with a profile starting at 110. It seems that the extension of free trade is almost incompatible with the political unification of Europe, and vice versa. This result is interesting in the current context of European doubts.

It is necessary to contextualize this conclusion. It is only the result of a collective vision in May 1993, as expressed by a set of European IT industry experts being questioned on the international context up to the year 2000. This vision can be seen as pessimistic. However, let us remember that a comparable exercise on the prospects of the steel industry in France by the year 2005 was done in 1990 and 1991. The hypotheses about growth were almost as pessimistic as in the current case (for instance the probability of keeping growth at less than 1.8% per year was 0.6).

In the current case the probability analysis with the Prob-Expert software confirmed the coherence and pertinence of the choice of the 4 scenarios (black, gray, blue and pink) elaborated in the morphological analysis. Nevertheless not all have the same likelihood to succeed; in addition, other scenarios on international evolution have been identified whereas the morphological analysis phase did not reveal them.

Scenario Building at Axa France [1]

The futures-thinking exercise and strategic scenario building was carried out in France from March 1994 to December 1995, under the direction of Planning and the leadership of Professor Michel Godet.

Until recently scenario planning was restricted, albeit unofficially, to a few specific sectors where long-term heavy investment was the norm, e.g. air and rail transportation, electricity, aluminium and petroleum production. In fact most service companies did not see the need to hold futures-thinking exercises.

Gradually, however, interest arose in the telecommunications and computer sectors. Soon areas like finance and tourism joined in because they too experienced growing uncertainty about the future given the threefold bind of deregulation, economic problems, and market globalization.

Certain forward-looking pioneers stood out from the start. One was Axa France, a leader in insurance. Axa France is actually an umbrella company for all the French subsidiaries of the Axa insurance group. In the early 1990s, the French entities had decided to look to the future in order to prepare the traditional four-year plan (1996-2000). The

---

1. Part of this case study first appeared in the international journal *Futuribles*, (Issue 203, November 1995). It was written by Paul Benassouli, Director of Planning, and Régine Monti, research-fellow.

previous plan (1992-1996) had focused exclusively on greater rationalization of resources and the reorganization of the new Axa, which had expanded through many buy-outs.

Given the company's objectives and focus on distribution, Axa's 1992-1996 plan had not taken into account how the general or competitive environment would evolve. The new plan (1996-2000) would, however, take into account the international objectives of Axa, its quality and profitability directives. Moreover, with a ten-year future horizon, the plan would integrate external challenges more readily and set the strategic course for the five years immediately following (1996-2000). Note that the futures-thinking exercise took place two years before Axa and UAP (Union des Assurances de Paris) merged.

A Pragmatic Approach

The procedure that Axa France adopted reflects how futures-thinking exercises have evolved and been applied to planning within major corporations. Today's companies have less time to think and feel an almost urgent need to act. Hence our mandate sounds increasingly like a bad self-help book – "how to conduct a meaningful exercise with managers on major future trends and uncertainties that is both coherent and realistic". In other words, what can we really achieve in six working meetings?

Axa France, a relatively recently established group known for its rapid integration of numerous acquisitions as well as its mobile and highly decentralized structure, could not consider anything time- or labor-intensive, like a specialized department that would require divesting and reallocating directors from various subsidiaries to take part in the process. On the contrary, the idea was to encourage the company's general managers to work together. The overall goal was to look to the future with a shared vision as they identified threats, opportunities and potential bifurcations thus preparing for expected changes and hopefully fostering desirable changes while fighting feared changes. In short, participants would have to identify possible futures and pinpoint which of these would be the most probable. The horizon adopted was 2005.

Given the nine-month deadline, we opted for efficiency and selected two main tools from the futures toolbox, structural analysis to find key variables and actors' strategies to explore possible changes. Three other methods mentioned in earlier chapters were also used, namely the futures workshops, morphological analysis and the Smic-Prob-Expert.

As emphasized earlier, selecting a methodology (workshops or structural analysis) to determine key variables is not a goal in itself. The first objective is to encourage participants to express their vision of the future. Otherwise this underlying future vision remains

Environmental scenarios were built following the ten-step schedule listed below:

1. Futures seminar: acquisition of analytical methods, identification and hierarchization of the factors of change affecting Axa, choice of the most pivotal environmental components for Axa in France (mid-March 1994).
2. Small group sessions: drafting of scenarios grouped into broad fields (April-June 1994).
3. Joint sessions: presentation of results from various groups and the construction of environmental scenarios (June 1994).
4. Survey on the future of insurance in France (July-September 1994).
5. Probabilization, selection and analysis of scenarios (October 1994).
6. Selection of one main scenario and identification of alternative hypotheses (November 1994).
7. Presentation of the main scenario and the alternative hypotheses to the various subsidiaries (December 1994).
8. Appropriation and integration of the main scenario and hypotheses in the plans of the different subsidiaries (January 1995).
9. Drafting of a plan in each subsidiary (February-June 1995).
10. "Arbitration" and allocation of resources (4th term 1995).

implicit. It is only by verbalizing that vision that the group can gain greater insight into certain member's stances or disagreements. Obviously having some idea of a future vision makes corporate decision-making more efficient.

Exploring Futuribles through Morphological Analysis

Once the key dimensions of the scenarios are set out, three or four scenarios must be drafted per component. These scenarios should be pertinent, coherent, realistic, and likely to occur within the horizon selected.

Morphological analysis was applied for each key area during a half-day meeting of a sub-committee composed of the three managers most affected. Preparatory work had been carried out, e.g. consultation of experts, documentation, interviews, etc. Once again it is a constant juggling act to get the management committee involved while taking up as little time as possible.

As we have seen, the principle of morphological analysis is simple: break the system under study down into sub-systems, components or fields, and then identify the resulting configurations. For example, the dimension, or key field, "demography and society", highlighted in the Axa France scenario-building sessions, may be broken down into components. In fact these components were identified during the futures workshops. In Axa's case, these are also the main factors of demographic and social change likely to have a major influence on the com-

---

Eleven Key Components

1. Demography and society.
2. European construction/structure.
3. Real interest rates.
4. Growth rates.
5. State interventionism.
6. Retirement system.
7. Taxation and life insurance.
8. Health system.
9. Demand for insurance.
10. Technology.
11. Distribution channels/means of distribution.

Note: In accordance with confidentiality agreements, only the first five may be detailed here.

---

pany's very future. These factors appear in the graphics that follow. They include aging, migratory flows, worksharing, taxation and work. Each of these components may take several possible shapes, commonly called configurations. If we take the horizon 2005 as an example, the migratory flows might be comparable to today's at 100,000 annually or they could rise sharply to 300,000 a year. Another possibility would be an even balance between immigration and emigration. If we keep these three configurations separately, we could say that we had explored the set of possible futures, at least quantitatively. This type of thinking was applied to each subcomponent. Highlights of the results follow as a diagram showing morphological analysis: of the component "Demography and Society".

In Axa's case, the group decided, whether right or wrong, that the following were not realistic:
– a drop in the French fertility rate to 1.4 children per woman;
– massive immigration;
– a net balance through emigration.

All the combinations with these configurations (18 scenarios) were thus eliminated. Certain paths were considered unrealistic. For example, the group did not envisage a worksharing program or system that excluded a section of the labor force and the development of family-related jobs.

After excluding these, only three scenarios for the component "demography and society" were retained in Axa's overall scenario-building process. (See broken, thin and solid lines within the diagram.)

The three scenarios read roughly as:

1) "Rigidity and Extended Duality"
This is a straight scenario with no social innovation or questioning of the limits weighing on the job market. Two worlds coexist: the offi-

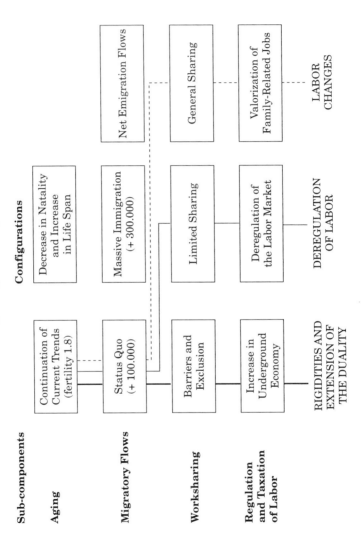

Demography and Society Component Morphological Analysis

Sub-components	Configurations		
Aging	Continuation of Current Trends (fertility 1.8)	Decrease in Natality and Increase in Life Span	
Migratory Flows	Status Quo (+ 100.000)	Massive Immigration (+ 300.000)	Net Emigration Flows
Worksharing	Barriers and Exclusion	Limited Sharing	General Sharing
Regulation and Taxation of Labor	Increase in Underground Economy	Deregulation of the Labor Market	Valorization of Family-Related Jobs
	RIGIDITIES AND EXTENSION OF THE DUALITY	DEREGULATION OF LABOR	LABOR CHANGES

Scenarios for This Component

cial work world, as regulated as ever and very traditional in terms of shifts and working hours; the underground economy in which a growing segment of the population gets by through under-the-table payment for small jobs.

2) "Deregulated Labor"

The name says it all. It is the "American plan" or a more flexible labour market where innovation remains localized in certain fields or regions.

3) "Changes in Working"

This is a scenario of collective voluntary efforts which leads to the recognition, organization and development of new types of jobs. There is also a serious reconsideration of social life, e.g. greater leisure time and different lifestyles.

Each of the components of Axa France's future scenarios was analyzed morphologically. The following outline summarizes the environmental scenarios foreseen by restricted groups of experts during April and May 1994. Note that use of the box "Others" is not only an attempt at exhaustive research but a reminder not to forget what may otherwise be easily forgotten. When determining probability for the configurations, we check to see whether the "Others" box is indeed unrealistic.

Outline of Environmental Scenarios for AXA France

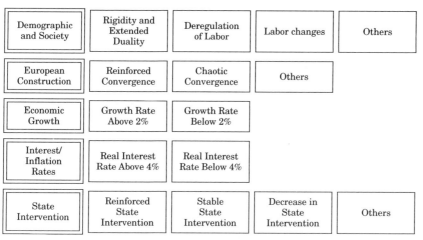

Demographic and Society	Rigidity and Extended Duality	Deregulation of Labor	Labor changes	Others
European Construction	Reinforced Convergence	Chaotic Convergence	Others	
Economic Growth	Growth Rate Above 2%	Growth Rate Below 2%		
Interest/ Inflation Rates	Real Interest Rate Above 4%	Real Interest Rate Below 4%		
State Intervention	Reinforced State Intervention	Stable State Intervention	Decrease in State Intervention	Others

In June of 1994, the management committee of Axa France collectively approved this outline of scenarios with a 2005 horizon.

Determining Probable Futures

The objective of Axa's management committee was to pinpoint uncertainties and major future trends as part of the 1995-2000 planning exercise. Naturally they wanted to go further in order to retain a limited number of scenarios with high probability ratings.

Construction of the Questionnaire (Scenario Probabilization)

The crossed-impact method consists of asking questions with simple and conditional probability on a limited number of hypotheses. Use of these methods means exploring possible futures across a restricted number of main hypotheses (5-6 binary hypotheses).

One of the main problems in using these approaches is determining the few hypotheses which represent the key components and subsequent configurations. Hypotheses are selected on the basis of the scenario outlines. One hypothesis per component is retained. This becomes the most probable configuration. The configuration is identified by an initial probabilization performed quickly by asking each expert his/her opinion. An average of these simple probabilities attributed to each configuration is then calculated. Let us take the component "demography and society" as an example. The highest average attributed by group members was that for the configuration "rigidity and extended duality" at 35%. This hypothesis was therefore retained as the main one.

**Probability Attributed to the Configurations
of the "Demography and Society" Component**

Component	*Configurations*			
Demography and society	Rigidity and extension of the duality	Deregulation of labor	Labor changes	Others
	35%	28%	27%	10%

*Average Simple Probability Rates
Attribued by Experts*

**Main Hypothesis Retained:
Labor: Rigidity and Extension of the Duality**

All the main hypotheses for Axa France were determined on the basis of the most probable configurations for each component. The list of hypotheses follows:

H1. In terms of aging (fertility rate of 1.8); migratory flows of one million more in the upcoming ten years; inequitable worksharing which leads to more and more exclusion, barriers or ceilings, and an extended underground economy.

H2. Reinforced Convergence for Europe. The Europe of Maastricht is effective and the single market becomes a reality. Member states respect the economic and financial criteria, e.g. low inflation, low interest rates, budgetary rigor.

H3. Sustained growth rate (above 2.2%).

H4. High real interest rates (above 4%).

H5. Reinforced state interventionism in France, e.g. predominance of a strong state. The French state increases its hold on the economy through organizations managed by its social partners. Social budgets are better mastered and labor regulations are reinforced.

H6. Retirement: budgeting maintains the distribution. The end of indexed pensions. Moreover, the level of contributions deducted from salaries remains constant. There is partial "budgetization". There is no sign of implementing a capitalization system using a tax incentive program.

H7. Tax advantages of life insurance are maintained.

H8. Health system continues to flounder. Technological progress spreads rapidly. Yet in parallel, the growing medical demand is a prevailing trend (or megatrend). Professional expenditures in the health system continue rising at the current rate. The state can no longer meet its obligations and withdraws.

H9. Unchanged demand in terms of clients. Expectations about prices (best value for the money), services (simplicity) and client needs do not really change.

H10. The traditional insurance distribution system continues to be eaten away on the edges.

Given the restriction on the number of hypotheses (maximum 5 or 6), it was impossible to probabilize in one questionnaire the full slate of Axa France scenarios using the Smic Prob-Expert method. Two questionnaires were needed: one on the social and economic environment; the other on the insurance context (H7, H8, H9, H10). Both questionnaires shared one hypothesis, H5, which was used to link identified changes and build the full scenarios with the 2005 horizon. However this part of the case study is not presented here.

The two questionnaires were circulated among members of the company's management committee during the summer of 1994. They were questioned in writing on the simple probabilities of each hypothesis $P(i)$: probability that the hypothesis i occurs, as well as on the conditional probabilities of the hypotheses taken in pairs $P(i/j)$: probability that hypothesis i occurs when hypothesis j occurs or $P(i/not\ j)$ and probability that hypothesis i occurs while knowing that hypothesis j has not occurred.

A sample questionnaire page follows.

Processing the Results with the Smic-Prob-Expert Software

We used the Prob-Expert software to process the two questionnaires and then probabilize the various environmental scenarios for Axa France with a horizon of 2005. The data were determined by taking an average of the answers provided by Axa France's management committee in the summer of 1994.

Questionnaire

Simple Probability
Question: **What is the probability that the hypothesis**
H3. Continued Growth from now until 2005 will occur?

Signification: I consider that it is probable that in ten years, the growth
rate will remain the same.
These hypotheses are evaluated with the following probability scale:
1) Very improbable event.
2) Improbable event.
3) Moderately probable event.
4) Probable event.
5) Very probable event.

Conditional Probabilities
Question: **Knowing that Hypothesis H3 (Continued Growth from now**
until 2005) has occurred, what do you think the probability is that each of
the following four hypotheses will occur?

	Improbable			Probable		
H1. Work World: rigidity and extended duality	1	2	3	4	5	Ind*
H2. Reinforced convergence in Europe	1	2	3	4	5	Ind
H3. High real interest rates	1	2	3	4	5	Ind
H4. Reinforced State intervention	1	2	3	4	5	Ind

* Independent.

Probabilization of the Hypotheses using Smic Prob-Expert

The initial result of processing is an average net probability and the
standard deviation, taking into account the correction indicated in the
diagram, attributed to each hypothesis by the experts.

Probability Rates and Scenario Selection

The beauty of the Smic Prob-Expert method is that it reveals the probability attributed to each of the 32 scenarios by each expert. These are
the 32 scenarios generated from the combinations of five hypotheses

Positioning of the Economic and Social Environmental Hypotheses according to their Average Probability and Standard Deviation

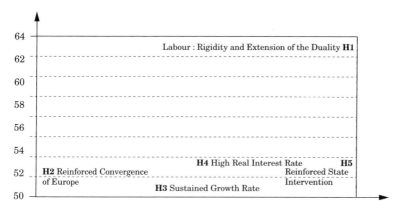

Legend:

H1. "Rigidity and Extension of the Duality" is the most probable hypothesis on average but the experts remain divided on this one. (high standard deviation).

H2. "Reinforced convergence of Europe". This is hypothesis is probable on average; i.e., one chance in two that it will occur. The expert opinions converge on this result (weak standard deviation).

on the social and economic environment of Axa France, horizon 2005. The most probable scenarios stand out, thus revealing the future visions of the various experts. We also calculate an average probability per scenario for the group itself. On the basis of this calculation, the most probable scenarios are selected.

The selection process seeks out combinations of two and then three hypotheses that group a minimum number of scenarios which represent the largest share of the field of possible futures. Here we find the greatest probability. In the case of Axa France, we found that four combinations of three hypotheses brought together 16 scenarios in four groups that indeed represented 70% of the possible futures. In concrete terms, according to the expert participants, we have more than two out of three chances of ending up in one of these combinations in 2005.

From each of these four groups, the most probable scenario was selected. As a result, we went from 16 to 4 scenarios.

Axa's four social and economic environmental scenarios with a horizon of 2005 appear in the following diagram. The first one, "Managed Crisis", represents 25% of the possible futures. This is a rare case. The probability rating for the other three scenarios is almost the same at 15% each.

It is also possible to identify, for each expert, the proximity of the various scenarios. The more probable the scenario, the closer it is and vice-versa. We end up with a fine snapshot of the different future visions of the experts surveyed.

Culling the Social and Economic Environmental Scenario Groups

E1. Managed Crisis (26%)
Work World: Rigidity and Extended Duality
High Real Interest Rates (above 4%)
Reinforced State Interventionism

E2. Inflationary Front (14%)
Work World: Rigidity and Extended Duality
Low Real Interest Rates (below 4%)
Reinforced State Interventionism

E3. Europe Embroiled in Social Tension (15%)
Work World: Rigidity and Extended Duality
High Real Interest Rates (above 4%)
No Reinforced State Interventionism

E4. Organized Liberalism (17%)
Work World: No Rigidity
Low Real Interest Rates (below 4%)
No Reinforced State Interventionism

Environmental Scenarios for AXA France

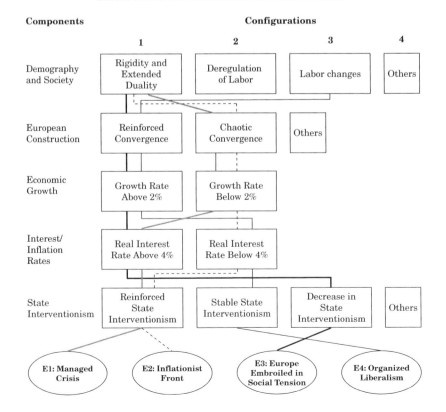

Environmental Scenarios for AXA France

E1. Managed Crisis: Here there is no consensus on main issues among the various European countries. The dream of a union fades. The French state faces an economic slowdown aggravated by social rigidity. It is the state putting out fires again. This context presents high real interest rates which are favorable to the insurance industry.

E2. Inflationary Front: The French government tries to jumpstart the economy through increased consumer spending. Social conflicts are temporarily avoided through wage increases which have disastrous effects on inflation. Real interest rates fall. The idea of European convergence fades. The state intervenes step by step in both the social and economic sphere.

E3. Europe Embroiled in Social Tension: In this instance, European convergence becomes an economic priority. France maintains high real interest rates; Brussels' power grows. Economically, Europe is a success. Growth rates exceed 2%. However, social crises, especially in the labor market, intensify. Europe does not implement reforms.

E4. Organized Liberalism: The social and economic context improves. Reforms succeed in promoting employment and battling other social ills without state intervention. A social hiatus seems to be taking shape. At the same time, the low real interest rates encourage productive investments. This healthy step can be seen in a growth rate higher than 2% and in an attenuation of previously seen social rigidities.

Analysis of Corresponding Visions
The Expert's Postions according to Scenario Probability

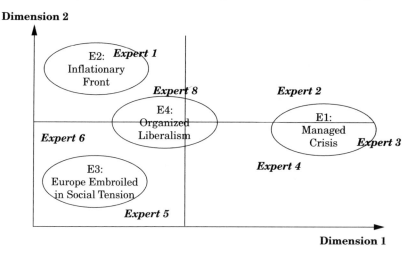

The Axa France 2005 scenarios were generated by crossing the four social and economic environmental scenarios and the five insurance industry scenarios (drawn from a questionnaire not presented here). Interestingly enough, by uniting these two scenario groupings, the participants found one shared hypothesis, H5 "Reinforced State Interventionism". Among the twenty possible scenarios, nine were selected, the others were eliminated because of incompatibility in terms of H5, e.g. H5 = 0 in one case and H5 = 1 in another.

The pure futures-thinking stage ends with the selection of nine scenarios that represent a significant portion of Axa's possible futures for the year 2005. Once the field of possibilities is reduced to what is probable, we turn to what is desirable. This is the start of the planning stage.

From Scenario Building to Planning

The shift from scenario building to planning is never easy. It is already no mean feat to select only one scenario that clarifies the array of possible futures. We understand just how confusing planners find working from several possible environmental scenarios. What can be done to retain the richness of the results of scenario building while remaining functional? The solution in the Axa France case consisted in keeping the most probable of the probable scenarios as the basis for the plan. This scenario became known as the "main scenario". This socio-economic environmental scenario "Managed Crisis" showed a probability rating of 25% and brought to the plan the risks and breaks (bifurcations) corresponding to the alternatives envisaged in the other scenarios considered highly probable and thus retained.

Some may object that this choice of a main scenario (the most probable of the probable) is simplistic in terms of the ambitions expressed at the offset of the exercise. However in terms of operationalizing a strategic plan, exploring the possible futures and pinpointing the probable ones is not a waste of time. In fact the participants became well aware of the risks of breaks or bifurcations in the trends that might affect their choices and cause them to rethink their course of action. The strategic plan will only become stronger in this sense.

The main scenario is used in two ways to build the plan. First, the scenario serves as the basis for environmental hypotheses that provide a backdrop to the plan itself. Some hypotheses are directly integrated into the plan, e.g. the real interest rates. Other elements are studied more, in a traditional fashion, to quantify the consequences of various combinations of hypotheses on the company's markets or market segments. In this sense, the main scenario can become a shared reference point that all the subsidiaries may use.

Afterward, with the main scenario in mind, each entity works toward its own strategic choices by asking the following two questions:
– what to do to reach our objectives, given our strengths and weaknesses and the conditions set by the main scenario? (In short, what to do to achieve x?);
– which moves should be made to prepare for possible breaks/bifurcations? (In other words, what to do if xyz?)

The first question leads to acting on the future environment and reflects a proactive attitude; whereas the second question requires adapting to an expected future environment and is a preactive attitude.

Of course it would be foolhardy to decide upon a strategy for the next five years on the basis of one main scenario. In fact, even if it is the most probable scenario, (25% in Axa's case), it remains not very likely since for Axa there are three out of four chances that the company will end up in another situation.

At this stage of making strategic choices, participants or managers must take into account the possible breaks or bifurcations that might occur given the situation described in the main scenario. Participants have to ponder each bifurcation highlighted in the analysis of the other highly probable scenarios and how that break or bifurcation would affect the conditions chosen within the hypotheses attached to the main scenario. Here, on the basis of the information provided, the tremendous uncertainty weighing on the industry in terms of developing trends was pinpointed for each hypothesis. For example, if the main scenario foresaw developing a certain market by making a heavy investment in computer technology then envisaging that market's disappearance for regulatory reasons, it would encourage participants to opt for a more rustic solution that would be easier to reconsider. (We might even ignore the fact that operating costs would be higher.) The decisions are made within the framework of the main scenario but they take into account the notion of ruptures. The decisions may thus speed up achievement of objectives or reevaluation of those objectives.

The virtual obligation to evaluate the consequences of these breaks or bifurcation points sheds new light on investment choices. In fact, occasionally the process may be halted to avoid exposing "irretrievable" costs. "Solid" solutions are thus preferred; in other words, solutions adapted to the contexts outlined by the most probable or most "flexible" scenarios, which can easily be revisited or challenged if there is a change in context. As a result, the company can better integrate uncertainty into its decisionmaking process.

Each subsidiary took the main scenario and probable bifurcations, or breaks, into account. Working groups were set up, again, to encourage that participants share their vision of the future.

The last stage, planning by scenario, or scenario planning, took place at the end of 1995. At this point, discussion turned to the plans presented by each subsidiary and the necessary resources for their projects. We were reminded that another contribution of the initial futures-thinking seminar is that it provides the criteria and weighting system (arbitration) used in this decisive stage.

All in all, what remains etched in the memories of the people in charge of corporate strategy and operations is the maturity gained through a futures-thinking exercise. Under fire, this "intellectual cross-training" will translate to strategic reflexes far sharper than those produced by a classical planning process with no prior reflection on the future.

Will Paris Need a Third Airport in 2030? If So, Where?

Site selection and scenarios seem particularly well-suited. However, choosing where to build a new airport for a large city, be it Athens, Paris or Montréal, raises many pertinent issues.

Over the past 25 years, we have been asked six times by various actors in government, the transportation sector, as well as the airport authority (Aéroports de Paris, or ADP) to consider the future air traffic situation in the Parisian region. The question boiled down to whether or not air traffic would make a new Paris airport necessary in the next few decades.

Each time the question came up, the reply was more negative, given the capacities of the provincial airports, e.g. Lille. It is worth noting here that regional hubs are underdeveloped in France, in comparison with other European countries. Nevertheless, the government mandate given to Jacques Douffiagues, former transportation minister, included a second, new question: Where should this hypothetical airport be built? The precautionary principle requires that appropriate, thinly populated land be selected, rezoned and expropriated for an airport. Otherwise, uncontrolled urban development may rob future generations of their choices. The following section presents extracts from Jacques Douffiagues' report to which we officially contributed.

The French ministries for supply and services, transportation and tourism created the Douffiagues Commission to study the air transportation situation in the greater Parisian area with the year 2030 as a horizon.

The commission's work followed two distinct yet equally necessary phases:

Phase 1: draft various scenarios and suggest that the seemingly indispensable measures be immediately implemented. The Commission proudly pointed out that almost all the measures had been enshrined by the French government during a ministerial council meeting in October 1995;

Phase 2: prepare an orientation document, primarily for the ministers, to guide them in the choice of a site for the new international platform which would be created outside the Ile de France (Parisian region) yet be designed primarily to serve that region.

The Third Airport Paradigm

After the first phase, the commission did not favor the idea of a third international platform. The commission's research over 15 months led the participants to confirm that current traffic conditions, and even the predicted conditions whether short-, medium- or long-term, indicated that the needs of the greater Parisian region would be amply met by

– coordination and moderate development of Charles-de-Gaulle Roissy Airport, as part of the scenario with the least noise impact;
– release of a portion of the traffic (mail and commercial) to other platforms in the region or bordering regions, e.g. Beauvais, Reims, Pontoise;
– redirection of a significant percentage of the medium and long-distance carriers to the major provincial platforms, e.g. Lyon-Satolas, Lille-Lesquin, and even possibly, Nantes-Notre-Dame-des-Landes (intermodal technique).

Potential Traffic for Provincial Airports in France

In 1995, one-third of the current traffic at Orly and Roissy airports was comprised of provincial residents in transit. The traffic at the second largest French airport (Nice) equals 10% of that of the first (ADP). Note that the second British airport, Manchester, enjoys traffic equal to 20% of the London airports.
The potential of Lille in terms of passenger handling is great (7 million passengers rather than today's 1 million); whereas the Satolas airport has a potential capacity of 15.5 million rather that the current 4.5 million.

On November 17, 1995, the ministers of supply and services, transportation and tourism, as well as the secretary of state for transportation, confirmed by letter their decision to move on to the second phase. Here the focus was on selecting sites within the greater Parisian region, but beyond the core. Given the situation, selecting a site was a major issue in regional development policy.

The initial goal was to analyze sites according to specific evaluation criteria including:
– quality of access by land and air;
– environmental impact;
– investment cost;
– regional characteristics;
– level of social risk associated with location.

The commission worked according to instructions within a strict timeframe. In order to structure their thinking, the participants used Multipol, a multicriteria selection method useful when the future is uncertain. The following pages trace how the group applied Multipol to a problematic and public choice.

A Wager and Its Risks

Choosing a better site for an airport that will open at the earliest in 2020 or 2030 is an especially difficult task. In 25 to 30 years, the basic elements at the heart of any choice will be considerably different.

Technology will have evolved, as well as the European and international supply and demand. The very face of air transportation will have changed along with airport systems, urbanization around the French capital, road networks, lifestyles, even public awareness of risks and disturbances. Futures-thinking efforts may well have been launched but they only quantify on the basis of various hypotheses, the market demand with horizons of 2015 or 2030. No one can guess what aircraft capacity or performance will be at that point. No one can be sure of the disturbances new aircraft may cause, just as we do not know about the precision, navigational power or control of new vehicles.

Forecasted Passenger Traffic and Flow Movements

1980-1990 Change in number of passengers
orly: 4.4% per year
roissy: 8.1% per year

Traffic in millions (PAX)	1995	2015	2030
Orly (capacity)	26.7	24-30	27
Roissy (capacity)	28.4	50-60	63-80
Demand	55.3	64-95	90-124

Movements	1995	2015	2030
Orly (capacity)	239 000	250 000	250 000
Roissy (capacity)	331 000	350 to 520 000	400 to 540 000
Demand	570 000	600 to 770 000	650 to 900 000

N.B. Hypothesis based on a simple average: 140 passengers rather than the current 120.

Even after the decision has been made, one of the main difficulties in this type of situation lies in the uncertainty created by the 15- to 20-year period required to set up the logistics of a new airport system. This uncertainty should be seriously considered when selecting a site. However, the context in which the new airport will develop can only be known when that decision is made and announced.

Developing a new airport outside a known region is a gamble in unsure future territory. It is not a classical case of a major project, like a container with a known content, e.g. large commercial stadium or an industrial plant relocation. Nor is it even an irreversible decision, a single major expenditure. Instead this decision requires reserving a site for an eventual air transportation center. The nature of this venture is not so readily defined and can not be evaluated for another ten years. It will not even start operations until 2020.

A Deficit of 250,000 Movements or a Surplus of 140,000 for the year 2030?

With this horizon, predicted traffic varies between 90 to 124 million passengers and 650,000 to 900,000 for the main centers. Just how relevant a new airport would be depends on how much air traffic grows during the period 2015 to 2030 and not the period 1995 to 2015. Obviously in the hypotheses that use low growth, a third airport would be totally unjustified, even in 2030. Given this highly uncertain context, the long-term must be kept foremost in mind. Actually, as we approach 2030, we can no longer exclude an increase in the demand higher than today's forecast, nor can we exclude a major technological or structural change in transportation or the impact of factors related to the environment or regional development that would make new air transportation facilities necessary even sooner.

The Procedure Adopted

The Douffiagues Commission developed its own procedure designed to take into account the inherent uncertainty. The commission began a "multicriteria analysis" comparing only the potential sites presented by the regions concerned. There were 13 sites spread over three regions. This study was carried out using the same questionnaire designed according to the needs of the commission and informed by the regions and analyzed by the appropriate departments of the federal ministries of supply and services, housing, transportation, tourism and the environment. On the basis of these elements, the commission proceeded to three successive screenings so that no site presented any major flaw and so that there was some basic hierarchy among the sites according to the objectives already given.

The first screening relied on technical feasibility criteria, in other words:

– basic data like soil, real estate and property values;
– quality of the air space in terms of weather patterns, obstacles, current and future route compatibility and approach paths;
– environmental impacts such as population, noise levels, natural and constructed historical or heritage sites, sensitive areas, etc.

The second screening used adaptation to the regional clientele as a criterion. Here the issues were ground access, employable population, commercial zoning. The main task here was to analyze the conditions for eventually developing an airport in terms of passenger or customer service while keeping the characteristics of the region in mind. The list included road systems, rail service, population served, commercial/shipping zones, regional characteristics, employment, and urban structure.

The third screening used the "demand scenarios" and airport operations. The objective was always to identify the most flexible sites in terms of airport infrastructure, e.g. support or satellite role, bipolar operations with an existing airport or an independent airport. At this stage participants also had to consider the consequences of reserving a site should the new project not materialize. The paradigm is essentially limited to the direct and indirect costs implied in merely reserving a site. It soon became apparent that the stakes are lower economically in this case than the cost of an airport or the cost of a poorly selected site. We are talking about investments of approximately 150 million euros in the first case versus 3 to 7 billion euros in the second. This aspect did not seem discriminatory to the commission.

The commission asked territorial or regional organizations and consular groups who had an interest in the greater Parisian region to provide data related to the technical-economic feasibility criteria for each site. These data were sent through the regional governmental offices.

The Regional Partners

Three regions submitted files which met the objectives of the commission; i.e., create a new large, international airport in the greater Parisian area, outside of Ile de France.
The Regions were as follows:
Centre: seven sites; three near Paris at Sainville, Santeuil and Beauvilliers along the ultrarapid Atlantic train route; four distant sites at Marboué, Bonneval, Arrou, Crucey-Senonches.
Haute-Normandie: two sites along the Seine, on the Vexin Plateau and the sother plateau of the Eure River.
Picardy: three sites along the northern ultrarapid train route, in other words, Hangest-en-Santerre and Vermandovillers between Amiens and Saint-Quentin and Rouvillers, a site near Compiègne. The regional management of the supply and services ministry identifies a possibility at Fouquescourt, not far from Hangest and Vermandovillers.

Evaluation and Multicriteria Choice using Multipol

The commission realized that any examination of the sites presented would be imperfect from the start and that further studies would be necessary. The specific location, for example, could always be optimized, but only through deeper analysis. The idea of picking two or three sites came up, in the case of a tie or some instability in terms of their advantages or, more likely, a feeling of comparing apples and oranges.

Within this context, it became important to present the actors (regional groups, etc) with the full set of elements behind the commission's rationale, e.g. criteria, files presented plus technical estimates, and also to develop a method that was sufficiently simple and convivial that people could appropriate it. Given the motives and context, the Multipol method was chosen.

Macrocriteria and Corresponding Sub-criteria

Macrocriterion 0.   Basic data, ground accessibility
Subcriteria:
– soil and subsoil;
– real estate and property matters.
Subcriteria for ground access:
– current distance by road from center of Paris;
– access time for the A 86 highway;
– the combining indicator for the commission related to the proximity of the sites;
– in terms of the A86 and the existing railroad network.

Macrocriterion 1.   Quality of Air Space
Subcriteria:
– meteorological conditions, geographical characteristics and obstacles;
– overall reorganization of the structure;
– available air space;
– airline routes;
– approach procedures;
– combined evaluation indicator for the commission.

Macrocriterion 2.   Environmental Aspects
Subcriteria:
– residents affected (a 40 to 8 km zone);
– residential areas affected;
– noise level per residential area;
– natural and manmade heritage sites;
– commission's combined evaluation indicator – environmental effects.

Macrocriterion 3.   Clientele and Site Region
Subcriteria:
– road access for the Ile de France region within a radius of 30, 45, 60, or 75 minutes (1995 or 2015);
– road access for the greater Parisian region outside Ile de France within a radius of 30, 45, 60, or 75 minutes (1995 or 2015);
– road access for those outside the greater Parisian region within a radius of 30, 45, 60, or 75 feet minutes (1995 or 2015);
– population 2015 greater Parisian area at 60 and 75 minutes;
– ratio between the potential market in term of the 60-minute zone around the greater Parisian area;
– commission's combined evaluation indicator.
Subcriteria for the region selected:
– employment within a radius of 30 to 45 minutes in 1995;
– commission's combined evaluation indicator;
– accounting issues, employment, urbanization, activities.

Each site was evaluated by the commission in terms of the five main dimensions: quality of air space, ground accessibility, environmental impact, clientele and employable local population, with several criteria, also defined by the commission.

The evaluation relied on a simple, familiar 1-5 scale ranging from 1, which meant highly insufficient or highly incompatible with the dimension considered, to 5, which meant very good or completely compatible. Note that 0 was not used since no site was excluded on the basis of one single criterion.

Moreover, the sites were not judged in a uniform fashion. Participants had to consider the various contexts related to the very objective of the study. With this in mind, the commission proceeded to judge the pertinence of the structures and corresponding sites according to the short-, medium- and long-term demand, the positioning of the Parisian region within Europe, the Paris-province relationship, the economy of the supply and the positioning of the French airline industry, the coherence and efficiency of the overall structure in serving the greater Parisian region, and lastly, the inherent costs and associated risks.

For the aspects related to the selection of a site based on feasibility and adaptability criteria, excluding an evaluation of airport structures, the variety of regional and economic development policies translated into a weighted system, with coefficients applied to the dimensions of the crtieria thus enabling participants to set up a hierarchy of sites according to possible policies.

Commission members distributed a weight of 15 points on five dimensions and again for four political orientations, or possible value systems. The four types of weighting criteria were as follows:
– weighting criteria to make air transportation a priority;
– weighting criteria to make regional development a priority;
– weighting criteria to make the environment a priority;
– weighting criteria with no differentiation of criteria (weighted average).

Multipol calculates the weighted score for each site for each set of criteria. As a result, we can draw up a chart and graph of the comparative profiles of the sites according to the weight given the criteria. Given the risk, the uncertainty surrounding the policies, a stability plan is carried out. Two dimensions are used: the average scores and standard deviations.

Multicriteria Analysis Grid

Regions	Sites	Macro Criteria Dimensions				
		Quality of Air Space	Quality of Ground Access	Environmental Impact	Clientele Base	Regional Employable Population
Upper Normandy	Plateau du Vexin normand	1	2	4.5	4.5	4.5
	Plateau sud de l'Eure	1	2	4.5	3.5	4
Center	Sainville	3	4	4	5	5
	Beauvilliers	3	4	5	5	5
	Santeuil	3	4	4	5	5
	Bonneval	4	1.5	2	2	2
	Marboué	4	1.5	2	2	2
	Arrou	4	1.5	4.5	1.5	2
	Crucey-senonches	1	2	4	3	4
Picardy	Vermando-villers	1.5	1.5	2.5	1.5	2
	Fouquescourt	1.5	1.5	4.5	1.5	2
	Hangest en Santerre	1.5	1.5	2	1.5	2
	Rouvillers	2	3.5	1.5	4.5	4

Chart of Weighted Criteria (or Coefficients)

	Quality of Air Space	Ground Access	Environment	Clientele Base	Employable Population	Sum of Weights
Air Transport Priority	4	3	1	4	3	15
Regional Management Priority	1	4	3	3	4	15
Enviromental priority	1	3	6	2	3	15
Undifferentiated	3	3	3	3	3	15

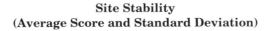

Site Stability
(Average Score and Standard Deviation)

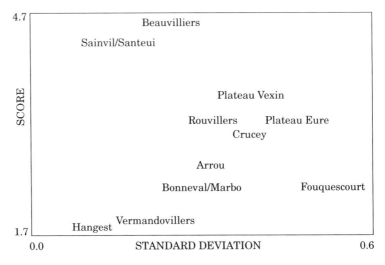

The analyses reveal that a major international airport is technically possible at any of the sites proposed. No differentiating element is politically insurpassable. Yet to commission members, certain sites appear better located than others. Any conclusion is obviously simplistic and any decision frustrating, but the wager – and it is a real gamble – is not a sure thing. Producing a proposal is in the commission's mandate; however, the decision belongs politically and exclusively to the political powers involved. The commission proposes; the government disposes.

The air traffic criteria lend a significant advantage to sites in the central region (exception: Crucey-Senonches) rather than those in Upper Normandy or Picardy. In these two regions, there is some risk of traffic problems, to varying degrees, with existing airports.

The criteria related to ground service do not favor sites like Upper Normandy and Crucey-Senonches in the central region. These sites do not have a new ultra-rapid (TGV) rail line.

Most of all, the commission believed that the basic choice, in terms of geographic position, should be founded on a market demand strategy and not on the supply side. One, the market demand strategy appears more coherent with the political will to follow market laws within the European context, an idea expressed repeatedly by successive administrations. Two, the supply strategy corresponds better to emerging sectors whereas the market demand strategy suits mature sectors. This would seem to be the case for air transportation (horizon 2015-2030).

Given these views, and on the basis of the elements available, the commission concluded that the best sites in terms of the clientele were the residents of the Beauce, the region closest to Paris. According to this hypothesis, the choice should be based on site optimization without any bias toward one region or another, as was the case with the commission and Beauvilliers. The commission defended its choice by pointing out that the classification process using most of the other criteria pointed in the same direction.

Distance to Sites from Paris Notre-Dame
(as the crow flies)

Sainville	64 km
Rouvillers	67 km
Santeuil	71 km
Beauvilliers	78 km
Vexin Normand	80 km
Bonneval	92 km
Plateau sud de l'Eure	92 km
Crucey-Senonches	94 km
Hangest-en-Santerre	100 km
Fouquescourt	106 km
Marboue	106 km
Arrou	113 km
Vermandovillers	114 km
Vatry	135 km

The commission recommended that the hypothesis of reserving the Beauvilliers site in Eure-et-Loire be validated and further developed by the appropriate goverment departments.

Actually, in each exercise using weighted criteria, the Beauvilliers site ended up on top. Sainville and Santeuil always followed. The Plateau du Vexin in Normandy and the Rouvillers site fought for the next rung on the ladder depending on policies (as seen in the weighting of the criteria).

This summary proposal had more nuances, implied certain limits and came with comments. The proposal must be understood within the context of "suggested sites". Deadlines limited the commission's choice of method and it could only call upon regional entities for lists of sites. Obviously this method does not claim to be exhaustive.

Another point to keep in mind, the conclusion is the result of a choice and weighting of criteria. These are the choices and weighting of the commission. The government will prove or disprove these choices and possibly substitute them with others. The method proposed will facilitate matters, should this be the case.

Ultimately the supply side of air transportation depends on how attractive the site is for airlines. This point can not be stressed enough and the market alone will decide on this point. Realistically, operators always prefer the closest site rather than the farthest, especially for short flights and medium-sized carriers. Experience in air transportation shows that it is difficult to nurture an airport designed for long flights without the support of a short- and medium-distance network. The conditions for a site far away thus remain doubtful and the possibility of operating three airports remains problematic.

The second airport in Montréal, Québec, reveals a great deal on this topic. The division of flights between the original airport (Dorval, 25 km from the city) and Mirabel (60 km) led to economic decline in the Montréal region as a number of operators turned to Toronto or northern US cities, especially New York. Openly declared a white elephant in the press, Mirabel never managed to gain a strong foothold in the world of air transportation. After February 20, 1996, however Mirabel became an airport for cargo, charter or night flights. The 1996 decision followed several in-depth studies which confirmed that maintaining intercontinental flights at a distant facility made Montréal vulnerable to the American hubs and its traditional Canadian rival, Toronto. The loss of more than half its intercontinental flights would have had an extremely negative impact on development in the greater Montréal region. Of course the Mirabel airport chapter also reflects the history of federal-provincial politics in Canada. Nevertheless, when the ADM, or Montréal airport authority, decided to bring transatlantic or international flights back to Dorval after twenty years, we were reminded that a problem can not be put aside easily.

The main advantage of this multicriteria analysis was that it imposed a systematic gathering of information and a collective thinking process that was far more rigorous than what could have been achieved without this logical framework (identification of sites, defined criteria, evaluation of sites by criteria, testing sensitivity of results against the possible policies). Note that the overranking of the Beauvilliers site was such that no better classified site could be found regardless of the policy tested, as seen through the weighting of criteria.

In the end, although the Beauvilliers site was finally selected by the government, it may never really become the third airport of the Parisian region. Yet someday on the horizon, Beauvilliers might stand out as a necessity if Orly were submitted to more drastic restrictions than today's. For instance, if a major crash occurred then the situation might change dramatically. However Beauvilliers as site is a conjecture among other possibilities in what are fortunately still the "open skies" of airport transportation.

Five years later (2000) when annual growth in air traffic volume reached 7 percent and more for the Paris airports, the question of a third airport reared its head once more. This time, we were called

Site Ranking According to Policies

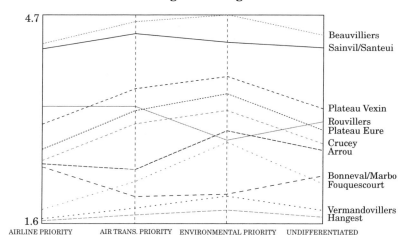

upon to ensure the methodological transfer of the scenario techniques previously employed. In the context of what is popularly called the new economy, the prospects for air traffic are more optimistic for the upcoming decades. The question now is clearly where to locate this third airport and perhaps even a fourth airport devoted exclusively to freight shipments.

8

BASF FACING AGRI-FOOD AND ENVIRONMENTAL CHALLENGES

The BASF case study shows how the future of agri-food and environmental challenges can be considered by the main stakeholders (corporations, farmers, consumer groups, etc.) over a long period (3 years). This innovative approach was initiated by one the former directors of BASF France, Bernard Lafourcade with methodological advice from Michel Godet (Cnam), and Pierre Chapuy (Gerpa). Of particular technical interest here was the use of the Mactor method. [1]

The Full Futures Process from Upstream to Downstream

Agricultural products occupy a significant rank among BASF's many sectors. In fact agricultural products represent over 15% of the BASF Group's overall activities. BASF manufactures ammoniac-based fertilizers, phytosanitary products utilised to protect crops, and food additives, including vitamins used in animal feed.

Within the European context, BASF's priority market is the French agricultural sector. The BASF Group currently leads the French market, which comes second to the American market worldwide. As a result, the agricultural products division at BASF France enjoys a certain independence and defines its own strategy.

Upheaval in the French agricultural sector in the early 1990s, caused by a redrafted joint agricultural policy and the shift from GATT agreements to the new World Trade Organisation led BASF France to rethink its strategy, especially product merchandising.

Relations between BASF and farmers follow the pattern of a traditional merchandising infrastructure – agricultural cooperatives, retailers and wholesalers – and require joint initiatives to supply the market better. Eager to consolidate its position on the French market, BASF sought to strengthen relations with the operations managers or officers of distribution companies in a lasting way. This step marked a break from the past when the focus was on purchasing managers.

Instead of offering some form of incentive travel (a common practice in this sector) and instead of drafting the umpteenth quality pledge, BASF decided to offer these small-to-medium-size business managers, who are usually caught up in day-to-day matters, an opportunity to reflect upon the future and the stakes which would determine their commercial success or failure.

---

1. This case study was prepared as a report, published in full as a Lips Working Paper (n° 11) and developed in the article "Scenarios and Actors' Strategies: The Case of the Agri-Foodstuff Sector" by Bernard Lafourcade and Pierre Chapuy in *Technological Forecasting and Social Change*, vol. 65, n° 1, September 2000.

A Participatory Futures-Thinking Exercise

Initially, a two-day seminar for training and futures exercises was offered to distribution managers. They were asked to consider as a group (suppliers and clients) the factors of both change and inertia that would affect the sector from 1997 to the year 2005, plus any pre-conceived notions on these two topics. After this exploratory phase, yet still within a workshop setting, participants identified the measures they would need to take to control some of the major stakes identified during the previous phase.

After the two-day event, participants had made enough progress to realise how effective this type of futures exercise can be. Yet they remained aware of the need to develop several themes, all of crucial importance for their own future. They also asked that the futures-thinking process continue under the auspices of BASF.

A summary of the two-day meeting was written up 1) to enable participants to repeat the process or something comparable in their own company and 2) to highlight priority topics for futures-thinking exercises. On the basis of these topics, working groups were set up including BASF operations executives and managers attending voluntarily from BASF client companies. This last group made up over 80% of the audience at the preliminary seminar in Venice.

Six meetings were scheduled over the following year so that each topic could be explored. The schedule allowed for the use of futures techniques (environmental scenario building, actor analysis, analysis of competence trees, etc.) in order to investigate possible futures in the agricultural channel, [1] winning strategies for distributors and, lastly, common goals on which both distributors and suppliers would do well to agree.

As part of the wrap-up stage, a seminar was held in Lisbon, in June 1996. Most of the participants from the Venice seminar attended as well as some important clients whose awareness of the exercise and its results was considered appropriate.

After the first phase, participants wanted to continue the collective thinking process by integrating new partners and by focusing on other major themes. As a result, the topics listed below were studied over the following two years:
– changes in the distribution profession;

---

1. Channel, sector, channel, chain, stream... depending on the context any one of these three words may be used to translate the French word *filière*. Sector is broader whereas chain reflects the interrelatedness of the actors, or stakeholders. Channel evokes the flow of goods and services. For the broadest, general sense, the *food* or *agri-food industry* has been used.

– impact of new environmental demands on the profession within the agricultural channel;

– consumer expectations in food security and how these influence future behavior of players in the sector.

A steering committee made up of volunteers from the sector carried out most of the studies. The topics were presented during seminars which brought together approximately fifty distributors each time. The research or results were then published in different formats in different collections, *Futuribles International* and the Lips Working Papers and also in the journal *Technological Forecasting and Social Change*. Professor Michel Godet and the Gerpa consulting team provided the steering committee with methodological support.

The past three years of futures-thinking exercises, led by BASF Agriculture with the participation of its clients, may be broken down into three phases according to the following four principles:

1) choose procedures that will specifically answer distribution questions;

2) use methods adapted to the time and means available;

3) select simple, concrete, appropriable tools that encourage reflection and group expertise;

4) enlarge the circle of individuals involved gradually as the themes develop.

The Future: What Stakes? Which Actors? What Are the Key Questions?

This particular process stemmed from BASF's openness to using Strategic Prospective methods and tools to answer the questions really asked by real agricultural distributors, who are also BASF Agriculture France's clients.

Three main questions came out of the studies based on the intial seminar which had brought together forty-odd managers from agricultural distribution firms in the Spring of 1995. The following three questions led to the first phase (1995-1996):

– what are the possible medium-term developments (horizon line 2005) in terms of farmers' expectations? *(N.B. these are the direct customers of agricultural distributors)*;

– given these expectations, what skills can distributors offer and in which areas should they develop?;

– more generally, what are the stakes for agricultural distribution in the ten-year period (1995-2005)? who are the main players on the field and what important conflicts can we expect?

After the first phase, the distributors wanted to consider the environmental factor and how both consumers' and citizens' demands related to environmental issues are evolving. Throughout the first phase during the spring of 1996, Mad Cow Disease [1] stole the spotlight from the environment and food safety in the collective thinking exercise.

The second phase included a futures-thinking exercise with the year 2010 as a horizon line. This phase was designed to enable participants to understand in detail how the environment [2] interacted with the various components of the agricultural sector in order to anticipate what would be at stake in this sector and to suggest possible medium-term answers.

Future visions developed during this phase also enabled the group to build three contrastive scenarios according to major issues.

Once again, the importance of food safety and the demands of actors downstream (agri-food, or agro-alimentary, industries and retail commercial distribution, especially mass distribution) in the agricultural channel became evident. Hence during the third phase in 1998, the steering committee decided to focus on actor analysis for the issues of food safety and the environment.

Methods Adapted to the Time and Means Available

The studies and methods chosen enabled participants to find answers to the questions raised within four to five group or steering committee meetings over five or six months of work. Whereas the initial two-day seminar used the workshop format so that forty agricultural distribution managers could all participate. After this seminar, thirty managers agreed to continue working as a group for four days staggered over six months.

The Delphi technique, based on three rounds of surveys, and the Régnier Abacus, based on a color-coded voting system, were used in the second futures-thinking phase. Some fifty agricultural distribution managers and forty BASF technical-marketing staff members were thus able to participate. The second phase was led by the steering committee which included fifteen people who met for four half-days over six months.

In the third phase, fifteen actors in the agricultural and agri-food sector spent four days carrying out actor anaysis on the topic of food safety.

---

1. The Mad Cow frenzy was not an environmental problem as such. It was the problem of a dysfunctional industrial channel and its control. Nevertheless, the Mad Cow Crisis revealed with particular clarity the notion of risk associated with agricultural and agri-food channels: food safety, conservation of the "environmentalized" production chains.

2. In terms of the struggle against pollution and harmful substances, nature conservation and protection of natural resources, preservation and enhancement of quality of life.

Simple and Appropriable Tools Reflect Group Expertise

The methodological procedures – especially the tools used – enabled groups of managers in distribution firms to work as a group by exchanging opinions, sharing information within a common framework and encouraging reflection through their professional expertise and that of other actors in the sector.

These thirty agricultural distribution managers built competence trees for their own companies according to type. The participants then profiled different types of farmers or growers, and detailed their expectations for technical areas, services or financing.

During phase 2, approximately 100 managers were polled. They gave their vision of the limits and opportunities created by the environment within their sector and of the development of these limits in the future. They also described the policies and courses of action that they envisaged adopting to meet the challenges on the horizon.

Similarly, professionals in the agricultural and agri-food sectors identified the food safety "battlefields". They also pinpointed the most important actors involved and the goals each one was pursuing. They created two synoptic tables that represent the influence capacity of the actors among themselves and the positions of the actors on each of the goals (see two matrices: actors/actors and actors/goals).

Lastly, after each of the three phases, forty-odd distribution managers and a few other participants (internal or external in terms of agriculture) attended a wrap-up seminar. This occasion enabled participants to present results plus test and complete the data. Joint working sesions have also helped group members to pinpoint pertinent areas for action in terms of relevence according to the stakes already identified.

Enlarging the Circle Downstream

Although futures thinking began with only agricultural distribution managers (co-ops and companies) and BASF Agriculture staff attending seminars, it gradually spread within the sector so that:

– a greater number (up to 100) of agricultural distribution managers could take part using the combined Delphi-Abacus technique during the second phase;

– farmers could be integrated as of the second phase;

– representatives from agri-food industrial groups (downstream) could join the steering committee during the third phase.

Fuller discussions were also held upstream, and representatives of several actors from outside the agricultural sector (e.g. consumer groups, public authorities, mass distributors...) were invited to react and participate during the wrap-up seminars.

The Future of the Agricultural Channel by BASF and Its Clients: the Three Stages of Futures-Thinking

Phase 1 (*) : BASF and Its Distributors: A Shared Future (1995-1996)
– Identify ongoing changes and the stakes implied for agricultural distribution, e.g., technical factors, economics, and training.
Clientele
– 3 working groups made up of distribution managers; 4 one-day meetings over six months.
Tools
– Understand the current demands of farmers and anticipate their future needs: *morphological analysis.*
– *Analyse the distributor's profession, strengths and weaknesses: construct competence trees* (both future and present) of the distributors' offering.
– Detail the main battlefields of the future, inventory the goals of the actors involved, and understand alliances and opposing interests: *analysis of the actors' game* inside and outside the agricultural channel.

Phase 2: Agriculture and environment with the horizon line 2010, "futures consultation" (1997)
– Understand the interfaces between agriculture and the environment now and in the past.
– Anticipate changes to the horizon 2010, reflect on measures that distribution can take.
Clientele
– A panel of a hundred-odd distribution managers (response rate 48 to 58%).
– An internal panel of 40 technical-sales representatives at BASF.
– A steering committee that unites distributors and farmers and experts at the wrap-up seminar.
Tools
– *Delphi-Régnier Abacus:* a Delphi questionnaire over three rounds (past, present, future) staggered over 5 months (votes and explanations), plus and efficient voting mechanism: the Régnier Abacus.
– A *morphological analysis* to construct *contrasted scenarios* of the relationship between agriculture and the environment, horizon line 2010.

Phase 3: Food Security and Environment, Analysis of the Actors (1998)
– Identify the battlefields related to food safety and the environment.
– Understand the manoeuvres of all the actors involved, analyse the forces active in the situation, pick out major conflicts, and identify necessary or possible alliances.
Clientele
• A Futures-Thinking Group including industrial suppliers, distributors and farmers that expanded to include downstream players, e.g. independent farmers.
• The other actors: mass distributors, public authorities and consumer associations brought together by:
– agreements as to fostering thought;
– the wrap-up seminar to comment, criticise, complete the data.
Tools
Actor analysis (stakes, battlefields, actors present, goals pursued) using the Mactor method.

(*) Proceeded by a seminar that brought together some 40 managers.

Environmental Issues (Horizon 2010)

As a result of Phase 1, environmental restrictions were pinpointed as one of the major threats in the agricultural sector. The regulatory agencies, e.g. Brussels, ministries, various boards or lobbies, and the agricultural sector itself, all of whom are in favor of the development of environmental demands, do indeed seem to be the most powerful actors.

Now more than ever, distributors must focus specifically on the environment. Of course the entire agricultural channel must pay attention, given that the environment, if not previously ignored, has only recently became an issue for many. Given the "recentness" of the issue, futures techniques were chosen accordingly.

The second futures-thinking phase for BASF and its clients ran from October 1996 to May 1997. Their objectives were the following:
– identify the main aspects of development for the medium term in the environment as a field;
  – evaluate potential consequences for the agricultural sector;
  – envisage possible measures to be taken.

In order to include a large number of distributors in this phase, the Delphi-Régnier Abacus was used. It combines the Delphi format in which a panel of experts answer and mail in a questionnaire with the Régnier Abacus, an expert consulting technique in which votes are color-coded and debated.

Later, on the basis of this analysis, which was complemented by contributions from experts and debates during the wrap-up seminar, three scenarios related to "agriculture and the environment, horizon line 2010" were generated. They present three possible interfaces between the agricultural sector and the environment, according to future visions of the profession.

Two Expert Panels

A hundred general managers of distribution firms (cooperative or commercial) considered representative of the diversity of French agriculture comprised the first panel. Categories included: major grain growers, specialized farmers, intensive or extensive breeders, arboriculturalists, vintners, and mixed-crop farmers... to name a few. The questionnaire was sent to a named addressee and the follow-up process handled by BASF's sales representatives/commercial agents in the various regions. The rate of return was high: 55%, 48% and 58% for the first, second and third rounds. [1]

The second panel comprised forty BASF Agriculture commercial technicians. They answered the same questionnaire, however, this

---

1. Some seventy percent of the managers polled answered at least one of the three rounds. Slightly more than thirty percent answered all three.

internal consultation allowed the company to develop the thinking process within its own walls, thus improving mutual understanding of the problems and enhancing the possibility of dialogue between BASF and its clients. [1]

The two panels were polled three times on a series of 22 questions presented as statements, for a total of 66 subjects consulted. [2] Ideas covered the past, present and future of the interface between agriculture and the environment, as well as the actions to be implemented. It was also requested that participants explain their choice briefly so that the problem-statement of the two populations surveyed could be elaborated.

Questions were developed for the second and third rounds on the basis of the previous round. The following five themes were highlighted:
– general, social, economic and environmental context;
– overall development of the agricultural channel, and subsequent impact on interfaces with the environment;
– restrictions related to the environment imposed on the channel;
– external actors and their roles or actions in terms of the enviroment;
– behavior and any measures related to the environment within the sector.

Future Visions of Agricultural Distribution

The medium- or long-term visions held by agricultural distribution managers reveal a certain degree of consensus in their votes and explanations. As the following examples illustrate:
– by the horizon line 2010, distributors expect (read hope for) a return in public trust in agriculture. They also believe that accountability (trackability) will play a vital role in regaining the public's confidence;
– overall they do not believe that reinforced environmental restrictions by the year 2010 could challenge the paths and trend-based growth of agriculture; however, they believe in limiting the most harmful forms of restrictions;
– they do think that environmental restrictions will have a major impact on agricultural trades or professions by the year 2010 (e.g. generalization of expenses, statements of requirements, or bids tendered, subcontracting/contractualization, safety goals, etc.).

Through the futures-thinking process, it became obvious that the year 2010 held several major areas of uncertainty in which develop-

---

1. For this panel response rates obviously reached almost 100 percent.
2. For the second and third rounds, questions took into account previous answers.

ment of the system remains open and the distributors' opinions diverge on the following aspects:
– societal agreement to pay for environmental quality;
– importance and clout of the environment in international trade legislation, especially in WTO regulations;
– development of specific areas of technology in the sector and the possibility that the technology will be implemented and accepted (especially in terms of genetically manipulated food processing).

This uncertainty also affects the behaviour of actors in the sector. Questions may be raised as to:
– the sectorial capacity to develop agriculture that remains intensive and productive but is much cleaner than it is today;
– the sectorial capacity to act as a coordinated unit in environmental measures and actions – obviously this implies significant and coordinated effort in terms of training and developing skills at the local level.

Building "Agriculture/Environment" Scenarios with the Year 2010 as a Horizon

On the basis of participants' visions of the future (either consensus or dissension) morphological analysis was used to draft full scenarios about relations between the agricultural sector and the environment up to the year 2010. Eight building blocks laid the foundation of these scenarios including major arbitration cases involving the economy, social demand, and environmental restrictions, e.g., regulation, commercial skill, demand, and their impact on agriculture, and farmers' taking the environment into account, possibly in their choice of agricultural techniques.

Three scenarios followed: the first is dark; the second, rosy; the third, considered trend-based by many.
– 2010 "conflictual relations" between "agriculture" and the "environment": the relations remain conflictual. Public trust in the sector did not come back, partly because the agricultural sector did not become sufficiently committed to environmental protection, e.g. water and chemical use. Also the sector failed to respond to public concerns about food safety;
– 2010 "rise of logical agriculture" ("integrated farming"): the profession and entire agricultural channel became strictly committed to taking back the environment and meeting society's expectations. The consumer's and citizen's confidence did return. This confidence is based primarily on contractualisation which became commonplace throughout the channel, and on professionalism among those active in the sector plus pertinent, broadly shared information;
– 2010, "plurality and discomfort": Through the efforts of a large segment of the sector, consumers were reassured, however their trust remains shaky. The environment is still perceived as a growing

restriction by the majority in the channel. Some are still uneasy about any improvement in terms of the environment.

The first scenario looks black, while the second seems rosy. The third scenario, according to current dynamics, might be considered the trend-based scenario.

Mobilize Actors on Environmental Challenges

The BASF-client futures process was carried out in a very decentralized way. Several dozen distribution managers as well as BASF employees took part, thus the group could build and refine reference points and ideas which favored integrating the environment into their commercial activities. The Delphi-Abacus method further contributed to the collective learning process. Indeed, often questionnaire answers were developed during real working meetings at the distributors'.

The questions were ordered so that participants were surveyed in a manner conducive to "prospective" and strategy. The following questions exemplify this approach:

– What can happen in the future? Why would the system develop in one way or another?

– What could the impact be on my own activities?

– What could I do to prepare for expected developments or to anticpate them?

– What could I do to make the system head in a direction beneficial to me?

Results of the exercises, especially the scenarios for 2010, were presented several times to general meetings of cooperative or commerical groups, to boards of directors, or to technical/financial staff at training seminars. These presentations further contributed to making actors aware of the importance of the environment among the actors.

Mactor Analysis Applied to Food Safety

Given the tremendous impact of food safety issues and links with environmental problems, e.g. chemicals, pollution, new technology like genetic manipulation, the steering committee decided at the third phase (1997-8) to continue with agricultural distributors on the theme "food safety and the environment".

The objectives were the following:

– analyse the stakes, short and long term, in food safety and the environment plus pinpoint the consequences in terms of either demands or opportunities for the sector;

– know well the downstream situation in both food safety and the environment;

– make downstream segments aware of the upstream situation;

– find possible short-term action to take in conjunction with down-stream actors.

The thinking exercises revolved around actor analysis, using the Mactor method.

Make the Entire Agri-food and Agricultural Channel Think Together

Given the significant role played by actors upstream in this channel, the steering committee decided to integrate actors from the agricultural sector as well as consumers and public authorities. Two methods were used:

– interviews with some twenty people during the initial survey;

– participation of representatives from agri-food industries in the Group.

The Circle comprised some fifteen people:

– distributors (half downstream in the agri-food channel);

– farmers;

– representatives from large food industrial groups;

– BASF members.

A smaller group within BASF worked in close cooperation with the Gerpa consulting group to prepare the meetings and prepare reports in between each meeting. Professor Michel Godet supervised the process.

Other actors, such as public authorities, consumers' groups and distributors were met during the initial questionnaire stage and became involved in the process during the intitial seminar and during the debate over the results in the fall of 1998.

The Four stages of the Mactor Method

The Futures Studies Group analysed strategies regarding food safety and the environment using the Mactor method. This method is structured around several components, which are described here as four distinct stages.

The first stage seek to identify the different dimensions of the problem, e.g. the issues at stake and potential battlegrounds, the main actors, and their objectives as they engage on the battlegrounds identified.

In this case, a detailed survey was conducted among all the actors (including industrial suppliers, agricultural distributors, farmers, representatives of the agri-foodstuffs industry and the mass marketing sector plus consumers). The Futures Studies Group then analysed and summarized survey findings.

The second stage involved analysing and describing the strategies identified, in two ways:

i) identifying the direct influences exerted by the actors on each other ("actors/actors" matrix), and;

ii) describing and measuring the position of each actor in relation to each objective ("actors/objectives" matrix).

This second stage was carried out as a joint effort by the Futures Studies Group, during two meetings lasting about ten hours altogether.

In the third stage, the two matrices are fed into the Mactor software for processing. The result helps us provide a more detailed picture of the relative positions of all the actors (dominant or dominated by others), to identify the objectives for which they feel the most concern, those which are controversial or not, and to highlight the diverging and converging interests reflected in the various positions.

Results are interpreted during the fourth stage. After this, of course, the results are made available to all the actors so that they can analyse them in the light of their specific situation or their own ideas on the issues involved, and draw out conclusions for their corporate strategies.

Ten Issues, Eighteen Actors, and Twenty-One Objectives

The basic construct for this analysis of strategies on food safety and the environment was built up in two stages.

First, some fifteen interviews were conducted with representatives from all segments, from industrial suppliers upstream right through to the mass marketing industry and consumers.

Interviews were thus conducted with farmers, representatives from agricultural cooperatives (with or without downstream activities), agri-foodstuffs manufacturers, representatives from mass marketing corporations and consumer observers.

In addition, documents were compiled to ascertain and include the positions of various other parties interested in the debate on food safety and the environment (conference reports, interviews in specialised journals, etc.), together with the results of opinion polls conducted among the general public and agricultural community.

The Top Ten Issues

Using these interviews as a basis, the Futures Studies Group identified the major areas where food safety and environmental issues emerge. These areas make up the "battlefields" where the future of the food system will be played out around the theme of food safety.

Depending on which way the stakes are played out, the story of the food chain will be very different. The same issues polarize the various actors as they take up their positions on a series of objectives and as they seek to protect their interests and achieve certain results.

Although the identification of the issues at stake is not used as direct input in the Mactor procedure, this is the foundation on which the two essential components of the method are established; i.e., the list of actors and the list of objectives.

The final list of issues identified by the Futures Studies Group included the following:
1. Consumer confidence in food products.
2. Consumer arbitration/participation on food quality and safety as well as on environmental protection.
3. Relevance and quality of consumer information.
4. Changing environmental and health standards.
5. Impact of new technologies (products and processes).
6. Degree of control over the system – or leadership – exerted by the mass marketing sector.
7. Upstream/downstream integration and increasingly frequent contractual arrangements in agricultural production.
8. Distribution of costs and added value within the system.
9. Overall competitiveness of French agri-foodstuffs (including environmental protection and food safety aspects).
10. Distribution of (legal) responsibility for food safety.

Eighteen Actors

Using the list of ten main issues, together with research data from previous years and findings from the interviews conducted in the first phase, the Futures Studies Group drew up a final list of eighteen actors who were considered key actors in terms of the future of food safety.

These actors were identified and differentiated in particular through the convergence or divergence of their positions with regard to the main battlefield areas.

Two types of actors in agricultural distribution (cooperatives or commercial enterprises) were identified in this way, those with and those without activities which would therefore integrate them within downstream segments. It was considered that those with experience and responsibilities in the manufacture of processed products, and especially in marketing them directly to the public, played a different role from that of distributors who are only involved in supplying products or collecting them from farmers.

Similarly, the Futures Studies Group made a distinction between consumer associations and environmental protection associations. Although some of their concerns lie in the same areas, e.g. the use of plant protection products or pollutant discharges into water, their behavior patterns and objectives are not quite identical. In addition, they do not initially place the same emphasis on some food safety objectives.

The final list of actors identified by the Group was as follows:
1. Industrial suppliers not involved in R&D.
2. Industrial suppliers involved in R&D.
3. Agricultural distribution (supply and collection only).
4. Agricultural distribution with downstream integration in agri-foodstuffs.
5. Farmers under contract to downstream agri-foodstuffs manufacturers.
6. Independent (non-integrated) farmers.
7. Large agri-foodstuffs companies.
8. Small agri-foodstuffs companies.
9. Mass marketing (including "deep", or "hard" discount).
10. Specialized distribution and retailing.
11. Catering.
12. National agricultural organisations (including advisory bodies).
13. National government (ministries).
14. Regional authorities (devolved state authorities, local government).
15. Supranational organisations (European Union) and international organisations (WHO – World Health Organization, WTO, FAO, etc.).
16. The media.
17. Consumer associations.
18. Environmental protection associations.

It should be remembered that this list, like the list of objectives further on, was drawn up by a Futures Studies Group in which the upstream segments of the system were represented only by the agrochemicals and agro-pharmaceuticals industries through to the agri-foodstuffs industry. Neither the mass marketing sector nor consumers were directly represented. Both lists may therefore be slightly biased.

Nevertheless, these downstream actors were fairly widely interviewed during the initial survey. Moreover, the upstream actors represented in the Forward Studies group – especially the agri-foodstuffs industrialists – are in daily contact with those not involved in the Committee's discussions and are well acquainted with their positions and strategies.

Twenty-One Objectives

As representatives of their category within the system, members of the Futures Studies Group identified objectives by describing their aims on the various "battlefields".

On the basis of this initial material (about fifty objectives identified during the workshops), the group drew up a final list of twenty-one objectives. These were the objectives that it considered were being pursued by the eighteen actors identified above, within the major issues at stake where the future of food safety will be determined.

The wording of these objectives needed to be formalized as much as possible. Because the method involves positioning each actor according to whether they are very much in favour, in favour, indifferent, not in favour or very much against, the objective have to be formalized as specifically as possible to allow the position of each actor to be assessed correctly.

The final list of twenty-one objectives identified by the Committee was as follows:

1. Ensure that all products supplied by the system are harmless to public health.
2. Ensure adequate transparency (good practice report, traceability).
3. Make continuous objective assessments of the "household shopping basket" to check on food safety and environmental compatibility "from table back to stable".
4. Educate and inform the public on the issues at stake in the food system, especially technological issues.
5. Protect brand name image (especially as regards product safety, "tradition" and environmental compatibility).
6. Promote the "environmental and safety" content of distributor brands.
7. Shorten supply channels (from farms to consumers).
   [Reduce the number of intermediaries (processing, transport, retail outlets, etc.) between producers and consumers. In other words, "cut out the middleman".]
8. Develop quality labelling and promote local specialities.
9. Inform public debate, even by "fostering controversies" over new technologies.
10. Restore confidence in institutions as well as in health and environmental monitoring procedures.
11. Ensure both nutritional quality and flavour in products.
12. Introduce new and rational regulations.
    [Which must be well founded scientifically as well as politically and socially applicable and economically sound.]
13. Focus on new technologies to enhance competitiveness through innovation.
14. Ensure that added value accrues to upstream segments (primary production and processing).
    [Added value to be shared in such a way as to ensure the survival of upstream segments, especially by justly rewarding their services.]
15. Reflect competitive sales prices downstream in purchase prices upstream.
    [Ensure that downstream competition or lower consumer prices are paid for by all those involved in the system.]
16. Develop contract-based arrangements between responsible partners
17. Develop integration from downstream segments (distribution).
    [For mass marketing corporations, to acquire or develop the means to integrate food production or processing with its suppliers upstream.]
18. Implement incentives and eco-taxes for the agri-foodstuffs sector.
19. Clarify the legal responsibilities of each level in the system and provide information on these responsibilities.
20. Avoid maximizing the use of the precautionary principle.
21. Maintain control over the environmental impacts of the system.

Four Main Types of Objectives

Most of the twenty-one objectives may be grouped into four main categories:
- protection of the public interest;
- internal system operation;
- information for citizens and users, and public debate;
- the "rules of the game" for the future.

Public interest objectives

Some objectives are fairly general and relate to the public or collective interest. These include objective n° 1 *[Ensure that all products supplied by the system are harmless to health]*, n° 3 *[Make continuous objective assessments of the "household shopping basket"...]*, or n° 21 *[Maintain control over the environmental impacts of the system]*.

Objectives concerning internal system operation

Other objectives relate more to the way the system operates. These include competition or internal technical or economic cooperation within the system, and include n° 14 *[Ensure that added value accrues to upstream segments (primary production and processing)]*, or n° 16 *[Develop contract-based arrangements between responsible partners]*.

Objectives concerning information and public debate

Several objectives involve education, information and awareness issues and public debate. Naturally they are important in confrontations between actors over the issue of food safety.

For example, objectives n° 4 *[Educate and inform the public on the issues at stake in the food supply system, especially technological issues]*, n° 9 *[Inform public debate, including by "fostering controversies" on new technologies]*, or n° 19 *[Clarify the legal and penal responsibilities of each level in the system and provide information on these responsibilities]* all belong to this group.

The fact that several objectives of this type exist demonstrates the importance given by the Forecasting Group to public awareness in strategic interplay among actors, both today and in the years to come.

Objectives likely to determine the rules of the game in the future

In the end, a number of objectives will determine how food safety "battlefields" are likely to evolve in the future. The battles taking place around these objectives and the way conflicts of interest are resolved will contribute to the laying down of new rules, which – depending on the direction taken by the system – will be more or less favourable to food safety, to maintaining control over risks to consumers, and to technical innovation.

These same objectives will affect how the future of food safety plays out.

Examples of these key objectives are n° 10 *[Restore confidence in institutions and in health and environmental monitoring procedures]*, n° 18 *[Develop incentives and eco-taxes for the agri-foodstuffs sector]* and n° 20 *[Avoid maximizing the use of the precautionary principle]*.

Two Input Matrices: "Actors/Actors"; "Actors/Objectives"

Professionals Exchanging Views to Fill In the Two Input Data Tables

How strategies on food safety and the environment are carried out will depend not only on the positions each one adopts for or against the various objectives, but also on the strengths of each actor, on the influence they have on each other and on the pressure they are capable of exerting on the system.

Two types of relationships therefore needed to be documented: the position of each actor with regard to the objectives, and the influence exerted by the actors on each other.

Two Mactor input data tables were filled in to obtain:
– the "actors/actors" matrix shows the direct influence each actor is capable of exerting on each of the others;
– the "actors/objectives" matrix shows the position (for or against) of each actor in relation to each objective.

These two matrices (see input data conventions below) were built up by the Futures Studies Group in the course of two working sessions, representing a total of about ten hours of discussion.

The discussions which took place among the members of the Futures Studies Group (upstream industrialists, agricultural distributors, agri-foodstuffs manufacturers) were extremely fruitful. All those taking part were able to explain clearly how they saw each issue, so that the discussions led all of them, as representatives of their "category", to give an accurate idea of their position regarding each of the objectives identified by the group.

By formalizing this input in table form after all the questions had been put systematically to all actors, on all topics, or objectives, the Futures Studies Group was able to build up a picture of the system and a jointly agreed "starting position".

This starting point, or common view, was reflected in the two matrices and subsequently used as input data for the Mactor processing package. This package not only provides different synoptic pictures, but also brings out various hidden parameters, which are otherwise masked by the complexities of the system (18 different actors and 21 different objectives, i.e. total of some 700 possible intersections between actors and between actors and objectives).

Conventions used to fill in the "actors/actors" matrix

The table showing the relative powers of influence of actors on each other was filled in using the following scale:

4: "i" is capable of jeopardizing the very existence of "j" is vital to the existence of "j";

3: "i" is capable of preventing "j" from carrying out his missions;

2: "i" is capable of jeopardizing the success of projects undertaken by "j";

1: "i" is capable of jeopardizing the management processes of "j" to some extent in time and space;

0: "i" has little influence on "j".

Conventions used to fill in the "actors/objectives" matrix

The table showing positions with regard to objectives specifies:

a) agreement or disagreement on the objectives, using the following conventions:
  (+) if actor "i" is in favour of objective "j";
  (−) if "i" is not in favour of objective "j";
  (0) if "i" has a neutral or indifferent position regarding "j";

b) four different levels of agreement or disagreement, revealing the degree of priority given to each objective:

4: the objective jeopardizes the actor's very existence/is vital to the actor's existence;

3: the objective jeopardizes the fulfilment of the actor's missions/is vital to the actor's missions;

2: the objective jeopardizes the success of the actor's plans/is vital to the actor's plans;

1: the objective jeopardizes the actor's operational processes (management etc.)/is vital to the actor's operational processes.

Highly Uneven Powers of Influence

Outline of the Methodology

The following table ("actors/actors" matrix) showing the direct influence of each actor on one another gives the total "influence" (horizontal sum of indice in the matrix) and total "dependence" (vertical sum) of each actor on the system. This makes it possible to calculate the indicators which position each actor in terms of "influence/dependence", thus showing their relative positions.

Influence may be exerted directly by one actor on another, but also indirectly through a third. These indirect influences (and dependencies) can be accounted for through a simple calculation to give a more exact picture of reciprocal influence.

Both the degree of influence and dependence of each actor and the feedback reactions that can affect them can be integrated in a single synoptic parameter expressing the balance of power. The more favourable this is to a given actor, the more power he has to influence both the way the system evolves and the other actors, and the less subject he is to the influence of others.

Actors × Actors Matrix

Actors	Suppliers with no R&D	Suppliers with R&D	Agricultural distribution with no downstream integration	Agricultural distribution with downstream integration	Integrated farmers	Non-integrated farmers	Large agri-foodstuffs Co.	Small agri-foodstuffs Co.	Mass marketing	Other distributors	Catering	Agricultural professional bodies	National authorities	Regional authorities	International organisations	Media	Consumer associations	Environmental protection associations
Suppliers with no R&D	0	2	1	1	0	1	0	0	0	0	0	1	1	1	0	1	0	0
Suppliers with R&D	2	0	2	3	1	1	0	0	0	0	0	1	1	2	1	1	1	1
Agricultural distribution with no downstream integration	3	2	0	1	2	1	0	1	0	0	0	2	0	1	0	1	0	1
Agricultural distribution with downstream integration	3	3	1	0	3	1	1	2	0	1	0	3	1	2	0	1	1	1
Integrated farmers	2	2	3	3	0	1	0	1	1	1	0	3	2	2	0	0	0	0
Non-integrated farmers	2	2	3	3	1	0	0	0	1	1	0	3	1	1	0	0	0	0
Large agri-foodstuffs Co.	3	2	3	3	3	1	0	1	3	3	3	1	2	2	2	2	1	1
Small agri-foodstuffs Co.	2	2	2	2	1	0	1	0	1	2	1	0	1	2	1	1	0	0
Mass marketing	1	1	1	3	3	1	3	4	0	2	1	1	2	2	1	2	1	1
Other distributors	0	0	1	3	1	1	1	2	1	0	0	0	1	2	0	1	0	0
Catering	0	0	0	1	0	0	2	2	1	1	0	0	0	1	0	1	0	0
Agricultural professional bodies	2	2	2	2	3	2	1	4	1	1	0	0	2	2	2	1	1	1
National authorities	3	2	3	3	4	4	3	3	3	3	3	2	0	0	2	2	1	1
Regional authorities	2	2	3	3	3	3	3	3	2	2	3	1	2	3	1	2	1	1
International organisations	3	3	3	3	4	4	3	4	2	2	3	2	3	3	0	1	1	1
Media	2	3	2	2	2	2	2	3	2	3	3	1	3	3	1	0	3	1
Consumer associations	2	2	2	2	2	2	3	2	3	2	2	1	2	2	2	2	0	1
Environmental protection associations	2	2	2	2	2	2	3	2	2	1	0	1	3	3	2	2	1	0

MACTOR

Actors × Objectives Matrix

Actors \ Objectives	Ensure health and safety	Ensure required transparency	Shopping basket assessments	Educate and inform the public	Protect brand name image	Promote distributor brand content	Shorten channels	Develop quality labels enhance local specialities	Inform public debate, foster controversies	Restore confidence in institutions	Ensure nutritional quality and flavour	Introduce new and rational regulations	Increase competitiveness through tech. innovation	Ensure added value upstream	Reflect downstream competitive pricing in upstream prices	Develop contracts and partnerships	Develop integration from downstream	Develop incentives and eco-taxes	Clarify legal and penal responsibilities	Avoid maximising the use of the precautionary principle	Control environmental impacts
Suppliers with no R&D	1	-2	0	-2	0	0	0	-2	-3	2	0	-2	0	3	0	0	-1	0	-2	3	0
Suppliers with R&D	3	3	1	2	0	0	0	2	-3	3	2	3	3	3	-3	2	1	1	3	3	3
Agricultural distribution with no downstream integration	2	2	1	1	1	1	-3	2	-3	3	2	3	2	3	-3	2	-3	-2	2	3	2
Agricultural distribution with downstream integration	3	3	2	2	2	2	-3	2	-3	3	3	3	3	3	-3	3	-3	-2	3	3	2
Integrated farmers	3	3	2	1	2	1	2	3	-3	3	2	2	2	4	-4	3	-2	-3	2	3	2
Non-integrated farmers	2	1	0	1	0	0	3	3	-3	2	2	1	2	4	-4	1	-4	-3	1	3	1
Large agri-foodstuffs Co.	4	3	3	3	4	-1	-2	0	-3	3	4	3	3	4	-4	3	-3	1	3	3	2
Small agri-foodstuffs Co.	4	3	3	2	4	0	0	2	-3	3	4	3	3	4	-4	3	-3	-1	3	3	1
Mass marketing	4	3	3	2	1	3	2	3	2	2	3	2	2	0	4	3	2	0	3	-1	1
Other distributors	4	3	3	2	2	-3	2	3	0	2	3	1	1	0	4	2	0	0	3	0	1
Catering	4	2	0	1	0	0	0	1	-3	2	4	3	2	4	4	1	0	-1	3	1	2
Agricultural professional bodies	2	2	2	1	0	0	1	3	2	2	0	1	2	2	-4	2	-3	-2	0	3	3
National authorities	4	3	2	1	0	0	0	3	-3	4	1	3	1	3	1	0	0	2	2	-2	3
Regional authorities	4	3	0	1	0	0	1	3	-3	4	1	2	2	1	1	1	-1	2	2	-3	3
International organisations	4	2	1	0	0	0	0	1	-2	3	1	2	1	0	0	0	0	1	2	-2	2
Media	0	0	3	3	0	0	0	1	4	-1	0	0	0	0	0	0	0	0	2	0	0
Consumer associations	4	3	3	2	0	0	3	2	3	3	3	2	2	0	0	1	0	2	3	-3	2
Environmental protection associations	3	3	2	2	0	0	1	2	4	2	1	1	-1	0	0	0	0	3	2	-3	4

MACTOR

The following diagram shows how influence and dependence can be mapped as a diagram.

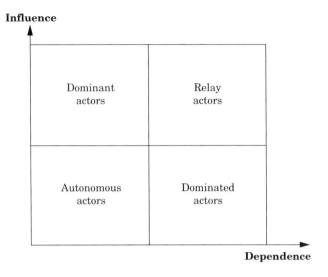

Dominant, Relay and Dominated Actors

This diagram, based directly on the input data compiled by the Futures Studies Group, shows the following:

– dominant actors, i.e. those who are capable of exerting strong pressures on the others without being subject to strong pressures themselves. These are primarily external to the system and include international organisations, the media and consumer or environmental organisations;

– relay actors, who are both highly influential and subject to strong pressures themselves: these are the other external actors (national and regional authorities) and, internally, the agricultural professional bodies, large agri-foodstuffs industries and mass marketing corporations;

– dominated actors, who have little influence on the others but are subject to strong pressures themselves. These include all upstream actors except the large agri-foodstuffs industries and distributors other than mass marketing corporations.

Only one actor, representing "catering", seems relatively autonomous (exerts little influence, but not much subject to pressure).

Which shows the indirect influence and dependence of actors on each other, is closer to the actual pattern of interplay. Here, three others have joined the group of dominant actors: national authorities, large agri-foodstuffs industries and mass marketing corporations.

Apart from the large agri-foodstuffs (AF) industries, all other actors in the upstream food economy are in a position of dependence within the system.

As both highly influential and highly dependent, the regional authorities and agricultural professional bodies (APB) are in an intermediate position. Either by virtue of their position as spokesmen for their profession at national level, or as public bodies with strong regional attachments, both play an essential role as relays in the system.

By comparing intersecting positions as represented by each pair in the analysis – such as industrialists, farmers and distributors – we can discern differences in their positions on the "playing field". Involvement in R&D (as in the case of industrial suppliers), integration with downstream segments (as in the case of agricultural distributors) and – to a lesser extent – integration within a sector of the system (farmers) increases potential influence within the system.

Relative Powers of Influence

The six influential or highly influential actors are mostly external to the system. These are the international organizations and national authorities, associations and the media, to which may be added the large agri-foodstuffs manufacturers and mass marketing corporations.

Two of the actors have average powers of influence: the agricultural professional bodies and the regional authorities.

In all the others, powers of influence are moderate to low; i.e. well below 1, or even very low as in non-integrated agricultural distribution, catering, suppliers not involved in R&D.

Taking average powers of influence as equal to 1, the figure for suppliers involved in R&D is 0.48; whereas integrated farmers stand at 0.53, and agricultural distributors with downstream integration at 0.61.

Involvement in R&D (distributors), downstream integration (distributors) and – to a lesser extent – integration within a sector of the system (farmers) increases powers of influence and therefore the actor's ability to exert pressure on the system.

The leading distribution companies score 1.39 and the major agri-foodstuffs industries 1.49. At the top of the power of influence league, the associations stand at around 1.9 and international organisations at 2.

Relative Influence and Dependence

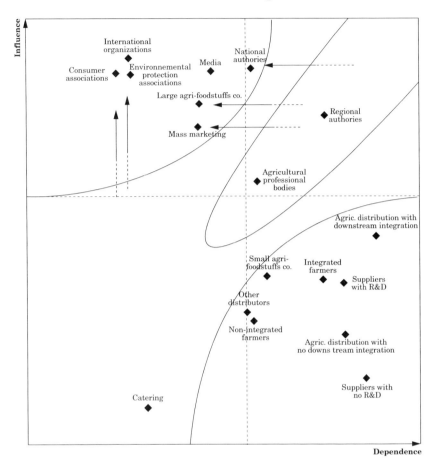

The arrows show the main directions in which secondary influences are exerted between actors. They show, for example, how national authorities and leading agri-foodstuffs and mass marketing corporations become part of the dominant group.

Relative Powers of Influence among Actors

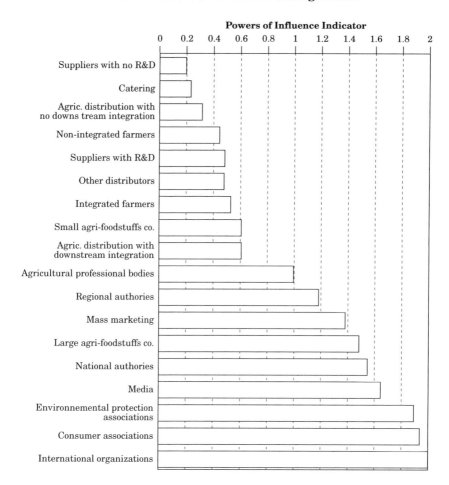

Example:
Consumer associations or environmental protection organisations have practically twice as much power of influence as agricultural professional bodies and three times as much as agricultural distributors.

Ambivalent Positions

One actor's position may converge with another's regarding specific objectives, while diverging from the latter on a different objective. If the same actor demonstrates similar ambiguity in relation to all the others, then he may be considered as highly ambivalent, and, preferably, should not be actively sought as a partner.

Overall ambivalence among the various actors was fairly moderate, with scores ranging from 0.18 to 0.72.

The least ambivalent, and therefore the most "dependable" as allies, include distributors other than mass marketing, international organisations and the small agri-foodstuffs manufacturers. At the other end of the scale, the most ambivalent, and therefore the least dependable, are suppliers not involved in R&D, the media, and environmental protection associations.

Ambivalence Ratings

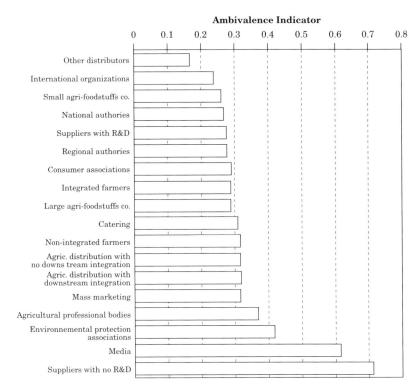

The more ambivalent an actor appears, the more caution should be exercised when considering alliances.

Legend: The ambivalence indicator - calculated here by integrating weightings by objective - may vary by convention from 0 (non ambivalent) to 1 (highly ambivalent).

Actors' Positions towards the Objectives

Outline of the Methodology

The data table ("actors/objectives" matrix) shows "valued" positions towards each objective. This reveals the extent of each actor's involvement in an objective, thus reflecting the importance they attach to each one.

The matrix of "non valued" positions (where positions towards objectives are shown only as positive, negative or neutral, regardless of degree) shows the number of actors concerned by each objective, whether they are for, against, or indifferent, and the number of objectives which concern each actor (for, against or indifferent).

In the matrix of "valued and weighted" positions, the power of influence of each actor is used to calculate a weighting for their involvement in the various objectives. This gives an idea of their degree of "commitment", or mobilization, and thus of their strength in relation to other actors.

Degrees of Commitment

Those concerned by all twenty-one objectives, and who are therefore to be reckoned with on all the battlefields, are the agricultural distributors (with or without food-processing) and the integrated farmers.

After these two groups come those highly concerned (by 18 to 20 objectives). They are the large and small agri-foodstuffs manufac-

Number of Objectives of Concern to Each Actor

21 objectives	– Agricultural distribution – Agricultural distribution with downstream integration – Integrated farmers
20 objectives	– Major agri-foodstuffs industries
19 objectives	– Small agri-foodstuffs industries – Mass marketing – Regional authorities
18 objectives	– Suppliers involved in R&D – Non integrated farmers
16 objectives	– Other types of distribution – Catering – Agricultural professional bodies – National authorities – Consumer associations
15 objectives	– Environmental protection associations
13 objectives	– International organizations
11 objectives	– Suppliers with no R&D
6 objectives	– Media

turers, mass marketing corporations, regional authorities, suppliers involved in R&D and farmers whose activities are integrated within a segment.

On the other hand, only six objectives concern the media. They are thus relatively independent in terms of the system. Obviously their stakes are elsewhere. The six objectives through which they interact with the system must be paid close attention, all the more so since they possess considerable powers of influence.

The least concerned are suppliers not involved in R&D (11 objectives) and international organisations (13 objectives). The remaining actors are still largely concerned by 15 to 16 objectives out of 21.

Objectives Involving the Largest Number of Actors

The objectives in which the largest number of actors feel involved are related to confidence, safety, controversies, and legal matters. These same objectives also have to do with informing the public: information, labelling and transparency.

Obviously, these are objectives of common interest, which are of concern not only to the technical segments, but also to the authorities at all levels, end users and associations.

Number of Actors Concerned by Each Objective

– Restore confidence in institutions	18
– Ensure health and safety – Ensure required transparency – Educate and inform the public at large – Develop quality labels, enhance local specialities – Inform public debate, foster controversies – Introduce new and rational regulations – Clarify legal and penal responsibilities	17
– Increase competitiveness through technical innovation – Avoid maximizing the use of the precautionary principle – Control environmental impacts	16
– Ensure nutritional quality and flavour	15
– Shopping basket assessments (safety, environmental impacts) – Develop incentives and eco-taxes	14
– Reflect downstream competitive pricing in upstream prices – Develop contract and partnerships	13
– Ensure added value upstream	12
– Shorten circuits – Develop integration from downstream	11
– Protect brand name image	7
– Promote distributor brand content	6

It would therefore be possible for the sector as a whole to establish cooperation strategies for these objectives, which are of concern to a high number of actors.

However, the objectives which concern the greater number are also those which will determine how the system evolves in the years to come, e.g. introducing rational regulations, mastering the precautionary principle or developing technical innovation.

Actors' Degrees of Commitment to the 21 Objectives

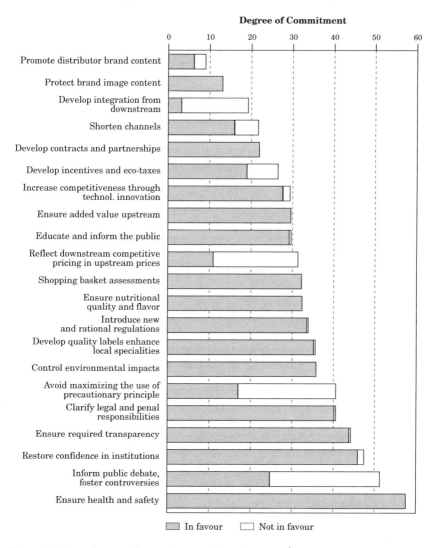

This table shows degrees of commitment (taking the balance of power into account), and which objectives create divisions (relative weight of positions for and against each objective).

On the other hand, the objectives which are of less widespread concern have more to do with internal issues of a technical, economic or managerial nature. These include distributor brands and brand-name products, integration from downstream segments and developing shorter channels.

When the balance of either power or influence are brought into play, we can go further and discern relative degrees of commitment for each objective for each actor.

The objectives which summon up the greatest degree of commitment, and around which the fiercest battles are likely to be fought when they are divisive – and which, *a contrario*, will rally the strongest support when they create a consensus – are those concerning safety, controversies, confidence and transparency, closely followed by legal matters and the precautionary principle.

Many Objectives Generate Agreement, Some Are Deeply Divisive

Depending on how positions for and against the objectives are distributed, they will generate either agreement or conflict in varying degrees. In addition, the actors involved in strategies specific to these objectives will have varying powers of influence. The scale of confrontation will also depend on the number of actors and their relative powers of influence over the system.

Divergence is obvious for the following two objectives, with about as many in favour of them as against:

– introduction of eco-taxes (7 pluses – those in favour – and 7 minuses – those against);

– ensuring added value downstream (5 pluses and 8 minuses).

Five of the objectives generate even greater conflicts of interest:

– fostering controversies (5 pluses and 12 minuses);

– shorter channels (8 pluses and 3 minuses);

– avoiding maximalist use of precautionary principle (10 pluses and 6 minuses);

– promoting the safety and environmental content of distributor brands (4 pluses and 2 minuses);

– developing integration from downstream (2 pluses and 9 minuses).

The table shows that several objectives bring a large number of protagonists into play and will therefore generate marked dissent. This is particularly true of the divisive objectives which are likely to weigh heavily on the way the system evolves in the medium- to long-term, and on the major mechanisms of arbitration:

– fostering controversies (17 actors concerned);

– avoiding maximalist use of the precautionary principle (16 actors concerned);

– introducing eco-taxes (14 actors concerned).

Other objectives are obvious causes of dissent within the system, but concern comparatively fewer actors:
– developing shorter circuits;
– protecting downstream added value;
– highlighting the safety and "environment" content of distributor brands;
– developing integration from downstream.

All the other objectives generate either a high degree of agreement (with only one against and all others in favour) or complete agreement (no opponents). This is particularly true of all the objectives of general interest to society as a whole – those concerning safety, confidence, transparency or environmental impacts, for example – and of those which are internal to the system, concerning partnerships, upstream added value and branded products (but not distributor brands). It should be noted that mass distribution needs branded products when consumers ask/clamor for them. However, this consensus does not apply to distributor's brands which independent farmers or small companies, but especially the other distribution channels oppose.

Varying Powers of Influence over Divisive Objectives

When powers of influence are taken into account; i.e., the capacities of those involved in various objectives to exert pressure and thus determine the outcome of battles over divisive objectives, this can reverse the powers of reciprocal influence between actors engaged in conflict or with opposing interests.

This does indeed occur for three of the most divisive objectives:
– avoiding maximalist use of the precautionary principle;
– introducing eco-taxes;
– fostering controversies over new technologies.

Moreover, these divisive objectives, together with the direction in which conflicts are resolved, will largely determine how the system evolves in the medium- and long-term.

Will the direction taken be rather favourable to the system; i.e., a tendency to rely on innovation, on possibilities for implementing new techniques and on the public confidence, or will the balance of power encourage trends in the opposite direction, with strict application of the precautionary principle, and constant uncertainty as to the risks or social usefulness of new technologies?

In the case of the three divisive objectives that are internal to the system, the powers of influence do not tip the balance either way between degrees of commitment hence:
– those in favor of shortening circuits are in the majority;
– those against reflecting competitive pricing downstream in purchase prices upstream seem to be more highly committed than those in favour;
– those in favour of integration from downstream are in the minority.

Towards Eco-Taxation

With the "eco-taxes" objective, the balance of power shifts towards those in favour of eco-taxation when degrees of commitment, where powers of influence come into play, are taken into account (+ 19 et – 8), but the situation is reversed when only involvement is considered (+ 12 and – 14).

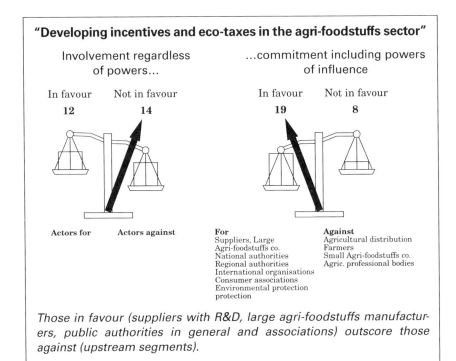

"Developing incentives and eco-taxes in the agri-foodstuffs sector"

Involvement regardless of powers...   ...commitment including powers of influence

In favour   Not in favour   In favour   Not in favour
12   14   19   8

Actors for   Actors against

For
Suppliers, Large
Agri-foodstuffs co.
National authorities
Regional authorities
International organisations
Consumer associations
Environmental protection
protection

Against
Agricultural distribution
Farmers
Small Agri-foodstuffs co.
Agric. professional bodies

Those in favour (suppliers with R&D, large agri-foodstuffs manufacturers, public authorities in general and associations) outscore those against (upstream segments).

Towards Maximum Use of the Precautionary Principle

The pattern appears the same for the objective on "promoting the maximum use of the precautionary principle". This objective was originally entitled "avoiding maximum use of the precautionary principle", but was changed here to "promoting maximum use of the precautionary principle" for greater clarity. However those against were in the majority when classified by involvement (– 28, + 14), the situation is reversed when degrees of commitment (bringing powers of influence into play) are considered.

The index of commitment for those against this objective is – 17. For those in favour, who are often opposed to the introduction of new technologies, the index of commitment is + 24.

Those in favour of maximizing use of the precautionary principle are in the majority and hence defeat their opponents.

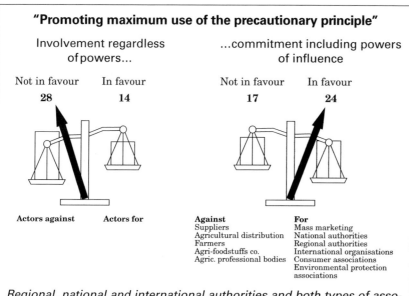

"Promoting maximum use of the precautionary principle"

Involvement regardless of powers...		...commitment including powers of influence	
Not in favour	In favour	Not in favour	In favour
28	14	17	24

Actors against	Actors for	Against	For
		Suppliers	Mass marketing
		Agricultural distribution	National authorities
		Farmers	Regional authorities
		Agri-foodstuffs co.	International organisations
		Agric. professional bodies	Consumer associations
			Environmental protection associations

Regional, national and international authorities and both types of associations outscore those against this objective (all of influence upstream segments).

Towards Permanent Controversy

In terms of "fostering controversies", the outcome (+ 15 and – 35) was more favourable to those against when involvement was considered (where bringing powers of influence are not taken into account). Bringing powers of influence into play merely results in a balanced situation, with commitment indices at + 25 and – 27.

These figures reveal a much weaker position than was previously thought among those opposing this objective.

The Three Divisive Objectives within the Sector

Three other objectives are divisive, but mainly concern issues that are internal to the system. Bringing powers of influence into play does not shift the initial balance between those in favour and those against these objectives.

Relative powers of influence as they emerge here from the interplay of strategies may be characterized as follows:
– favourable to those supporting shorter distribution circuits;
– favourable to those opposing any reflection of competitive pricing downstream in purchase prices upstream;
– unfavourable to those supporting the development of integrated activities from downstream.

"Supporting public debate, including by fostering controversies over new technologies"

Involvement regardless of powers...   ...commitment including powers of influence

In favour   Not in favour   In favour   Not in favour
15   **35**   **25**   **27**

Actors for   Actors against

For
Mass marketing, Media
Agric. professional bodies
Consumer associations
Environmental protection
associations

Against
Suppliers, Farmers
Agricultural distribution
Agri-foodstuffs co.
National authorities
Regional authorities
International organisations

Upstream segments and public authorities on the one hand, and mass marketing, APBs, the media and the associations on the other (in favour of controversy).

"Shortening distribution channels (from farmers to consumers)"

Involvement regardless of powers...   ...commitment including powers of influence

In favour   Not in favour   In favour   Not in favour
15   **8**   **16**   **6**

Actors for   Actors against

For
Farmers
Agric. professional bodies
Mass marketing & other
Regional authorities
Consumer associations
Environmental protection
associations

Against
Agricultural distribution
Large Agri-foodstuffs co.

Those in favour (local actors) outscore those against (agricultural distribution agencies and large agri-foodstuffs manufacturers).

"Reflecting competitive downstream pricing in upstream purchase prices"

Involvement regardless of powers...

In favour	Not in favour
14	**29**

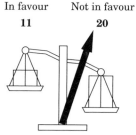

...commitment including powers of influence

In favour	Not in favour
11	**20**

Actors for   Actors against

For
Mass marketing & other
Catering
National authorities
Regional authorities

Against
Suppliers with R&D
Agricultural distribution
Farmers
Agri-foodstuffs co.
Agric. professional bodies

Those against (upstream) outscore downstream actors and the authorities.

"Developing integration from downstream"

Involvement regardless... of powers...

In favour	Not in favour
3	**23**

...commitment including powers of influence

In favour	Not in favour
3	**16**

Actors for   Actors against

For
Mass marketing

Against
Agricultural distribution
Farmers
Agri-foodstuffs co.
Agric. professional bodies
Regional authorities

Those against (upstream and regional actors) outscore mass marketing.

Main Results Regarding Food Safety and the Environment

Strong Actors, Weak Actors and Four Future Battlefields

Participants from the agricultural sector walked away with the following lessons, as summarized below:
- actors upstream are dominated;
- many objectives are consensual and only a few are very conflictual;
- mass distribution plays a lynch pin role,
- four battle lines will shape the future: distribution of added value, application of the principle of precaution, implementatin of eco-taxes, scientific and technical controversies.

Actors upstream are dominated

Actors dominating the system include public authorities (international and national), associations, the media and mass distributors. Contrary to popular belief, large companies in the agri-industry branded products play a role equal in importance to that of mass distribution. As a whole, with influence on the system is largely outside the actual agricultural channel of suppliers, agricultrual distributors and farmers.

Many consensual objectives and few conflictual objectives

Overall, the actors' role in food safety and the environment reveals a large number of subjects which generate consensus, e.g. "guarantee innocuity" "clarify legal and penal liablity", "master environmental impact" and "implement new rational regulations".

In fact, the number of conflictual objectives is small and includes "development of incentives and eco-taxes, redistribution of added value, controversy, precautionary principle".

In this context, those active in the agri-food sector must avoid two parallel pitfalls: first, hushing up diverging viewpoints and talking only about commonground; second, splitting up on a conflictual goal to the detriment of converging interests.

The pivotal role of major food distributors

Given the stance adopted by major food distributors on various issues and goals, they are in a position for double-dealing since opinions converge significantly between distributors and players upstream in the market as well as with the consumer, who seems very close to distribution. The role played by distribution in changing the system will therefore be a key one. Distributors will have to make some choices in order to ensure a coherent strategic front.

The four battles of the future: distribution of added value, precautionary principle, eco-taxes and controversy

If we take into account the balance of power among the actors the most involved in the goals that create dissent potentially serious conflict in four areas arises, namely:

– the main issue of the distribution of declining added value in the sector, given the consumer's decreasing willingness to pay plus the additional costs linked to food safety and environmental conservation;

– a very favourable balance of power for those who support developing eco-taxes on the use of chemical products, water usage, etc.

– similarly, a favourable position for those who support a maximialist application of the precautionary principle. This should generate greater restrictions in technical innovations;

– an equal balance of power in terms of controversy because the food safety debate is likely to become permanent.

Let us consider then constantly renewed controversies and a permanent state of doubt, as well as a rather maximalist application of the precautionary principle, lastly, the implementation of eco-taxes and increased integration of environment-related external costs by the sector. In a mature market, the struggle for added value will only intensify.

Three Topics for Strategic Thinking

This section describes the main points arising from the comments and discussions on these findings within the Futures Studies Group on food safety and the environment.

The Future Role of Integrated Farming

Discussion focused mainly on the likely role of integrated farming in crop production, over both the medium- and long-term. On the one hand, industrial users of agricultural products, who occupy an intermediate position in the sector, must ask whether integrated farming is likely to become the dominant norm in agriculture. This would obviously have an impact on agricultural practices and techniques, and in turn, on the nature of plant protection products and fertilizers and their sales volume. On the other hand, in the area of food marketing, would distributors decide to turn integrated farming to their competitive advantage, or would it become the norm for everyone, with only a few companies benefitting from their image as pioneers in the field?

Food Safety and Environmental Issues as a Key to Common Interests

There is also the question of the different actors' responsibilities with regard to food safety and the environment. Judging by the results and the number of topics generating consensus, it would seem that food safety and environmental protection are "pre-competitive" objectives. The fact that these objectives are supported by all the actors involved is a key to the economic future of agriculture and foodstuffs, and to long-lasting consumer confidence.

There is some doubt as to whether all the economic actors in the sector, especially in downstream activities, are fully aware of this fact. Some tend to take an immediate stance which parrots that of consumer associations – sometimes as a short-term reaction – and thus ensures favourable public opinion.

The Crucial Role of Communication

Communication and information, particularly for the general public, will therefore play a crucial role in shaping strategies on food safety and the environment. The public is often convinced that scientific knowledge on a given topic exists but remains concealed for economic or political reasons. This is the basic problem underlying the question of expert independence, or differences in expert opinion.

At present, inadequate information and communication is a fundamental problem. While food safety is improving objectively, perceptions of the food sector are increasingly negative.

The key question is therefore how to debate an issue which has not yet reached crisis proportions early enough to prevent it from ever developing into a crisis. What form should the debate take, and how should the public be encouraged to take an interest in it? There are three possible tacks to take in dealing with the public's lack of confidence: provide information, provide "science lessons" to increase public knowledge, or throw open a debate. The first two solutions have been tried, albeit unsuccessfully as measures were taken in haste, and with no attempt to anticipate results.

With regard to communication about what goes on in upstream segments, appropriate responses may include meeting controversies head-on or opening up farms and factories to public inspection. At present, communication on agriculture is often too fragmentary and many representatives of agricultural organisations are too defensive in their arguments, which tend to reflect an urge to justify past practice ("it's what we do already"). What the sector needs is to move forward and communicate differently as a coherent whole, rather than as isolated segments.

Four Avenues to Explore in Future Discussions

The Futures Studies Group felt that it would be useful to extend discussions in the four directions that were further explored by the four workshops organised during the Hendaye seminar:

– the future role of integrated agriculture and its consequences for the farming profession;

– guidelines for a charter setting out initiatives and responsibilities to be taken within the sector, regarding food safety and the environment;

– other practical initiatives for the short term, in areas that are common to all those involved in upstream activities (packaging, traceability, etc.);

– objectives and main lines of mutually agreed communication activities to be developed by the sector as a whole to target external audiences.

Summary of Discussions: Ten Key Points

Ten key points emerged from the discussions and workshops organised as part of the seminar in which the Futures Studies Group presented its findings to other members of the sector and external actors (public authorities and consumer associations). These ten points are summarized here, in no particular order of importance.

Dominant actors under pressure

Those who were not members of the Future Studies Group felt that the analysis of the influence exercised by the different actors on each other credited them with more influence than they possessed. One participant, Vincent Perrot, who heads a consumer protection group, felt that consumer associations had far less influence on the mass marketing sector than was suggested by the Group's findings. Consumers only appear to be able to act – and to put pressure on the industry – when major problems arise. Of course his impression would argue in favour of the need to anticipate problems that are likely to emerge.

Similarly, Nicole Zylbermann [1] thought that the amount of pressure brought to bear by public authorities, international organisations and consumer associations was overestimated. There is a possibility that this discrepancy in the perceptions of relative powers of influence stems from a lack of awareness of the way administrative bodies and government authorities really work. The authorities do not have absolute power, and they can be influenced, especially by the media and lobby groups. They are generally amenable to discussion and, in matters coming under their scope, they prefer to gain the best possible understanding of the interests of the different parties involved.

Exerting pressure on international organisations

The same is true for international organisations, which are not autonomous entities as the powers vested in them are those of their member governments. Anyone wanting to exert any influence on these organi-

---

1. Head of the health and safety department of the General Directorat for Competition, Consumer Goods, and Food Inspection, or DGCCRF.

sations has to take part in the major debates taking place within them. This means preparing material, identifying areas of common interest with other countries or governments, forging alliances, taking an active part in both formal and informal discussions, and following up the practical enforcement of all decisions in detail.

Active participation is particularly necessary in the technical and scientific discussions designed to establish a *Codex alimentarius* under the authority of the Food and Agriculure Organization (FAO). This *Codex* is being referred to more and more frequently by the World Trade Organisation (WTO) as a basis for its technical decisions, especially when disputes arise concerning the food industry.

Reversing traditional attitudes to agricultural production "from table back to stable"

Agriculture is experiencing profound changes as those involved become increasingly aware that they need to look at production from a completely different angle if they are to understand what is going on in the farming and agri-foodstuffs sectors. Farmers must realize that their job is to meet the needs of society, in other words that they have to match production to the markets associated with these needs. This means reversing traditional attitudes to agricultural production, taking downstream demand as a starting point and following through "from table back to stable" rather than the other way round.

Meeting the consumer's demand despite its contradictions and diversity

There is no single consumer profile, but rather a wide diversity of different and sometimes contradictory expectations which all must be met. The food system has to be in a position to meet many different types of demand, using organic as well as intensive methods, and by promoting integrated agriculture as well as local specialities.

Consumer perceptions of food safety and the environment are changing fast. For example, people are becoming more aware of some of the external costs or "externalities" involved in the food supply chain, particularly in the area of water use. Increasingly consumers feel that as their water bills steadily rise – as they have in France for the last few years – they are being made to pay for all the pollution for which the farmers are partly responsible.

In view of these changing attitudes among consumers, we need ways to gain a better understanding of how collective behaviour patterns and consumer sensitivity are changing. What worries consumers today is "all those chemicals in the food we eat", but a clear distinction must be made between actual risks and risks as perceived by consumers.

Consumer attitudes can be contradictory indeed, as in the case of those who have high expectations with regard to organic or "natural" products, but completely different attitudes in other areas. A common example would be the amateur gardener who uses inorganic fertilisers and plant protection products to grow his own vegetables, [1] and whose attitudes could be summed up as "no chemicals please, except in my backyard garden".

To address these fears and contradictions, reciprocal feedback between consumers and those involved in the agri-foodstuffs system is essential, together with regular debates organised through the various channels of opinion. The associations have a key role in this respect. Opportunities have to be created to listen to people's concerns, and provide, or seek, any relevant technical or scientific information that will answer their questions.

Food safety arguments should not be a competitive advantage

According to the foodstuffs industry – and this is corroborated by the other actors – while quality is obviously a valid argument for competing agri-foodstuffs companies, marketing approaches should exercise caution with regard to food safety and environmental protection objectives, both considered "pre-competitive".

Since any market is only as safe as its products, any suspicion regarding a given product – whatever the commercial brand – is a threat to the market as a whole. Marketing arguments based on product safety are therefore entirely inappropriate, since they are liable to have direct negative effects on other products marketed by the same company or by the sector in general. Similarly, from the consumer's point of view, environmental protection is no longer a negotiable option. In a sense, these two dimensions make up the foundations for sustainable development within the sector as a whole.

Seemingly, what the sector needs are more systematic efforts to develop integrated farming, so that this form of agriculture ultimately becomes the norm for the entire profession.

The pivotal role of the mass marketing sector

There have been many debates on the relationships between mass food marketing companies and the public. This sector will play a vital role in the future of the system, partly because of its economic and commercial strength, partly because of constant close contact with consumers, but also because of the acute competition among the different mass-marketing groups.

---

1. The same goes for heavy smokers or people who drink a lot of alcohol, or – in the United States – people who have no qualms about taking Viagra, despite the high risks which appear to be involved for those prone to cardiovascular diseases.

Contrary to conventional thinking in various quarters, the position of the distribution sector in the food supply chain, between the agri-foodstuffs industry and the consumer, is neither neutral nor intermediate. Survey results show that consumers see the mass marketing sector as a separate entity within the system, which is linked to the other segments of the food supply chain through the consumer's own concerns and demands.

Nevertheless, the discussions did bring out the various diverging interests involved, particularly with regard to the "appropriation" of added value, which determines how payment is made for services rendered among the different segments in the system, from farmers to mass marketing corporations.

The workshops organized during the seminar also contributed the following four points for further discussion:

Informing the public before problems emerge

The ultimate purpose of communication in this sector is to restore consumer confidence in the agricultural system. Priority actions and targets have both been identified: consumers should be given information on the means employed throughout the system to ensure food safety, and on the technical, scientific and managerial capacities used to do so. Communication activities should target the younger generations as a priority, together with teachers as opinion relays. Lastly, to prevent consumer rejection, timely information must be provided to the public on emerging technologies and their soundness (advantages and disadvantages), well before their marketing and general distribution is actually on the agenda.

Internal debate within the system — as a form of self-assessment — should take place both to evaluate past communication strategies and to analyse the reasons for their success or failure. These joint discussions should also help to improve reciprocal information networks and contents within the system, and strengthen its ability to construct consistent messages for external audiences.

The agricultural sector needs to take on more initiative and responsibility

The sector should not take action purely to meet legal requirements or expectations from downstream segments and consumers. A voluntary charter on initiatives and responsibilities should be established, which might include the following:

– the need to comply with current laws, regulations and codes of sound agricultural practice;

– encouragement to non-polluting techniques and efforts to reduce waste of all kinds;

– development of partnerships between different actors within the system, as a means of encouraging transparency, efficiency and proper observance of mutual undertakings;

– the need for communication strategies and as much transparency as possible throughout the system, in particular by implementing full traceability procedures, through to each finished product;

– commitments towards training and information for partners and other members of the sector to strengthen their involvement.

Upstream segments with enough leverage to implement practical actions in the short term

Other practical initiatives of common interest to upstream actors may be implemented in the short term, for example on traceability, certification or recycling. A short list is included:

– common reference documents could be drawn up on a partnership basis, to avoid tendencies towards over-specification from downstream segments;

– agricultural training and information on sound practices could be developed, particularly on product storage, shipping and handling, equipment adjustments and, more generally, on environmental protection techniques;

– approval criteria for agricultural distributors could be strengthened;

– more specifically, a number of immediate practical measures could be encouraged, such as rinsing out jerricans, recycling used packaging, organising visits for the general public to farm "headquarters" and head offices of upstream companies (e.g. farm visits or open house days organised jointly by farmers and members of the agri-foodstuffs industry).

Integrated agriculture will either become dominant or dormant

Clearly the big issue in the years to come will be establishing an agricultural system that guarantees food safety and environmental protection. The means to this end involve what has become known in France and other European countries as "integrated farming" *(agriculture raisonnée)*.

The working group on integrated agriculture concluded that if integrated agriculture is to succeed, the proportion of farmers adopting this method should ultimately reach 50 to 60%, but about 25% of all farmers should do so as soon as possible. This would counter any threat of marginalization or lack of recognition of the integrated approach in public opinion, and help to avoid unwanted effects, for example, on perceptions of product quality in relation to other types of agriculture.

If the integrated approach were to become widespread among farmers, the likely consequences would include the systematic use of specifications, compulsory traceability documentation, and possibly farm certification.

This shift would tend to enhance farmers' perceptions of their profession and strengthen their solidarity, as members of a group whose value is recognised by society at large. Training and information activities would be crucial to this change in perceptions. The use of specifications or certification procedures may in some cases cause prices to rise above the norm.

The countryside stewardship plans *(contrats territoriaux d'exploitation)* currently being discussed as France prepares to enact its new Agricultural Planning Law *(Loi d'Orientation Agricole)* may well encourage this type of agriculture. However, this does not mean that integrated farming should rely exclusively on such plans or programes to become established.

From Anticipation to Strategic Management Processes

Futures Research and the Sectorial Procedure

Futures-thinking exercises proved extremely valuable as a means to animate interprofessional debate or discussion in which highly competitive actors find themselves obliged to consider one another's opinions.

Indeed, at the initial meeting in Venise, we brought together fifty-odd distributors who often compete amongst themselves. However, the methods adopted not only generated a series of avenues to explore together, as a group, but also encouraged half of the participants to ask for further futures-thinking opportunities.

During later sessions, it became clear that the tools enabled us to purge preconceived notions, poll the actors present, and list future issues. Once again, we allowed each participant to tease out avenues or immediate measures to be taken according to his/ her own company.

BASF particularly appreciated the fact that a large number of companies located in all four corners of France were open to having their managers participate in this futures-thinking exercise and enrich their own files. In fact, we polled participants on their participation while consulting them on the environment through the Delphi questionnaire method.

We also measured the importance of outside input from interviews with experts, specific speeches or discussions during meetings of the steering committee, *extramuros* skills or any research, in terms of enriching files.

Lastly, when a theme surpasses that set out at the beginning of the exercise, it is particularly important to expand the circle to actors other than those intially selected. In this case, experience taught us that by opening up a circle composed primarily of distributors to include other partners (farmers, industrialists, mass distributors), we gained in power through a broader base of confrontation.

Futures-Thinking Exercises: the Strategic Utility for BASF

The initiative BASF undertook to meet its distribution partners' expectations through a futures-thinking process makes perfect sense for any corporate leader who wants to anticipate an uncertain future within the context of the global agricultural economy, the expected upset caused by EU structures and the arrival of the euro.

Given France's privileged geographical position, the French agricultural context provides the fullest range of the various aspects of European agriculture. The French scene thus serves as a point of reference for the BASF Group whether in terms of increasing productivity, enhancing the quality of agricultural production or improving agronomic procedures while integrating various ecological, environmental and economic characteristics.

The lessons learnt from this futures-thinking exercise helped BASF clarify its perception of a number of hypotheses. The company were thus able to contribute handsomely to the collective thinking process. Examples cover several fields; for instance, in terms of developing basic research, the BASF Group had decided several years previously to commit to genetic engineering as a means of improving agrochemical processes.

Reflection confirmed our position and encouraged BASF to take specific orientations. The decision to invest heavily in R&D led BASF to sign agreements with several research centres in Switzerland and Germany, in 1989. The initial thrust of the research consisted of injecting plants with genes capable of resisting chemicals, e.g. herbicides, infections or insect attacks. However, this had not been BASF's original priority.

BASF's goal is to improve its knowledge of genomes, genetic mutation and the introduction of genes into vegetables as well as come up with concrete applications that will complete the action of fertilisers and phytosanitary products on plant growth and quality.

On the basis of future needs, BASF decided to orient its research toward a more complex field. More specifically, researchers are making plant behaviour change so as to meet chronic or sporadic stress situations caused by climatic or pedological phenomena or other external factors.

Another research area involves using plants as tools capable of synthesising and creating interesting substances that will improve food products or health, intensify protein production and develop other substances such as aminoacids.

BASF has also opted to continue developing management of environmental factors, notably through intensified research on nitrification inhibitors designed to manage nitrogen better. There is also the battle against insects using "sexual confusion", a technique which helps limit reproduction.

Futures thinking has helped us not only in R&D but also more locally in making decisions and reorienting our merchandising procedures in the French agricultural context.

BASF has thus integrated the notion of a production channel. The company is committed to taking into account each crop in its marketing and commercial structures in France. This "crop" process, implemented for flower, vegetable and tree growing enables BASF to offer distributors and growers a full range of products so that the entire channel can meet new needs. The same process has just begun in the French winegrowing market.

BASF has also redefined procedures in terms of grains and industrial crops by developing the "channel approach" which goes beyond the farmer and co-op to include the processor, the regulator, and tomorrow, even the superstore or any other agri-foodstuff distributor.

While progressing through these various stages, BASF strengthened ties with its distributor-clients. The company is currently moving from a "buyer-seller" to a "actor-actor" relationship. In fact, the "channel" *(filière)* approach led us to integrate parameters from expertise garnered at different levels. The readymade solution is simply not satisfactory anymore.

Indeed, alongside its partners, BASF learnt to evaluate what will be at stake in the future. With each partner, we tried to study the best positions to take in order to meet farmers' expectations.

Of course, "conventional thinking" and "preconceived notions" die hard. As creatures of habit, we all change and break down barriers slowly.

Futures Thinking and Managing Corporate Collaboration

Beyond the initiatives mentioned, we found it necessary to take into account how BASF could appropriate the results of the procedure its collaborators had undertaken. Obviously a new strategic orientation may be acquired intellectually with little trouble; however, its implementation by the players involved requires an adapted, voluntary, managerial approach. On this point, BASF suggested that perhaps they were too optimistic and did not integrate enough corporate actors in the futures exercise.

This was the conclusion that we reached after two years of work. Although the team which made up the strategic orientation committee participated fully in the futures-thinking process at BASF France, and teased out the guidelines for a new approach at BASF, most corporate collaborators did not readily see the basic changes that this process would have on their own behaviour.

Through daily contact with their usual cohorts, both internal and external, our collaborators often remained "under the influence of the event". It should be added that the increased power of ecological restrictions, the Mad Cow scare and the uncertainty in which famers live, contributed to this type of attitude.

The question that corporate managers and their mangement team must ask when starting a futures-thinking exercise is how and when should corporate collaborators participate. The thinking process does not stop at the highest echelon of the company instead it must be cultivated at each level of the organisation likely to set up its own managerial procedure.

The notion of a channel obliges technical teams, assigned the task of implementing a developmental program for new products, to take into account new factors which may require additional partners and lead to setting new goals. The same may be said about a team mandated to develop agri-business in the grain or any other crop sector with a clientele concerned about the future of products on the market.

Marketing teams must also integrate this new approach in drawing up their strategy. Of course many other examples may be found up and down the corporate ladder.

In fact, two years ago, the need to integrate the channel approach throughout the company led BASF to commit to a follow-up program as part of training for executives. BASF hopes to develop managerial aptitudes in each executive by accentuating management by leadership so that they will take on a project individually and ensure its implementation as an entrepreneur rather than as a mere group leader or the supervisor of old.

The futures process provides the means to develop this managerial aptitude and the individual capacity of each executive in his/her own position to anticipate future developments, identify as well as implement the appropriate responses and initiatives.

Futures thinking has become part of the BASF France way of doing business on a daily basis. Naturally the company is eager to take its research futher in order to anticipate decisions better. Consequently, in 1999, we will continue working on the theme of food safety within a Circle expanded to include mass distribution representatives. Their inclusion should help determine the impact of distribution in setting up a statement of requirements that links all actors along the agri-food channel. Hopefully, all of the Futures Studies Group's endeavors will serve to judge the performance of products or techniques better.

Furthermore, within the company, BASF has decided to improve its ability to appropriate the new marketing orientations of our collaborators. BASF will try to improve its ability to take into account the expectations and reactions of actors or stakeholders playing a role in the company and with whom it shares both the same stakes and battlefield.

9

THE HUMAN FACTOR MAKES THE DIFFERENCE

Thinking collectively about the present and future is an important step, but reflecting upon changes in the environment should not become an end in itself. Similarly, we do not want to shine a spotlight on the exterior while leaving the interior in the dark. Yet sometimes people do just that and fool themselves by believing that the future of a company depends on smart strategic choices alone without any change whatsoever in internal structures and behaviours. However, this necessary transformation of structures and behaviours is conditioned by the answers to the following basic questions:

– How far should the subsidiarity principle be applied? In other words, should we decentralize or "recentralize"?

– How should we weigh and balance out short-term profitability and long-term development objectives?

– Should financial profitability and employment be considered a restriction or the result of a strategy?

The last question often proves crucial for the future. Should a company subordinate its strategy to maintain current staff, structures and behaviours? If so, what form of development should be promoted and what results should be expected? What strategic deficits should be accepted? In the opposite case, what are the consequences on the personnel, qualifications and structures according to the needs expressed in the strategy? Simply asking the question points to the answer: Activity is what creates employment and employment should not hold development strategy in check.

Any change in structures and behaviours depends not only on external changes but also on a corporation's identity, culture and history. In general, environmental complexity of the environment seems to be more readily mastered by simple structures, organized in a network according to the subsidiarity principle. This change sparks a veritable "mental revolution". In this chapter, we consider the revolution that change implies and then seek the out keys needed to motivate people. Motivation is a permanent challenge yet motivation makes everything possible. The future is truly the fruit of human will and initiative, as the examples presented herein have shown. Each example bears the same message: The difference between successful and unsuccessful companies lies in the human factor. A seemingly obvious fact of life, the human factor was found to be at the root of excellence and growth in a study carried out by an international consulting firm in 1998. [1]

Out of what we call "1001 individual initiatives", one movement might rise up in which people march toward the future differently. This is the hopeful message our last chapter gives.

---

1. Bain & Company France Lettre d'information, n° 7, 1998.

Our "Growth Champions"...
Their Performance and Related Myths
Results from a 1998 International Comparative Survey
of 9,000 Companies
(Carried out by Bain and Company in conjunction
with Business Week magazine)

Growth does not depend on the economic sector.
In fact, only 20 percent of our "champion companies" are active in the so-called high growth sectors.
Growth does not come from size; in fact the correlation is low.
Growth does not depend on technological breakthroughs; in fact only 6 percent of the "champs" are in the high-tech sector
Lack of opportunity is not an obstacle or barrier to growth.
Fewer than one-quarter of executives give this reason or excuse.
Therefore it is not economic sector, size, technological breakthroughs, nor is it the opportunities available to the company that determine growth.

It is managerial behaviour that makes the difference.
What are the priorities that "growth champions" set?
1. Focus on core competences and a leadership position
2. Seek out ways of expanding into neighbouring activities or areas
3. Maximize or fight turbulence in the sectorial environment
4. Eliminate "growth inhibitors" within the company in a systematic way.

Changing Worlds and Adapting Structures and Behaviours

Strategic flexibility is a firm's capacity to adapt to changes in its environment. (This statement assumes that the firm has made a permanent effort in technological, commercial and economic foresight.) However, we know that flexibility does not suffice. Remaining competitive requires performance in terms of the price and quality of products or services. Of course performance must be constantly renewed through innovation. It soon becomes obvious that there are a multitude of possible strategic consequences of changes within a company's environment.

Without even attempting to be exhaustive in this chart, we have listed nine main trends that characterize change in the general business environment. Also indicated are the consequences for the organization and its corporate strategy.

Main Environmental Trends and Strategic Consequences

Uncertainty in the environment not only requires flexibility but also reinforces the need for a vision and projects, even if only to figure out where a company stands in terms of its objectives.

Environment	Strategic Consequences
1. Uncertainty	Flexibility
2. Interdependence and complexity	Overall view and simple structures
3. International Imbalances	Regulation via information and financial networks of "world systems"
4. Globalization	Internationalization of activities Local implantation
5. Irregular unequal growth	Struggle for market shares, Productivity, quality, differentiation
6. Technological Change + 7. Deregulation	Progress in processing rather than in products New competitors
8. Economy based on diversity Mass production of variety + 9. Autonomy, differentiation	Multi-small is profitable Independent, responsible teams Entrepreneurs and intrapreneurs

END OF HABITS
START OF MENTAL REVOLUTION

In the face of uncertainty, the rise in interdependence of phenomena makes understanding them all the more complex. More and more any action that should be taken requires panoramic vision. Actually, in attacking environmental complexity, complicated structures are definitely not needed; simple, light forms are preferable.

Persistent international imbalances (whether geopolitical, ecological, demographic or economic) within an international regulatory vacuum are compensated in part by new forms of regulation and new "world-systems", to use Fernand Braudel's term. The international financial network operates around the clock as well as around the planet. The same goes for information. Various international disturbances and non-tariff trade barriers have not prevented globalization, e.g. processes, products, markets, from developing and spreading. Every single year since 1945 has seen manufactured or finished product export figures rise faster than production figures. Companies are obliged to operate on a world scale. The result is globalization of the executive suite. However it takes time for foreign executives to be trained and "imbibed" in the corporate culture.

Basically the following three trends combine to stimulate competition:

1) irregular growth;

2) technological changes in processes, and;

3) deregulation.

In fact the struggle for market share is fought on the basis of the best price/quality ratio. Yet a company must simultaneously stand out, strive for greater automation wherever possible in order to reinforce productivity (progress in terms of process) and, last but not least, confront new competitors.

The human (and organizational) factor remains determining in terms of competitiveness. Equally decisive is the use of new information technology and communication networks according to the philosophy of "small is beautiful AND profitable". We have already entered the age of economic diversity so that the future trend is one of mass production of diversity and profitable production on a small scale. This technical and economic development is in sync with independence and differentiation. What does this mean for companies? It means setting up small, autonomous teams of responsible intrapreneurs. In this sense, new forms of management will progressively emerge and be seen in attitudes and behaviors throughout the organization.

External and Internal Front: Same Challenge

For many struggling companies, the reasons for sinking into the red can be found in internal managerial inadequacies rather than in the storm raging outside. As on the playing field, there can be no winning team without a good captain. Similarly strategy requires more than just the right game plan. It also needs a trained, motivated team to do the job. Hence the internal and external challenges of a company are really one and the same opponent in a battle that must be won on both fronts simultaneously or not won at all. In other words, when faced with strategic environmental changes, the future of a corporation depends largely on its internal and external strengths and weaknesses.

Of course the distinction between "strategic gap" and "performance gap" must be made, without forgetting "management gap". Let us consider, as an example, the following question: Is it absolutely essential to grow in order to be profitable?

In the late 1970s, automakers believed that only two or three large manufacturers in the world would survive up to the year 1990! In the name of this myth of minimum critical size within the global marketplace, PSA (Peugeot group) embarked on its Chrysler adventure and Renault followed suit with AMC (American Motor Car). Fiat, on the other hand, restored its competitiveness by withdrawing from the American market and refocusing its efforts on Europe. It may well be that the scale effect is becoming less and less dependent upon size, given the existence of network organizations.

In reality, smaller companies with better business figures do still exist in the same sector. The correct question, revised version of the previous one, is how can a company be profitable given its current size? In other words, the strategic gap; i.e., the ratio between growth objectives and volume, is perhaps less important than the performance gap. What counts is being profitable at the level where you are. It is worth noting that adopting a more Eurocentric strategy (even if only due to the enlargement of Europe) should not blind managers to the fact that in certain mature sectors like automobiles or electronics, an international company owes it to itself to be dominant at least in one of the poles of the triad and present in the other two, as Ken'ichi Omae (1985, 1991) demonstrated.

One of the conditions required to close the performance gap is, of course, catching up with the "management gap". The latter poses the question of adapting structures and behaviours within the company. The main factor limiting corporate development is the human factor; i.e., the time required to train men or women and create efficient teams. Yet wherever there is weakness in management or strategy, there is an opportunity to close the gap and catch up.

Of course management also implies considering an individual's fulfillment in his/her personal and professional lives, which are distinct yet indissociable. In this sense, during the 1980s, firms were able to reclaim a certain element of citizenship over and above their economic objectives. People were able to find a privileged place of fulfillment and shared objectives in the workplace. In many cases, however, the dynamics wound down, due to restructuring in the 1990s or because the procedures did not survive the departure of the individuals who had introduced them. Moreover, the general corporate climate deteriorated greatly in companies during the 1990s versus the 1980s. It seemed that the dream had faded, leaving many disillusioned.

In these circumstances, how can we (re)motivate people? Before attempting an answer, let us go back to the history of a corporation, or its roots, because the future always depends partly on the past.

Roots of the Future: Identity and Corporate Culture

Contrary to the popular belief held until recently, it is impossible to "mix and match" human resources like stock parts or machinery in modern corporations. People want to know why they are working, what their efforts achieve, and what kind of future they can expect within the company. They have ideas about what they do and react to the behaviour of their supervisor, team leader or colleague.

In order to understand why certain organizations succeed while others flounder, we need to pay attention to the culture, history and identity of each organization. As the popular expression goes: To know where you are going, you have to know where you came from. Marc Mousli (1984) summed up this powerful idea in the following analogy:

identity is to the company as personality is to the individual. Identity is recognition by difference and is defined by opposition. In this sense, identity operates on the zone between what is self and what is "other". Identity provides a sense of belonging and even existence to the corporation and its members (employees and executives) hence it offers them self-recognition through their differences. This identification process may be expressed through a logo, e.g. Renault's lozenge or Coca-cola's scripted lettering, through a successful product or a technological process that is solidly linked to the organization.

The corporate culture is a set of shared values, know-how, collective living habits, as well as a fairly strong sense of identity within each member or employee. The culture is based on a corporate image, collective memory, and, in many instances, on stories, myths and even legends. The organizational culture may be summed up in a few impactful words, e.g. quality, daring, tradition, and innovation. The exact words may vary from one organization to another but are not actually decreed anywhere. Remember, it took years to imprint them on the "corporate genetic code"!

Yet the corporate culture should not become a cult. All too often a corporation becomes a new church and the founding president becomes a self-styled prophet dictating his commandments. The nuance between religion and sect is not easily made, hence we find individuals scrambling to fit a mold, e.g. the white shirt plus blue blazer and red tie uniform, and giving the impression that they exist only for the glory of the company, now a totalitarian state of sorts. One anecdote describes the reaction of a Japanese businessman who landed in Paris with the firm conviction that Japanese civilization was superior to the French or, more broadly, the Western. As he put it: "We think that in all our activities we have reached the "five zeros"; i.e., zero defects, zero breakdowns, zero delays, zero inventory and zero dust. However after living for a while in your country [France], I realized that our system also had its flaws: zero vacation, zero humor, zero sex, zero space and zero freedom."

The vital harmonious relationship between strategy and culture must necessarily flow through structure. In the trilogy – structure, power and environment – power is attacked by changes in the environment and defends itself through structures. One characteristic of structures is that they become the property of those who actually constitute the structures. In fact they tend to grow rigid for precisely that reason.

Adaptive or anticipatory structures? The debate continues and the jury is still out. Nevertheless Igor Ansoff's suggested dual structure, in which new forms coexist with old ones, seems realistic. Once again we have to consider that structures are influenced not only by strategy statements and the corporate environment but also by the intricate weave of company history and culture.

There is a conception of the company, its policies, goals, priorities and power plays behind the structures. As a result, an efficient structure must be adapted to the culture of a company as well as to the type of behaviour displayed by its actors. Any reference to structure must be linked to behaviour and management, but obviously there is no ideal structure just floating around somewhere. Blue chip and Fortune 500 companies have simply managed to harmonize strategy, culture and structure. If future performance depends on this harmony then past performance influences strategy, unites structure and shapes culture.

Subsidiarity and Simple Structures to Manage Complexity

Changes in the environment demand quick reaction time and flexibility. These capacities stem primarily from corporate structures. Now structures must not only adapt to such changes but also anticipate them because the inherent inertia in structures slows down adaptation to change.

Any and every structure runs the risk of becoming sclerotic, even fossilized, if it does not undergo reorganization and redistribution of its advantages and powers. Wherever possible, companies must introduce "habit busters", or factors to break habits within structures. Between the rigidity-sclerosis described above and agitation-alibi, which stirs up preoccupations and inefficiency, there has to be a suitable pace of transformation that can respond to changes in the corporate environment without upsetting the established balance unnecessarily. Seeking harmony implies a voluntary process which takes time and inertia into account. However these inertia should be lesser if we are dealing with simple, light structures.

Let us apply to corporations what has become known as the "subsidiarity principle", a key component of the EU's approach to handling administrative redundancy. In other words, we will decentralize everything that can be decentralized and centralize everything that must be centralized. To reach the point of "strategic centralization-operational decentralization", we have to blend rigour and flexibility, adopt a firm line or orientation while maintaining maximum individual autonomy.

The above paragraph raises the well-known debate over decentralization. Here decentralization means more autonomy and responsibility at the grass roots level but supposes that for consistency and overall efficiency, a certain central form of coordination is necessary.

Decentralized structures are best adapted to complex, evolving or geographically distant situations. Conditions within this type of structure may require some centralization beforehand. The key to successful decentralization is twofold:

– maintain a firm, central guideline on a certain number of basic values, e.g. production and service quality, internal rules;

– base the autonomy and responsibility of individuals or units on clear, respected rules through such processes as objective statements and contracts, evaluation of results, penalties, etc.

For example, responsibility means that each member of the team rather than one special department is responsible for quality control. Autonomy means development of an internal competitive spirit. The future belongs to flexible, decentralized, project-based structures made on a human scale. Autonomy and responsibility go hand-in-hand, and can be confirmed by the market reaction, balance sheet or performance review by objectives.

The End of Habits and the Start of a Mental Revolution

The trend of appropriation by individuals or groups of intrapreneurs within a company means that its executives and managers should have different qualities. For many corporations, the problem stems from inadequacies in internal management more than any outside danger. How else can we explain that some firms actually flourish under the same conditions?

Among the catalogue of internal weaknesses, we find an absence of power created essentially by permanent power struggles. It may sound paradoxical or not, but the fact is power struggles paralyze action. In these situations, the notion of power is less important than its twisted use or abuse. In other words, the pleasure of dominating others is often sought-after to the detriment of the power of self-domination, or self-control, which enables one to focus on creating or planning. The leader who knows how to base his/her authority on competencies and on motivation can let his/her team or employees take initiatives. The goals would not even need to be negotiated; they would be naturally generated or present.

The subsidiarity principle trickles down and throughout the organization. This operational decentralization assumes goal-based contracts or contracted goals, evaluations and monitoring later. In this new way of sharing responsibilities according to competence (sometimes called the German model), the operational units or inviduals should be remunerated since the hierarchical levels are fewer. If we are to apply a model that is open to communication and change, the size of production units should not be neglected, e.g. do not go beyond 300 people in an industrial or administrateive unit.

Of course within this ideal organization, responsibility is no longer hierarchical but rather collegiate. Although the boss and authority remain, the top of the corporate totem pole rises because of his/her leadership capacity; in other words, the ability to mobilize people, solve problems, and deal with human conflicts as well as financial risks. Co-opted rather than named, this leader's authority is earned through competence. Management is thus open and plural. Rather than challenge traditions, beliefs and values, mangement uses them as means of adaptation in specific regions or countries.

The entire organizational structure feels the tremor of the "mental revolution", similar to the revolutionizing effect of F.W. Taylor's "Scientific Management". The company is thus a grand social experiment. The bureaucratic rules of the game fall away as executives seek to acquire the same responsibilities that they have in their associative life. The economic efficiency of a company is not incompatible with individual aspirations if they draw upon autonomy, initiative and responsibility.

Training certainly plays a key role in this revolution; however, the type of training offered must promote collective self-teaching whenever possible. There is truth in the old adage that you only really learn or know something when you have to teach it. Hence this type of training should go beyond the banal to put theoretical knowledge into practice quite quickly.

Any training not followed up by action is just another drop in the ocean. Furthermore internal trainers should be the best, as was the case of executives acting as trainers at IBM, while awaiting promotions in the 1980s. In fact, being a trainer should be one of several stages in a career.

How can you spot the companies where this mental revolution has already begun? One simple test is to ask how things are going, as the work week begins. If the answer is "like a Monday", then the company is not faring well. Although it may sound simplistic, we stress that if people are unhappy in their work environment then they are not happy in the general social environment.

Towards Sustainable Motivation

Throughout this book, we referred to the human factor as a key to excellence. A double-edged sword, the human factor can spell success or failure.

According to the contingency principle, a key depends on the context. In which case yesterday's success might actually become the cause of tomorrow's failure. In order to adapt to a changing world, we have to know how to change habits, structures and behaviors. Fortunately change is also vital in motivating people.

Out with Routine, In with Motivation

When faced with future challenges, people will only mobilize if motivated. In the same vein, people only do really well what they understand. In the words of Henri Fayol, "if governing is foreseeing then obeying is understanding". Similarly, the ideal manager of pioneer management writer Mary Parker Follet does not issue orders but rather encourages initiatives which go along the same lines as the orders that could have been given. The quality of the leader remains a determining factor in business as well as in sports.

During the past two decades of consulting with clients in corporations or ministries, we have met a few of these ideal leaders. They were frequently but not exclusively in small firms. They were also usually in sectors experiencing difficulties rather than healthy ones. One law of human nature seems to be that when things are going well, companies can afford the luxury of mediocre managers or uselessly domineering ones. Similarly, a fundamental law of strategy states that generals should never fight their own army.

Multi-Small Is Profitable

The age of behemoth industrial groups or departments is not yet history, as the major corporate restructuring plans and mergers implemented or signed each week prove. Company size within a sector often expands like an accordion. If specific research functions, production units and marketing groups require greater strategic centralization within the context of the global economy, others may need to remain decentralized and "human size" in order to be efficient.

Like motivation, innovation requires stimulation. Operation structures assigning responsibility per project or per market seem preferable to structures that assign responsibility by larger function, e.g. studies, methods, purchasing, sales, etc. The most difficult thing is trying to cross two of these into so-called matrix structures. There are, of course, some corporate examples in which matrix structures do achieve harmony.

Usually the collection, boutique or shop organization works better. In this structure the departments/functions operate like an array of "almost small-to-medium-sized businesses". In some instances, a company can imitate outside competition in order to stimulate innovation and better performance. Organizing a company in small operational units, or what we call a human scale, may be the secret of constant adaptation as well as the key to ongoing innovation.

Moreover, globalization highlights the need for differentiation in terms of culture and local identification. These two feed off each other, as seen in the organization of the ABB Group, product of a merger between the Swedish ASEA and the Swiss Brown Boveri. At least this was the view of the company's president, Percy Barnevik. Since his successor took over the helm, ABB has since returned to a highly traditional organizational structure.

People are more easily motivated when part of small, independent, responsible teams in which individuals know one another, at least by sight, than when in large anonymous groups. We should remember that the longevity and performance of companies are not related to their large size. Remember how IBM, the big blue machine, learned a lesson or two about size when threatened by Apple then Microsoft.

There are countless other interesting examples to prove that companies operating on a human scale are more apt to motivate people and develop team spirit among staff. There must be some logic to numbers in that a football team rarely exceeds 11 players and the army covers territory by dispatching squadrons of 12 soldiers. What a difference from the mammoth corporations paralyzed by their elephantine proportions! Inside most of these dinosaurs, internal energy is spent on turf wars and executive power struggles. Employees are considered like weaponry by leaders chosen for their particular allegiance rather than their competence. In companies with a human face or operating on a human scale, individual employees can meet other employees and recognize something of themselves in their managers, who, in turn, are capable, open, accessible or simply well-adjusted.

Of course flexibility requires a certain amount of rigour to be efficient and to distinguish between that which must remain centralized and that which may be decentralized. Also required is a shared values system within a vision and along side corporate projects which act like living cement to bond the small units inside the company.

One Future Vision and Several Short-Term Projects

Our conviction has long been that it is far better to start a corporate project without saying so than to talk about it without really doing anything. Similarly, it is better to initiate small concrete projects rather than an illusory megaproject because the appropriation process counts more than the project itself. In fact, by the end of the 1990s, little appropriation and lots of talk had cheapened the concept of the corporate project in Europe. This situation likely contributed to the replacement of the term "project" by "vision", a similar word that seemed "new and improved" when introduced as an American import.

Regardless of terminology, a corporate future vision must be ambitious yet sufficiently realistic to be translated into concrete projects at the company's many levels. This future vision, although shared, must not claim to translate one grand, unique project that will be imposed uniformly upon one and all. The vision should be translated to a host of projects within the multiple facets of the company or group.

We believe that a vision and projects are necessary both as privileged vectors, capable of mobilizing intelligence within the company and as decisive advantages in the quest for competitiveness and excellence.

The discourse of the top brass, the attention paid to inhouse communication and the talent of consultants can not justify a coporate vision and ensure the success of corresponding projects. Prior serious reflection and proper precautions are also required at all levels of the company. In the end, the corporate vision fashion is not "ready to wear" but rather "made to measure". Each company must define the moment, form and content of the most suitable vision and projects.

With respect to corporate vision and projects, we turn to the following three questions: Why? how? and what are the pitfalls to be avoided?

Why one future vision and several short-term projects? The answer is twofold. First, a project is needed to avoid going off into never-neverland. Flexibility alone leads nowhere. Faced with uncertainty and a turbulent environment, reactivity may be desirable in the short-term but if not oriented toward long-term corporate objectives, it leads nowhere, too. In fact flexibility is not really strategic unless it helps a corporation stay on course. If we indulge in one last ship metaphor: when buffeted by contradictory winds, you do not necessarily change course but you do adjust the sails.

Strategic flexibility can only be fruitful and profitable if it becomes part of a shared ambition or what Harrington Emerson called "a clearly defined ideal". In fact, Emerson made flexibility the first of his twelve principles of efficiency. He felt that if all the ideals driving the organization, from top to bottom, could be aligned to pull in the same direction, the resulting force would be extremely powerful, but if these ideals pull in different directions, the resulting force could only be slightly positive, insignificant or occasionally even negative.

Yet the connection between foresight and strategic will is not enough to put companies on track to competitiveness and excellence. The third dimension that a project can bring is missing; i.e., the collective mobilization of intelligence to target strategic objectives as well as to confront threats or opportunities in the environment.

The Four Dimensions of a Vision Explained Clearly

A corporate vision normally includes four dimensions: an ambition for the future, a collective desire, a shared values system, major medium-term strategic axes.

The first dimension, ambition, rides on the aims and overarching objective that a company must define through debate then state both openly and clearly. There are several courses of action open, but there are also the uncertainties in the environment to consider. For example, a major corporation could have leadership in specific markets for certain products/services/techniques as a long-term ambition. Often expressed openly and qualitatively, this ambition is part of the dream needed to build any reality.

The collective will to stay the course especially when the seas are rough implies that each partner or participant maintain the same open communication under all circumstances. This will, or desire, to reach the objectives that correspond to the company's aims must be everybody's business. It must be permanent and functional across the board.

A values system shared by the corporate partners or actors in terms of recognition of roles and differences is vital. Such a system ideally includes
- listening;
- dialogue;
- access to information;
- trust in others' behaviour;
- pride in belonging to the same group, in creating quality products or services, in being competitive and in playing a key role in innovation despite social, economic and technological changes.

Here the idea is to prefer a few major projects, set as short- and medium- term priorities, e.g. self-financing, investment, market share, training, and working conditions, but also to have a few long-term projects in R&D, for example.

All in all, a corporate vision can not be summed up as a statement of goals or aims but rather an expression of a collective will to achieve them. It is thus the recognition of a shared values system and the mobilization of people moving towards objectives and their corresponding overall aims which have been debated and clearly stated.

Five Pitfalls to Avoid

A lengthy catalogue of pitfalls can discourage any reader, so we have drafted a short list that will, hopefully, help lessen the number of abandoned efforts at corporate visions and projects.

These pitfalls put the corporate project out of fashion, although the concept occasionally resurfaces with the name "future vision". The unfortunate demise of the corporate vision or project represents a lost opportunity for companies looking for other ways to initiate the necessary transformation in structures and behaviors in the face of change.

The Future: Fruit of Will and Initiative

Throughout this book, we have worked to keep futures thinking or scenario planning "fresh" while underscoring the rigour applied in our approach. The fact that tested methods exist is an essential asset. The accumulated heritage of *la prospective*, foresight, futures studies, scenario building, as well as strategic analysis reveals the converging forces and complementarities among these approaches along with the possibility of listing the thinking tools in a single container, a "mental" toolbox. We can thus define our problem and look for the right tool. Contrary to popular opinion, the disorder of creative thinking does require some organization.

Five Pitfalls

• The first pitfall is to confuse collective mental gymnastics with strategic mobilization. Group mobilization and any warm-ups involved do not ensure flexiblity and performance in all circumstances. With hindsight, the intellectual gymnastics should be considered as efforts that were necessary to avoid threats and take advantage of opportunities arising from changes in the environment. Strategic culture can not be reduced to jogging on the spot.

• The second pitfall is the absence of any real content. In this sense vision is used as an executive toy or gadget because communication is poor. Worse, any vision in this case does not engage the life force within the company through a futures-thinking exercise. There is also the risk of seriously demotivating those who initially expressed interest in working on a corporate vision. One way of avoiding this trap is to build a corporate vision without saying so and then start the collective process without revealing the result in advance.

• The third pitfall would then be to consider a corporate vision as the be all and end all rather than a mere means to an end. The main advantage of developing a corporate vision is the opportunity for structured thinking and debate that it provides the group. How else will the company really know its strengths and weaknesses when facing the present and future threats or opportunities in the environment? As already mentioned in this chapter, the process counts more than the result.

• The fourth pitfall would be to contract out the vision or buy off the rack from specialists who reduce complexity to a few simple, attractive, images. In their enthusiasm to shed light, they can easily dazzle clients. The idea of adopting a vision and projects according to a menu of corporate lifestyles may appeal to some. However, is it reasonable to play with the future of a company on the basis of a fleeting snapshot? Would it not be better to ask about changes in the environment that might affect peoples' aspirations and behaviors? This type of question, based on mechanisms that link and oppose the forces of change with the forces of inertia, is vital to both understanding the inevitable resistances to change and to identifying the levers, or drivers, which may start the necessary shift in structures and change in behaviors.

• The fifth and final pitfall appears as a shortcut to most. The idea is to launch a corporate project while hoping to not go through the change in structures and behaviours necessarily implied. This change metamorphosis is more accurate here – involves executives and managers first. A corporate project forces them to undergo a real mental revolution which will place authority on competence and leadership rather than function or title. The true power of a leader is measured not through domination but through the capacity to develop intitiative and responsibility among his/her subordinates.

Of course the tools mentioned are neither panaceas nor ends in themselves. They should be used as needed according to the problem presented, the time allotted and funding budgeted. Unlike some kind of deck of cards for solitaire, they should be used to provide some shared language and method for collective thinking exercises.

Note that these methods have proven effective time and time again in Europe. They do not guarantee the quality of ideas but they do structure thinking by stimulating the imagination. Futures thinking and scenario building are an art which requires many talents, e.g. nonconformism, intuition and common sense. To use an analogy, playing scales is not enough to create a great pianist, but a pianist must practice scales everyday to remain great.

Of course there are other possible approaches. In fact it is a good idea for researchers and practitioners to keep trying to innovate while using established approaches in scenario building or strategic analysis. Their innovation will represent real progress if it makes their questioning or that of the participants more relevant, if it reduces inconsistencies in logic, and if it enhances the realism and importance of the conjectures. However, these new methods must be sufficiently simple to be appropriated. Complication is not the best weapon in fighting complexity. As primary school teachers used to tell their pupils: Clear thinking is clear writing.

Nevertheless, we need progress in the pedagogy of implementation more than we need new methods of analysis and thought to understand the world around us. For most major problems, e.g. training, unemployment or health, the diagnosis and prescription are well known. What is not known is how to take action before it is too late.

This leads to another question: How to replace urgency and reactivity by foresight and preactivity? If futures thinking, or scenario planning, is to be translated into action, it can no longer be the art of enlightened captains of industry but must be the concern of the largest number. Everyone should be interested in the future because that is where he/she will spend the rest of his/her life!

If there is no appropriation, there is rejection. This logic applies to ideas in that the best ideas are not usually the ones we have but rather the ones that we generate or encourage. Throughout this book, we have referred to motivation and talent as the distinctive feature that actually makes the difference between successful companies or regions and their unsuccessful counterparts. As a corollary, problems are also often part of the human factor. Without a good leader or captain, there is no winning team. In this sense, people are not only social animals, to paraphrase Aristotle, but also animals with desires. Dreams and projects are needed to build reality and, more prosaically, to score goals. In other words, the passage from futures thinking to strategic action can not take place without debate and awareness (group and individual) of the responsibilities that we share *vis-à-vis* the generations to come. We owe them at least some hope for an open world in which liberty and initiative thrive.

People need challenges and projects to give some meaning to their lives. Forward-looking people, who are moving towards the future unconventionally, find along the way what they seek in life – social links and mutual recognition – two elements found in any shared adventure. As the German proverb goes, *der Weg ist das Ziel* or the path is the goal. Some might say that "the aim of life is living".

Organisations will increasingly need to shed light on their actions according to possible and desirable futures. They will be able to do so in an even more effective manner since people's concerns will be a priority and, of course, individuals are necessarily behind all problems, solutions and wealth. In short, *strategic prospective* has acquired a solid heritage and has rediscovered the importance of Socrates' lesson, "know thyself". We must use our skills and know our strengths and weaknesses before setting out to conquer the future. As the French philosopher Vauvenargues observed: "knowing our strengths increases them; knowing our weaknesses reduces them".

Still open, the future will always be the fruit of the labours of those who care to work unconventionally towards it in regions or organizations. In the end, each one of us must take a stand: resignation, passive resistance or collaboration for an unconventional future. Collaboration has long been our choice, even though we know the long road stretching ahead of us.

As mentioned earlier there are two major roadblocks. The first stems from an excess of rationalism which leads to a blind, mechanical reliance on the very tools that were forged to spark the imagination, encourage reflection and facilitate communication. The second, almost symmetrical, comes from excessive pride; in other words, just because the tools are insufficient does not mean the mind alone is sufficient. It is a question of multiplying the strength of analysis and synthesis within the human brain through the use of "manmade" tools.

In sum, futures thinking helps us recapture a childlike curiosity and awe while applying rigour to our thinking. It keeps the human factor at the heart of matters and serves to shed light on people's actions thus guiding them towards a desirable future. Indeed, while creating futures, people find the social links and meaning they seek in their lives.

10

How I Became a Futurist

Young professionals who are interested in entering the field of *la prospective* or futures studies will find this chapter particularly useful. Here you will discover the personal and professional stories of two of the most prominent futurists in the world, Joseph Coates, author of the preface of this book, and Michel Godet, the author. Both of these Renaissance men have an incredibly large breadth of knowledge and mastery of their craft. Both have lead enormously productive lives in the service of their respective nations – the United States and France. Both have published numerous books and articles; and continue to work as top-tier consultants to some of the largest corporations, foreign governments, and regions. Both have taught or continue to teach as university professors and are actively engaged in philanthropy. In summary, both men embody the title of this work, *Creating Futures*.

Michel Godet and Joseph Coates are natural allies. Few people care more profoundly or have done more for the profession of futures studies than these two men of action. Take advantage of the collected wisdom contained in this chapter and draw inspiration from their success. The following interviews, conducted by my colleague Philippe Durance and me, belong to a larger set of interviews with prominent futurists which will be available on the Lipsor web site [http://www.cnam.fr/lipsor/eng/] in upcoming months.

Adam Gerber

Joseph COATES interviewed by Philippe Durance and Adam Gerber

Paris, the 16ᵗʰ of January 2006

Philippe Durance: Joe, can you tell us about your personal path to futures studies, your formal education, and professional experiences? How did you get started with futures studies?

Joseph Coates: I trained as a chemist at Brooklyn Polytechnic and Pennsylvania State University. I also had parallel interests in the history and philosophy of science, which I explored a bit at Penn State, and at the University of Pennsylvania. My first professional employment was as a chemist in the research unit of Atlantic Refining Company which is now a unit of ARCO. I was looking into the longer-range research opportunities for the company, rather than the short-term product improvement stuff. I worked there for a long time, and I decided that – judging by the way they structured their business – they were never going to build my factory. In other words – it was very unlikely that my work was going to lead to a major new product. So I went to work for a more entrepreneurial small chemical company. I was there for about a year or a maybe a year and a half, when I got an invitation by telephone from a man who had been my boss' boss at ARCO. He had left ARCO to join one of the military think tanks and he called me and invited me to spend a year with him. I thought this was a great opportunity, so we moved to DC. Within a few months, it was clear that I loved the place and they found me to be pretty good. So, I got an open-ended appointment and I spent eight years there. That was a substantial introduction to the future, because the Institute for Defense Analyses [1] with which I was connected was looking at military R&D. The central notion that everyone agreed on was that the dollar spent on military research today can not have any significant effect in less than fifteen years. Research, development, testing, evaluation, procurement, training, and so on, all take time. Consequently, we weren't interested in the first fourteen years, our interest was: what's the fifteen year future of conflict about? That was an institutionalized professional commitment to looking at the relatively longer term – in the vocabulary of that time. I also had no interest in nuclear war or war on the great German plains, and so on. My real areas of interest were the short-term conflicts among nations and within nations. Also along the way, we got an interesting assignment to do the technological side of the President's Crime Commission study. That was a landmark piece of work and the futures contribution was really quite interesting. It led to the first systems diagram of the criminal justice system in the United States. The diagram illustrated how the criminal moved from

---

1. The Institute for Defense Analyses may be found online here: http://www.ida.org/

crime to rehabilitation to next crime, etc. Laying it all out was a real eye-opener. That diagram has since become a standard item in police training, and in the whole criminal justice system. The Institute for Defense Analyses was a marvellous place because it was made up of people that government couldn't hire – either they didn't want to work for government, they wouldn't work with government, or they had academic careers. The wages were good, the environment was great and the staff was just outstanding. You couldn't arrive in the morning and not find somebody to talk with about something in which you were interested. Moreover, their talk was with some authority, because of both their professional and avocational interests.

I left there to go to the National Science Foundation [1] where I was a program manager in a new unit of the foundation. New units are always interesting because it takes awhile for the concrete to set. That gave us tremendous flexibility, in a program called *Research Applied to National Needs*. What we did was disperse grants to those we thought had fruitful ideas about national issues. We also had a particular interest in something the Congress was concerned about – the unintended consequences of new technologies. Congress was seeing, time and time again, the adverse affects of technology, particularly in environmental and social affects. The need to better anticipate the consequences of technological change was called *Technology Assessment* by the relevant congressional committee. The Congress was interested to know how one could anticipate the social, economic, political, etc. consequences either of a new technology or a substantial expansion of an existing technology. Ours was, I think, the first program to put research money into looking at that, and it was to a large extent my responsibility. When Congress finally set up its Office of Technology Assessment [2], I was invited to join them as assistant to the Director. After my five years at the National Science Foundation I spent the next five years at that new OTA. What was exciting about that was the uniqueness of the client. The client was only 535 people, the members of the US Congress. Furthermore, it wasn't even all of them; it was individual committees in which Congress developed its responsibilities. Having one single client for each project was an enormously powerful way of shaping what we did – not to cater to their preconceptions, but rather to target their conceptual and information needs to lead to action. In the five

---

1. The National Science Foundation awards grants to scientific projects in the United States. With a $5.6 billion (fiscal year 2006) budget, the NSF is the largest agency of its kind in the world. The National Science Foundation may be found online here: http://www.nsf.gov/

2. The congressional Office of Technology Assessment (OTA) closed its doors September 29, 1995. For 23 years, the nonpartisan analytical agency assisted Congress with the complex and highly technical issues that increasingly affect our society. Archives and more information may be found here: http://www.gpo.gov/ota/

years that I was there, it was interesting to see that OTA became the best science policy research organization in Washington, because of its unique relationship to its unique client. It had a hard time getting started, due to the fact that most of the initial top managers had no experience with technology assessment. They were mostly brought in on the basis of their Congressional connections, and so they were not the ideal first choice for running such an organization. Anyway, they survived and did quite well for about 25 years.

I left after five years, and at that time, I decided to satisfy a long-term desire to have my own think-tank. I opted for a micro-miniature think-tank. I got to do that in what I feel is an interesting way. I first identified 17 people who ran think-tanks in the size range in which I was interested. I didn't want to interview directors of firms with more than 25 staff members; my previous experience taught me that there's a critical number – about 25 – when once exceeded you have to break up into subunits. In any case, I interviewed these 17 people, and I learned some interesting things from a managerial and business point of view. I was surprised to find that they unloaded all kinds of stuff on me related to their business. They weren't all futures organizations; some were economics think tanks, etc. But anyway, I was the only person that anyone of them had ever known who was thoroughly interested in their business experience, and so they just dumped everything in their experience on me. All of these people had tremendous ego-strength. Short ones, tall ones, fat ones, thin ones, good looking ones, ugly ones, it didn't make any difference. They all had tremendous ego-strength. So I paused about after the 9th or 10th interview and thought to myself: Do I have the kind of ego-strength that these people have in order to go through all of this? That really paralyzed me for about three or four weeks as I thought through the implications of what they were telling me. I decided that I could probably find the strength for the struggle and I completed my interviews. Then I announced to everyone I knew my decision that I was going to start a business, because I wanted to create an artificial social pressure on me to prevent procrastinating. I called up everyone I knew and told them about the new business and I got all the pats on the back and all their good wishes. That led to the company *J.F. Coates Inc.* We later changed the name to *Coates and Jarrett* after Jennifer Jarrett joined the firm. Jennifer Jarrett had been a British journalist, who earned a Masters Degree in Futures Studies at the University of Houston at Clear Lake. Jennifer worked out to be quite a competent futurist, and I wanted to keep her from jumping ship or taking an offer to teach, hence I added her name to the company. Anyway, the bulk of my full time futures career has been with that firm that I set up in 1979. In about 23 years it grew to about 19 people. In growing to that size, it created a problem for me. I was spending more and more time reworking other people's work, and less of my time actually thinking fresh thoughts about the future. So I gave the firm away to two of the longest tenured employees, Jennifer Jarrett and John Mahaffie. I trained them over a three year period on the parts of the business that I thought they should know about.

The day I left, I reincorporated myself as *Joseph F. Coates, Consulting Futurist*, Inc. [1] There my goal is to work on projects that I can handle by myself, or perhaps just call in someone for assistance, write articles, give lectures and seminars and consult – a one-man band.

Adam Gerber: Much of your work focuses on technology. You also mentioned your interest in, and study of the philosophy of science and technology. Do you think there is a special affinity between philosophy of science and technology, and futures studies?

Joseph Coates: No. The philosophy of science or the history of science, both have relatively little to contribute to futures thinking. There's a widespread belief that you need to get a running start on the future by understanding the history of your subject. No way. Most of the history of any field a futurist is interested in is irrelevant. Often times you find people making foolish historical comparisons in trying to draw lessons from the past and applying them to the future. The flaw in that approach is that what they see are four or five apparent matches of events or situations, but that historic situation didn't consist of four or five variables, it consisted of 50, 60 or 100 variables to understand and consider. But because you can see three, four, or five similarities, then to think that the outcome of the present situation can lead to the alleged historical parallel is just intellectually specious and practically stupid. But you see people doing it all the time. What they're trying to do is reduce the number of variables to be understood and considered, whereas the practical concern for futures studies is to learn how to embrace more and more variables. If you had only one variable, any fool could solve the problem; when you have five, then you can think about it, and come to some interesting conclusions. What if you have 25 variables? That really gets to the point where historic analogies and oversimplification can mislead you.

The interesting point you raise: Why the emphasis on technology? If you look at the long-term drivers of change, population tends to be number one, and science and technology are number two. Pretty soon, we're likely to see a reversal of that order. The one thing that you can be absolutely sure of – the one thing that will deliver changes in society is developments of science and technology. You'll notice the subtitle of my book, 2025: *Scenarios of US and Global Society Reshaped by Science and Technology*. [2] If you look at other areas

---

1. More information may be found here: http://www.josephcoates.com/

2. The content of 2025: Scenarios of US and Global Society Reshaped by Science and Technology is available for download free-of-charge here: http://www.josephcoates.com/2025_PDF.html

of intellectual or social activity, none of them are as definitive as the physical sciences. Coming up rapidly in this respect are the biological sciences, and far, far behind are the social sciences. When you look at role of the natural sciences in the future, you can pretty well count on Moore's law operating, you can count on the law of gravity, you can count on blood being the way we transport and use oxygen in the body in the future. When you get to the social sciences, few people can even claim to be definitive in any area. So how do you deal with that disparity in their intellectual power? Conjecture and plausibility of fit with other factors is the solution. The emphasis on technology is not because I was trained that way, but because the reality is that it is the number-one or number-two certifiable driver of change.

The other element to keep in mind is the following. When I evaluate futurists who come from different backgrounds, I find that the ones who have the most difficulty in dealing with complex issues are the ones who don't have scientific or technological training. There is simply an asymmetry in their training and the ability to understand complex issues. You can not understand an engineering problem without a substantial amount of engineering background. On the other hand, if you have an engineering background, and you're concerned about the social effects of building a bridge and how that might influence traffic – that's not a skull-cracking problem. There is an asymmetry there. You see this nicely if you look at patent law – almost all patent lawyers are technologically trained and pick up the law as a second degree. I know of none who have done it in the reverse direction.

Adam Gerber: You mentioned that population and technology are among the most important drivers of change. I wonder if you can speak to Paul Ehrlich's formula, *Environmental Impact = Population × Affluence × Technology* [1]. Would you agree that more technology is positively correlated to greater environmental impact?

Joseph Coates: No. These kinds of things are intellectually disgraceful. Because what is that *times* symbol supposed to imply, if it's supposed to imply a multiplier effect, then no, it's simply not there. Most of these quick pseudo formulaic things are intrinsically, not accidentally, misleading. Now to say that A, B & C all enter into and interact in an important way in creating environmental problems (and solutions); now that's important. But that declarative sentence doesn't have the cute, false appeal of an A *times* B *times* C. Note also that in Ehrlich's use, "impact" connotes or at least suggests "bad consequence".

Philippe Durance: What is your definition of foresight?

---

1. Ehrlich, P. and J. Holdren. (1972) *Impact of population growth*. In Population, Resources, and the Environment, edited by R.G. Riker. Washington DC: U.S. Government Printing Office. pp. 365–377.

Joseph Coates: "Foresight" is interesting because it reflects a larger vocabulary problem. When I first got actively interested in being a futurist, I heard the word futurologist being used, and that sounds much more like a palm-reader than anything else. But I think it's a good, popular name. Nevertheless, I know of no American who ever wanted to be called a futurologist. But then the question becomes, what are you? "I'm a student of the future – oh, what school are you at?" That creates something misleading. "I'm involved in futures studies – well what's there?' Every bit of nomenclature creates more problems. "Is a futurologist like being a podiatrist; like being a school teacher?" So a number of people have settled on futurist. Now what happens when institutions get involved and they have to put money on the line to do something? They have to have a label for everything and they want a safe label. Safety is the safeguard of institutions. So, is some conservative organization going to talk about futures studies?, systematic studies of the future?, I'm bringing in futurists? No. They want a good solid old-fashioned word, that carries with it a sense of knowing what you're doing – foresight. "Foresight" has been in the English language for seven hundred years. It's the sort of word that everyone feels that he or she understands, but in reality, they do not. What happens is that a number of activities that deal with the future or explore the future, need a new umbrella term, so you choose something bland and safe, like foresight. But it's driven by the economics and institutional economics of the study of the future – the client wants to be safe. All those terms are perfectly OK to use. You just want to be sure not to mislead someone. If A is selling foresight and B is selling futures work, and C is selling futures studies. It isn't just a matter of product differentiation – it's a matter of what term the clients are comfortable with.

Philippe Durance: Do you make a distinction between foresight and the French term, *prospective*. Do you use the term *prospective* in your practice?

Joseph Coates: Yes. Let me make a sharper distinction first. There's a difference between studying the future and making predictions. The prediction concept has with it a degree of precision which is alien to most strategic futures work – such and such will happen with probability X by date so and so. That kind of prediction is of relative little value when you're dealing with strategic futures. However it may be enormously important for others who look at the future – and I'll get back to that in just a moment. What I do is called strategic futures, which has a time frame of generally 10+ years. What characterizes strategic futures in contrast to short-term futures is that there are few data and virtually no significant mathematic or quantitatively based models, and therefore we are moving into a set of domains in which there is little that you can call hard data. Therefore what you move to is not prediction, but rather identification of alternative futures. The future is really wide open. So you move away from the notion of fore-casting a single future, to forecasting alternative futures. What is central to strategic futures is the concept of alternative futures. The concept of alternative futures is separate and distinct from the delivery mechanism, which may or may not involve scenarios. You may have a scenario for each and every one of those alternative futures, but you can deliver your work without them. Scenarios are a presentation tool.

In the whole range of short term futures work, the largest numbers of people employed in that sector are by corporations and government. They are the folks who are looking out six months or perhaps one year, perhaps maybe three years. You find them in manufacturing, agriculture, commodities, and financial services, etc. They have short-term interests, they have enormous amount of data, and they have extremely sophisticated mathematical models. Furthermore, they can come down often to a second or third decimal. I've never spoken to a decimal in my life – at least not when dealing with the future. Nevertheless, these are the people who drive the short-term activities of enormous numbers of businesses. I don't discount them; in fact, I really hold them in high regard. But it's a kind of work that I have absolutely no interest in performing. I make a distinction between short-term futures in contrast to what I do, which is strategic futures. To summarize, strategic futures have little data and few models and focus on helping organizations-, or occasionally an individual, understand what's driving change and help them how to respond to that.

The fundamental underlying beliefs of a futurist are really three things. 1.) We can see the future to a degree that's its useful. Useful for what?… useful for planning. 2.) We can take actions to make the desirable futures more likely and the undesirable futures less likely. Notice that neither of these is a claim of omniscience or omnipotence – they are both very modest claims. You can see the future to a degree that's useful, and you can take actions to improve your situation. And then there's a third assumption. 3.) We have a moral obligation to use that capability to anticipate and to influence. Now that's the centrepiece of my thinking.

My work universe is made up of clients – people who want to understand the future in order to improve their decision-making, planning, or thinking. In dealing with them as a futurist, there are three separate things which are lynchpins of the work. Now almost all of my clients are bureaucracies. The central feature of bureaucracy is the division of labour. In other words, everyone is a specialist and of course, everyone wants to succeed. Most people in corporations keep to their knitting and learn more and more about their specialty. That's what keeps that enterprise healthy. In looking at the future I have one objective, which is to break them out of their specialty box and make them more and more aware of things they may normally not be aware of. In other words, where unfamiliar developments can converge on their interests and either create a threat or an opportunity. Widen their horizon is objective number one. Second in bureaucracies, the time horizon is usually relatively short. That's what keeping all the short-term futurists so busy. What I want to do is give them greater depth of field. Show that their are things 5, 10, 15, 20, 25 years in the future that are going to present opportunities or risks. If it's 25 years in the future, why should I care about it now? Because the actions you take today have consequences for the future. Do you want to work against the future or do you want to work with the future? Futures studies can help an organisation understand one of three things about any of its short-term actions: is it neutral to the future, is it pro-future or is it anti-future? The second objective is to create greater depth of field.

The third objective, which as far as I know, no other futurist makes central to his or her thinking, comes out of the observation that every field of activity has a history of failure – businesses go out of business, projects, plans, and government agencies fail. Failure occurs in every organizational format. The central observation that links all organizational failure together is that a single person or a small group of people at the top of the organisation had assumptions about the future that were unsound. That's the key to organizational failure. So the third objective is to pry out of the client's mind their assumptions about the future. If I just ask you about future assumptions, I get prosaic reactions. In order to elicit someone's views, they must be provoked. When dealing with clients I want to deal mostly with things that are fairly comfortable and familiar, in order to legitimate myself and legitimate the work. Then I have to hit them with things that are going to provoke them. I'll give you a typical dialog. Client says, "I couldn't possibly believe woman could ever…, not in my lifetime…" Futurist replies, "Ah, Charlie, you really acted strongly to that point… could you develop that thought a little bit further, why don't you think women could ever…" If he takes the bait, I've got him. One can't react negatively or reject any concept about the future without revealing some of their own assumptions. The third and in some sense, most important thing that I do, in my lifelong career is – change minds. I don't care how they are changed. My fundamental belief is that if I can change your mind about anything, in any way, you're going to be better-off. I don't have an agenda, I don't have a goal I want to change you mind to. I don't have a specific objective; I just want to change your mind, because changing has to be fundamentally good for you. No other futurist will tell you that, partially because there is no one training them about the fundamental or underlying objectives of the study of the future are. The training tends to be at the instrumentality level, rather than at the more philosophical level.

Philippe Durance: I'm interested to know which methods you use. Do you use scenarios?

Joseph Coates: Conceptually, anything whose future is worth studying is a system. That's central. If you were to reorganize the intellectual world from scratch, futures research would be subsidiary to systems analysis. Since the system is the central unit in a futures study, you have to put a great deal of attention to developing the description of the system. This wall [2 × 5 meters] might be just about the right size as you work out a diagram of the system. A system is to a collection of elements or parts connected to each other by a variety of different means. You have to understand that system and come to the point where you can say: I understand the system.

I find that the system diagramming is easy to do, about 90% relatively quickly. But keep the system concept open, until the very end of the project, because you're continually going find things you missed and others that change in your judgment in importance. Since the system is the most important thing, how do you do it? You do it by doing it. How do you dance? I can tell you how to dance and I can show you how to dance. But how do you dance? You dance by dancing. And how do you start off dancing? Awkward, being laughed at, but you dance. You do the system the same way. Whatever resources you have at your disposal you use them to pull it together. You might start out with an encyclopaedia. You might start with your client's annual report. You might go to the library and do some research. None of those will have your system, but they may have significant components of it. For example, what's the system of McDonalds? It's different from that of a French restaurant right around the corner here. What's the system of the French national railway company [SNCF]? It's altogether different from the system of United Airlines. Nevertheless, you can often observe that systems share certain components. Some futurists are so unaccustomed to thinking systemically that every project is like dancing, but starting a new dance where you haven't heard that music or taken those steps before.

With that in mind, step two is: What are the forces operating on each of the elements of the system? There are a half-dozen generic clusters of forces that are nearly universal drivers of change. For example, demographic factors are an absolute universal. Information Technology is the second absolute universal. But then you get down to social values and other clusters such as areas of science and technology, their relevance varies. Trends in business practices have become more important the last ten years. Globalization is a trend area. These half-dozen broad categories might have three to 30 trends driving change under them. Then you have to add to those categories others specific to the client's enterprise. If you are dealing with a client who manufactures ice cream, you'll have a lot more things to add to that list of drivers than if you're modelling a system of a government agency that builds bridges in the United States. If you're studying the future for someone who makes window glass, you'll have a set of fac-

tors different from those relevant to an organization that grows toma-
toes in Italy.

Once I have the forces at play, how do they affect the components of
the system? I'm able to move to the critical point of how might they
interact and how might the system change. Incidentally, keep in mind
that you must not neglect those forces that promote stability. There is
a tendency on the part of many futurists to see only those forces acting
for change, but the forces for stability are often far more powerful.
You've go to keep them in mind. Now we get to the point, as I mentioned before, of rejecting the concept of the single future. All of the
forces of the system come together to create some interesting new
alternative futures. What do I mean by interesting? Relevant to policy
and decision-making. We don't want to concentrate on the most likely
future, nor the least likely future. We don't want only the most desirable future either... We want a range of futures that will be rich in policy implications. How do you select them? We're back to dancing. You
do it by doing it, and do it by making mistakes. You do it by eventually
getting it right.

Now you've got your alternative futures. How many are you interested in? You should do an even number because someone will always
try to look for the one seemingly in the middle and pick that one as
most likely. Somewhere between four and six, is useful for most purposes; when you begin to get to 8 or more, confusion sets in. On the
other hand, we did 14 for a car company. However those 14 were not
all comparable at the same level of generality.

With that in mind, I make a distinction between the next stage
implications: What are the most general implications of each of these
alternatives, and derivative of that, what are the actions that could be
taken? The reason I break it up that way is I want the client to understand the implications. Go back to the car company. "The largest
future car market for cars will be China." I want the client to understand that implication, but I don't want to confuse him by saying you
must open a plant in China, or he must do X in China because he'll
focus on those actions, If he reject them he may forget or also reject the
big implication that China is the biggest emerging market and manufacturer of cars. I separate all the implications in terms of implications
and actions. When you look at your alternative futures and you work
out these implications, some will be applicable to more than one the
alternatives – that tells you that's a pretty important implication. On
the other hand, some implication might only show up once, and that
could be extremely important if that alternative is the one that's going
to be realized. It's not just the frequency with which the implication
shows up. The one that shows up multiple times, you can be pretty
sure that is going to be important. The one that shows up only once or
maybe twice, don't dismiss it.

Once you've done all of that, then you have got two other things to consider. You've got to consider the wildcards – what could happen that could upset the whole analysis. And they are often surprising numerous; 25, 50, 75, is not unusual. We had one project that had 110 wild cards. The way I like to treat them is perturbations on the previous analysis.

The other thing we need to consider are stakeholders. In this whole system you're dealing with: Who are the people who either affect the system or are affected by it? That's how I define stakeholder; you either affect the system or you're affected by it. The central notion you want to get for each of them, with regard to your analysis is: What are the implications for the client? Is it important to them? What is their coinage, i.e., what is it that can make them change? Some stakeholders are neutral: Are there things you can do to shift them to being more favourable? Some stakeholders are already favourable: Can you use that in some positive way? Some stakeholders are or will be hostile: Is there some way you can mitigate or change their minds? But you must understand what they represent, what they stand for and what their coinage is. What is it that they're looking to do? How are they looking to bring about change? When you understand that, then you understand what that stakeholder's concerns are and what they mean to you. That finishes a future study.

Let me address methodology. With each of those pieces and components I already mentioned, you may use different methods to get what you want, but the structure is the same. In some cases you will want to use a mini-Delphi [1] study, in other cases you might want to make some phone calls, in other cases, you might have a conference or a workshop. Now remember, if we're doing the fifteen or twenty year future, then mathematical models are laughable. Sometimes when treating demography you can make useful 10, 15, 20 or even a 30 year forecast, depending upon the subject. But once you get past that, it's hard to find anything that is really respectable. What I tend to do is try to find surrogates, when we can't answer he question directly. For example: What will be chocolate consumption in the US 15 years from now? In other words, do I really want to go into the chocolate business? How the devil is anyone going to know chocolate consumption in the United States 15 years from now? However, what you do know is who consumes chocolate now. Look at the system demographically, 15 years from now, what will be the number of old people, young

---

1. "The Delphi method has traditionally been a technique aimed at building an agreement, or consensus about an opinion or view, without necessarily having people meet face to face, such as through surveys, questionnaires, emails etc. The Delphi method was developed at the Rand Corporation at the beginning of the cold war to forecast the impact of technology on warfare." http://en.wikipedia.org/wiki/Delphi_method

people, children and so forth, and then integrate that. In other words, assume some continuity or overlap, but then say what else will come along to compete with chocolate, what will come along to enhance chocolate, etc. So you now use the population as a surrogate to allow you to forecast chocolate and to give you a framework in which to add the things which might enhance or reduce chocolate consumption. Like what? Dark chocolate has the same kind of chemicals that are in red wine allowing the French to live forever – or at least until they die. They live forever healthy because of the antioxidants in red wine. Researchers now find in dark chocolate those same antioxidants. Chocolate is likely to move from a confection to a health food. Anyway, finding a surrogate is important. Nevertheless, there is no one technique that we use. The one central thing is the systems approach, but the data gathering, interpretation and analysis of it, is either our own craft and our own discussion, or the result of interacting with other people. Also, sometimes clients don't want to interact. Sometimes clients want to hear only the results of a project. Other times they want to be closely involved. If you can get them closely involved, the clients become primary inputs into your thinking – not determining what you're thinking, but rather giving you insight into the stuff that's so hard to get otherwise.

Adam Gerber: How important is cultivating a public persona – in other words, publishing and speaking – with respect to creating a successful consulting practice?

Joseph Coates: Two good ways for a futurist to draw attention to the future and to useful work with regard to the future are through public speaking and publishing material.

Public speaking is a particularly effective way to lead people into wanting to know more, and to display one's scope and clarity of thinking about the future. On the other hand, writing is less ephemeral and in many regards calls for much closer attention to completeness and clarity. In my firm, I encouraged everyone to write, but not of course about the work in our proprietary projects. Working steadily on projects left many of them with too little time and energy to write. I always believed that publishing an article was a satisfying ego booster for the author. In my firm, Coates & Jarratt, for years we averaged a published article every 17 days. We also used the articles to mail to current, past, and potential clients to keep them abreast of our thinking and also aware of us as a potential service provider.

Philippe Durance: What is a desirable future?

Joseph Coates: For whom? One of the things that becomes clear, if you take, for example, the technology assessment perspective: almost anything new has negative consequences for some, and positive consequences for others. One of the nice things that could happen for those for whom the change would be bad is to figure out how to move them

into potentially positive outcomes. I remember when I was an under-
graduate, and we had these beautiful, marvellous, slide rules, which
cost 18 dollars in 1949. There were beautiful and made from aluminium. Within five years, there was a $350 handheld calculator. Within
ten years, the slide rule manufacturer was out of business. Was that
some moral defect in technology? Was that something we ought to cry
over? Is that something we should have prevented? Should we have
compensated people? Or should we have said, the slide rule manufacturer was pretty dumb not to look at what was going on? Going on
where? Where? Where would they look? How would they know about
Texas Instruments? What do they do?... monitor cows? The point is
that every change has adverse affects on some and benefits for others.
Do you want to look at it from the point of view of the social calculus?
Is the government or the commonwealth your client? Or do you want
to look at from the point of view of the slide rule manufacturer or
Texas Instruments, or from the point of view of the engineers? A lot of
people get all caught up with negative effects, as if some how or
another that new technology was primarily bad and preventable.
From the social perspective, in contrast to a stockholders' view, you
often get a quite different view of what things should or could be like.

Adam Gerber: Can you speak to your scanning methodology and
some of your favourite resources?

Joseph Coates: The purpose of scanning is to find out what you don't
know, or to enhance what you already know, or think you know about
trends and developments. It's convenient to divide continuous information screening into monitoring and scanning. You do the very same
things, except in monitoring you may have an immediate focus to what
you are looking for.

Suppose we were doing a study for a chocolate company. I'd be very
close to monitoring to what's going on in chocolate and competitive sectors and I'd also be interested to know what was happening with the
medicinal properties and benefits of French wine. But, while I'm doing
that, I have to look at things I'm not working on now, which is the scanning part. What I find is that in the US, at least three newspapers have
to looked at, the New York Times, the Financial Times – I'm not particularly keen the Wall Street Journal, the FT is so much better – and
a local newspaper. Since we live in the centre of the galaxy, I can read
the Washington Post. Some other important resources are the national
news magazines, of which there are three, and about 40 other publications which represent different socio-economic points of view. Publications like Atlantic Monthly and Harpers, which are middle-of-the-road
politically – sometimes accused of being liberal, but not too liberal – the
New York Review of Books [1], which is probably the more liberal of the

----

1. More information here: http://www.nybooks.com/

central publications, etc. Then you have a group of science and technology publications, all the way from Science News to Scientific American. Various societies publish magazines for their own membership, For example, the American Chemical Society publishes Chemical and Engineering News [1]. It is mostly business news and rather uninteresting from a futurist's point of view But it usually has background articles and review articles about something important in chemistry that might be of interest in relation to the future. The electrical engineers have similar publications. They are all important things to read.

Then there's some which are a cut above merely popular, like Scientific American, but it tends to be a bit faddish. The current fad is space and cosmology. The American Scientist [2] is published by a scientific society, Sigma Xi, and it has highly credible review articles and outstanding book reviews. Book reviews are important. Your reading list depends a lot on your personal interests, where you see your futures business going and where you think you need to keep current. You must keep an eye on the social science literature and the arts and humanities publications as well as international affairs. These are the kinds of the things that comprise a list of 50 to 75 publications one must keep up with. Some of them are meant to be dipped in and some are meant to be clipped, while others are meant to be noted. I'm a clipper; I usually clip things and then throw away the publication, except for 15 or 20 of them which I keep for from one to several years. I have – the last time I counted – 160 categories, all gross categories into which I file things. I have one file on bureaucracy, but nobody writes about bureaucracy. I don't think there's a single article in that file that has the word "bureaucracy" in it, but all are about bureaucracy; i.e., how an agency or corporation behaves. My file on information technology, for the moment, is three boxes big with unsorted information. I don't have an information technology project going, so I haven't sorted that all out. I dip into that file when I need information on IT for a different project. The thing that I find that I need to be wary of is to not wasting time filing too finely. I have a long-term interest in *sports, leisure and recreation* and I've done some projects in that industry. That file is just a collection about seventy cm thick. I don't want to make this file any more fine-grained, because in 15 minutes I can go through 300 articles and see which ones I want to reread. To file them into 7 subcategories would take several hours of work. The point is economy of time. Some people prefer to set up a computer database of scanning resources. Personally, I just find that is a waste of time unless you have infinite staff resources. Better to read one thing and understand it, than to file 5 things and not understand any of them. You only have 24 hours in a day.

---

1. More information here: http://pubs.acs.org/cen/
2. More information here: http://www.americanscientist.org/amsci.html

Philippe Durance: Joe, is there anything we've overlooked?

Joseph Coates: Yes, three points. First, you asked how does prospective differ from American futures practice. They are not congruent with just a change in naming. Prospective as illustrated by Godet's book [1], is a well integrated set of methods and techniques, which can be used in a total approach, or piecemeal as the situation calls for. The American practice tends to be made up of a group of relatively independent techniques closely matching but not identical with those in prospective, and generally drawn upon in a much more arbitrary way. For that reason there is a great opportunity for cross-learning, by experimenting with each other's new or preferred specific tools.

Second, I should mention one of the techniques that I find very valuable. When we are looking at a future technology, let's say something under advanced research or something whose characteristics are already being spoken about, we try to do the following. We create an inventory of the new technology's characteristics: colour, size, shape, activities, functions, etc., and then more or less scan the universe (slight exaggeration) to see where each of those characteristics, or sets of them, could be used, and the consequences thereof. It's easiest to see this with a physical technology but the technique can be used with any social, political, or economic change, anticipated or planned.

Third, further material on my thinking and orientation to the future can be found in the 300 or so articles posted or noted on my web site, www.josephcoates.com.

Philippe and Adam, it's been great talking with you.

Michel GODET interviewed by Philippe Durance

Paris, the 24th of August 2004

Philippe Durance: Prospective, or foresight as it is sometimes translated, is your passion, one that has been your career for over 30 years. How did you discover this vocation?

Michel Godet: In 1971, I was 23 and developing rigorous scientific methods with mathematical probabilities. This was before the oil crisis. I was working then at the CEA [2]. Later at SEMA [3], I had the chance to travel

---

1. first edition of *Creating Futures*, by Godet, Michel
2. CEA: Atomic Energy Commission
3. SEMA: Society of applied economics and mathematics. The SEMA was created in 1954 by Jacques Lesourne. It was a research group for companies and administrators. SEMA focused on economic problems including future studies, operation research and cost comparisons for different solutions, to name but a few specific topics. Michel Godet met Christian Goux there in 1970. Goux, the "master of conjecture" of that era later initiated Godet in prospective and supervised his French State PhD in economics.

round the world as a member of various missions. One stop was North Africa. There, I realized that the keys to industrialization in Algeria were agriculture, education, mastery of urban development and demographics. Soon thereafter, in 1978, in the Far East, I saw that Confucius had got it right long ago: Teach people to fish rather than to give them fish. In other words, good ideas are not those that we have or give but those we elicit. The word is appropriation. The French all know the story of the Parmentier potato. Only by creating an elaborate set-up and having soldiers guard the field did people want to appropriate, or steal, Parmentier's potatoes. Yet from a more basic point of view, we need to ask a few questions. Besides How to? or How? we need to ask Who am I? We need to remember the ancient Greek advice: Know thyself, thyself. We often forget to ask or forget the actual questions. Let's get two things straight. First, what will happen is not written down somewhere. Second, thinking about the future does not eliminate uncertainty. Instead it prepares us better. Everyone will face the same changes; the real differences lie in how each one of us reacts. The elements of both success and failure lie within. All in all, learning how to maximize your strengths and minimize your weaknesses is more effective than trying to change the world.

Philippe Durance: Let's backtrack to how you started out.

Michel Godet: I started as a research engineer at SEMA in 1974. A year later [1], I was promoted to senior engineer and headed a profit-making center within the SEMA. In 1976, I became head engineer, and then in 1978, I led the Prospective department that I had initiated. Only then could I really apply and develop the prospective methods and systems analysis that I had studied as an intern in the CEA programs from 1971 to 1974 [2].

During the same period, I carried out vast projects on the future of energy, industrialization in developing countries, and air transportation. It was around this time that I began leading teams and going further afield; literally, on missions in the USA, Algeria, Egypt, and most of Southeast Asia, an area really taking off then.

At age 29, I became SEMA's youngest director and was in charge of its second profit-making centre. At that time, I began wondering how useful all those interesting reports that usually ended up lining drawers were [3].

---

1. That same year, Michel Godet received his doctorate in economics (Paris I, Pantheon-Sorbonne). Much of his doctoral research would appear in the book, *Crise de la prévision, essor de la prospective* (1977).

2. In 1974, Michel Godet had obtained a PhD in statistics and mathematics (Paris IV) on the development of new methods of systems analysis and scenario probabilisations.

3. This situation would become the subject of an article by Michel Godet and J-P Plas, "L'Entreprise sur le divan" that appeared in *Le Monde* on October 14, 1978.

I answered an ad in the newspaper Le Monde and found myself working as deputy project leader of an EEC program on the future from 1979 to 1980: Ricardo Petrella had recruited me to launch the FAST program [1]. Already then, almost a quarter of a century ago, computerized communication technology and the information society were our main interests. At this time, I wrote a report called, "Europe en Mutation". Over 10 million Euros were spent, but little remains for our collective memory and the general manager of the research department launched Technology Foresight without realizing that the same questions asked by new teams are not necessarily better. Once again, we have evidence of the lack of collective memory.

Back from Brussels, I tried to get into the CNRS as a prospectivist, often called a futurist in English, but to no avail. Why? There was no department and there still is no such department. I tried the same thing at the Plan, another French government planning centre, with the same result. From 1980 to 1981, I worked alongside Jacques Lesourne as a full-time lecturer at the Institut Auguste Comte [2].

For six years, until 1987, I served as scientific advisor for the Centre de Prospective et d'Evaluation (CPE) at the French ministry of research. There I handled international relations. My duties enabled me to participate in several missions and exchanges related to technological change and economic development in Japan, Canada, and the USA, as well as Europe, of course. Some missions were carried out further to requests from the foreign affairs ministries of the American and Canadian governments. This was the case in 1984 and 1993, when our focus was technological change and its impact on growth and employment. In 1986, I also led a mission on the Japanese model, both in society and business. This mission would lead to Radioscopie du Japon, published in 1987.

From 1982 to 1987, I was also an assistant professor at the CNAM. In 1987, I became a full professor and the holder of the chair in industrial foresight. This chair had been created with me in mind when I came to the CNAM in 1982. Concurrently, I have served as a consultant in prospective and strategy for major corporations such as

---

1. FAST (Forecasting and Assessment in Science and Technology) was a program directed by Riccardo Petrella from 1978 to 1994. The FAST mission was to study the links between science, technology and society. The focus was on the socio-economic consequences of scientific and technological developments in the short and long term.

2. In 1972, Giscard d'Estaing founded the *Institut August Comte*, which sought to train managers from large corporations or very large administrations to solve complex problems by treating all dimensions: legal, economic, social, and international. The *Institut Auguste Comte* has had five research directors including Jérôme Monod, now in the French government, and Michel Crozier, a well-known sociologist. Jacques Lesourne introduced Michel Godet, who was bored by the situation in Brussels, to the institute.

Renault, ELF, Pechiney, Electricité de France, Sollar, Chanel, Bongrain, Lafarge and AXA. I have also acted as a consultant to local or regional administrative groups. During the same period, I managed to maintain an international perspective through regular missions to North and South America, as well as several European centres.

Philippe Durance: Many people consider the 1970s as the golden age of prospective in France. They also lament the fact that prospective is little taught at the university or post-graduate level elsewhere. What do you think?

Michel Godet: Personally, I do not see a decline in prospective, or foresight. On the contrary, I find the field more open and less specialized than when I began. The golden age was actually the work of a handful of individuals — Bertrand de Jouvenel[1], Pierre Massé[2], Jérôme Monod[3] and Gaston Berger[4]. They did not try to fit this "intellectual undiscipline" into the academic categories nor did they train followers.

Prospective, as I prefer to call it even in English, has a broad cross-cutting nature that is a handicap for compartmentalized organizations. However, the cognitive sciences share this breadth and have received research funding from the CNRS and ministry of research.

------

1. Bertrand de Jouvenel (1903-1987) served as a diplomat, journalist, economist, jurist and professor at several universities in France and abroad. De Jouvenel ran the SEDEIS, or Society for the study and documentation of social and industrial economics from 1954 to 1974. The SEDEIS had been created by a group of managers. Bertrand de Jouvenel was one of the main players in the rise of prospective in France and abroad. He wrote *L'Art de la conjecture* and founded the international association called Futuribles (1967).

2. Pierre Massé became an engineer in public works and in the electrical sector in 1928. He was in charge of building hydroelectric plants. He was director of electrical equipment in 1946, then director of economic studies at Electricité de France (EDF) in 1948. In 1957, he became president of Electricité de Strasbourg. He served as general commissioner of the Plan from 1959 to 1966.

3. Former delegate at the Datar and president of the Groupe Suez, Jérôme Monod is now advisor to the president of the French Republic, Jacques Chirac.

4. Gaston Berger died in 1960 just before a research and teaching program in prospective was inaugurated at the school of higher commercial studies (*Ecole pratique des hautes études*), under the direction of Fernand Braudel. Fernand Braudel wrote the following for a speech: "*Gaston Berger should take his place among us today. He was excited in advance, happy to no longer be just another professor. He also had fun, not to excess, though, with the reversal of our respective roles. He treated me with an amused deference, as one would treat an administrative superior. He proved to himself in this way that he was once again a free man. (...) This fragile science called prospective, that he had created and baptized, he intended to consolidate it and enhance its structure here, in our school.*" (Braudel, 1962).

Prospective could be considered within this same category. All in all, the learning curve for anything requires patience, persistence, and preparation of the next generation of practitioners. We also need to offer theoretical and practical instruction to those interested so that they can capitalize on experience and maintain the collective memory. I am saddened by some practitioners, often the best, who consider prospective a profitable business, and do not try to pass on their know-how. They forget that knowledge is to be shared.

The same applies abroad, especially in the English-speaking world where there is no collective memory, and a noticeable withdrawal from rational methods. Again, the terms create a problem as prospective is translated as foresight usually and reduced to participatory scenario building exercises during which group dynamics and communication take over. As a result, the questions covered and the level of research involved suffers. You can see this in France, too, with "scenario entertainment", which is part of the "future of the present" trend. We should all remember pioneer Gaston Berger's words of wisdom: See far, wide, deep, and think of Man.

I have added three more pieces of advice: 1) see differently, to avoid conforming to conventional thinking, 2) do it together, to facilitate appropriation and the balancing of differences, 3) use rigorous methods to deal with complexity, and pinpoint the group's collective inconsistencies.

I am glad to see that the past 30 years have been marked by the appropriation of our methods in corporate and regional management, here and abroad. I'm optimistic about prospective; that is to say, the French version. It has taken root and developed well in other countries where romance languages are spoken. The French and international expansion of prospective does, however, stem from the ongoing efforts to disseminate concepts and methods of French practitioners belonging to the international association, Futuribles [1]. These compatriots have kept alive the tradition of volunteering from the sixties, along with the rigorous approaches to exploring and evaluating ideas that the RAND Corporation [2] and SEMA developed during the post-war boom and the space race. What we need now is something equal to Erich Jantsch's book on forecasting and technological evaluation. This book was state of the art in 1967 [3]. Of course, Futuribles contributes tremendously through its journal and training seminars. Also the founding of the Laboratoire d'investigation en prospective, stratégie et organization (Lipsor) at the CNAM in the early 1990s, and the doctoral training program in prospective, strategy and organization which I

---

1. *Futuribles* was created by Bertrand de Jouvenel in 1967. The current president is Jacques Lesourne and the acting director is Hugues de Jouvenel.

2. Cf. *infra*

3. Available on the Lipsor website in French and English: http://www.cnam.fr/lipsor/recherche/laboratoire/memoireprospective.php

lead with Yvon Pesqueux, assisted by Jacques Lesourne and Rémi Barré, have provided training to several dozen professionals in France and the world. As far as I know, there are some twenty former students of CNAM who are living quite successfully plying their craft in France.

The publication of my manual in 1985, with updated editions in 1991, 1997, and 2001, as well as translated versions in English, Spanish, Portuguese and Italian, has also helped spread the methods of the French school. Writing a manual is an author's effort to help others, although it's more of a thankless task than it seems. Each revised edition represents more than a year of work. In fact, I spent a year and a half on the English adaptation in which I was assisted by a translator who worked on site and attended my corporate workshops. This translation, like those for South America, received partial funding from the French Ministry of Foreign Affairs, which has a translating tradition. In fact, it helped fund a special English issue of Futuribles (Prospective and French Futures) and in 2001, a special issue of Technological Forecasting devoted to scenario planning.

During the 1990s, I tried in vain to get the Commission in Brussels to structure some form of European prospective. I could not generate interest in research through doctoral scholarships, either. These scholarships would have been funded by the CNAM, Plan [1] and Datar [2]. Yet I do remain optimistic and intend to try again at every opportunity [3].

The status of prospective remains fragile, though. Far too much still depends on the good will and persistence of a few people, like Hugues de Jouvenel and Jacques Lesourne, to name but those two. Chance has always played a role in preparing the ground for projects. In fact, this is one of the lessons that I can draw from my own experience in the field. I remember that SEMA's prospective department had produced numerous and voluminous studies on air transportation, the post office, etc. Many of these studies stand the test of time, too, but lay buried in filing cabinets. Given the lack of academic recognition, training in prospective happens by chance, often at the whim of circumstance.

In the early 1990s, given all the seminars organized by Futuribles, and in light of the development of some form of prospective in the European Commission, a doctorate in strategic prospective was needed and created at the CNAM. Again the same question: which

---

1. Commissariat General du Plan is a French governmental agency.
2. The Datar is a French paragovernmental delegation for regional action and territorial organization.
3. A European college for regional prospective opened in April 2004. The proposal came from the *Conseil de prospective et de dynamique des territories*, a forward-looking council focusing on regional cooperation. This new council is headed by Michel Godet. The college seeks to open up to Europe by reinforcing skills in regional prospective through the Datar's and its partners' efforts.

academic niche? Economics, history, management? Management actually offered more possibilities than the others. It is a more open field with an applied strategic dimension well suited to prospective. This relationship with management enabled us to network with other centres and thus form credible doctoral thesis defence juries. Credibility is important as the jury legitimates the doctoral program as a whole.

Through this program, I was able to create two full lecturer positions; however, it eventually became clear that teaching prospective, like teaching strategy, required the practical experience that a young academic can never have. The academic world is increasingly compartmentalized. In fact, the demands inherent in a university career prevent the further development of prospective. One must publish abstract theoretical articles in juried academic journals to be recognized. Well, prospective does not fit this type of logic. Today's practitioners usually did not follow a traditional academic path; in other words, they came to the field by chance. This often makes them excellent "deviants", fresh from many different horizons.

Philippe Durance: You talk about the French school of prospective, but few people agree with you that it exists. Can you clarify this?

Michel Godet: Let's start with the scenario method as an example. Given American cultural domination, the Americans tend to self-attribute the roots of scenario thinking. But, after all, we do share with the Americans some common historical background. To muddy the waters further, we face the terminological problem of the word, prospective, which does not translate fully into one English word. Futurology is the term that dominates in the English-speaking world. Now you also find foresight and even strategic prospective. In any event, the concept of the scenario remains central to the entire process, especially as the scenario appears to be less of the rigorous scientific method that it once was in the 1950's and 60's, under the influence of the RAND Corporation [1]. In those days, the RAND had several researchers, often European immigrants like Olaf Helmer (Delphi method) and Fritz Zwicky (morphological analysis in scenario building). At the same time, Gaston Berger and Bertrand de Jouvenel founded the French school of prospective and the Plan in France was an official priority. The peak in this period was the publication of Jantsch's book.

The French school simply kept alive and further developed this legacy of Cartesian methods of systems analysis. It was inherited indirectly from the RAND Corporation, and furthermore combines broad historical, global and voluntaristic perspectives.

---

1. Initiated as a military project in 1945, the RAND Corporation was officially incorporated as such in 1948. Its name is a contraction of research and development. This corporation became a lab and an incubator for the tools used in prospective. Examples include Herman Kahn (scenarios), Olaf Helmer (Delphi, 1950s) and crossed impact analysis.

Without going into detail, the Vietnam War created a deep mistrust of rational methods of systems analysis. The Americans had failed in their effort to analyze conflict scientifically, so they threw the methods, like the proverbial baby, out with the bath water. You can more or less date a certain decline in logical thinking in the USA from that point on. From one extreme of scientific approaches, the Americans went to the other, intuitive even irrational techniques. This attitude is illustrated beautifully in what they call "New Age" thinking. As a result, the English-speaking world reduces prospective to little more than scenario entertainment. I don't think that gathering a few intellectuals together to play at pleasing or scaring one another with a concept equals research. It is entertainment in the Pascalian sense — a distraction really. In terms of content, though, this approach is simplistic, often binary, so that the future is divided according to two hypotheses (yes or no), hence four scenarios. Scientifically, this comes close to some kind of mystification, especially when people claim that the strategy of such and such a big group was enlightened by these scenarios. As far as I know, Shell built scenarios on communication and information technology but never invested a penny in that sector. In American practice, scenario building is like bodybuilding! The collective and participatory process of futures thinking, as I call it, is positive in its own right but all the more useful for strategy if we ask real questions that are not simply reduced to two possibilities chosen to suit the latest fashion.

Actually, corporate scenario building is an excellent participatory management tool that can get the whole staff involved. Although not all issues are suitable, because of confidentiality, it is possible to have people think not about the company's strategic choices that their employer faces, but rather about the environment affecting those choices. If structured properly, not only the executives use this approach but the rank and file as well. At Renault, in 1983, I was involved in Mides, a futures-thinking exercise involving 3,000 people. The scenario process has been successfully applied to regions, too, as seen in the Pays Basque 2010 project [1]. Nowadays, group learning is an integral part of knowledge management; however, in management terms what counts is involvement. A popular American phrase sums it up well: the reward is the journey. The goal is a pretext, almost an excuse, for the group effort, shared experience and ties created among the participants.

Last but not least, I'd like to point out that English-speaking authors and researchers themselves speak of the French school of prospective [2].

---

1. This regional exercise has been published as a Lipsor Working Papers (Mousli, 2004).

2. In 1999, the British magazine *Antidote* produced a special issue on scenarios and forecasting methods. It included an article entitled "Creating the Future: a French School, La Prospective, argues against taking a fatalistic approach" (CSBS, 1999). This piece profiled the French school and described the methods developed by Michel Godet.

Philippe Durance: The future being what it is, primarily uncertainty, how can prospective separate itself from futurology or future studies?

Michel Godet: Futurology claims to be a science of the future, just as history would be the science of the past. Although the past is as multisided and uncertain as the future, and although we constantly rewrite history, the past remains gone. On the other hand, the future is open, and any form of prediction is tantamount to fraud. For prospective, the future is the fruit of desire, in other words, a dream that motivates present action and drives reality towards a desired future. And we know that an action without a goal is meaningless.

As we asked in the English adaptation of our book: Do we want the world to change with us, without us or against us? Simply asking that question begs the answer. It is up to each of us to take charge of our future, to conspire for a better future, one closer to our desires and farther from our fears.

Determinism of any kind does not resist determination, and chance. Pasteur said it best when he said that chance favours only the prepared mind. When you have projects, you are young and alive. As Gaston Berger, creator of the very term, prospective, once said: old age is the shrinking of the field of possibilities. This explains why you find 20-year-olds who seem dead and 70-year-olds who are still planting trees in their garden.

Fortunately, the future is indeed open and uncertain. A totally certain and foreseeable world would be intolerable. However, the clock is ticking and each minute lived is one less to live yet one more at the same time. Now you see why happiness is possible only where there is some degree of uncertainty. Uncertainty is life; certainty is death.

Philippe Durance: What key lessons can you draw from your many years of practical experience in prospective?

Michel Godet: First, it is an art – an intellectual art that requires a poet's imagination, knowledge, common sense and a healthy dose of non-conformity. Second, although it is an art, prospective requires rigour and methods designed to enlighten our action and direct us toward a desired future.

Those who seek our services are large corporations, governments and regional authorities. They are looking for someone to help answer five basic questions: What can happen? What can I do? What will I do? How will I do it? Who am I?

Each of these questions is a source of errors, though. If you do not get the diagnosis right from the start then you get the prescription wrong. In other words, there is no correct answer to an incorrect question. Yet a good question may also require being aware of conventional thinking, or cookie-cutter ideas. These are the ones that we all know, that are never discussed and that often turn out to be false.

Let me give you an example: change. We tend to overestimate the speed of change, especially technological change. We think that we are living in a period of unprecedented tumultuous change after which nothing equally important will ever occur. Some people go so far as to say that we have entered the "end of history"[1]. There's nothing strange about this feeling because every generation thinks its era is exceptional. And it is, to them, simply because it is the only chance that generation has.

We probably tend to overestimate change because we underestimate inertia. In reality, the world changes, but the problems remain. Why? Human nature. History's great invariable is the human component. Our driving forces, e.g., power, money, love and hate, have not changed since ancient times.

Let's go back to those five questions. We should begin with Who am I? Then we can study and know human nature to understand what is happening. We need to recover our memory of the past in order to illuminate the future. This makes me think of a line from a Visconti film, The Leopard (1963): "Everything must change for everything to being again."

Man is always at the heart of difference, so why look for other scapegoats outside us. One example is globalization or technology. For many floundering companies, the cause of the shipwreck lies in internal management deficiencies rather than the storm raging outside. Without a strong captain there can be no winning crew. The ideal leader must know how to anticipate events as well as instil a sense of enthusiasm and belonging. He/she must act firmly and react calmly. The correct destination is not an adequate strategy. If we extend the metaphor: we need a crew that is not only prepared but also motivated to make the journey. For any firm, the home and foreign fronts are actually one strategic segment. The battle must be won on both fronts or it is lost. In other words, when confronted with change in the strategic environment, a company depends primarily on its internal strengths and weaknesses. As Vauvenargues, the nineteenth-century French philosopher put it: knowing our strengths increases them; knowing our weaknesses decreases them.

Prospective in a company acts like a mirror. A good prospective exercise teaches one to ask the right questions but most of all to know thyself better. Strategic analysis is rediscovering Socrates' dictum, know thyself. So, before asking Where do we want to go? What can happen? What to do?... We must know who we are and know it well.

Philippe Durance: The role of experts in society is increasingly questioned. They are criticized and appear less credible. Does that bother you?

---

1. Note the title of Francis Fukuyama's best-seller, The End of History.

Michel Godet: In this field, a trait that I call intellectual imperti-nence is necessary. If we want to ask the right questions, these must necessarily be the questions that upset. We are not asking questions full of politically correct gobbledygook. It is easier to think like every-one else, not rock the boat and never have to defend one's ideas. In fact, this explains why experts often are wrong while in agreement with one another. On the other hand, swimming upstream against the dominant thinking is difficult because one has to explain reasons to a massive majority of conformists. In the end, a visionary often stands alone, little heard.

I'm not saying that a minority view is necessarily correct. However, consensus is suspect and should be examined more closely. Some thirty years ago, after the first oil shock, people spoke of an energy cri-sis. Suddenly we had the diagnosis and Rx at the same time. Energy was the root of the crisis and solid economic growth means guarantee-ing energy independence. The underlying logic was clear: no more oil, so develop nuclear power. In reality, though, I managed to demon-strate my idea, later verified, that there was an overabundance of energy. Again, the logic was clear: what is rare is cheap energy and what abounds is expensive energy. Why? Because is it expensive.

Another widespread corporate cliché is critical size. Major invest-ment decisions are justified with a mantra: we don't have the critical size to compete on an international scale. Yet somehow there are always smaller, more profitable companies. Actually, the real question is whether or not the company is profitable at its current size. Often we have to start by growing smaller; in other words, cutting out the dead wood. In short, we often confuse growth with profitability. We need to remember that companies are like trees that need pruning to grow better.

Philippe Durance: As a prospectivist, you have a vision of the 21st century. Can you share it with us?

Michel Godet: Thinking about the future has always been a special opportunity for us to let our minds run free. We may have dreams or nightmares. Essentially we will be either pleased or frightened by the new technological developments that supposedly will bring about unprecedented changes. The new millennium generated so many pre-dictions, just as the year 1000 did. Of course, the world was supposed to end in 1000! The major issues at this end of one century and begin-ning of a new one already have known diagnoses and prescriptions. What is needed is an answer to the question: how should we take action before it is too late?

The politicians are informed. In fact, they often tell me that I am correct, but that they cannot say much if they want to stay in office. They are there, it seems, to answer to opinions. We need to change opinions by being brave enough to say loudly what others just think softly. The only censorship is really self-censorship. If everyone, each of us in our own corner, becomes aware of the realities and does appropriate the diagnoses, then preventive policies will naturally fall into place. The expert in prospective reminds me of the lookout on the Titanic. From the crow's nest he sees the iceberg coming closer. His job is to alert the captain and crew so that they change course and avoid a collision. In short, good foresight is foresight that leads to action.

I do not hope for change to come from above. No. It must come from below, if we are to anticipate, act, experiment and innovate. In other words, the future interests all of us greatly. Remember that the future is where we will be spending the rest of our lives.

Yet that which is essential is often ephemeral. To paraphrase Karl Marx in his early writings (Grundrisse): the productive forces are not only material but are also spiritual. Economic growth alone does not bring happiness. People want to find social affinities and some meaning in their lives. Otherwise, there is despair, real despair out there; as people feel that they are alone. The great paradox of modern life is that information technology makes us more connected to the entire world, but there is nobody next to us for a chat. Of course, some people pay therapists a lot of money for a regular chat. People are always at the core of our thinking on the future. I remember a father's words to his son: if you don't live like you think, you will think like you live. It is up to us to decide what we want for tomorrow. Do we want to be like the ancient Romans with their bread and circuses or like the ancient Athenians (without slaves, thanks to modern technology)?

Both the worst and the best are possible. Ghosts must no longer rule the living and we must leave future generations a true legacy. We should bear in mind that we did not inherit the earth outright; we are only borrowing it.

My ambition is to inject people with a healthy dose of prospective so that everyone can hold up his/her compass and lead others toward a shared destination. In the end, initiatives and common projects provide us with social ties and a meaning or direction in our lives. The German proverb sums it up well: der weg ist das ziel. The journey is the goal.

Philippe Durance: Practising the art of prospective basically means using methods and tools. Is there more to it?

Michel Godet: Tools are available to deal with the uncertainty and complexity of problems. These tools have been honed over time and remain useful today for even if the world changes, certain invariables and similarities in the problems remain constant.

The tools employed in strategic analysis and prospective are useful in stimulating the imagination, decreasing inconsistencies, creating a common language, structuring group reflection and enabling appropriation. There are limits, though. There are also the illusions of formalization. Tools are not substitutes for thoughts. They should not block freedom of choice. As professionals, we face the double-edged sword of presenting tools then trying to avoid the errors people make in using those tools incorrectly. For example, the hammer is a useful tool, but only if we need to drive a nail. Just because we know how to wield a hammer, we do not need to apply it everywhere, on every problem. We want people to use the tools that prospective offers, but we also spend a lot of time dissuading beginners from using them incorrectly.

These tools should be simple enough so that people can appropriate them; otherwise, they will reject them. As I said before, the best ideas are not those we have but rather those we generate in others. Leaders and managers have forgotten this, but I try everything to get them to appropriate this very idea. A problem presented properly and shared by those involved is already partly solved. The French author and researcher, Michel Crozier, said it best: the problem is the problem [1].

Philippe Durance: Where would you tell young researchers to focus in prospective today?

Michel Godet: There are many potential research areas. If we start with the most difficult, there is the link between game theory and actors' games, begun by Francois Bourse. There is also the integration of prospective tools in operational research. More broadly, there are the mathematical specialties, such as diagonalisation, proper values, unknown number systems, fractals, graph theories, and many more.

In the soft sciences, there is cognition and organization learning, something Philippe Bootz (2001) has developed.

But we have to remember the zero question, the Who are we? This dimension enables us to make projects happen, to build the bridge between the individual and the collectivity.

Last but not least, we need to bring history and prospective together. The past is as multiple, uncertain and controversial as the future, but it affects both the present and future. History, the novel of the real, as Paul Veyne [2] put it, is constantly being rewritten according to the needs of the present. The whole issue of climate change takes on another light when we are reminded of the past by authors like Emmanuel Leroy Ladurie in his work on the history of climates. If prospective aims to enlighten our actions in light of possible futures, the goal of history is to do the same, but in light of past futures.

---

1. Former director of research studies at the *Institut August Comte*, Michel Crozier is a sociologist. As research director at the CNRS, Crozier founded the Centre of organizational sociology (CCSO), at the Political Science Institute in Paris.

2. Author, historian and professor at the *Collège de France*.

BIBLIOGRAPHY

Ackoff, R. *A Concept of Corporate Planning*. New York: John Wiley & Sons, 1970.

Alba, P. "Prospective et stratégie d'entreprise", *Futuribles*, n° 18, feb. (1989).

Albert, K.J. *The Strategic Management Handbook*. New York: McGraw-Hill, 1983.

Allais (Maurice), 1989, "La philosophie de ma vie", *Annales des Mines: gérer et comprendre*, June.

Ansoff, I. *Corporate Strategy, An Analytic Approach to Business Policy for Growth and Expansion*. New York: McGraw-Hill, 1965.

Ansoff, I. *From Strategic Planning to Strategic Management*. New York: John Wiley, 1976.

Ansoff, I. *Strategic Management*. New York: McMillan, 1979.

Ansoff, I. *Implementing Strategic Management*. Englewood, NJ: Prentice Hall International, 1984.

Apostol, P. "Marxism and the Structure of the Future", *Futures*, vol. 4, Sept. 1972.

Archier, G. H. Sérieyx. *L'entreprise du 3ᵉ type*. Paris: Seuil, 1984.

Artus (Patrick), Cette (Gilbert), 2004, *Productivité et Croissance, La Documentation française*.

Asher (François), 1995, *Metropolis ou l'avenir des villes*, Odile Jacob.

Baudry (Paul), Green (David), 2000, *Population Growth, Technological Adoption and Economic Outcomes: A Theory of Cross-Country Differences for the Information Era*, University of Columbia.

Barel, Y. *Prospective et analyse du système*. Paris: Collection TRP, La Documentation Française, 1971.

Beaufre, A. *Introduction à la stratégie*. Paris: Ifri-Economica, 1963.

Bébéar (Claude) (Dir.), 2002, *Le Courage de réformer*, Odile Jacob.

Bechmann, R. *Des arbres et des hommes, la forêt au Moyen Âge*. Paris: Flammarion, 1984. [Available in English. *Trees and Man, the Forest in the Middle Ages*. New York: Paragon House, 1990.]

Bell, D. "Prévision contre prophétie" in *L'historien entre l'ethnologue et le futurologue*. La Hague: Mouton, 1972.

Bell, D. *The Coming of Post-Industrial Society, a Venture in Social Forecasting*. 1st. ed. New York: Basic Books, 1976.

Benassouli, P., R. Monti. "La planification par scénarios, le cas AXA France 2005", *Futuribles*, n° 203, nov., 1995.

Berger, G. "Sciences humaines et prévision", *La revue des deux mondes*, n° 3, feb., 1957.

Berger, G. *Phénoménologie du temps et prospective*. Paris: Presses universitaires de France, 1964.

Berger, G. *Étapes de la prospective*. Paris: PUF, 1967.

Blake, William *The Marriage of Heaven and Hell*. Mineola, New York: Dover Publications; 1790, reprint edition 1994.

Bonneuil (Michèle, de), Cahuc (Pierre), 2004, *Création d'emplois dans les services*, La Documentation française.

Boyer, L., N. Equilbey. *Histoire du management*. Paris: Éditions d'Organisation, 1990.

Brender (Anton), 2000, "La réalité du New Age n'est pas prouvée", *Revue de Rexecode*, n° 66, 1er trimestre.

Brundtland (Gro Harlem), 1987, *Notre avenir à tous*, Commission des Nations Unies sur l'environnement et le développement.

Calot (Gérard), 2002, "Le vieillissement de la population: un sujet qui fâche", *Panoramiques*, n° 57.

Camus, A. *Le mythe de Sisyphe*. Paris: Gallimard, 1962. [Available in English. Trans. O'Brien, J., *The Myth of Sisyphus and Other Essays*. New York: Vintage Books, 1955.]

Cannac (Yves), Godet (Michel), 2001, "La bonne gouvernance", *Futuribles,* n° 265, June.

Cazes, B. *Histoire des futurs*. Paris: Seghers, 1986.

Center for Strategic Business Studies, 1999, "Scenarios: The search for foresight", The Antidote, n° 22.

Chaize (Jacques), 1992, *La Porte du changement s'ouvre de l'intérieur,* Calmann-Lévy.

Chandler, A. *Strategy and Structure: Chapters in the History of the Industrial Enterprise*. Garden City, N.J.: Doubleday, 1966.

Chesnais, J.-C. *Le crépuscule de l'Occident*. Paris: Éditions Robert Laffont, 1995.

Coates, J.F *What Futurists Believe*, World Future Society 1989.

Coates, J.F. *American Business in the New Millenium: Trends Shaping American Business*. New York: Coates & Jarrat, Inc., 1994.

Coates, J.F. *2025: Scenarios of US and Global Society Reshaped by Science and Technology. Akron, OH: Oakhill Press, 1997*.

Coates, J.F. *Issues Management: How to Plan, Organize, and Manage for the Future*. Mt. Airy, MD: Lomond, 1986.

CNAF, 2004, "L'Allemagne veut investir dans la petite enfance", *Horizon 2015*, n° 3, September.

Commission européenne, 2002, *Attitudes of Europeans towards fertility: ideals, desires and realizations*, Eurobarometer, n° 56.2, Bruxelles, 75 p.

Commission européenne, 2004, *Rapport du Groupe de Haut Niveau sur l'avenir de la politique sociale dans une Union européenne élargie*, Direction générale de l'emploi et des affaires sociale, mai, 104 p.

Commission européenne, 2005, *Face aux changements démographiques, une nouvelle solidarité entre générations*, Livret vert, COM(2005) 94 final, 16 mars, 26 p.

Cournard, André and Lévy, Maurice, 1973, *Shaping the Future, Gaston Berger and the Concept of Prospective*, New-York Edited by Cournand, Lévy, Gordon and Breach. Current Topics of Contemporary Thought Vol. 11.

Crozier, M., E. Friedberg. *L'acteur et le système*. Paris: Seuil, 1977. [Available in English as *Actors and Systems: the Politics of Collective Action*. Chicago: University of Chicago Press, 1980.]

Daguet (Fabienne), 2004, "La fécondité dans les régions à la fin des années quatre-vingt-dix", *Insee Première*, n° 963, avril.

Davezies (Laurent), 2002, "Les limites de la contribution des mécanismes fiscaux à la cohésion territoriale", CNAF, *Informations sociales*, n° 104.

Delattre (Lucas), 2000, "Michel Camdessus fait le bilan de son action à la tête du Fonds monétaire international", *Le Monde*, 21 juin.

Didier (Michel), 2000, "Quelle croissance longue pour l'économie française?", *Revue de Rexecode*, n° 66, 1er trimestre.

Doliger (Cédric), 2003, *Démographie et croissance économique en France après la Seconde Guerre mondiale: une approche cliométrique*, LAMETA, Faculté de Sciences économiques, Université de Montpellier I.

Drucker (Peter), 1957, *La pratique de la direction des entreprises*, Edition d'Organisation.

Drucker, P. F. *Concept of the Corporation*. New York: New American Library, 1985.

Drucker (Peter), 1973, *Management tasks responsibilities and practices*, Harper & Row, New-York.

Dumont (Gérard-François), 2001, "Départements: les 'six' France", *Population et Avenir*, n° 654, septembre-octobre, p. 4.

Dupuy, J.P. *Ordres et désordres*. Paris: Seuil, 1982.

Durance (Philippe), Godet (Michel): "Europe Grey Hair and Low Growth", *Foresight*, vol. 8, n° 2, 2006.

European Commission, 2002, *Attitudes of Europeans toward fertility: ideals, desires and realizations*, Eurobarometer, n° 56.2, Bruxelles, 75 p.

European Commission, 2004, *Rapport du Groupe de Haut Niveau sur l'avenir de la politique sociale dans une Union européenne élargie*, Direction générale de l'emploi et des affaires sociales, May, 104 p.

European Commission, 2005, *Face aux changements démographiques, une nouvelle solidarité entre générations*, Livret vert COM, 2005, 94.

Faujas (Alain), 1998, "Des vitamines pour l'innovation", *Le Monde*, 12 mai.

Fauroux (Roger), Spitz (Bernard), 2002, *Notre État: le livre vérité de la fonction publique*, Pluriel.

Follett, M.P. *Creative Experience*. New York: Longman's Green and Co, 1976.

Giget, M. "Arbres technologiques et arbres de compétences. Deux concepts à finalité distincte", *Futuribles*, n° 137, nov. 1989.

Giget, M. *La dynamique stratégique des entreprises*. Paris: Dunod, 1998.

Gille (Laurent), 2002, *Partager et échanger, les valeurs du lien et du bien*, thèse de Sciences de gestion soutenue au Conservatoire National des Arts et Métiers.

Giraud (Pierre-Noël), Godet (Michel), 1987, *Radioscopie du Japon*, Economica, coll. CPE-Economica, 165 p.

The Global 2000 Study: *"Report to the President of the United States: Entering the Twenty-First Century"*. New York: Pergamon Press, 1980.

Godet (Michel), 1978, "Va-t-on vers une surabondance d'énergie?", *Le Monde*, 5 septembre.

Godet (Michel), Plas (J.-P.), 1979, "La banque pourrait être la sidérurgie de demain", *Le Monde*, 22 février.

Godet (Michel), 1987a, "Dix idées à contre courant sur le Japon", *Politique industrielle*, avril.

Godet (Michel), 1987b, "Regards sur la japanosclérose", *Futuribles*, n° 112, juillet-août.

Godet (Michel), Pacini (Vincent), 1997, *De l'activité à l'emploi par l'insertion, rapport au ministre du Travail*, Cahiers du Lips, n° 6, janvier.

Godet (Michel), 1998, "La France malade du diplôme".

Godet (Michel), 2001, *Creating Futures : Scenario Planning as a Strategic Management Tool*, Paris: Economica.

Godet, M. "Smic: A New Cross Impact Method". *Futures*, vol. 7, Aug., 1975.

Godet, M. "Smic 74: a reply from the authors". *Futures*, vol. 8, August 1976.

Godet, M. Scenarios and Strategic Management. London: Butterworths, 1987.

Godet, M. "Integration of Scenarios and Strategic Management". *Futures*, vol. 22, Sept., 1990.

Godet, M. *From Anticipation to Action*. Paris: Unesco, 1994.

Godet, M. P. Chapuy, G. Comyn. "Global Scenarios of the International Context on the Horizon 2000", *Futures*, vol. 26, April, 1994.

Godet, M., F. Roubelat. "Creating the Future: the Use and Misuse of Scenarios". *Long-Range Planning*, vol. 9, n° 2, April, 1996.

Graff (James), 2004, "We need more babies!", *Time*, November 29, pp. 40-41.

Grimaldi, N. *Le désir et le temps*. Paris: PUF, 1971.

Guillerme, A. *Les temps de l'eau: la cité, l'eau et les techniques (fin IIIᵉ-début XIXᵉ siècles)*. Paris: Champ Vallon, 1983. [Available in English. *The Age of Water: the Urban Environment of the North of France, A.D. 300-1800*. College Station, TX: A&M University Press, 1988.]

Hall, D. J., M. A. Saias. "Strategy Follows Structure", *Strategic Management Journal*, vol. I.2, April-June, 1980.

Hamel, G., C.K. Prahalad. *Competing for the Future*. Boston: Harvard Business School Press, 1994.

Heijden, K. (van der) *Scenarios, the Art of Strategic Conversation*. London: John Wiley & Sons, 1996.

Interfuturs. *Face aux Futurs*. Paris: OECD, 1979.

Jantsch, E. *Technological Forecasting in Perspective*. Paris: OECD, 1967.

Jouvenel, B. (de) *L'art de la conjecture*. Paris: Éditions du Rocher, 1964. [Available in English, Trans. Lary, N., *The Art of Conjecture*. New York: Basic Books, 1967.]

Juppé (Alain), 2000, *Intervention sur l'Europe*, Assemblée nationale, 9 May.

Kapferer, J.N. *Rumeurs, le plus vieux métier du monde*. Paris: Seuil, 1987. [Available in English. Trans. Fink, B. *Rumors: Uses, Interpretations, and Images*. New Brunswick, NJ: Transaction Publishers, 1990.]

Keynes, J.-M., *The General Theory of Employment, Interest and Money*, London: Macmillan, 1974.

Kok (Wim), 2004, *Relevé le défi, La stratégie de Lisbonne pour la crois-sance et l'emploi,* rapport du groupe de haut niveau, Communautés européennes, November, 60 p.

Lacoste, J. "Abondance pétrolière, jusqu'à quand?" *in: L'énergie. Commissariat Général du Plan, Collection Plan et prospectives.* Paris: Armand Colin, n° 6, 1970.

Le Roy Ladurie, E. *Histoire du climat depuis l'an mil,* vol. 1, Paris: Flammarion, 1967. [Now revised and updated in English as *Times of Feast, Times of Famine: a History of Climate since the Year 1000.* Garden City, New York: Double day, 1971.]

Lesourne, J. *Les mille sentiers de l'avenir.* Paris: Seghers, 1981.

Lesourne, J. *Éducation et société pour demain.* Paris: La Découverte, 1988.

Lesourne, J. *L'économie de l'ordre et du désordre.* Paris: Economica, 1981.

Lesourne, J. "Plaidoyer pour une recherche en prospective", *Futuribles,* n° 137, nov., 1989.

Lesourne, J., M. Godet. *La fin des habitudes.* Paris: Collectif, Seghers, 1985.

Lesourne, J., D. Malkin, "L'exercice interfuturs, réflexion méthodologique ", *Futuribles,* n° 26-27, sept.-oct., 1979.

Linstone, H.A., M. Turrof. *The Delphi Method, Techniques and Applications.* Reading, MA: Wesley Publishing Co. 1975.

Lussato, B. "La culture en danger" (An interview with Prof. Michel Godet), *Futuribles,* n° 122, 1988.

Lussato, B. *L'échelle humaine: contre le gigantisme technologique et bureaucratique.* Paris: Robert Laffont, 1996.

Martino, J. P. *Technological Forecasting for Decision-making.* New York: North Holland, 1983.

Masse, P. *Le plan ou l'anti-hasard.* Paris: Idées Gallimard, 1965.

Mayo, E. *The Human Problems of an Industrial Civilisation.* New York: Viking Press, Compass Books Series, 1960.

Mintzberg, H. *Structure et dynamique des organisations.* Paris: Editions d'Organisation, 1982.

Mintzberg, H. *The Rise and Fall of Strategic Planning: Reconceiving Roles for Planning, Plans, Planners.* New York: The Free Press, 1994.

Morgenstern, O. *Précisions et incertitudes des données économiques.* Paris: Dunod, 1972. [Available in English. *On the Accuracy of Economic Observations.* Princeton, NJ: Princeton University Press, 1965.]

Nanus, B. "QUEST – Quick Environmental Scanning Technique", *Long Range Planning,* vol. 15, n° 2, 1982.

OECD, 2001, *International Mobility of the Highly Skilled.*

Orgogozo, I. *Les paradoxes de la qualité*, Paris: Éditions d'organisation, 1987.

Pascale, R. T. *Le management, est-il un art japonais?* Paris: Éditions d'Organisation, 1984.

Pawley (Martin) "The Private Future" New York: Pocket, 1977.

Pesqueux (Yvon), Durance (Philippe) (coll.), 2004, *Apprentissage organisationnel, économie de la connaissance: mode ou modèle?*, Cahier du Lipsor, série Recherche, n° 6, September; available on the Lipsor site (htlp://www.cnam.fr/lipsor/).

Poirier, L. *Stratégie théorique II*. Paris: Economica, 1987.

Porter, M. *Competitive Strategy: Techniques for Analyzing Industries and Competitors*. New York: The Free Press, 1980.

Porter (Michael), 1985, *Competitive Advantage: Creating and Sustaining Superior Performance*, New York: The Free Press.

Postel-Vinay, O. *Le Taon dans la cité: actualité de Socrate*. Paris: Édition Descartes et Cie., 1994.

Prigogine, I. "Loi, histoire et désertion" in: *La querelle du déterminisme*. Paris: Collection Le Débat, Gallimard, 1990.

Prigogine, I, I. Stengers. *La nouvelle alliance*. 2nd édition Paris: Gallimard, 1987.

Putnam (Robert D.) "Bowling Alone: The Collapse and Revival of American Community" New York: Simon & Schuster, 2001

Revel, J.F. *La connaissance inutile*. Paris: Grasset, 1988.

Ringland, G. *Scenario Planning*. New York: Wiley and Sons. 1998.

Rosenau (James N.), 1997, *Along the Domestic Frontier, Exploring Governance in a Turbulent World,* Cambridge University Press, p. 145.

Roubelat, F. *La prospective stratégique en perspective: genèse, études de cas, prospective*. Thèse de doctorat en Sciences de gestion, Cnam, Paris, 1996.

Saaty, T.L. *The Analytical Hierarchy Process*. New York: McGraw-Hill, 1980.

Sardon (Jean-Paul), 2004, "Évolution démographique récente des pays développés", *Population,* INED, n° 59 (2), p. 305-360.

Sauvy (Alfred), 1980, "Démographie et refus de voir", *in L'enjeu démographique,* Paris, Éditions de l'Association pour la Recherche et l'Information Démographique (APRD).

Schröder (Gerhard), 2001, "Familles, progrès, bonheur", *Le Monde,* 14 March.

Schwartz, P. *The Art of the Long View*. New York: Doubleday, 1991.

Sérieyx, H. *Le zéro mépris*. Paris: InterÉditions, 1989.

Simon, H. *Models of Bounded Rationality*. vol. 2, Cambridge, MA: The MIT Press, 1982.

Todd, E. *La troisième planète: structures familiales et systèmes idéologiques.* Paris: Seuil, 1983.

Toffler, A. *Future Shock.* New York: Random House, 1970.

United Nations, 2004, *World Population Prospects: The 2004 Revision,* Population Division of the Department of Economic and Social Affairs of the United Nations Secretariat.

Valaskakis (Kimon), 1998, "Mondialisation et gouvernance. Le défi de la régulation publique planétaire", *Futuribles,* n° 230, April, p. 5-28.

Ville, J. *Étude critique de la notion de collectif.* Paris: Gauthier-Villars, 1937.

Wack, P. "Scenarios: Uncharted Waters Ahead." *Harvard Business Review,* Sept.-Oct. 1985, vol. 63, n° 5.

Wack, P. "Scenarios: Shooting the Rapids." *Harvard Business Review,* novembre-décembre 1985, vol. 63, n° 6.

Zwicky, F. "Morphology and Nomenclatura of Jet Engires", *Aeronautical Engineering Review,* June, 1947.

INDEX